'For Only
Those Deserve
the Name'

To Tania

# 'For Only Those Deserve the Name'

## MARK CALDERBANK

T. E. Lawrence and
*Seven Pillars of Wisdom*

A literary biography & study

**sussex**
ACADEMIC
PRESS
*Brighton • Portland • Toronto*

Copyright © Mark Calderbank, 2017, 2018.

The right of Mark Calderbank to be identified as Author of this work has been asserted in accordance with the Copyright, Designs and Patents Act 1988.

2 4 6 8 10 9 7 5 3

*First published in hardcover 2017, reprinted in paperback 2018, in Great Britain by*
SUSSEX ACADEMIC PRESS
PO Box 139
Eastbourne BN24 9BP

*Distributed in the United States of America by*
SUSSEX ACADEMIC PRESS
International Specialized Book Services
920 NE 58th Ave #300
Portland, Oregon 97213

All rights reserved. Except for the quotation of short passages for the purposes of criticism and review, no part of this publication may be reproduced, stored in a retrieval system or transmitted in any form or by any means, electronic, mechanical, photocopying, recording or otherwise, without the prior permission of the publisher.

*British Library Cataloguing in Publication Data*
A CIP catalogue record for this book is available from the British Library.

*Library of Congress Cataloging-in-Publication Data*
Names: Calderbank, Mark, author.
Title: "For only those deserve the name" : T.E. Lawrence and Seven Pillars of Wisdom / Mark Calderbank.
Description: Brighton : Sussex Academic Press, 2016. | Includes bibliographical references and index.
Identifiers: LCCN 2016027734 | ISBN 9781845198084 (hb : alk. paper) | ISBN 9781845198428 (pbk : alk. paper)
Subjects: LCSH: Lawrence, T. E. (Thomas Edward), 1888–1935. Seven pillars of Wisdom. | Lawrence, T. E. (Thomas Edward), 1888–1935. | World War, 1914–1918—Campaigns—Arabian Peninsula. | World War, 1914–1918—Personal narratives, British. | Arabs—History—20th century. | Bedouins—History—20th century. | Wahhabiyah—Saudi Arabia. | Arabian Peninsula—Social life and customs.
Classification: LCC D568.4.L43 C35 2016 | DDC 940.4/15—dc23
LC record available at https://lccn.loc.gov/2016027734

Typeset & designed by Sussex Academic Press, Brighton & Eastbourne.
Printed by TJ International, Padstow, Cornwall.

# CONTENTS

*List of Illustrations*     vii
*Acknowledgements and Note on the Texts*     ix

**Introduction**     1

**PART ONE**
**SEVEN YEARS OF STRUGGLE, 1919–1926**

1. Genesis in Paris, 1919     11
2. Writing the Book: London, Oxford, Pole Hill, 1920     30
3. In the Political Arena, 1920–21     47
4. From the Oxford Text to Enlistment in the Ranks, 1922     62
5. Literary Mentors, 1922–24     79
6. Bovington Camp, 1923–25     98
7. The Subscribers Edition, 1924–26     107

**PART TWO**
**SEVEN PILLARS OF WISDOM**

*The Arab Revolt: Participant Accounts*

8. Lawrence in the Arab Revolt: A Summary     129
9. Lawrence & Ronald Storrs in Jeddah     135
10. The Battle of Tafileh: Subhi al-Umari & Lawrence     142
11. Kirkbride's Account     152

*The Drama of the Self*

12. The Outsider (1)     171
13. The Climax at Dera'     181
14. The Outsider (2)     199
15. The Biographical Environment and Sequel     210

*Between Myth and Reality*

16. The Arab Mirage     227
17. The Presentation of History     243

18  The Problem of Autobiography                                    260

**Epilogue:*Was that all it was, then?***                          274

*Appendices*                                                        291
Appendix 1: Chronology of Text 1: Four Versions
Appendix 2: Nesib al-Bakri and the Syrian alternative
Appendix 3: The Demonisation of Abdelkader
Appendix 4: Abbreviated References
Appendix 5: Key Chapter Numeration in Successive Editions of
*Seven Pillars of Wisdom*

*Notes*                                                             301
*Bibliography*                                                      317
*Index*                                                             324

# List of Illustrations

**Cover Illustration**
Eric Kennington's "ghost portrait" of T.E. Lawrence: Image of a reproduction of the original. By permission of the Warden and Fellows of All Souls College, Oxford.

**Plate Illustrations (after page 124)**
Illustrations 1–4 are of Lawrence uniformed, 1918 to 1925. The four images are reproduced by permission of the Imperial War Museum, London.

1   3 October 1918. In Damascus. Painted by James McBey. This is the only painting made of Lawrence during the war. Copyright © Imperial War Museums (Art.IWM ART 2473).
2   1919. Paris. A formal portrait of Lawrence in the uniform of a Colonel at the Versailles Peace Conference. Copyright © Imperial War Museums (Q73538).
3   1923–25. Bovington. Private T.E. Shaw of the Royal Tank Corps. Copyright © Imperial War Museums (Q83977).
4   April 1921. Amman, Transjordan. "The wild ass of the desert" as a civil servant in suit, white collar and Homburg hat. From left: Gertrude Bell, Major Welsh, Lawrence, Sir Herbert Samuel, Emir Abdullah. The person between Samuel and the Emir is probably Subhi al-Umari. Copyright © Imperial War Museums (Q60171).

Illustrations 5–7 are of various Arabs of importance in the text or as art.

5   October 1918. Subhi al-Umari, in Bedouin dress, on the outskirts of Aleppo during a truce. This is the photograph widely misidentified as Lawrence, which persuaded Subhi to write his own book, *Lurens kama' areftuhu* (Dar al-Nahar lil Nashr, 1969) from which this image is reproduced.
6   1918. Guweira. Emir Zeid (centre) and Nesib al-Bakri holding

ceremonial swords. Reproduced from a photograph in *The Memoirs of Emir Zeid: The Jordanian War 1917–18* (ed. Suleiman Moussa), Jordanian Studies Centre,1990 (Arabic).

7 Nawaf al-Sha'alan by Eric Kennington. Pastel. One of the Arab portraits made by Kennington during his trip to Amman in the spring of 1921, which were exhibited at the Leicester Galleries. Nawaf was the eldest son of Nuri al-Sha'alan, paramount Sheikh of the Rualla. See Chapter 17. By courtesy of the Trustees of the *Seven Pillars of Wisdom* Trust.

# Acknowledgements and Note on the Texts

My thanks to Gaye Morgan, Librarian in charge and Conservator of the Codrington Library of All Souls College, Oxford, for the help she gave me with the copy, held by the college, of Kennington's 'Ghost' portrait of Lawrence, on the cover of this book. I am grateful to Emily Dean of the Imperial War Museum for the amazing efficiency and patience with which she handled my frequent changes of mind over selection of prints. I thank Mr Carey of the Seven Pillars of Wisdom Trust for the congenial manner with which he considered my pleas to reduce copyright expenses for the large amount of quotation I have made from the 1922 text of *Seven Pillars* and his help with Lawrence's correspondence. The Houghton Library of Harvard University Imaging Services (Mike Mellor and Mary Haegert) were most helpful in colour photocopying free of charge from the original of the Garnett-Lawrence annotated copy of the 1922 text, which was necessary in order to distinguish Lawrence's amendments from Edward Garnett's. Dr Helen Smith of East Anglia University kindly read through my chapter section on the literary relation between Lawrence and Garnett and provided her expert comments on Garnett. At the British Library I particularly wish to thank the Curators of Rare Books for granting frequent access to the original editions of Seven Pillars of Wisdom, Colin Harris of the Bodleian Library Special Collections Department, and the Oxford Public Library for putting at my disposal the complete Journals of the TE Lawrence Society, frequently referred to in this book. I thank Kate Pool and Sarah Baxter of the Society of Authors for their advice on guidelines concerning permissions, copyright, etc. My editor and publisher, Anthony Grahame, hammered into shape a book which was written in total ignorance of academic norms or publishing procedures or techniques. My grateful thanks.

Among friends and family: I would like to thank Maurice Larès for generously giving me, among several other books, a copy of his *T.E. Lawrence, la France et les Français*, which was indispensable for its account of the Paris Peace Conference. Layla Al Durrah kindly helped me with my translation of extracts from the book on Lawrence by Subhi al Umari. Jeremy Wilson helped me generously by allowing me to read in his home the copy of the earliest known fragment of Seven Pillars and for copies of other early Mss, and much useful advice; my wife and I remember Jeremy and Nicole for their much appreciated hospitality at Woodgreen Common. Among the early readers of the biographical section I would mention my sister Liz Earl and Carl Earl for their feedback and encouragement. Two people have helped me enormously: One is June Rathbone of University College, London. As an expert on the whole field of masochism who also knew a great deal about Lawrence, her support and criticism have been invaluable overall. Of course, what I have written on masochism in this book, while it owes a vast amount to others, is, as it applies to T.E. Lawrence, entirely my own creation. I also owe her the correction of my memories of Hampstead! Finally, Dick Long, an old friend and a specialist on Middle East history, has provided over the years much appreciated comment on the text, encouragement in hard times and a good deal of practical advice on publishing.

## A Note on the Texts

The writing of *Seven Pillars of Wisdom* occupied Lawrence for nearly eight years and saw the creation of three complete versions: the *Oxford* text of 1922, the *subscribers'* edition of 1926, and a popular abridgement of the latter, *Revolt in the Desert* (1927), the only version published in his lifetime. *Seven Pillars of Wisdom* was not published until after his death in 1935, in accordance with his wishes. The subscribers' edition was promoted by Lawrence as the definitive version. However, in 1997, J.M. Wilson edited and published for the first time the 1922 Oxford text. The Oxford text has made its mark as a serious alternative to the standard edition so there are now two versions to choose from.

In this book I have chosen the Oxford text as default. The question of the author's original intentions is decisive. The passage of time changes writers' attitude to their work, and the Lawrence of 1924–26 was not the Lawrence of 1920–22. There is also no doubt that the earlier text is generally more transparent than the later, which makes it slightly easier to interpret, and the style less mannered.

My decision will make it slightly less simple for readers who know and possess the standard edition rather than the Oxford; however, the vast majority of the discussion relates as well to the one as to the other. Wherever possible (i.e. where the original passage has been retained, with or without alteration, in the standard text) I give both page references. The symbol employed for the Oxford text is OX; the symbol R (revised) is employed for the texts based on the subscribers' edition. Page references are taken from the 2003 edition of the Oxford text and the 1940 edition of the revised text. I would recommend the Oxford text, to those alike who have read the standard version or have not. It is more informative, more revealing about himself, and closer to the time of the events it relates. It is also easier to read. I am confident that those who know only the standard edition will find it refreshing to see samples of the original full text.

    I assume that some of my readers will have read neither version and for this reason I have added a list of all the most important chapters discussed and where they are to be found for, in the words of E.M. Forster, "as we penetrate its vast interior, and are bewildered by contrary effects, it is natural that we should ask for a guide"!

MARK CALDERBANK
Quimper, France

I looked back on the *Seven Pillars*, and gave up my ambitious hopes of being a writer: a great writer, I should say, for only those deserve the name.

T.E. Lawrence

# Introduction

This book is about *Seven Pillars of Wisdom,* T.E. Lawrence's memoir of the Arab Revolt. It is part biography, part essay in interpretation.

*Seven Pillars* is part and parcel of the Lawrence phenomenon. There is the war, there is the life and letters, and there is the book. For many a biography, it is the major source relied on; This book is one of the longest, the most heterogeneous, and the most personal to be centred on a history of a military campaign. It is also mysterious. The lack of clear definition, as well as its heterogeneity, explains why, to a far greater degree than most books, it means different things to different people. For some, it is a historical account, for others it is essentially an autobiography, for others again a literary creation, but perhaps still for the majority simply a splendid adventure story. And there are plenty of important subjects within these genres or outside them: military history, desert war, travel, ethnography, and above all the author himself – as hero, as military genius, as expert operator in foreign interventions, as orientalist, as psychological case history, as exemplar of the modern consciousness.

My approach to this vast work is comprehensive, in the sense that I have determined to neglect none of the three major aspects: neither the historical, nor the autobiographical, nor finally the literary. The reader will find that these aspects are rarely independent one from the other, in fact, they are very much mixed up together. I follow the book through its genesis and development, how it was influenced by post-war political developments and Lawrence's own moral crisis. *Seven Pillars* was at the centre of Lawrence's life; and even more so, of his legend. It is difficult to imagine how the mythology would have developed without it.

Can one read this book without having read *Seven Pillars*? Certainly one can, but it is preferable to have a copy of the book on the table. My text regularly gives the page references concerned to both the earlier and later editions and there are over 3000 words of text quoted.

My book has two parts. The first half is a biography of the seven years and ten months during which he was occupied, usually intermittently, with the writing and production of the book; these are the most eventful years of his life and the most socially interesting and varied. The way his book was written is extensively documented, especially since the discovery of an early fragment, and I believe that my book is the first to give any kind of analysis of it. The book's development continues through the unfinished 1920 abridgement, the 1922 'Oxford' text, to the subscribers' edition of 1926. There is a chapter on the 'literary mentors', those famous men of letters who tried to help him, which throws light not only on the book, but also on contemporary attitudes. Outside his struggle with *Seven Pillars*, there is his political engagement and the outcomes in the Middle East arena, which had a drastic effect on the tone of the book and the drama of betrayal and guilt. There is a sunny side of the street also, full of art galleries and their artists, new friendships, some lifelong, with painters, writers, politicians, great ladies, soldiers and airmen; his room at All Souls College at Oxford, the journeys on his beloved motor-cycles, the classical music over tea with his fellow soldiers in his cottage in Dorset, the visits to the Shaws or to the Hardys, the free expansive letters to Charlotte Shaw. Yet over it all hangs a certain mood of restlessness, stress, depresssion, remorse and pessimism; and the dark shadow of a masochistic compulsion accompanies him. He is dogged by his past and hopeless about his future. For freedom he has to pay everything.

The second part looks at *Seven Pillars* from various angles: through accounts written by other participants; through the parallel text: the drama of the self; and finally through three essays in interpretation of major themes. Outside this I have added an epilogue: a literary evaluation, and appraisal of the meaning of literature in Lawrence's life, in the form of a commentary on an essay by André Malraux written between 1940 and 1943.

For those who have had too much of *Seven Pillars*, alternative accounts are a breath of fresh air. One of the accounts is an Arab account – one of the few and all the more valuable for that. The comparison of narratives of the same event has the purpose of showing the extent to which *Seven Pillars* is one man's version of events and, as far as historical truth is concerned, invites one to ask to what extent one can rely on Lawrence's accounts in *Seven Pillars*. They also enable us to see how Lawrence later personalised his accounts to give them a significance beyond history.

The drama of the self traces the 'parallel text', the introspective epic that moves to its own climax (or anti-climax) and provides the material for the 'real' autobiography. The term 'parallel text' is a little misleading; the drama of the self is more like a *leitmotif*, erupting suddenly at various stages of the narrative and in various ways. It is structurally a bundle of fragments. Edward Garnett talked about "strange free disclosures". He found them vital, but inadequate and fragmentary. Nonetheless, they form the basis of a psychological portrait of universal interest. They are difficult to decipher without a knowledge of masochistic behaviour. They also raise all kinds of questions over truth and Lawrence's attitude to truth.

The last section of Part II deals with three major themes: Lawrence's multi-faceted attitude towards the Arabs, his presentation of history, and the meaning of his autobiography. The first two subjects remain highly topical and controversial The chapter on history works outward from one particular incident, exploring its context in depth; what we have learned about Lawrence's psychology is key input to the interpretation, both here, and in the subsequent chapter, where we hope, but without much sense of certainty, to have finally pinned down this Proteus, this bag of tricks.

One simple reason for writing a book on *Seven Pillars* (but not in my view the most interesting) is the use made of the book as a source, both a biographical source on Lawrence himself, and yet more so as a source on the history of the Arab Revolt. In a book published in 1962, the first biography by an Arab, Suleiman Moussa wrote in truth that all Lawrence's biographers relied heavily on Lawrence's own statements and writings (whereas his own research included an impressive array of Arab personalities who played a role in the Revolt). Even since that date, in spite far greater coverage of the Arab Revolt from all sorts of sources, they have continued to be indiscreet. The reason is, as I hope this book will show, that it is extremely difficult to write *anything* about Lawrence or Lawrence's version of history or the Arabs without *Seven Pillars of Wisdom*. It is there that we have his final view of things, very carefully worked out and presented. That is what he wanted us to believe. A number of Lawrence scholars, headed by Jeremy Wilson and Malcolm Brown, have claimed that the gradual release of classified documents have vindicated Lawrence's claim that his book is essentially accurate. It would seem, however, that they mean only those documents that refer to sources which in some way involve matters of interest to the British or sources of which Lawrence himself is the original source, although this may not be stated. I have quoted reports in this book written and sent to Cairo by Lawrence which are highly questionable or misleading or incomplete and which have no independent witnesses, but they have been filed as official information about the war and decorations awarded on the strength of them. The insoluble problem is that a great deal of Lawrence's activity in Arabia and Syria was carried out and reported on without any independent British witnesses (and Arab witnesses were never sought). See especially Chapters 10 and 17 and Appendix 3.

Historians do not want to get bogged down in a secondary research as to whether what they are citing from Seven Pillars is reliable or not. They assume it is, if there is no contrary evidence, even when the sole source is Lawrence himself. A book on Lawrence can hardly avoid relying on his own documentation. An interesting case is James Barr's *Setting the desert on fire* (2006). This is an excellent and sober biography-cum-history of the Revolt. However, the author obviously has his doubts about the veracity of the notorious Dera' incident, as he devotes a whole chapter (17) to testing a hypothesis about Lawrence's diary entry. On the other hand, he accepts the entries in his notes about the dubious shooting in Wadi Kitan (108–9), which could also be forgeries. When Robert Bolt, the screenwriter of *Lawrence of Arabia*, was accused of taking Lawrence literally in *Seven Pillars*, he retorted: "if we are to doubt his veracity here, why not elsewhere?" That riposte is not a little unsettling!

Robert Bolt also stated in his *Apologia* that "*Seven Pillars of Wisdom* was my prime, almost my only source for the screenplay." That is definitive. It means that, *pace* quite a number alterations and distortions, *Seven Pillars* is for all but a fraction of our population the basic history of both the Arab Revolt and of T.E.Lawrence.

Interest in the T.E. Lawrence saga, which I date from 1919, the year of the Lowell Thomas lantern slide lectures, has never seriously flagged. It has seldom been stronger than it is now. The impetus for this, apart from the spread of media and the internationalisation of the Lawrence legend, has been the Middle East wars and allied interventions, which continue almost unabated for twenty-five years and have intensified since 2003. In our plight, the name of Lawrence has been invoked as the man who understood how to deal with the Arabs, how to conduct a campaign of guerrilla warfare in the desert, and more. The question: "how would Lawrence have dealt with this?" is everywhere. It has led to a wider association of one man with the war in the Middle East. From being a key source for authors, *Seven Pillars* has become relevant for generals, politicians, and centres of strategic studies. Even the 'narrative of betrayal', which to some extent *was* his creation, and which belongs to the psychological domain as well as to the historical, has never been more popular, especially in the West.

But is *Seven Pillars* a reliable source? And how do we judge whether information in *Seven Pillars* is reliable or not? To answer these questions will take us much further than we might imagine. And this is part of the deeper answer to the question: what is the book about?

In spite of all that, I do not think that the main interest of this book is history. I am less interested in Lawrence's version of history itself than in his motivation. Why does he present history (including of course his own history) in this very idiosyncratic fashion? Originally, I had intended to do two things: to dethrone the work as a literary creation; and to show the mismatch between historical and literary aims. I hope I have achieved the first up to a point, but I got so involved in discovering Lawrence's *intentions*, what exactly he wanted the book to say, to show, (and what he wanted it to half show and half hide), in a word: interpretation, that the psychological puzzle became overwhelming and took me far and wide. It is autobiography that is at the centre of this book.

What about the phenomenon of heterogeneity itself, and how it is handled by the author? For this heterogeneity does not operate simply at the level of topic; it is a general phenomenon; it affects style, genre, attitude. There is the indefiniteness with which ideas and themes appear and disappear or are metamorphosed; the confusion and cross-contamination of genre; the contradictory attitudes expressed; the confusion between author and actor, and the different time zones they represent; the ambiguities, mystifications, concealments, oblique statements, signposts pointing the wrong way; the changes in the author's aims. All this needs puzzling out across the book, or it will not yield up its secrets; and certainly there are secrets.

I do not think that many of my facts are new. I have tried to cover a lot of ground and that means gratefully accepting the discoveries of others. The interest of my book lies in the way a wide variety of facts, events and narratives have been connected to one another so as to show a new or unexpected significance. I am concerned more with insight than with new findings. I do not seek certainty so much as intelligent speculation. With Lawrence, certainty is in any case hard to come by. I am fascinated by the different ways in which people perceive the same events. I am also fascinated by deciphering puzzles, and Lawrence's are in a class of their own since they bring in such a vast range of accessible data (an example is part of my Chapter 17). And a new fascination I have acquired as a result of this project is the question: what is truth? Lawrence's truth shakes one's assumptions to their foundations and opens up vistas of freedom.

The sole area of knowledge which I have exploited more deeply than has been done hitherto, as far as I am aware, is masochism. It is probably fair to say that this is a key to my interpretation of Lawrence's book. I have given attention not only, not even primarily, to physical acts with another participant, but to what Freud called 'moral masochism'. By this is meant (here I am using my own terms, not Freud's) an entire behavioural 'character', an attitude to life, marked conspicuously by guilt, redemption, self-punishment, egoism, social apartness, and fantasy (to name some of the more important traits discussed in this book). This is not, however, a book on masochism. The important thing is that all the traits I have mentioned – and not only those – are linked, and make up a behavioural character that is consistent and even predictable, and has provided a surprisingly comprehensive basis for a meaningful interpretation of the book.

It is a book we are talking about, not a real-life person; a book is an artefact formed within the author's mind; it can tell us about that person's mind and what he chooses to tell us, but we can easily be deceived. The writer of a book controls everything in it, he is free to select or reject whatever aspect of experience he wishes, to present it in whatever light he wishes, to present himself as hero, villain, sufferer. He can conceal, distort, invent. In the case of a book written by the same person as its subject, we have a persona created through introspection, and the masochistic character assumes a far more unbridled deployment than in everyday life. And in Lawrence's case, the exploitation of the material as redemption is infinitely magnified and encouraged by the need for what Liddell Hart has called the purification of the legend, an aim regarded as entirely legitimate and desirable in 1926.

One must not, then, confuse the Lawrence of *Seven Pillars* with the Lawrence of life. Many an accusation of denigration has been based on an error, a failure to distinguish between the two. One of his old schoolfriends, E.F. Hall, referring to the 'Myself' chapter, wrote: "That self-analysis in the *Seven Pillars* is too severe, too one-sided, introspective. It leaves out entirely the generosity and magnanimity of the man." Exactly. There are two Lawrences: the physically real Lawrence of social life and the solitary introspective Lawrence of

*Seven Pillars*, a Lawrence unsympathetic to himself. I cannot overemphasise this point.

One theme insistently intrudes almost everywhere you look. It is the notion of Truth. "The truth was his own business", wrote his friend Vyvyan Richards. It was indeed, and his contemporaries respected it. Now, on the contrary! Those readers or writers, and they are very many, who out of belief or convenience (it is often the latter) follow Richards' dictum will remain outsiders to his book. It is not a straightforward choice between lies and truth. We need to concern ourselves with the distinctions between historical truth, psychological truth and spiritual truth, as understood by Lawrence. The depiction of Lawrence wallowing in Turkish blood in the film *Lawrence of Arabia* and the protests that followed, especially from his former fellow officers and even biographers, arise from a failure to examine that question in *Seven Pillars of Wisdom*.

MARK CALDERBANK<br>
Quimper, France<br>
June 2016

PART
# ONE

# SEVEN YEARS OF STRUGGLE, 1919–1926

"To the vast majority he was a figure, legendary, elusive, whose master motives lay far outside their cognizance. So true is it that men often admire most what they are least able to understand."

*An address by Lord Halifax in St Paul's Cathedral for the unveiling of a bust of T.E. Lawrence.*

CHAPTER

# 1

# GENESIS IN PARIS, 1919

### THE IDEA IN THE MIND

*3rd October 1918.* The Emir Feisal arrives on horseback at the Victoria Hotel in Damascus. Pushing his way through the jostling crowd of fezzed Damascenes, Bedouin and Druze tribesmen, he encounters for the first time the British Commander-in-Chief, Allenby, with Lt. Colonel Lawrence among others. The war in Arabia and Syria against the Ottoman Turks is virtually over. Lawrence, never a man to hang around, would leave Damascus the very next day, never to return. All that remained to do, it seemed, was to write the story.

There could have been no more likely sequel than a book about it by himself. As George Lloyd, his wartime colleague, had predicted as early as August 1917, Lawrence would "some day be able to write a unique book. Generally, the kind of men capable of these adventures lack the pen and wit to record them adequately. Luckily Lawrence is specially gifted with both."[1]

He was indeed quite extraordinarily well equipped for the task. He was deeply conscious of being the unique witness to a major part of what he was to relate; such a privilege gives an enormous freedom to any writer. His contact with the Bedu leaders had been so close as to be of a different order to that of any other Englishman during the war and yet, at the same time, he could justly claim to have been at the centre of high level decision making on the British side concerning the Arab Revolt. For nearly two years, as liaison officer between the Emir Feisal and General Headquarters Cairo, he had been right at the centre of things. The adventures in which he had participated were both exciting and exotic, and thus a blessed relief, in a war memoir, from the deadening quagmire of the trenches; yet they were also, as a description of a new kind of warfare, of real military interest.

Apart from his unique wartime experience, he also had the expert knowledge to give depth to the historical narrative. His erudition about the Arabian peninsula embraced its history and religion, its cultural traditions. He had an up-to-the-minute appreciation of the political forces at work there and their interface with Western intentions and influence. He was so widely travelled in the region as to be considered one of the explorers of Arabia. He was a trained observer and thoroughly practised in geographical and topographical observation: he had done a thorough survey of Crusader castles in Syria, been a member of a group of military surveyors in Sinai, and a mapping expert in London and Cairo. His notebooks are full of topographical notes and map sketches made on the march.

On top of all that, he was literary. He was steeped in European literature about the Orient, both medieval and modern. He had before him the example of Doughty, whose *Arabia Deserta* he profoundly admired. But his secret ambition, unknown to Lloyd, went far beyond Doughty.

The book he would write would not be merely a memoir that would follow naturally from a war experience in a position of responsibility, like the countless *mémoires pour servir* produced by the generals, officers and a few soldiers of World War I; nor merely a war adventure story in exotic surroundings; nor a history (the only one of its time) of the war in Arabia; nor, essentially, a traveller's book about Arabia and the tribes; nor a social document of historic change and the clash of cultures. It would be all these things – and yet none of them.

He had read the great modern writers of the Western world and felt their power: Tolstoy, Dostoevski, Melville, Nietzsche, Conrad. These were works of the imagination, not of history; nonetheless, he yearned to emulate their achievement. It did not seem unattainable to a person like Lawrence. In Arabia his ambition had swept aside all obstacles, why not now?

Composing a first book is always difficult. In 1919 he was already 30 years old and, whatever the skill with the pen detected by Lloyd, had never made a serious attempt at a work of literature. Finding the key to enrich a complex historical narrative with such a range of heterogeneous knowledge would be taxing enough for any writer. But Lawrence intended to enter a different kind of territory, where the subject matter of the narrative, and its treatment, would somehow transcend its historical significance. He would create a literary masterpiece. "The story I have to tell is one of the most splendid ever given a man for writing", he was to write to a friend in 1923. The unique circumstances of the Arabian experience and the unique qualities of the writer that would generate Seven Pillars of Wisdom were once and for all. This was the heroic challenge. There would be no second chance.

## FAILURE AT VERSAILLES

After leaving Damascus Lawrence wrote to Major Scott, the base commander at Aqaba: "the old war is closing, and my use is gone". He continued: "We have, I expect, changed history in the near East. I wonder how the powers will let the Arabs get on."[2] But had history already been changed? In an obvious sense, yes. The Arabs had helped their British allies to topple a 460 year-old empire, the old Arab east was suddenly projected onto the stage of Western international politics and a new future awaited them.

That was what Lawrence intimated to Scott; but otherwise, everything was very far from clear. Lawrence's engagement had been political from the start. For him, changing history meant the achievement of Arab independence, the end of the old colonialism. But the making of this history was still at Square One. He did not intend to sit back and "wonder how the powers would let the Arabs get on". He would be in the midst of the fighting, once again. The heroism of Lawrence was a classical heroism; it lies in action; and in his unquestioning response at that moment to what destiny laid in his path, regardless of his mental and physical well-being.

He made straight for England to engage immediately in the political battle for the Arab future. He spent just one weekend at home in the house at 2 Polstead Road, Oxford, with the family he had not seen for four years and which had lost two of his brothers in the war, the place where he had grown up and prepared himself so assiduously for whatever Fate would lay in his path. One wonders what his parents made of this survivor whom that war had so changed. Did they have any idea who he now was? It was the last time he would see his father alive.

Throughout November 1918 into the new year of 1919 Lawrence lobbied without sparing himself for British support for the Arab claims. He attended meetings of the Eastern committee, submitted memoranda and maps, wrote an article in *The Times*, and, in the teeth of French opposition, went to France to look after Emir Feisal, who, on 26th November, had arrived at Marseille on a British warship. He was there to represent his father, Sherif Hussein bin Ali al-Hashemi, former Grand Sherif of Mecca and now King of the Hejaz, at the upcoming Peace Conference in Paris. He had won that right through his revolt against the Turks, being granted belligerent status by Great Britain, though this was at first contested by the French. Back in England, after being refused any status by the French, and now wearing ceremonial Arab dress, Lawrence interpreted for Feisal at his reception by King George V, who decorated the Emir with the Chain of a Knight Grand Cross of the Royal Victorian Order. He was becoming a glamorous figure.

The British government, and especially the Eastern Committee under Lord Curzon, were ready to listen and sympathetic to Arab aspirations, which were seen as by no means completely incompatible with British interests. On the other hand, there were French interests in Syria, to which the British government was committed. A secret treaty had been made between the British, French, and Russian governments in the spring of 1916 over post-war arrangements for the future status of the Eastern Ottoman territories, assuming the defeat of Turkey in the war. It was referred to in Britain by the names of its negotiators Mark Sykes and François Georges-Picot: the Sykes–Picot treaty. For Britain and France, this document was essentially a map of the Middle East illustrating the tripartite carve-up of the Ottoman Empire. As far as Syria was concerned, the coastal region and some of what would become Lebanon had been assigned to France; the Arabs would be left the government of Damascus and the interior up to Aleppo, on condition they accepted French 'advisers' and entrepreneurs. There was to be a similar arrangement in Iraq for the British and a tripartite sharing arrangement for Palestine.

In November 1917, the new revolutionary government of Russia betrayed, denounced and withdrew from the treaty. It therefore became a very unsecret Anglo-French affair. Arab aspirations were obviously quite incompatible with this treaty. However, some members of the British government, conscious of having made promises to both sides, hoped they would be able to wriggle out of their commitments to the French, and indeed they had plenty of plausible arguments for doing so.

D.G. Hogarth, an Oxford don and archaeologist, former head of the Arab Bureau in Cairo and well connected in political circles, thought that the treaty was no longer relevant. The victorious British occupied all of Syria, Mesopotamia and Palestine except the coastal area of Syria where the French had been allowed to set up an administration (but still under the supreme command of General Allenby); the facts on the ground in the Ottoman territories had so changed since the spring of 1916 that this treaty now seemed an embarrassment which would impede the consolidation of all that Britain had achieved by our arms and diplomacy. The Arabs had fought in the war as our allies, were ready to govern themselves and were totally hostile to a French occupation. The French, with due respect to the gallant participation of a faithful few, had done little to merit a claim to Syria. Lawrence was hopeful, perhaps optimistic. He may not have realized, however, that there was in both the India and Foreign Offices vehement opposition to Arab interests being preferred to those of France.

On January 9, 1919 Lawrence arrived in Paris for the Versailles Peace Conference. He was to remain until mid-May, when he travelled to Cairo. He returned briefly to Paris in July, but was back in England by mid-August.

He had a typically Lawrencian status: that is, ambiguous. He held the official position of 'technical adviser' to the British government and, ostensibly for that purpose, was attached to the so-called Hijaz delegation and worked as Emir Feisal's adviser, but was he under appointment to the Foreign Office? Nobody seemed to know and the French were far from happy about it. For the British government, however, which needed Arab support for its ambitions in Mesopotamia (Iraq) and Palestine, it was essential to keep Feisal in the British camp until the upcoming contest with the French over the future of the Middle East was settled, and perhaps even longer if it proved necessary to pour oil on troubled waters. Only Lawrence could achieve this and it would be easier (and safer for the Foreign Office diplomatically) if Lawrence was not an official member of their delegation; he could then be given a freer hand, and disowned if he became embarrassing. He was. It was a bit like the arrangement he had worked under in Arabia and Syria, with responsibilities in both camps and a nebulous status; but there he had been a man of power; in Versailles, he was a merely a brightly coloured pawn on a chessboard.

Much to the fore in Paris was his companionship of Feisal who, although he had learnt French in Constantinople, was heavily dependent on him as translator, guide and advisor. Except on ceremonial occasions, Lawrence wore khaki with a kaffiyeh, which could hardly have pleased him; he disliked the Army uniform and it emphasised his shortness by comparison with those similarly attired. With the Corps Diplomatique at large, he was a big hit. His blazing blue eyes, his wit, his flamboyance, his energy and quickness in conversation, and his occasional striking appearances in spotless white, accompanying Feisal to receptions or banquets, gave a dash of glamour to the otherwise drab post-war scene. Gertrude Bell, who wrote to her mother that she was spending much time with Lawrence there, described him as the Conference's most picturesque figure. No doubt, and all this surface glamour hid from those he met his growing sense of frustration.

The work with Feisal was spasmodic. To begin with, there was the drafting of the plea for Arab independence before the Council of Ten, and the meeting of the Council itself, in early February, where Lawrence had to make an impromptu translation from the Arabic into French before the rulers of the world; but after this general plea, the question of the Ottoman territories was discussed by the Big Three: President Wilson, Clemenceau, and Lloyd George. Feisal was in the wings waiting to be called, like Rosencrantz or Guildenstern. He was approached only in April, when the French were assured that the British and Americans would not block their claims in Syria. In the meantime, TE, as Lawrence was known to his friends, searched for support behind the scenes, in the form of a deal, from the Americans in general and the Zionists in particular. We do not know exactly whom he saw or where he went. Winston Churchill claimed that he had spoken with Clemenceau several times; perhaps that is what TE told him. He also claimed to have spoken with Woodrow Wilson.

From late March onward, Lloyd George became increasingly reluctant to stand up to French demands over Syria. His own greed for territory both in Palestine, for strategic reasons and more emotional religious ones, and in Mesopotamia, made him to resort to a kind of diplomatic swapping game with Clemenceau. In late March, the big Four (France, GB, the USA and Italy) were arguing about President Wilson's proposal to send a Commission to Syria and Iraq to sound out the views of the populations on their future government; and here, Lawrence appears to distance himself from Arab self-determination, and move decisively towards the Foreign Office and French point of view which opposed any such thing. A volte-face? It was certainly the opposite of Feisal's position, who regarded the Commission as the sole initiative which might save Syria from a French mandate. In a note attached to a letter from Gertrude Bell to Major Bonsal, a member of the American delegation (March 24), Bell and Lawrence wrote: "the movement for Arab unity has no serious political value either now or in the future". The next day, Lawrence attended a meeting of prominent rightist personalities (French and British) with the aim of unifying the British and French position on

Syria. The British participants were Wickham Steed, the Editor of the Times, who arranged the meeting, Gertrude Bell, Lawrence, and a representative of the F.O., Sir Valentine Chirol; the major French member was Robert de Caix, a hardline imperialist, and architect of the policy of the partition of Syria into so-called autonomous regions, one of which would later become the home base of the Assads, Hafez and then his son, Bashar. The unofficial anonymous memorandum which the participants produced opposed the sending of the Commission and, against that, supported the French mandate on Syria unequivocally, and the creation of a separate state within Syria, also under French suzerainty, to be known as 'Lebanon' [3]. This apparent volte-face shows Lawrence at his most ruthlessly pragmatic, perhaps desperate, in the attempt to broker a deal but what it brought him in subsequent self-disgust we can only guess at. Feisal in Paris was almost completely dependent on Lawrence, whose tactics were becoming increasingly suspect to Arab members of Feisal's delegation, perhaps even to Feisal himself. His efforts were successful, but only superficially so. On April 13th Feisal did meet with Clemenceau but achieved nothing. He left for Syria a week later. Lawrence helped to draft the valedictory letter to Clemenceau.

## THE DEATH OF ROBERT TIGHE CHAPMAN BT

A few days earlier, he had received a telegram that his father was dangerously ill. Ned, as he was always known at home, had rushed back from Paris but arrived two hours too late to see him alive. His death was sudden and unexpected. He had been struck down by Spanish flu. Although Ned was unusually reticent about the death of family members and their effect on him, it must have been a psychological blow. Absorbed as he was in the diplomatic battle in Paris, he did not realise at the time all that his father had meant to him. His father was the member of the family with whom he had a confident, if slightly distant relationship, whom he liked to respect, whom he had been able to take for granted. An Anglo-Irish gentleman, "on the mind and imagination of T.E. Lawrence his influence was enormous", wrote V.S. Pritchett.[4] His death destroyed whatever hopes TE may have had concerning happiness within his family and removed a last prop of psychological assurance. His relationship with his mother was full of fear and resentment.

He said nothing about his loss on his return and later Feisal, with typical generosity of mind, was to praise as courageous his extraordinary ability to stay any demonstration of personal grief in the call of duty. Less generously, it may be seen as another demonstration, not only of that totally single-minded involvement in action, until the battle is won or lost, but also of an inability to express grief, as in his reaction to the news of the death in France of two of his brothers; but, as Lawrence was coming to know, when action is exhausted, repressed emotional expression takes its revenge. And there was more to come.

He had long suspected that his father and mother were not married. But it was not until he returned home again, a week later, that his mother indicated to him a letter from the deceased:

> My dear Sons,
> I know this letter will be a cause of great sorrow & sadness to you all, as it is to me to write it. The cruel fact is this, that your mother & I were never married.[5]

He learnt in black and white that his father was not Mr Lawrence but an Anglo-Irish aristocrat named Sir Thomas Chapman. Later, he was to romanticize him as "naturally lord-like. He had been thirty-five years in the larger life, and a spendthrift, a sportsman, and a hard rider and drinker." The humiliation that is evident in his father's letter was blamed by the son on his mother.

※

Versailles, "the peace to end all peace", breathed, and still breathes today, an atmosphere of retrenchment, bitterness, fatal revengefulness, petty wrangling and cynicism. The opening pages of *Seven Pillars* are eloquent against it. In those pages, Lawrence evokes the solidarity of companionship in battle and danger, both Arab and British; but in Versailles, he was alone. Mistrusted by the French to the point of paranoia, suspected also as an imperialist manipulator by some of the Arab delegation, alternately disowned or used by the British, Lawrence played without self-pity the role of scapegoat, lobbying with increasing hopelessness for the Arab cause represented by Feisal, the cause he had chosen to make his own. The chickens had come home to roost with a vengeance. Lawrence's statements should rarely be taken as permanent positions, but there is some reason to accept his retrospective judgement that "those five months were the worst I have lived through".[6]

John Maynard Keynes, a member of the British delegation, has seemed to disagree: "The first part of 1919 was the only time when I was really acquainted with T.E.L. I agree with you strongly that it was subsequent events that twisted him. I have always thought that the view which attributed his state of mind to the privations and experiences of the war years, was wrong. When I knew him in the spring of 1919, I should say that he was a man fully in control of his nerves and quite as normal as most of us in his reactions to the world".[7] However, there is no contradiction. Lawrence's 1927 judgement is a retrospective view of himself, and is doubtless coloured by a sense of disgust, failure and humiliation. The moral consequences of Versailles would not be immediately apparent.

It was difficult enough to play the role in Paris of the British agent behind the scenes, arranging and manipulating in the interests of Britain and her Empire. This was essentially the role he had played with such success in Arabia and Syria. During the war, in spite of his knowledge of the duplicity of Whitehall, Lawrence believed yet (until near the end, at least) in the compatibility of the double role he was playing, that of a friend to the Arabs, their guide and leader; and the adviser to Feisal, even manipulator, in the interests of British aims. He may have deceived, but he believed it was all in a good cause. He was comforted by the moral support he received from his like-minded colleagues, both at the Arab Bureau in Cairo, and in the field from fellow officers such as Stirling and Newcombe. The former, like him, were anti-French and wanted to bury the Sykes–Picot agreement. Here in Paris, surrounded by British diplomats who had no sympathy for Arab aspirations, it was increasingly obvious that his role of adviser to Feisal under British auspices was morally unsustainable, and he was isolated. His behaviour in Paris and up to the final British hand-washing of Syria in September shows him moving into deeper and deeper compromises. The humiliation and guilt nourished by the unfamiliarity of failure, the knowledge of his false position, and perhaps the doubtful loyalty (to Feisal) of some of his actions, were absolutely devastating and had a profound influence on his book.

The curse of divided loyalties haunts the pages of *Seven Pillars of Wisdom*. His sublime dream of creating a new Arabia, which had begun in the Wadi Safra in October 1916, and seemed so close to fulfilment in Damascus, had failed. His book could be no longer be simply an epic story of his triumph; it would be, in the words of André Malraux, a 'speech for the Defense'. The theme of betrayal would be exploited to the full.

In these circumstances, at first hopeful but always uncertain, he began the writing project that he would take seven years to finish and which would perpetuate the legend of the Arab Revolt and of himself. The book about the Arabian adventure was never out of his mind and his impatience is attested by his beginning it in circumstances which would have put most writers off, especially a beginner. He stated that he began to write the book in his room in the Continental Hotel, Room 98 from mid-February, in the midst of his spasmodic but demanding diplomatic and social activity, using what time he had in the early morning and free evenings. He wrote fluently from memory and claimed that he completed 250,000 words in Paris in three months. Later, however, he would tell Liddell Hart that he had merely sketched out his history in this first effort. He soon realised he needed more documentation, which meant returning to Cairo. With his usual skill at getting what he wanted, he obtained permission to fly from Paris with a flight of Handley Page bombers, destination Cairo, in order to consult files in the Arab Bureau,[8] to retrieve any notes and papers he had left behind, and probably, numbers of the *Arab Bulletin*, to which he had contributed much on his experiences of the war and his views on various issues. In the middle of May, he took off for Rome.

The spiritual birth of *Seven Pillars of Wisdom*, at least as we know it, took place in the air. As the plane rose over Paris, his spirits rose also, and the failure and moral doubt of the conference fell away. He felt that elevation of the spirit once celebrated by a poet of the city below him:

*Envole-toi bien loin de ces miasmes morbides;*
*Va te purifier dans l'air supérieur,*
*Et bois; comme une pure et divine liqueur,*
*Le feu clair qui remplit les espaces limpides.*[9]

An almost mystical ecstacy for the air, which the poem evokes, would remain with him and influence the direction of his life.

He had with him a book by Sir Robert Vansittart called *The singing caravan*. On a fly-leaf, he began to jot down in pencil his thoughts, random snatches:

The wind had been born somewhere over the far Euphrates, and had slowly dragged its inarticulate way across the many hollows of this Hamad to find its first obstacle in the palace of ibn Wardani, against whose gaping window sockets it fussed in a steady column of air filled with the childish murmurs of first speech.

Alan Dawnay had that faculty, so rare among Englishmen, of making the best – not only of a bad job, but of a good one also.

Let my excuse be that I have introduced such trivia, just so that no one should mistake this narrative of mine for History. The book of battle is a large one, and each of us sees only a little page. I have written down what I thought, and saw and did, fully conscious myself that as I sometimes did ill and saw imperfectly, so also my thoughts must often be wrong. This book is the bones of history, not history herself.

Any thought of Naser was always a good thought.

A    I wrought for him freedom to lighten his sad eyes: but he had died waiting for me. So I threw my gift away and now not anywhere will I find rest and peace.
*Written between Paris and Lyons in Handley Page*

Five samples that to a strange degree represent a selection of topics and styles of the book. Many readers will recognize notes 1 and 3, which found their way into it.

It is also not difficult to recognize in (5) the elements of what was to become the famous dedicatory poem *To S.A*. It has been assumed that these lines refer to this S.A, whoever he was.[10] Here, for the first time, we see Lawrence practising this art of veiled identity, along with the tone of melancholy, which characterise the dedicatory poem.

Then, in the same exalted mood, as the plane flew down the valley of the Rhone, he began the lyrical opening of *Seven Pillars*. He would like later to recall that moment and the throbbing of the great engines which, he claimed, inspired the rhythm.

We lived for years anyhow with one another in the naked desert under the indifferent heaven, fermenting by day in the heat of the sun, dazed by the beating wind, and at night stained with dew, and shamed into nothingness by the innumerable silences of stars.[11]

On May 17, the Handley Page, attempting a night landing on a downhill lie, hit a tree while trying to get airborne again, at Centocelle, near Rome. The pilots were killed but Lawrence, sitting behind, survived with concussion and a cracked shoulder blade. He recovered quickly and left Rome in another Handley Page but that one broke down in Crete and Lawrence, never one to miss an archaeological opportunity, missed its departure when visiting the ruins of Knossos. Only on June 28th does he reach Cairo, in company with the great Arabian explorer Harry St. John Philby, who had been sent out, on another bomber, on a placatory mission to Ibn Saud of the Nejd, who had just inflicted a crushing defeat on Abdullah, Feisal's elder brother. This defeat, which confounded Lawrence's assessment of Ibn Saud's strength, announced a new power in the Middle East. Lawrence will meet both Philby and Abdullah two years later, again in the Middle East, when history will have moved on.

He spent only a day or two in Cairo and was back in Paris for most of July and August ("neither we nor the War Office ever know where he is", memoed an aggrieved F.O.) but, with Feisal still in Syria and Woodrow Wilson, whose advocacy of the self-determination of the peoples of the former Turkish empire was Lawrence's main hope, now ill and out of the reckoning, his role at the Peace Conference was effectively over. He was able to move out of his hotel to Feisal's headquarters in Neuilly where, left to himself and armed with notes and documents, he made his first big surge in the writing of *Seven Pillars*. In mid-August he returned definitively to England.

Lawrence was back in Oxford. The Paris Peace Conference had ended with the Arabs being denied any formal recognition of independence in Syria, Palestine, or Iraq. Feisal retained a degree of fragile autonomy in inland Syria. Lawrence himself was being attacked in the French media as an agitator and in British diplomatic circles for being "to a large extent responsible for our troubles with the French over Syria".[12] On September 8th, in a last-ditch effort to move public opinion, he published a letter in the Times. But on the 13th, Lloyd George announced the British withdrawal from Syria, piously endorsing the arrangements of the now amended agreement with the French. Demonstrating once again a very flexible attitude, Lawrence had come round to accepting Sykes–Picot as the best solution the Arabs could hope to get. He had recommended a very similar solution to the F.O. within a day or two of Lloyd George's announcement and told another F.O. official, Kidston, that he regarded the agreement as a personal triumph for himself![13] He was moved to write to Lloyd George:

> I must confess to you that in my heart I always believed that you would let the Arabs down:- so that now I find it quite difficult to know how to thank you. . . . Now in your agreement with them you have kept all our promises to them, and given them more perhaps than perhaps they ever deserved, and my relief at getting out with clean hands is

very great. . . . My first sign of grace is that I will obey the F.O. and the W.O. and not see Feisal again.[14]

There is something rather pathetic here. It is true that his pragmatism has led him to concede more and more but surely he was naive to believe, even for one moment, that a British withdrawal would leave intact a viable Arab government in the Syrian interior, without access to the sea, and alongside a French one which would now be immediately reinforced by a French army. Either his judgement is yielding to wishful thinking or he is looking for a conscience-salving exit from the hopeless situation in which Feisal now found himself. The central statement in his letter, and especially the words *clean hands,* suggests the latter. We shall see this expression frequently repeated in the future – in *Seven Pillars,* in letters to his friends, to F.O. officials – whenever the issue of the Arab settlement arises. The hope of Arab independence in any part of Syria was now dead, and even a limited autonomy highly unlikely. As for Feisal, he was under no illusions. He arrived in London, an unwelcome visitor, on 19th September, too late. He protested bitterly about the British withdrawal, which would leave him cut off from the Mediterranean and thus at the mercy of the French. He was told it was no longer the British government's responsibility; he must negotiate with France.

Lawrence had done what he could, and was at last free. The familiar Oxford scene, which had been so much his, did not give him much comfort. He was not yet, would never be, a person who could allow his mind to relax or his soul to respond for more than a fleeting moment to the beauty of a scene or the love of the familiar that is such a profound human need, a part of oneself. Besides, something essential was missing. His father. In the melancholy of an Oxford autumn, in the now half-empty house in Polstead Road with his mother and two surviving brothers, he would sometimes sit the entire morning between breakfast and lunch in the same position, without moving, and with the same vacant expression on his face.

The dangerous dreamer of the day had woken from his dream "to find that it was vanity". His future, his great hope, now was the book he was writing about it.

## THE FIRST TEXT

On the streets of London, even as Lawrence was staring motionless into the Oxford autumn, the people of England sought the pleasures that would put the war behind them, or at least show it in a more chivalrous light. A new show on an unknown war in romantic Arabia had opened at Covent Garden in August, ahead of the main season. "At this moment", exulted the show's American presenter, a publicist named Lowell Thomas, "somewhere in London, hiding from a host of feminine admirers, reporters, book publishers, autograph fiends and every species of hero-worshipper, is a young man whose name will go down in history beside those of Sir Francis Drake, Sir Walter Raleigh, Lord Clive, Charles Gordon, and all the other famous heroes of Great Britain's glorious past."[15]

Our latter day Raleigh (he was said to be related to the original Sir Walter), if depressed, was by no means destitute. Powerful friends, on whom he had always been able to rely, were busy pulling strings. In June, through the good offices of D.G. Hogarth, he had been elected to a Research Fellowship at All Soul's College, Oxford. There, he was able to avoid the depressing atmosphere of home, and the madding crowds of Covent Garden, in its exclusive precincts. A more comfortable and scholarly abode for writing his book could not be imagined. Therefore, he did not write it there.

An alternative retreat – even more secluded than All Souls, and more spartan – was offered him by Herbert Baker, an architect, whom he met in the common room of New College; they had discussed Syrian archaeology. It was an attic flat above the architect's offices at 14 Barton Street, Westminster, leased from Westminster School. There, in the autumn, according to his own account, he continued to expand the draft he had completed in Paris. Meanwhile, he showed the original Paris manuscript to Hogarth in Oxford, and then sent it to Colonel Alan Dawnay (see above), the senior British staff officer attached to the Arab Revolt, who now held an appointment at the Royal Military College, Sandhurst.

Then on November 28th, the MS disappeared. Lawrence had gone down to Camberley by train to hear Dawnay's comments on it. To bring it back, he borrowed an attaché case. He then, in an act of extraordinary absent-mindedness, left the case behind at Reading station, either in the refreshment room or on the train. There was no copy. The whole manuscript, except "the Introduction and drafts of Books 9 and 10"[16] was lost and was never recovered. Whether the MS was lost on purpose or by accident, or not lost at all, has become one of the classic controversies of the Lawrencian canon.

Would it have told us anything new? Some terrible secret? Lost MSS always seem more valuable than existing ones. Most books go through several drafts. He would certainly have destroyed the MS in any case, once he had revised it, just as he did subsequent ones. The copy of an early draft of the Introduction and Book I which came to light in 1997 (see below) and was hailed as a fragment of the lost text, provides no startling revelations. The attaché case also contained, as Lawrence claimed, photographs, negatives, and wartime notes relevant to the later chapters. Given the extraordinary, almost photographic detail of the narrative in *Seven Pillars*, one would hardly place huge importance on the loss of these documents.

Why did Lawrence not keep his drafts or, if he is to be believed, even the wartime notes on which they were based? Many writers do not bother to keep drafts, but they rarely destroy original sources before a book is at least finished, if not published. Lawrence makes a point of announcing in his Preface that he destroyed his notes as he went along, as if he was still involved in secret work. Giving wrong dates, confusing systems of Book or chapter numeration, using terms ambiguously, studied carelessness, and producing irreconcilable or subtly different versions of the same events, may be part of the same habit or obsession of the secret intelligence officer. For June Rathbone, however, both the loss of the MS and destruction of the notes signal the perversity of the masochist: "Who but a masochist could possibly have lost almost the entire book, a year's concentrated work, almost a quarter of a million words, whilst changing trains at Reading station? What academic, apart from Lawrence, an erstwhile archaeologist employed by the British Museum, would have been perverse enough to destroy his wartime notes as each section of the book was constructed"?[17] He wished to be known, but to control absolutely what would be revealed about himself. This is one of the constants of this story; and a decisive constraint on the fate of his book.

Lawrence gave four accounts of the chronology of this first version, of which no two are identical. Three are written accounts and one a later verbal account to Liddell Hart, his biographer. For those who like Lawrence puzzles, see Apppendix 1. It is certainly a fine example of his seemingly compulsive need never to give the same version of a story twice.

From these various accounts and other sources I have drawn the following conclusions:

1. He sketched out his memoir of the Revolt in Paris between mid-February and mid-May, largely from memory. He referred to this as the first draft. It had seven Books.
2. He travelled to Egypt in mid-May to get needed documentation. He wrote the first version of Chapter 2 on the plane to

Rome and the rest of the Introduction (nine chapters) between Rome and Cairo, and the return to Paris in July.
3. He completed Text 1 in Paris on July 25th, in Feisal's absence, writing intensively with the aid of documentation, putting flesh on the bones.
4. On his return to England, he added more to the beginning and end of the narrative, creating drafts of at least two new Books, before the loss occurred. This indicates that the original draft of Text 1 was already being superseded by the time it was lost.[18]

There is one very important conclusion we can draw from this history of composition: Text 1 was composed amid constant interference from other activities, written here and there as time and circumstances permitted. There was no period of unmolested leisure of more than two weeks until he returned to Oxford and he insists that he did not write a word of it there. From this we can make a strong claim that it could only have been a series of accounts written from memory expanded by material copied more or less directly from diaries and notes or reports. What he was about was getting it all down while the experience was still close to him. At the other extreme, however, there was at least one chapter of a quite different inspiration, much more personal and imaginative, probably two. *The Spirit of the Revolt* (Chapter 2) we have already traced; the piece on his capture and beating by the Turks at Dera' may be another. He claimed it was one of the first chapters he wrote. Both these chapters stand out in bold contrast to the rest of the book. Overall, however, an absence of premeditated structure capable of easily accomodating chapters like this remains a striking characteristic of the book.

Lawrence's own indications on his sources and method of composition confirm this hypothesis. He relied on wartime notes and diaries and, undoubtedly, after the return from Cairo, on information in the Arab Bulletin and other documents retrieved there, especially his own reports written from Arabia and Syria. Evidence of this is the early fragment mentioned above. The first part of Book I 'The Discovery of Feisal' begins with a description of Lawrence's first desert journey. Lawrence had written a detailed report of the journey at the time,[19] and this report is closely adhered to, almost copied, in this early draft. The fact that some of Lawrence's reports were, like this one, semi-literary pieces made this easier.

The diaries helped him with a chronology of his activity, the names of places, and the dates when he had been there; the notebooks contained very rough jottings made on the march. They contained an abundance of names and notes on tribes and individuals and places, and a great deal of topographical detail. Nearly all of this finds its way into the book. Although he claimed in the Preface to have destroyed these notes as each section of the draft was completed, some of the notebooks survived this fate and are still extant.[20]

TE told Liddell Hart something about his method of composition after his return to Paris: "Sketched out expedition to bridge again – from memory. Then took diaries and notes, and wrote on the other side – took days. A composite process. Then 'planing off into one smooth run'." This method sounds entirely sensible, but it is time-consuming to combine memory with other sources into a single version.

### THE CURTIS DRAFT

In 1997, as indicated above, there was sold at Sotheby's a typed copy of a document, either a typescript or a MS, originally sent by Lawrence to Lionel Curtis, one of his closest friends after the war.[21] It is a fragment, and there are no chapter breaks or titles. It is an early version of what became the Introduction and the first five chapters of Book 1. These last describe Lawrence's first journey up-country whose climax is the dramatic meeting in Feisal's tent in Wadi Safra which ends, as in *Seven Pillars*, with the legendary exchange:-

FEISAL: *And how do you like our place here in Wadi Safra?*
LAWRENCE: *Well, but it is far from Damascus.*

Is this a fragment of the original Text I of which all but the Introduction was lost, according to Lawrence, at Reading station? When the fragment came to light, the news was published by Philip Knightley in the *Independent on Sunday* under the title *Found: Lawrence of Arabia's lost text*. It is a headline in tune with the legendary landscape of Lawrencian mysteries but, in fact, very little is known of the history of this document, a typescript, other than that it, or another document on which the typescript is based, was apparently sent to Lionel Curtis by Lawrence on an unspecified date. I refer to it as *The Curtis draft*. It may contain fragments of Text I (1919) or early 1920 (Text II) or some of each. In any case, it is the earliest fragment we possess.

This is how it starts:

> This is the narrative of what I tried to do in Arabia, and of some of what I saw there. It is a chronicle no more skilled than the tales of the old men who marched with Bohemond or Coeur de Lion. It treats of daily life, mean happenings, little people. In it are no lessons for the world, no events that will shake peoples. It is not the history of the Arab movement but just the story of me in it. I have filled it with trivial things, partly that no one should mistake it for history, (its place is among the bones from which some day a fresh man will extract history) and partly for the great pleasure it is to me to recall the free fellowship of those who with me made the revolt. We were very happy together, and this story is just an edition of the notes jotted down daily on the march, added to some reports sent in to Cairo, and filled in with my memories of the sweep of the open places, the taste of their wide winds, the sunlight and the hope in which we worked. It felt like morning and the freshness of the world intoxicated us. We were wrought up with ideas, inexpressible and vaporous, well worth fighting for, and indeed necessary to fight for.

There is nothing here that is unfamiliar. But the feel is different. It is less bookish, more confiding than the later 1922 version:

> We were fond together, and there are here memories of the sweep of the open places, the taste of wide winds, the sunlight, and the hopes in which we worked. It felt like morning and the freshness of the world-to-be intoxicated us. We were wrought up with ideas inexpressible and vaporous, but to be fought for.

It has become more stylish and there is a first hint of a mannered archaic vocabulary. Also, there is no reference to notebooks and reports. This original introduction was overwhelmingly a personal story, 'the spirit of the Revolt' in fact; only later was it divided into two chapters: *How and Why I wrote* and *The Spirit of the Revolt*, as it appears in the 1922 text.

> I have written down what I believe I thought and saw and did, fully conscious that as I sometimes did ill, and saw imperfectly, so also I must have thought wrong. However that is not for me to say but for you to tell me. And if there is evil in the tale, as some say there is, I would have you remember that we lived for years anyhow with one another in the naked desert, under the indifferent heaven, fermenting by day in the heat of the sun, dazed by the beating wind, and at night stained with dew, and shamed into nothingness by the innumerable silences of stars.

The last three lines, copied from *The singing caravan* fly-leaf, will remain virtually unaltered from their original form. Here, the idea of *evil* is slight, and tentative; later it will be the first word in the book, presented as something commanding, esoteric, even beautiful. The later text suggests that we are about to read a story of evil which is sublimated by the purity of the desert environment. Here, there is less sense of certainty, most notably a tendency to appeal to an imaginary audience or readership. There is indeed a Conradian feel to these early samples, an appeal to an unseen audience about the judgement of difficult moral dilemmas in colonial environments.

> To give yourself to the possession of another people, people on whom you can react only by difference is selling your soul to a brute. You are not of them. You may imitate them, and do it so well that they imitate you back again, which is what I did; or you may stand against them, persuade yourself of a mission and beat and twist them into something which they, of their own accord, would not have been. In neither case are you doing a thing of yourself. In one you are giving away your own environment and pretending to theirs (all pretences are hollow worthless things): in the other you are exploiting your old environment to press them out of theirs. The chapter of the Houyhnhnms is the gravest lesson ever read to us on our colonial governance.

Chapter 36 of *Lord Jim*, has the identical phrase 'selling your soul to a brute'. Lawrence may have been reading *Lord Jim* at the time he claimed to have written the first draft of this passage in May 1919.[22] The connection between Lawrence and Conrad is both obvious and mysterious; on the one hand, the parallels between Lawrence's interpretation of his situation and Conrad's fiction are obvious; not only in *Lord Jim* but also *Nostromo* and *Heart of Darkness*; on the other, Lawrence has never directly admitted specific influences on his writing.

He has, however, made a general admission about "borrowed phrases and ideas" (OX 4).[23] The Curtis draft shows how much the Marlow presentation of a man's moral predicament, in so far as it assumes the imaginary presence of an unseen jury, must have appealed to Lawrence, and helped him to create the manner in which the colonial dilemma is presented.[24] In his later versions, especially 1926, Lawrence suppressed a good deal of this kind of language of a man among friends, which jarred with the remote and Olympian style he was developing. But the overall feeling of a man pleading before a jury remains overwhelming. Lawrence's Marlow was himself.

# CHAPTER 2

# WRITING THE BOOK: LONDON, OXFORD, POLE HILL, 1920

### TEXT II

The book was begun when the history it relates was still in the making, right in the midst of wrangling and uncertainty about the Arab future, in which Lawrence was directly involved. Did this have any specific influence on the book at this point? Certainly, it did. As we have seen, it was in September that TE wrote to Lloyd George congratulating him on having made an honourable settlement. This means that he had already discounted Feisal's original claim to greater Syria (Feisal had not) and was happy with the once reviled Sykes–Picot treaty. In an anonymous letter to the *Times* on September 8th, giving full details of all the British and French commitments made to the Arabs during the war, he even supported the treaty as the Arabs' 'Charter'. This was published by the Editor, Wickham Steed, on September 11th. However, Steed, who supported French claims to Syria, suppressed the last part in which Lawrence expressed his anger at the way Feisal and the Arabs had been treated, and bitterly reproached the British government for putting him in a false position with the Arabs through having authorised him to make promises to them which they had no intention of honouring. The two parts of this letter illustrate the self-contradictory element in Lawrence's character: flexible pragmatism on the one hand, emotionalism on the other. *The Times* article shows that a *personal* sense of betrayal was already very much in evidence, and it would still be there when he sat down to re-write his book.

The draft had been lost but he was persuaded to rewrite it, by

Hogarth, who reminded him that no-one but he could write the story of the Arab Revolt, and he got down to work at once. Here begins another heroic labour in which he sat for three or four months in the unheated flat in Barton Street, Westminster, starting apparently in January 1920. In this place he wrote 400,000 words, writing Book VI (the Yarmouk Bridge and Deraa incident) in a single 24-hour sitting: 34,000 words, giving an average of over 1400 words an hour. These are his own statements and estimates; Lawrence's estimates, where his own exploits are concerned, are often considerably exaggerated. However, the exact figures do not matter. What is important is that this second draft was written at a feverish pace.

"His record run was over the Easter holiday", wrote Vyvyan Richards, a schoolmaster friend from his undergraduate days, who was the only person whom Lawrence permitted to stay there with him. "He had forgotten that most shops would be closed and so he wrote for four days and most of the nights at a stretch without food – though a little further afield he could easily have found a restaurant open, of course. He sat, fireless, in very cold weather, wearing a leather, wool-lined flying suit, with the fattest fountain pen I have ever seen . . . and wrote in a splendid great Kalamazoo note-book, leather bound and secured with a patent lock that delighted him."[1]

When he left the flat for a break, he walked the wintry pavements of the small streets, to buy a sandwich at a station refreshment bar, keen to avoid meeting anyone he knew. "Westminster", Richards tells us, "provided excellent sixpenny hot baths for him round the corner, and for his washing, . . . he lugged it down to a taxi and off to the Savoy Hotel. Then he explained, you had but to stay one night, give your washing to the lift boy in the evening and it would appear next morning superbly laundered at your door". And the thrifty schoolmaster added: "What this method cost per collar, I never worked out"![2]

Not far away, across Hyde Park, the American showman was making his pitch every night to a new capacity audience, this time at the Royal Albert Hall, an audience that on one night included Lloyd George, and on another Prince Feisal and his retinue, while the King of England himself requested a private performance: "At this moment, somewhere in London, hiding from a host of feminine admirers, reporters, book publishers, autograph fiends, and every species of hero worshipper, is a young man whose name, etc . . . ." Lowell Thomas continued to announce. He was absolutely right this time. He wrote later that on at least five occasions the "Prince of Mecca" was sighted by his wife in some shadowy corner of the very theatre (Covent Garden) where he was uttering these words. The apparition had vanished before the show ended. Why did he go there? To be diverted from his enslaving task? Or did it intrigue the writer in him to see himself portrayed as a romantic hero, as someone so unlike his real self? Or was it the intoxicating taste of fame?

Lloyd George, the man who had thwarted Lawrence by dividing up the old Turkish Arab empire with France, commented in *Strand Magazine* in a preface to some of Lowell Thomas articles: "Everything that Mr Lowell Thomas says about Colonel Lawrence is true. In my opinion, Colonel Lawrence is one of the most remarkable and romantic figures of modern times." A legend was taking hold.

This period was one of the most secretive of Lawrence's always discreet life. He was indeed hiding from fiends but also from friends. For almost the only time in his life he gave absolute priority to his writing. He had learned that the task of writing a masterpiece must be given more exclusive attention than hitherto.

The manner in which this draft was written left its mark, not only on the finished product but also on the man himself. It was the latest stage in a self-destructive progress: first came the extraordinary physical ordeals and nervous exhaustion he exposed himself to in the Arab campaign; second, the demoralising failure at Versailles; and now, the ruthless attack on his physical endurance in the Barton Street flat. There seems to be something willed in it. What motivated this frenetic race to finish?

Impatience is a characteristic of the novice writer, and, in this case, there was the urgent need to rewrite his entire text. Whether he *had* lost it or merely abandoned it, he had something to prove and he was determined this time to get through to the end before he rested. Its very recent disappearance would in any case help him to write the new draft faster. However, the immediate circumstances are not the whole answer. He had chosen from long ago only to do things by extremes; it seems he knew no other way. More crucially, he had convinced himself that were he not to force himself in this way he might not succeed in writing the book he had failed to write at first attempt. The sudden deliberately enforced loneliness in a strange empty flat, with the bitter humiliation and self-disgust of Versailles immediately behind him, and the absence of any discernible way of life in front, gave to this extraordinary enterprise its peculiar zest. Creation was the alternative to an intolerable void. By the end of February he was able to write to Richards:

It is on paper in the first draft to the middle of Book vi: and there are seven books in all. But the first draft is a long way off the last one and I feel hopeless about ever finishing it. I work best entirely by myself: when I speak to no one for days.[3]

He claimed that when he once went without food or sleep for two days he wrote at his best, until he became delirious. Was he not following the glorious precedent of the Romantic period, the unknown starving genius forging his masterpiece in an attic? The feverish *pace* and the physical deprivation would raise the *pitch*:

I thought that the mind I had . . . if joined to a revival of the war-passion, would sweep over the ordinary rocks of technique. So I got into my garret, and . . . excited myself with hunger and cold and sleeplessness more than did de Quincey with his opium.[4]

It was a dangerous assumption and it is not clear that he succeeded. Undoubtedly, he was inspired by previous example. Nietzsche (in *Thus spake Zarathustra*) and Dostoevski, two of his icons, were both writers whose passion seems to sweep over the rocks of technique.

What exactly he wrote in this garret was a closely guarded secret locked in the Kalamazoo notebook; not a single word has been revealed. However, the same letter to Garnett tells us something. "It gave me a foundation, and on that I worked for two years, biting the lines deeper." What he had to do this time was to express the whole experience as an existential reality: the whole narrative of his life in the desert – every action, every journey, everything he did, brought about, saw, felt, thought, suffered; the outside and the inside – the events themselves, his reaction to them, their effect on him. From this would emerge, alongside or within the historical narrative, the drama of the self, of the sentient individual, to form the essential interest of the book. He used the *Arab Bulletin* and his existing wartime notebooks, but above all he relied on his astonishing memory, his perception of everything in relation to himself, the writer.

In the aftermath of Versailles he was also much concerned with the dubious historical legacy. Feisal would be in London in December/January begging for his help. One need not be astonished at the intensity of Lawrence's approach. Or his anxiety. Inevitably, the writing was emotional and self-justificatory. He wrote, passionately, the speech for the defense:

"The book (is) just a designed procession of Arab freedom from Mecca to Damascus."

"(The Arabs) achieved a deathless thing, a lasting inspiration to the children of their race."

"In this book also, for the last time, I mean to be my own judge of what to say."

"Seven Pillars of Wisdom: A triumph."

In this he succeeded, giving a version of history that influenced contemporaries and later generations down to the present day. The Arab Revolt has become almost synonymous with the name of Lawrence of Arabia. For all but the Arabs, that is.

This time, at the second attempt, he succeeded in completing the 400,000-word draft. He gave the date July 12th for the completion of Text II but he had got the full story down by April. This text formed the basis of the *Seven Pillars* as we know it; Text III, which was effectively the Oxford text, was essentially a revision of Text II, which he burned as soon as the third draft was finished.

"The first draft (of Text II) is a long way off the last one", he had written to his friend. Yet he could not have dared to imagine just how far that would be. He knew the text would have to be revised, but in what way exactly? Many writers greater than Lawrence find this beyond them; they are too tired from the effort, psychologically washed out, too close to the material to achieve the necessary detachment. If unsure, they may turn to a friend to get an objective view. For Lawrence, this was difficult. He was far too diffident to show anything less than the best he could do. Besides, some of the material was personal and shocking. Who would understand what he was trying to do? Did he even want them to know? Not yet anyway. He had always been a man who pursued his objective alone and to the end. There was no problem in existence that could not, should not, be solved by himself.

In this unique case he was wrong. Writing was somehow different and Lawrence would spend many subsequent years trying to work out why. His self-questioning would fill a small book in itself. Had he been able to overcome his pride and secretiveness after completing Text II, and confide the draft to a few trusted critics, as he eventually did with the finished text, he would in theory have had a better chance of perceiving earlier on the immense gap between the real and the ideal, between what he had wanted to write and what he had actually written. By the time he did show his work, the creative inspiration was over and could never return. Now that the book was written, it would be a kind of double of himself, sometimes an enemy, always disturbing.

He was buffeted by two quite different problems that were to constantly get in the way of his book: what to do with his life once the book was finished; and the unresolvable conflict between the desire to reveal himself and the shame and fear of it. The book became a source of stress and he was only too happy to escape from it into the real world. It is one thing to improve a book in which the self is safely hidden from the reader; quite another when one's self is the very subject of the book.

## AN OXFORD FRIENDSHIP

On April 15th Lawrence wrote to Robert Graves from All Soul's College inviting him over for lunch. He had called a halt to his ordeal in Barton Street, he felt he had broken the back of the book. There is no recorded reaction of joy. That blissful rest, however short, after a great effort, seems to have been outside his experience. But there is a return to normal life. There was time for social life, the only circumstance that sometimes permitted him to relax. For the first time since before the war he has prolonged freedom from an all-embracing commitment. True, the book was not quite finished, but was it not just a matter of tidying it up? Improving the style?

It was at All Souls, in that melancholy November of 1919, that TE had first met Robert Graves, seven years his junior, and an undergraduate at St. John's. He owed to his father, Richard Perceval Graves, a man of letters, the invitation to the dinner at All Souls where their first meeting took place. Lawrence was in the coffee room talking to the Regius Professor of Divinity about the influence of the Syrian Greek philosophers on early Christianity. "He happened to be wearing full evening dress ... evening dress concentrates the attention on the eyes, and Lawrence's eyes immediately held me. They were startingly blue, even by artificial light, and never met the eyes of the person he addressed," recalled Graves.[5] Graves knew at least as much about the poet Meleager and the city of Gadara as did Lawrence, and joined in the discussion. "You must be Graves the poet?", guessed the well-informed Lawrence. Graves, a largely unknown poet, was warmed by this recognition. What with Herbert Baker, Lawrence, the Regius Professor, and now Graves, the Syrian

Greek philosophers of Gadara[6] seem to have been well represented at Oxford that year. Between Lawrence and Graves the theme would remain alive. They shared a wide knowledge of the Hellenic culture of the East.

They quickly became friends. Graves was awed by the scholar-warrior, and flattered by his friendship. Although he had the war in the trenches behind him and had seen everything (he was having intermittent attacks of shell shock), Graves had a natural youthful exuberance and trust. At that first meeting he had felt "a sudden extraordinary sympathy" with Lawrence and now, in October, he wrote proudly to his brother John how he was spending "most of my time at Oxford with Col. Lawrence the man who smashed the Turks in Arabia & Palestine: he is at All Souls and a great man on poetry, pictures, music & everything else in the world".[7] His nephew and biographer was to write: "The truth is that Lawrence had a great gift for reflecting back to people the best of which they were capable; and he sustained Robert's sense of worth both as a poet and as a human being at a time when he was increasingly full of self-doubt."[8] Graves was already committed to poetry as a vocation but he was overburdened by money problems, marriage problems, too many children, and too little time. Lawrence's life looked beautifully simple by comparison.

He wrote in *Goodbye to All That* of their early friendship. He would visit him around 11 o'clock between lectures, just as Lawrence had got up after working all night. In his oak-panelled room were "pictures, including Augustus John's portrait of the Emir Feisal, which Lawrence bought, I believe, from John with the diamond he had worn as a mark of honour in his Arab headdress; his books, including a Kelmscott Chaucer; three prayer-rugs, the gift of Arab leaders, one of them with a lapis lazuli sheen on the nap; the Tell Shawm (i.e. *Shahm*) station bell from a raid on the Hedjaz railway; and on the mantelpiece a four-thousand-year-old toy – a clay soldier on horseback from a child's grave at Carchemish".[9] An idiosyncratic display of unique objets d'art.

And they behaved as if 1914–18 had never happened. Graves sensed that Lawrence disliked the subject of the Arab Revolt, and there was a tacit agreement between them never to talk about the war: "We were both suffering from its effects and enjoying Oxford as a too-good-to-be-true relaxation." The foolscap pages of the *Seven Pillars* "were always stacked in a neat pile on his living-room table" but Graves sensed that TE did not want to talk about that either. There were to be limits.

What they did talk about was poetry. Graves was still finding his feet as a poet and Lawrence was soon to become an important source of feedback to him. He sent Lawrence almost all his new poetry in those days and Lawrence sent back highly detailed reactions like (from *The Gnat*): "I don't like 'tyrant's use': it's become a phrase now: not crisp enough: also the rhyme of 'fare' and 'hair' is rather wanton, I think."[10] These were the kind of minute corrections Lawrence was to make, *ad nauseam*, to his own work. But Graves acknowledged: "for years he was very serious about my work. Because of this he stood as a sort of guardian angel over me: if anything went wrong he was always on hand to help". It was often money.

Graves also helped Lawrence. Banished to the political wilderness, Lawrence was focussing his tireless will on literature and the art of writing. All his life had been learning and the practice of what he had learned, and now he was going to learn how to use words. Sure, he had written a book – but how to make it into a masterpiece? He was keen to meet poets (especially the younger ones) and there was no lack of them in Oxford. Graves knew them all. He introduced him to the poet laureate, Robert Bridges, who lived on Boar's Hill, and to Robert Nichols and Edmund Blunden. Graves also brought him into renewed contact with his closest friend, Siegfried Sassoon. And in October, Graves got him to invite the American Vachel Lindsay, "one of the best bad poets of the day," to lunch in his rooms after a poetry reading at the university. Appropriately, this event took place by gracious permission of the eponymous Sir Walter Raleigh: Merton Professor of English History at the University.

Lawrence's interest in poetry was not just practical. Years later Graves was to write: "Lawrence frankly envied poets. He felt that they had some sort of secret which he might be able to learn for his own spiritual profit. This secret he envisaged as a technical mastery of words rather than as a particular mode of living and thinking."[11] A revealing comment.

## THE-BOOK-TO-BUILD-THE-HOUSE

Alas, it would be misleading to give the impression that Lawrence was quietly and happily cloistered at All Souls during the latter part of 1920, busy with improving his book, having learned discussions with professors of divinity, or learning style from Oxford poets. In fact, he was never there for more than a month or two, and was frequently in London and elsewhere. It would be more true to say that he was "of no fixed address". He seemed to want it this way. He made a point of writing to friends that he was only at All Souls' because he could live there free. "I've hopped off here – more or less broke – for a month. They give one credit", he wrote to Lord Winterton in April. And in August, to Wilfrid Scawen Blunt, whom he had never met, "Unfortunately I have been driven down into Oxford (here I live on credit: elsewhere I need cash!)". These unsolicited revelations were made to express his willed independence from bourgeois convention; also to shock (Lawrence of Arabia broke!) and to make his wealthy acquaintances feel uncomfortable or sympathetic, and then to complete the trick to his satisfaction by refusing the loans they then offered to him. "He is extremely difficult to help," wrote Hogarth.

There is also here a foreshadowing of the future – the life in the ranks with the otherwise jobless poor, the short back-and-sides, and the Union Jack club. He would later come up to London to meet with a King who loved him, and stay for that purpose in a boarding house.

For nearly three years (August 1919–August 1922) Lawrence went through a period when he was uncertain what to do with the rest of his life, and this led to his being pulled in different directions. Through it flows the *Seven Pillars*, at first a headlong flood (first half of 1920), then meandering and sluggish, but persistent; then again swift and impatient (first half of 1922). One discerns a constant urgency to clear the decks of the paraphernalia of the past: the 'Arab business' on the one hand and the Book on the other – they are of course inextricably linked. Until he had settled these, and emptied his mind of the motives that inspired them, he was not free. In these years, he was living between a past which weighed on his conscience and a future to which the doors were still closed.

What would he do, where would he go, how would he live his eventual freedom?

There was a dream, even a plan. Vyvyan Richards was Lawrence's oldest friend. They had formed a close friendship during TE's undergraduate years at Jesus College from 1907 and TE had kept in touch with him, even during the war. Richards was the faithful friend, Pylades to TE's Orestes. "I was the kind of foil he liked. All that he did and said was so completely fresh to me that I constantly reacted with a delight that stimulated him too." At Oxford they had shared a dream of medieval living as expressed by William Morris and the pre-Raphaelites. And they obtained a living symbol of it when a medieval hall (appropriately named Laurence Hall) was pulled down by the College and TE managed to acquire some of the old timbers. "We planned and planned to build ourselves such another hall and crown it with these carved oak kingposts and their rafters and purlins", wrote Richards. Lawrence had kept the kingposts. They had made many excursions, including one to Broad Campden in search of a Morris house.

> We found the house, an old Cotswold stone building which seemed to us just right for Morris. . . . There was a low gallery at one end screened with Morris chintz, a long polished refectory table and shelves full of the Kelmscott printings. Here and there were Morris tapestries. Above all, on a special oak lectern lay open the great Morris— Burne-Jones *Chaucer*, the book we had come specially to see, a feast to us then in itself. We were shown all about the rest of the quaint building, and, to crown all, found that it contained the very hand-press that Morris himself had used.[12]

Here, from example, were the ingredients of a simple semi-monastic life of craftsmanship that seemed to suit Lawrence so well: hand printing fine editions in a purpose-built medieval hall. Ten years later, just before the end of his war service in the Middle East, he wrote nostalgically, recalling Morris from far Arabia:

> This is a very long porch to explain why I am always blowing up railway trains and bridges instead of looking for the well at the world's end.[13]

During the war and afterwards, Vyvyan Richards had a job as a schoolmaster at Bancroft's, near Pole Hill on the edge of Epping Forest. He actually lived in a timber hut on the hill with a number of heraldic shields round the walls. Pole Hill, bare save for a couple of Nissan huts and with a fine view over London, had been proposed by Richards before the war as the ideal place for setting up their printing establishment. In September 1919 Lawrence had written to him from Polstead Road: "I'm out of the army today: and today I have paid for 5 acres 2 rods 30 poles of Pole Hill:"[14] It seemed like the first step towards that new life of quiet craftsmanship, the renewal of a pre-war enthusiasm. At the end of February 1920, in full steam on Text II, he wrote Richards, who was busy enclosing the plot, that he could contemplate building there in 1921:

> It seems monstrous that you should have to put up the fence yourself, while I sit at peace and dream of having written a book. Why can't Rogers hire a man? I can afford that easily.

He had begun to go out to Pole Hill quite frequently. Pole Hill, rather than All Souls, was his escape from the toils of Baker Street. Richards had established a permanent camp for the boys near the school. McKenzie Smith, who was one of those boys, remembers that time:

> It consisted of a a small bell tent with an open fire on which we cooked sausages and boiled a dixie of tea after football on Saturday afternoons. Here Richards brought Lawrence on a number of occasions . . . . He sat with us around the fire with a mug in one hand and a sausage in the other, and the talk was often of Arabia and the Bedouin Revolt. My schoolboy impression was that he was a quiet studious little man – by no means the glamorous hero type.[15]

Lawrence's land purchase included the hutments of an old gun emplacement which were occupied by an Old Bancroftian, another Morris enthusiast, to make Gothic oak furniture.

> A room was reserved for Lawrence when he was in London. It was sparsely furnished with a bed, a white sheepskin on the floor, and a portrait in oils by Augustus John of Lawrence in Arab dress, on the wall. A tiny bookshelf completed the furnishing. I was most impressed by its simple austerity![16]

Later, Lawrence stored here a massive house door of teak which he had transported from old Jeddah on his final return from Arabia in 1921.[17] Around the same time, Richards' hut was burned down but he took advantage of this by replacing it "with the help of a camp of boy volunteers from the school, by a cloister and diving-pool, which became rather beautiful and pleasant by the time Lawrence seriously contemplated settling on the hill with me." It was a labour of love, the nearest he could get to that hall dreamed of long ago by the two friends in Oxford:

> His dream of the perfect hall, to crown our perfect hill, was often in our casual talk up there . . . . Its walls were to be quite three feet thick; two walls with a space between, so that all should keep evenly warm . . . The roof was to be open, but yet with a mystery of structural parts interwoven, rafter and truss and purlin, and just a little carved ornament for the king-posts. As for the garden, there would be a little court with a covered and flagged walk round it . . . No fountain should break the silence – 'silence more musical than any song' to his worn nerves.

... All was to be for deep quietness in that hidden court ... the very cutting of the lawn was to mean but the swish of a scythe.[18]

He had not forgotten the letter Lawrence wrote to him near the end of the war from Cairo:

Those words, peace, silence, rest, and the others take on a vividness in the midst of noise and worry and weariness like a lighted window in the dark.[19]

The work in progress, the book, he calls "the-book-to-build-the-house". It was a brave idea and for a moment it fired his enthusiasm. A letter to an American publisher, F.N. Doubleday, dated 20 March 1920, confirms what he had written to Richards: that he is hoping to make money out of it. "My present burst of labour is only to get enough cash to build myself a house." He goes on to talk of fine bindings and hand-made paper. "If you print my *Seven Pillars* I'll send a ream across, and then we can pull a large paper copy for you and one for me."[20]

Lawrence met F.N.D. – Effendi as he called him – at a dinner party given by Sir Evelyn Wrench in London in December of 1918. Effendi did not know who was sitting next to him, which doubtless pleased Lawrence, and they hit it off at once. "Why shouldn't we see each other again?" said TE. Doubleday published important British writers in America, including Kipling and, later, Conrad. The upshot was that Doubleday, now aware that he had to do with the war hero, immediately contacted Kipling and invited him to dinner with Lawrence. The great man of letters was already engaged but he cancelled for the sake of "the most romantic figure that had come out of the war" – only for Lawrence to turn up at Brown's Hotel on the evening before. Mr and Mrs Doubleday managed to persuade him that there was no mistake. Kipling came the next evening, as did Lawrence, and Effendi was dazzled by the brilliance of the conversation. They talked politics rather than literature. Convinced by Lawrence's arguments, Kipling used his top level American connections to try to interest them in the Syrian mandate, coveted by France. In vain.

It was Doubleday who suggested to Lawrence that he should write something for *The World's Work*, the first excerpts from *Seven Pillars* to appear. Later, when the Oxford text was printed, Lawrence asked Kipling to read it. He accepted with a good deal of reluctance and, behaving rather like Lawrence himself, insisted that it should be done in secrecy.

Lawrence's next letter to Doubleday, just one week later, is the first mention of publishing. It makes clear why he was interested in an American publisher. This is the first sign of his fear of the consequences of publishing his work:

> Unless I am starving (involuntary) there will be no London publisher. My whole object is to make money in the U.S.A. And so avoid the notoriety of being on sale in England. One gets, inshallah, the goods without the publicity.[21]

Doubleday sent him his best edition of the works of Kipling and TE's expression of thanks is simultaneously an expression of his love of beautiful artefacts, and of his interest in the production of books:

> First of all, very many thanks for your luscious Kipling. It's very good to have the three volumes as one in such excellent type, and on good paper. Did you print it from plates, or was it re-set? It's beautifully done anyhow. Then the binding. I'm very glad to see your Frenchmen's work. . . . . I think it's very pleasantly done, technically as good as anyone ever wants, and the style of tooling is so quiet and respectable. One is ashamed of a Cobden Sanderson on one's shelves: it shouts out its virtue so loudly. This is a self-respecting binding, which will mellow and improve every year it is handled.[22]

His own writing is mentioned only in a post-script. By this time he has been made aware of the piracy problem. He intends to get round the problem of an American edition being pirated in England by publishing in both countries, but in England at £1000 a copy! This is the tactic he eventually used, in the reverse direction, to prevent piracy in the United States. He ends: "I think my MSS may be ready for abridgement about 1921 autumn – or 1922: and I'm aiming to give you about 150,000 words." This is the first time he mentions the idea of publishing only an abridgement. On their next visit to England the Doubledays, with their stepson and his wife, visited Lawrence at All Souls. Lawrence dined with them at their hotel, showed them round the colleges the next morning, and gave them lunch in his rooms at All Souls. "It was a delightful lunch party", wrote Florence Doubleday, "afterwards Lawrence pulled out his valuable books and sat on the floor and showed them to us like a small boy." Effendi must have enjoyed handling the Kelmscott *Chaucer*.

By the end of June the timing had telescoped. He was now offering

Doubleday "an edition 150,000 words long" by September or October. "Only it's just a boy-scout sort of book, not good or deep (the strong bits all left out), produced in the hope of making enough money to build a house in Epping Forest. . . . I haven't any illusions about the rotten book it is, and will feel delighted if you find it below your standard. However perhaps its faults may help it sell." So he now intends to go straight into the abridgement before revising the "original-and-to-be-kept-secret version". For the first time he starts to run the book down and to distinguish between a "boy-scout" version abridgement and a full unexpurgated edition, a contrast which would eventually become *Revolt in the Desert* versus *Seven Pillars of Wisdom*.

Lawrence continued with the abridgement for America idea and at the end of July he gave a firm date, August 11, for beginning the "American or boy-scout version. It should be ended by September 30 . . . I want to publish only one volume, and propose to leave out half, mending the gaps skilfully, and making it fit for family reading. The boy-scouts will be my best public, for my reputation is of a melodramatic and very bold swashbuckler." He then went into details, proposing seven 'books' of seven chapters each (in harmony with the title of the book, presumably) and various printing requirements, maps and illustrations. Once again, his interest in book production is to the fore.

With his mind thus settled, Lawrence set to work almost immediately and in August he wrote to Richards: "To finish my 'Boy-scout' book by Sept. 30 will mean my spending August & September in All Souls: solid: the more you can come down in that time the better I will work: . . . Your critical faculty would be invaluable: because though it's only a cheap book written to buy Pole Hill & build its house, yet it's got to have my name on it – therefore I don't want it to be despicable." [23]

## THE 1920 ABRIDGEMENT

He did indeed work at it in August and September, completing eight well-written pieces, something of the order of 45,000 words. So we are still far short of the 150,000 word abridgement. The following table lists the topics[24] and where they occur in the finished work:

| | |
|---|---|
| Journey from Rabegh to Feisal's camp | Book I |
| Feisal's camp in Nakhl Mubarak | Book II |

| | |
|---|---|
| A train mining near Wadi Ais | Book III |
| The camel charge at Abu Lissan | Book IV |
| A train mining near Mudowara | Book V |
| The battle of Tafileh | Book VII |
| The destruction of Mezerib station | Book X |
| Mopping up in the Deraa area | Book X |

They are a series of set pieces and all have their origin in reports published in the *Arab Bulletin*. With one exception (no.2) the eight excerpts are action pieces: they provide a chronology of a sort from the beginnings to the end of the war. Because of this, and because they were easy to compose, one might wonder whether Lawrence intended to write more, or considered it finished. Whatever, he lost the desire to continue. The last story ends with Lawrence's making contact with the British forces advancing into Dera'.

A 'boy-scout' abridgement he called it but, although most of the topics are adventures of war, it does not read like a story for the innocent. Each piece contains all the variety that it possesses in the finished book, and there is no censoring of the obscene horrors of the Tafas massacre and its aftermath.

The description of the journey up to Feisal also exists in the earlier text (Curtis fragment) so it is possible to see how much work has been done to the earlier draft. It has been revised in detail but without any important alteration of content, except that it is 30 per cent shorter. All the major incidents are there and the great majority of the minor ones, and there has been little reordering of material. On the other hand, a lot of small work has been done on the text, much of which is descriptive. Here are three examples opposite, including their final form in the Oxford text, at this point still in the future. There is evidence of a constant striving for the perfect word or expression, and, in dramatic scenes like the meeting with Feisal, for effect.

The MS, seven chapters according to Doubleday, was sent or given to him in London and deposited in the safe at Brown's Hotel.[25] But that was all. No further chapters were written. The idea of an abridgement simply dried up without explanation. The prospective partnership with Doubleday did not materialise either. In 1925 FND was astonished to learn that his partner Doran had acquired American publication rights through Raymond Savage, Lawrence's London agent. Not surprisingly, Doubleday was baffled by Lawrence. "He had the most peculiar notions . . . he made a dozen different plans", he wrote in 1928 in a book of recollections.[26]

| Draft 1 (Curtis) | Draft of Abridgement | Oxford text |
| --- | --- | --- |
| (Feisal's) black beard and *white* face looked like a mask | ... black beard and *colourless* face | ... close black beard and *colourless* face |
| Then he [an unidentified Sherif] strolled rather delicately over towards us, and sat down under our wall, after affecting to look at us easily. | He strutted over to us, and sat down by me with an affectation of unconcern. | Then he strolled over to us and sat down under our wall, after glancing at us with an air of affected unconcern. |
| There was a dead silence for some minutes; the others waited for Feisal to speak, holding their breath ... | There was a shiver, and everybody present held his breath for a silent minute ... It was a sudden flame into their midst. | There was a quiver, and everybody present stiffened where he sat, and held his breath for a silent minute. ... It had fallen like a sword into their midst ... |

The abridgement was effectively damned. And with it the-book-to-build-the-house on Pole Hill. And Vyvyan Richards. And the whole dream of medieval living and working. Only Oxford itself, which would mean less and less to him, now remained of his spiritual past. He had clung tenaciously to the dream of the printing idyll. But the future, after Lawrence's journey, could not lie in the past. It would be elsewhere. But nobody could have guessed where.

Why did he give it up? There is a clue in the words he wrote to Richards in August: "I don't want it [the abridgement] to be despicable". As we have seen, this was no quick cobbling together of ready material. A great deal of work has been done on the text. And yet only the simplest parts, those built round single actions and relying on reports in the *Arab Bulletin*, had so far been written and these amounted to a mere 45,000 words. Lawrence came to realize that a complete abridgement would involve him in a lot more work than he had bargained for. As always with *Seven Pillars*, he hopelessly underestimated. There were also qualms of conscience. What he wrote for Doubleday was good stuff but was not the very idea of an abridgement despicable? An abridgement that would present him as a hero who blew up trains and made camel charges? He was too interested in the literary project to waste time on a boy-scout abridgement. It would not be the last of his hesitations and changes of mind.

However much he may have been comforted by the thought of the printing idyll, his ambition was to *be a writer*, to produce a masterpiece. The time he spent on these passages was not wasted. He had moved closer to the style he was striving for. He worked on with the book, working right through Text II once more. Yet it would take him another 18 months before he would send the Oxford text to the printers, double the time it had taken him to reach this point.

The pre-war past was now quite behind him and, as if to seal the matter, the big family house in Polstead Road (with Ned's bungalow at the end of the garden) was sold a few months later. The eldest son, Bob, left for China as a missionary and Mrs Lawrence would follow him.

CHAPTER

3

IN THE POLITICAL ARENA,
1920–21

LONE WOLF

In 1920 the victorious European Powers set about governing the former Turkish Arab Empire, formally dismembered among themselves. In a process described by President Woodrow Wilson as "the whole disgusting scramble" for the Middle East, the administration of these territories, (to be named Syria and Lebanon, by France; and Iraq, Palestine, and Transjordan, by Great Britain), was formally endorsed at San Remo in April and enshrined in unimpeachable legality as mandates granted by the League of Nations. It would not be the last time that Western intervention in Arab countries for reasons dishonestly advertised would be legalised by an international body.

Not least because he was writing a book which unashamedly advertised the Arab achievement and political betrayal by Great Britain, Lawrence had been unable to put the Middle East out of his mind. He was furious at the translation of the hated Sykes–Picot treaty into the irrevocable imposition of mandates on these five new territories. Once Text II was on paper, he vented his rancour and contempt in a series of articles written for newspapers, some of them of a rare ferocity. The assault began on May 28. Ten articles had appeared by August 25, in the *Daily Express*, the *Times*, the *Sunday Times*, the *Observer*, and the *Daily News*.

If he needed a bone to gnaw, he had one: Iraq – or Mesopotamia as it was known then. This new preoccupation totally replaced his concern for Syria, which had occupied him throughout 1919. As he had written (but not posted) to Lloyd George, he had washed his hands of Syria and promised no longer to intervene. He was as good as his promise. Iraq offered better possibilities for an aggressive intervention in the Press – of achieving results, and if nothing more, for letting off steam. The timing was perfect since the journalistic assault started just before the Intifada in Iraq broke out in June. Lawrence knew Iraq, having been there during the tragic surrender of Townshend to the Turkish forces of Khalil at Kut in April 1916. Although on a special mission – a last-ditch attempt to save Townshend by diplomacy suggested by Lord Kitchener himself – Lawrence had been treated in a mistrustful manner by senior personnel, both civil and military. What he saw in Iraq branded on his mind a fundamental contempt for traditional imperialism and strengthened his belief in Arab self-determination. On that occasion he had excoriated the Indian army in a report to Cairo. Now, he targeted the Anglo-Indian administration in Iraq: the India Office, the Government of India, its officials and all its works. He specially singles out A.T. Wilson, the acting High Commissioner, whom he attacked and ridiculed as the typical old-fashioned colonial administrator. Perhaps there was indeed a psychological connection between the humiliation of Versailles, the diplomatic defeat over Syria, and the vehemence with which he set about the British-Indian administration in Iraq; it fits, for it was Sir Arthur Hirtzel, his implacable foe in Paris, who had gone "as far as to say that the India Office hope that Lawrence will never again be employed in the Middle East in any capacity".[1] Lawrence's attacks reach a climax in August and September, beginning with comments on Syria which, however, play second fiddle to his attack on the policy in Mesopotamia:

> ... we really have no competence in the matter to criticise the French. They have only followed in very humble fashion, in their sphere of Syria, the example we set them in Mesopotamia. (to *The Observer*, August 8th)

> These risings take a regular course.[2] There is a preliminary Arab success, then British reinforcements go out as a punitive force. They fight their way (our losses are slight, the Arab losses heavy) to their objective, which is meanwhile bombarded by artillery, aeroplanes, or gunboats.... It is odd that we do not use poison gas on these occasions. By gas attacks the whole population of offending districts could be wiped out neatly; and as a method of government it would be no more immoral than the present system. (Ibid.)

The sins of commission are those of the British civil authorities in Mesopotamia (especially of three 'colonels') who were given a free hand by London. They are controlled from no Department of State, but from an empty space which divides the Foreign Office from the Indian Office. (*Sunday Times*, August 22nd)

How long will we permit millions of pounds, thousands of imperial troops, and tens of thousands of Arabs to be sacrificed on behalf of a colonial administration which can benefit nobody but its administrators? (Ibid.)

Where does one draw the line between the personal and the political ? This vituperative propaganda campaign, which was successful, undoubtedly had a personal motivation. The 'rebellion' in Iraq (mistakenly so called as Iraq did not belong to the crown) gave TEL the opportunity to revenge his humiliation and he took it. But as so often, Lawrence showed the ability to simultaneously act coolly and with deadly effectiveness on his conviction that the method of administration in Iraq must be changed to a much more Arab-centred approach. He brought this about by gathering together influential supporters of change and by political lobbying, in which he showed all his old expertise. He renewed contact with Lord Winterton, his former subordinate in Syria, Lord Robert Cecil, and Sir Hugh Trenchard, head of the R.A.F, whom Lawrence expected to play a role in Iraq. He was also the driving force in getting together a group of people with knowledge of the Middle East: St.John Philby, Hogarth, Lionel Curtis, Arnold Toynbee, and Aubrey Herbert. The deputation lobbied for a separate clearing house for Middle East affairs. By August 10 he was able to write to Cunninghame Graham that "it did some good and the Government (very grudgingly and disowning me every step of the road) is doing absolutely the right thing by Mesopotamia".

But Syria was lost. The climax of the European contempt of their commitments to the Arabs came in July 1920, when General Gouraud, the French High Commissioner, ignoring Feisal's late acceptance of his ultimatum, rode into Damascus and forced him out of Syria after a battle at Maysalun, in which many Arab patriots, poorly armed and facing 80,000 French and colonial troops; died.[3] George Antonius commented that "where the betrayal (of the Arabs) occurred" was not at Versailles or even San Remo, but when the British government "looked on and assented" to the French occupation of Damascus and eastern Syria.[4] Feisal's position in Damascus had never been strong; "the verb 'ruled' is probably too strong for the uncertain authority that Faysal was allowed to exercise".[5] The withdrawal of British troops in late 1919 led to popular mobilisation to fight the French, as Lawrence had warned in his audience with King George V one year earlier. Pressured on one side by the belligerent Gouraud, and on the other by the Arab nationalists within and outside his own government (including officers who had fought in the Arab Revolt) who found him woefully weak, and without support from either the Americans or the British,[6] Feisal's position became completely untenable. On July 27th he was given 24 hours to leave Syria by Gouraud. He was transported in a special train to Dera'a and from there went down to Haifa, Egypt, and then to Italy. The British mounted him a guard of honour at Lydd. He must have found it poignantly ironic.

If there was one person whom one might have expected to react, surely that was Lawrence ? No, the event is passed over in silence.[7] Nor does there appear to have been any attempt to contact Feisal in his distress. Was not Feisal his close friend and the very embodiment of his Arab policy towards Syria? Had not Damascus been the lodestar of the Arab Revolt? Had he not refused a decoration from the King because "he had pledged his word to Feisal, and that now the British Government were about to let down the Arabs over the Sykes–Picot agreement? He was an Emir among the Arabs and intended to stick to them through thick and thin and, if necessary, fight against the French for the recovery of Syria."[8] A lot of dirty water had flowed under the bridge since those bright heroic days.

First, he had a low opinion of Syrian politicians and nationalists; this is clear to anyone who reads *Seven Pillars*. In fact, his opinion was by now little different to that of the British government. The more the situation in Syria deteriorated, the more frightened the latter became of the increasingly uncompromising political demands of the nationalists (who were demanding that Palestine be recognized as part of Syria) and of the increasing anti-French violence and breakdown of public order. Equally to the point, perhaps, he knew that the Arab nationalists had mixed feelings about him; at Versailles, as we have seen, his behaviour had aroused the suspicion of other members of Feisal's delegation; he had signed a memorandum approved by the French colonial party, which denied the political value of the Arab unity movement, thus dissociating himself from the concept of an Arab nation; he had supported the partition of Syria; he had put pressure on Feisal to accept the terms proposed by Clemenceau and possibly connived with Clemenceau behind Feisal's back; he had courted the Zionists and helped to promote an important meeting between Feisal and Ezer Weizmann. None of this (what they knew of it or suspected) was in the least to the liking of the men around Feisal in Damascus, of whom one of the most influential was Nesib al-Bakri, with whom Lawrence had quarrelled in Arabia.

Do we need a psychological explanation? He had written to Lloyd George ten months prior: "My relief at getting out with clean hands is very great": so great, it seems, that even the base acquiescence of the British government in the illegal annexation of Syria would not stir him to action. He had 'got out' and felt great relief. One can hardly blame him for staying out. Between these two events, there is a letter to Fareedeh al Akle, his former Arabic teacher in Syria, dated 16 February 1920, in which he wrote: "I can't ever come to Syria again. Because I failed." These two letters point to paralysis over Syria. He would never again show any interest in the place.

Once again Lawrence's work on his book had been sidelined by the temptation, indeed the necessity, of the real world: action, the deployment of what one would now call his 'interpersonal skills', and the use of power – which undoubtedly suited his temperament better than trying to write a great book. He was still independent but, on December 4th, he was invited to meet Mr Churchill, who had just been appointed Colonial Secretary, and to whose department had been transferred unambiguous responsibility for sorting out the government of Iraq and Palestine. Churchill must have learnt at that meeting of Lawrence's views on the management of Iraq and the Middle East and had the insight to appreciate that these pointed to the only realistic way forward. He was insistent that Lawrence should join his new team.

## LONDON LIFE: IDEALISTS AND PAINTERS

All was not bad. In 1920, Lawrence's acquaintance was expanding on all fronts. One beneficial fall-out from the press campaign was that it brought him into contact with Arabophiles, political radicals or idealists, or their friends.

One of these was R.B. Cunninghame Graham, a well-travelled Scottish aristocrat, adventurer, great friend of Joseph Conrad and himself a writer. On July 18th he took Lawrence to meet Conrad at his last home – Oswalds, a lovely house in the charming old village of Bishopsbourne, near Canterbury. There were few contemporary writers who were more important to him than Conrad. It is strange, therefore, that Lawrence scarcely referred to this visit, even (apparently) to Edward Garnett, who was also an old friend of the master. If it were not for a diary entry by Hugh Walpole, who was also there, we would have no clear knowledge that the visit took place. Walpole wrote that they discussed printing and the Crusades. However, according to Herbert Baker, to whom Lawrence must have mentioned the visit, TEL "probed him on the methods of his craft" but Conrad "admitted but little conscious design".[9] It is a disappointing summary.

A later article by Walpole suggests that the visit was not a success for Lawrence:

> I saw him on several occasions, but I remember principally a weekend at Joseph Conrad's. I was alone there with Conrad, Cunninghame Graham and Lawrence. And Lawrence seemed entirely blotted out by the other two men – blotted out and willing, even anxious to be. . . . I remember that on that Sunday in Conrad's garden, by a trick of light (it was high summer) Lawrence, walking in front of a sun-shining tree on the lawn, seemed to disappear into it. Cunninghame Graham commented on it. 'You damned well near vanished, Lawrence.' And Lawrence might have answered: 'I couldn't vanish – because I am not here.'[10]

In August 1922 Lawrence contacted Conrad again in the hope of getting hold of a copy of the crown 8vo. edition of *The Mirror of the Sea* (his favourite book of Conrad) and received in return a second-hand copy of a different edition, but inscribed by the author. In spite of the exciting similarities between Conrad's interpretations of the danger of living in remote native environments, and Lawrence's own, that is all we know of what they either wrote to one another or discussed.[11]

In December 1920 Feisal arrived in London for the first time since his humiliating expulsion from Syria. He had been nursing his humiliation by the Italian lakes and colluding with the new Turkish leader of the very country he had fought against with the British, Mustafa Kemal (Ataturk), and other opponents of Franco-British imperialism, including Indian and Afghan nationalists and Bolsheviks, through the 'League of Oppressed Nations'. Lord Curzon was anxious and welcomed Feisal to England once more "to remove him from dangerous anti-British influences".[12] Curzon believed that pan-Arab nationalism in Syria was unsettling the Middle East, especially Iraq. As soon as Churchill took over at the Colonial Office, Feisal again became interesting to the British. Cunninghame Graham asked Lawrence for an introduction. Afterwards he wrote to thank him, saying of Feisal: "He is a charming man & the only Oriental I ever saw, who looks really well in European clothes."

Another new acquaintance was the poet, Wilfrid Scawen Blunt. Blunt, with his wife Anne, was one of the explorers of Arabia and a translator of classical Arabic literature. They also had a stud of Arab horses. He was passionate about the Bedu and the Arab cause. Cunninghame Graham, a like-minded adventurer, called him 'a prophet, who like Cassandra, was never believed'. He invited Lawrence in these terms: "Any one who can talk to me of Arabia & the desert life finds a free seat at my coffee hearth & you especially who know so much".[13] He was by now eighty years old and Lawrence wrote to him with that special respect he reserved for the old, addressing him always as *Mr*. Blunt's Arabophilia stands in contrast to Lawrence's. While they had both stood for Arab liberty, Blunt's commitment was whole-hearted, comprehensive, and inspired by old-fashioned Garibaldian principles, and the flame never died. In his last letter to Lawrence, just before his death, the unrepentant Blunt wrote: "Liberty is the only thing worth a wise man's fighting for in public life". Lawrence, on the other hand, was more ambivalent, switching with ease from the preaching of liberty to neo-imperialism, and his determination to prevail could be stronger than any political principle. His pro-Arab stance was selective; and his Arabophilia seems to have depended on emotional nourishment; it was exhausted with his active involvement. In the long run, he loved Arabia more than he loved its inhabitants.

In 1919, at the peace conference, and yet more so in 1920, Lawrence was sought out by famous painters and sculptors and he was only too happy to meet them. Augustus John and William Orpen had painted him in Paris, William Rothenstein was painting him in Arab robes in June, and in the autumn he met Eric Kennington, who was to become one of his very few really close friends. John's first portrait of Lawrence is a head in half-profile wrapped in a keffiya; a pencil drawing, remarkably economic in line and striking in its sponaneity, done, according to Lawrence, "in two minutes" while he was gazing out of a window in John's Paris flat. It immediately became a favourite among portraits of him. Two paintings of Lawrence in Arab dress, also made by John at the peace conference, were a sensation when exhibited at the Alpine Club Gallery in London in March 1920.

Lawrence was fascinated by the larger, more famous one which he nicknamed the 'wrathful' or the 'rebellious'. Three-quarter length, with Lawrence in princely Arab dress, and wearing the golden dagger, it might be better designated as the 'Olympian'; if there is a portrait which personifies the romantic legend of Lawrence of Arabia, this is it. "Again and again", writes Charles Grosvenor, "he returned to the Alpine to view the painting."[14] He came either alone or with friends. Christine Longford recalled seeing Lawrence there "staring long and fixedly at John's portrait of him . . . , friends would come in, and Lawrence would converse with them, but from time to time gazed back over his shoulder, as if he were checking to see that the painting was still there".[15] Lawrence wished to buy this painting but it was beyond his means. It was sold "for a thousand", according to Lawrence, to the Duke of Westminster, who donated it to the Tate Gallery. Lawrence saw it there with an RAF comrade, Sgt. Pugh. A large number of people surrounded it, wrote Pugh, "some admiring and some doing the other, while Lawrence stood, looked, listened, smiled broadly and walked away. Such, as he said, is fame".[16]

Graves saw that not only poets but also "the painters and sculptors seemed to Lawrence to have a secret". It has been suggested that his love of being painted, sculpted or photographed was motivated by curiosity about himself, by the hope that, through the artist's insight, they would reveal to him his nature, deepen his self-understanding. Kennington also observed that "he had a droll belief in the artist's power of sight".[17] To this Lawrence added another reason. It was because artists were "the one class of human beings I'd like to belong to. I can salve the regret of not being an artist by watching artists work, & providing them with a model".[18] Altogether, there are fifty portraits of Lawrence: paintings, pastels, line drawings, sculptures.

This new interest led to another important development for *Seven Pillars*: the illustrations. "I've written a book", he told Kennington at their first meeting, "a poor thing without illustrations to help it through. Do you know any artist who could make portraits from photographs?" He meant portraits of the Arab participants in the Revolt. Kennington, an adventurous spirit, volunteered to go to Arabia himself and paint them from the life.

Eric Henri Kennington had worked as a war artist in France where he had met Robert Graves. It was Graves who, in the autumn of 1920, had taken Lawrence to an exhibition of war artists at the same gallery where John had exhibited: the Alpine Club. Lawrence had admired Kennington's art. They met in Oxford in November and immediately hit it off. Kennington was "a sturdy, upright, basically simple, but highly intelligent man of great physical presence: a complement to Lawrence's withdrawn complexity".[19] He was also outspoken and uninhibited. Although educated at a public school (St. Paul's), he had none of that veneer of superiority that Lawrence secretly detested. In this freedom from the characteristics of class he was similar to Bernard Shaw, whom Lawrence also felt easy with. Kennington, Shaw and perhaps Lady Astor were the only people who dared to confront Lawrence's equivocations directly and with humour, which was just what he needed since it enabled him to see *himself* with humour. From this time to the end of 1926, these two men, with Shaw's wife, Charlotte, were his closest friends.

Kennington regarded Lawrence as an exceptional being. He was, in the felicitous phrase of Charles Grosvenor, "a hero of daily human life", a being of "complete integrity and limitless compassion for all living souls"[20] who inspired him as an artist like no-one else. He painted, drew and sculpted him many times, beginning only a matter of weeks after their first acquaintance in Oxford with a pastel portrait, the famous head on a dark-blue background, and not ending even with Lawrence's death, which Kennington commemorated with the recumbent stone effigy in Wareham parish church. The bust of Lawrence in St.Paul's Cathedral is also Kennington. He was one of the six pall-bearers at the funeral. Lawrence chose the pastel portrait as the frontispiece for the *Seven Pillars*. For the other portrait of himself, he chose John's pencil drawing. Grosvenor believes that these two portraits represent the two veils through which Lawrence saw the Revolt: the Arab persona and the English.[21]

They arranged to go together to Amman in Transjordan in the early summer of 1921 but, in the event, Lawrence was unable to travel with him because, by then a civil servant in the Colonial Office, he had to travel to Cairo, on his first post-war trip to the region, in accordance with official instructions; so Kennington, who had become enormously enthusiastic about the project, went alone. There he made the pastel portraits of Arabs that have become an enduring feature of the book, since at least a few have been published in all of the early editions. When Lawrence first saw the portraits, he was thrilled. "To me they were drawings", wrote Kennington, "he exchanged with them as with living souls". The exhibition he mounted at the Leicester Galleries in London in October 1921 was a sensation and an outstanding critical success. "They are akin to the portrait drawings of Holbein",[22] wrote Charles Marriott. Lawrence, who was unable to attend because he was on a second mission in the Middle East, nonetheless wrote the introduction to the catalogue: "I saw first one then another of the men whom I had known, and at once learned to know them better ... These drawings are deep and sharp renderings of all that Western Arabians are".[23]

Not long after, Lawrence chose four portraits and sent them to the firm of Whittingham & Griggs of Chiswick, to be reproduced as colour plates by chromo-lithography. These four plates, which crop up constantly in his correspondence, dictated by their size the page size of the subscribers' edition. The decision to make portraits was the first sign of the new direction of Lawrence's enthusiasm concerning *Seven Pillars*. There is the book itself, still in preparation, but essentially exhausted as a creation; and its potential as an artefact, a *Gesamtkunstwerk*, a total work of art. The illustration of the book would also be an exciting and time-consuming hobby from this time onwards, and would go way beyond portraits. The more he chafed at the revision, the more he sought compensation in the artwork.

## GOODBYE TO ARABIA

The year 1921 was the final act in Lawrence's involvement with Arabia and the Arabs. There was little development in other directions, including *Seven Pillars,* though he continued to revise Text II and build the final text when he had time, in such unlikely places as Jeddah and the Transjordan. He also wrote the dedicatory poem "to S.A." and continued to develop his plans for an illustrated edition.

One week after writing "I've long given up politics", he joined the Colonial Office, in January, as advisor on Arab affairs in the newly created Middle East department. Attracted by the personality of Churchill himself, who had no less high an opinion of Lawrence, as well as by what he now saw as a chance to create a new Middle East based on his own ideas, the 'wild ass of the desert' let himself be harnessed as a civil servant in a suit, white collar, and Homburg hat. To begin with all went well as Churchill lost no time in planning a settlement and Feisal, idle after his banishment from Syria, was immediately cast in the lead role, that of king of Iraq. Obviously, nothing suited Lawrence better; it was at once an opportunity to repay a debt and to vindicate the most passionately and consistently held tenets of his Middle Eastern policy: the first, that the India Office should be put out of business in the Middle East; the second, that the Hashemite princes were the loyal and self-evident rulers of the post-Ottoman British Middle East and the perfect candidates for the experiment in 'Brown dominion'. This idea in power-sharing he had developed in an important article, 'The changing East', which he had published anonymously in September 1920 in the *Round Table*, a political monthly of which Lionel Curtis was the guiding spirit. He had private meetings with Feisal in London, but Lawrence found him uncertain. Finally, his friend Lord Winterton offered his country house as a venue and invited two more Lords to help. Winterton reports that Feisal was difficult. "He had been abominably treated in Damascus; was there any reason to believe we should treat him any better in Baghdad?" Feisal had asked. After five hours of resistance, Feisal once again put his fate into the hands of Great Britain.

In his report of his first meeting with Feisal on January 17, Lawrence comes over as a very different man to the morally indignant propagandist of the previous summer. Now, all is political pragmatism. After listing four points which Feisal wanted regulating, which did not include the key Middle Eastern regions of Syria and Palestine, he writes:

> The advantage of his taking this new ground of discussion is that all questions of pledges and promises, fulfilled or broken, are set aside. You begin a new discussion on the actual positions today and the best way of doing something constructive with them. It's so much more useful than *splitting hairs*. [my italics][24]

In March, with the essential details of the power-sharing in Iraq agreed in advance, Lawrence was back in the Arab world. Cairo had been chosen as the venue for Churchill's grand Middle East conference. "Everybody Middle East is here except Joyce and Hogarth", he wrote enthusiastically to his mother, "we're a very happy family." He could afford to relax a little as the conference had no Plan B to that of adopting his recommendations. A conference photograph shows the new Lawrence. Sitting in the centre of the large group, wearing a suit with an ineffable casual elegance, he stands out as a man apart, the figure you would choose to point your finger at and ask: "I wonder who that is?"

Another letter to his mother follows on April 12, reporting extensive shuttling by air round the area – Gaza, Jerusalem, Amman: "living with Abdullah in his camp. It was rather like the life in war time, with hundreds of Bedouin coming & going, & a general atmosphere of newness in the air".... "Some of (Sir Herbert Samuel's) party want to see Petra, so perhaps after that I'll go down there for a night or two to show them round . . . I am trying to buy (Hogarth) some bronze weapons from tombs on the Philistine plain, axes and daggers".[25] He seems to be enjoying himself and the letters to his mother, with their crowded detail and old enthusiasms, are like in prewar times.

He met Kennington in Amman and smoothed the way for him. Kennington has described Lawrence's reception there by the tribesmen:

> Their cries ... became a roar, Aurens – Aurens – Aurens – Aurens! It seemed that each had a need to touch him. ... Easily self-controlled, he returned a percentage of the pats, touches and gripping of hands, giving nods, smiles, and sudden wit to chosen friends. He was apart, but they did not know it. They loved him, and gave him all their heart.[26]

But there had also been a lot of lightning diplomacy. Emir Abdullah, who had occupied Amman and was recruiting tribesmen to march against the French in Syria, was invited to Jerusalem. Through a judicious mixture of promises and threats, in which Lawrence played a leading part, and a rosy and reassuring picture of the future of Palestine painted by Herbert Samuel, he was persuaded instead to accept to be ruler (Emir) of Transjordan, part of the British mandated territory as agreed (without the Arabs) at San Remo in 1920. Another Hashemite prince had come on board. So far, Lawrence had got his way in everything.

He was home for some weeks and by this time, with the settlement implemented, he was beginning to get tired of being a Whitehall official. But Churchill insisted on his going out again. It was a pity, he had already had enough. There were two problems remaining: first, Abdullah was having difficulties in Transjordan, which might fall apart; and the old King Hussein of the Hejaz, who had become deeply disillusioned with Great Britain, had to be persuaded to accept the terms of the political settlement, in particular that concerning Palestine, already accepted by his sons. Lawrence was given plenipotentiary powers.

It was late July when Lawrence left, and he spent August and September in hot clammy Jeddah trying to persuade the King to accept an agreement based on what he construed (and Lawrence also in *Seven Pillars*) as broken pledges made to himself during the war. Here, together once more and for the last time, were "the only two men for whom the resurrection of the State of the great caliphs had been their raison d'etre".[27] Hussein, unlike Feisal and Abdullah, was not prepared to discount the past and start afresh under the aegis of a new form of British imperialism. "The language he used to Lawrence was the same as Lawrence used to Great Britain on his return to Europe [in 1918]: 'YOUR PROMISES!'"[28] The refusal to agree to the loss of all Arab control in Palestine and to the special arrangement with the Zionists was not seen by the old King as 'splitting hairs'. So Lawrence spent two fruitless and tiring months there, on a mission that he thought no longer counted for much except in relation to the King's sons. So desperate was he to smooth Feisal's enthronement in Iraq that he suggested to Percy Cox, High Commissioner, the suppression of a telegram from King Hussein to Feisal and its substitution with an entirely fictitious one, ostensibly from his younger brother Zeid, saying that all was going well – a shocking instance of professional and personal dishonesty, but it would not be the first time he had done diplomacy by means of forged telegrams. Cox refused to co-operate. The stubborn, but principled, Hussein also refused to co-operate, and his British government allowance, as Lawrence had threatened him, was stopped. In practical terms it did not much matter. In 1924 the Hashemite Kingdom of the Hejaz, where the standard of the Arab Revolt had been raised in June 1916, and without which the *Seven Pillars of Wisdom* would never have been written, was overrun by Ibn Saud and ceased to exist.

As for Lawrence, who now stood for the new imperialism, he learned that his great mission with the Arabs, which had started just four months later, in October 1916, was over in every sense. "He had gambled. He had gambled against the order of the world; he now found himself, himself of all people, charged to defend it, not because he had betrayed what he had fought for, but because the order of the world is stronger than all human will."[29] So wrote Malraux, a writer with a sense of fate. But the fires were never quite put out and smouldered on. Two years later, Lawrence apparently still had it on his mind.[30]

The sole trophy from Jeddah was the teak door (two leaves of a single door) from the old town, which Lawrence had transported back to England and which were taken out to Pole Hill, to await the inauguration of the 'workshop beautiful'. The style of decoration exemplifies Lawrence's description in *Seven Pillars* that Jeddah was not really Arab in its cultural background.

Lawrence was equally skeptical about his second mission, to Transjordan. He wrote to Kennington from Cairo: "Tomorrow I go to Trans-Jordan, to end that farce. It makes me feel like a baby-killer ... I'm bored stiff: and very tired, and a little ill, and sorry to see how mean some people I wanted to respect have grown." He follows this dig – at Hussein? – with a Conradian echo, which is also a profound autobiographical comment.

> The war was good by drawing over our depths that hot surface wish to do or win something. So the cargo of the ship was unseen, and not thought of.[31]

He arrived in Amman on October 12th. Action soon made him more upbeat, less pessimistic. Indeed, it was in large measure due to him that Abdullah won through in Trans-Jordan and that the entity was given a separate official status, rather than being united with Palestine, as the pro-Zionist High Commissioner in Palestine, Sir Herbert Samuel, and indeed Lawrence himself, had recommended. Rarely in his office, he drove all over the familiar countryside to find out and see for himself and soon became aware of a "distrust of the honesty of our motives" with regard to a British Zionist policy in the region. He therefore recommended to Churchill that Trans-Jordan should remain independent of the High Commissioner's control. Churchill took his advice. The saving of the Trans-Jordan, though perhaps not entirely due to Lawrence, was probably the most significant tangible historical legacy of his activity in and concerning the Middle East; unlike in Iraq, the Hashemite monarchy of Jordan (as it became) survived and has remained a bulwark, for better or for worse, of conservative pro-western policy. It is fitting that Lawrence's success was due, not to his political ideals, but to his ability to get things done – his political and practical realism.

But he was not happy there. Already in May he had written to Graves: "I wish I hadn't gone out there: the Arabs are like a page I have turned over: and sequels are rotten things." F.G. Peake, who with Lawrence's support was raising and training the tiny defence force that would become the famous Arab Legion, describes him as sometimes staring listlessly out into the desert, as he had done at Polstead Road two years before. He was tired to death of Arab and Whitehall politics. This time, as a government plenipotentiary, he had been batting for the right team, unlike in Paris, where he had been fighting a lone battle. He had every right to be proud of his achievement, but the result was no better. The end of action still led to disgust. He was still conscious of the ethical dubiousness of his double role, he had felt the bitter irony of meeting tribesmen who believed he had come to support their cause. And what about the treaty he had tried to force on the old King to sign away Palestine to its dubious fate? He claimed "to be quit of the Eastern adventure with clean hands." But he repeated this *clean hands* expression so often in his letters and other writings that one cannot help thinking of Lady Macbeth trying in vain to clean hers.

He recommended Philby as his successor; the two men of the desert understood one another. He got home just before Christmas. In the words of Philby, "He shook the dust of Arabia from his feet for ever." It would take longer – to the last full stop of the *Seven Pillars* – to shake it from his mind.

CHAPTER

# 4

# FROM THE OXFORD TEXT TO ENLISTMENT IN THE RANKS, 1922

> If you do not have this,
> Only this: *Die and become*
> You are only a dismal guest
> On this dark Earth.[1]
> Goethe

So what now? He was not yet quite footloose. His contract stipulated no fixed term of service at the Colonial Office, but Churchill was loath to let him go. So, although he took three months' leave in March, he continued into April, with increasing frustration, to go into the office from his little eyrie in Barton Street. As usual, he gave himself no real holiday, and he did not get his official release until July 1922.

His mind was on other things: first, the book. He was determined now to bring this long saga to an end. He still hoped he would see greatness in it. In January of the new year he sent out chapters from his abridgement to Robert Graves for comment and wrote the poem of dedication, which he also sent to Graves. But there was also something new afoot, the most audacious idea he had had since his decision to write a challenging book, and of so totally different an orientation that nobody could possibly have guessed at it.

In *Seven Pillars* Lawrence wrote: "There was a special attraction in a new beginning, an everlasting endeavour to free my personality from its accretions, and to project it unencumbered on a fresh medium." This is one of the keys to his psychology. Almost the first thing he did when he got back from Cairo was to write to Sir Hugh Trenchard, Head of the newly created Royal Air Force. "You know

I'm trying to leave Winston on March the first. Then I want about two months to myself, and then I'd like to join the R.A.F. – in the ranks of course. I haven't told anyone . . . People wouldn't understand." They wouldn't indeed! This included Trenchard. He might well have appreciated Lawrence's wish to join for he knew of his enthusiasm for the air. Indeed, he was in his debt; it was Lawrence who had championed his ideas on the potential of the air force at the Cairo conference and ensured its policing role in Iraq. But in the ranks? He would try to talk Lawrence out of it. To make himself credible, Lawrence mooted the idea of his writing a history of the RAF from the inside "and the best place to see a thing is from the ground. It wouldn't write from the officer level".[2] Trenchard, though he could hardly have been convinced by such an argument, wrote a sympathetic reply and suggested a meeting. Lawrence won. After it, Trenchard told him that he had no objection in principle to his joining as an Aircraftman.

Lawrence wisely kept his own counsel until he had actually enlisted. Even to Kennington, he merely said that he had been offered an interesting job. At the time he was probably unsure whether he would really do this. It was a drastic step. He had not yet made up his mind either about the *Seven Pillars* or, in theory, about Pole Hill and the printing of fine books. For the moment his mood was one of deliberate uncertainty, nicely expressed in a letter he wrote to his mother in February. Her departure from Polstead Road was one more break with the past and made it possible for Ned (he signs the letter "N") to be more confiding than usual concerning himself; one would not guess from it how strained had been their relations for years. He even mentions, in a remote key, the subject of the Air Force:

> I'm perfectly well & very comfortable in Barton Street which is quite beautiful. The quiet of so little a place in the middle of a great mess has to be experienced a thousand times before it is properly felt. I will be very sorry to leave, but it is altogether too pleasant to be allowed to go on too long.
>
> My own plans are still doubtful . . . If I get away finally from the Colonial Office about May my plans are to do nothing for a little, & then perhaps to consider the Air Force. Of course I'm too old to join it, but I think that the life & the odd mind (or lack of mind) there might give me a subject to write about. This long drawn-out battle over my narrative of the campaigns of Feisal has put an ink-fever into me. I find myself always going about trying to fit words to the sights & sounds in the world outside me.

However all this remains uncertain, and will remain uncertain for me till I do it. That's a new course I have: of trying to prevent myself making up my mind till afterwards, when the need for action is over. Let me know what you yourselves do, please, now & then. It's odd you know how impossible it is to be altogether alone. It's the one experience that humanity has never really worked towards: and I'm quite sure that we can only manage it in a crowded place. The difficulty is to keep oneself untouched in a crowd: so many people try to speak to you or touch you: and you're like electricity, in that one touch discharges all the virtue you have stored up.[3]

Allowing for the duty of reassuring an always anxious mother, there is more truth and less evasion or distortion in this letter than in many others. About the RAF he says both much less and something more than he told Trenchard: less in that he disclaims an intention to enlist; but more in giving a hint of what subject he might be really interested in depicting – not an official history of the Air Force but "the life & the odd mind (or lack of mind) there" that would lead him to write *The Mint*, his bold account of service life. The last paragraph may refer to his mother having expressed a fear of loneliness, either for herself or for him. The allusion to being touched in a crowd may be a memory of his recent experience among the Arabs in Amman. But his mother would have surely seen in it an allusion to Christ during his ministry.

### A NEW ACQUAINTANCE

Early in 1922 Lawrence was more frustrated than at any time before. He was fed up with the Colonial Office and pressing Churchill to let him go. He was fed up with the book, desperate to get it finished with, but endlessly revising it. He was in fact in a state of metamorphosis, keen to shed all his previous lives but not yet ready for the new one. The desire to finish with everything, to disappear into the RAF as soon as possible, yet the fear of it, the constant uncertainty, the lack of any proper address or companion, led to self-neglect: few meals, little sleep.

John Bruce, whom Lawrence first met in London in early 1922, has provided testimony of Lawrence's condition and way of life in London.[4] A young working-class man from Aberdeen, John Bruce met Lawrence early in 1922 in the Mayfair flat, he said, of a Mr Murray, a friend of Dr Ogston, the Bruce's family doctor. He had gone there to be interviewed for a vacant position. Lawrence happened to be there. Bruce returned to Aberdeen, but he was soon invited down to London again, to a meeting with Lawrence.

Lawrence said, "What I'm looking for is someone like you, young, strong and alert who can be trusted with highly confidential personal matters, and to do what he is told without question." Bruce hesitated but Lawrence said: "Sleep on it; we will talk further tomorrow". They met again the next day at the Union Jack Club, the famous servicemen's club in Waterloo Road. Bruce himself was staying there and it was a place where Lawrence was unlikely to be recognized. Later, it would become Lawrence's favourite overnight place on visits to London:

> He arrived at one o'clock, looking very ill and worn out, so ill that I suggested he saw a doctor. His reply was, "When I left you last night I walked back to Barton Street, wrote all night, and was at the office at eight-thirty this morning. Does that sound like a sick man?" At lunch he said that he was going to have a few hours sleep in the Union Jack Club and I was to wake him at six. I let him sleep on, and he did not wake up until mid-day Sunday, twenty hours later. This made all the difference to him; he was a charming and delightful person. He came to King's Cross station and saw me on the train; homeward bound for Aberdeen, I was puzzled but pleased. . . . From then on I received £3 a week in cash in an envelope sent to my home.
>
> I heard nothing further for three weeks, then in June a telegram came saying – UNION JACK SUNDAY WITHOUT FAIL. I saw him for less than half an hour. He told me he had to give up his job, and gave me a package containing twelve letters addressed to various people. Each letter had a wrapper round it with instructions for the posting; date to be posted, post offices, time of posting.

One is bound to be impressed with the very convincing description of Lawrence's behaviour: his skill in using a chance opportunity, his physical condition and his explanation for it, his change of mood, his invariable courtesy, the tests he designs to prove the young man, and his weirdly secret service methods.

## ROBERT GRAVES AND THE POEM TO S.A

Robert Graves was the first person Lawrence approached for advice over his book, an honour he owed to his being a poet. Lawrence's friendship with Graves had remained strong though he had seen less of him after he had joined the Colonial Office. Graves' life, unlike Lawrence's, had changed little. He was still trying to do too many things at once: raising an increasingly large family on little money, spending too much time on domestic affairs with a wife who was 'difficult' and frequently unwell, trying various foredoomed money-making ventures, and writing poetry (frequently after washing up and putting the children to bed) that brought in very little money. He was still a student at Oxford and likely to fail his exams. By the spring of 1921 he was in desperate straits and seeking psychiatric help. At that low moment, Lawrence generously helped him out of debt with gifts from his salary. He also made him a present of four chapters from the 1920 draft abridgement of *Seven Pillars*, which he had originally sent him for an opinion. Graves sold three of them in America for £200 – about £10,000 in current purchasing power – and they were published in *The World's Work*, a Doubleday publication. Lawrence was disappointed that Graves had got so little.

"I had meant to publish the enclosed muck in USA, to raise £1000", he had written Graves at the end of the year. Graves wrote that he found the chapters "admirably strong and certain". But this response was too favourable, perhaps too simple, and got only this brief acknowledgement: "Thanks for what you said about my chapters. You know me, so I don't trust your judgement."

At the end of January 1922, when he was making his final assault on Text III, they met at Graves' cottage in Islip, where Robert found him looking "so bad that I told him he must take himself in hand. . . . Lawrence said, jokingly, that the only settling down he could contemplate was enlistment in the Army or Air Force, where he would be compelled to eat and sleep normally, and would have no time to think". Graves little imagined he had been told the truth. He told him he should look for a wife. Lawrence must have found Graves' marital hardships rather poor supporting evidence for this recommendation but would have felt pleased that his friend so little understood his nature.

A week later, Graves received an absurdly mysterious letter with an MS in verse that the writer half disclaimed as his own (he said it was dictated to him by "S.A") and asked ingenuously: "Is it prose or verse"?

To S.A
I loved you, so I drew these tides of men into my hands
    and wrote my will across the sky in stars
To gain you freeedom, the seven-pillared worthy house,
    That your eyes might be shining for me
When I came.

Death was my servant on the road, till we were near
    and saw you waiting;
When you smiled, and in sorrowful envy he outran me,
    and took you apart
Into his quietness.

So our love's earnings was your cast-off body,
    to be held one moment
Before Earth's soft hands would explore all your face
    and the blind worms transmute
Your failing substance.

Men prayed me to set my work, the inviolate house,
    in memory of you;
But for fit monument I shattered it unfinished, and now
The little things creep out and patch themselves hovels
    in the marred shadow
Of your gift.

Graves answered the question as posed, giving Lawrence a short lecture on the subject:

> The poem is neither prose nor verse, but poetic quartz in which the veins of metre run. To be prose, the ear must not be drawn at all where into (sic.) blind-alleys of iambic rhythm; you tempt and disappoint with blank-verse promises.
>     To be verse, the ear must be kept under control, & the delight one gets is in the variations from a norm or a sequence of norms; where there is no norm the hypnotic spell has no chance of taking effect.[5]

He enclosed with the letter an example, a rewriting of Stanza 2.

THE CRUSADER ON HIS DEAD MISTRESS
Death, eager always to pretend
    Himself my servant in the land of spears,
Humble allegiance at the end
    Broke where the homeward track your castle nears,

> *Let his white steed before my red steed press*
> *And rapt you from me into quietness.*

"The last couplet about the horses is a miracle", wrote Lawrence enthusiastically. But "what is to be done with it? I feel like a new whoever it was, whose middle finger has been suddenly tipped with gold. The rest look idiotic, yet one can't eat with one finger".

One can see Lawrence's point; the stanza is a fresh wind disturbing the careful building up of an atmosphere of melancholy. One can also see Graves' point: for him, the poem is a largely sentimental and dreary linear narrative in an outworn mode. Against this, he transposes the metaphor of the race with Death to a fresh but still relevant context (the Crusader) that makes for a coherent series of more striking images. The lexis of romantic chivalry *defines* the Crusader theme, and the red and white of the steeds make one aware that Lawrence's poem is colourless. Graves might have acknowledged, though, the indubitable grandeur and rythmic beauty of the opening stanza.

Lawrence evidently felt he needed more advice of a less adventurous nature and wrote to Laurence Binyon, author of the famous war poem *For the Fallen*. Binyon's reply is polite. He restricts himself to the meter, emphasising its irregularity, but ends encouragingly: "I think the movement of the whole poem is quite successful: it comes out when read aloud, as all poems should be."[6] It was evidently enough to convince him.

Lawrence made no changes to the poem for the Oxford text; nor did he send it to the printers. Instead, he added a typescript to each of the eight printed copies before binding. Later, he did make a number of small changes and rewrote the third stanza; images of morbid, almost grotesque physical contact – an original Lawrencian cocktail:

> *Love, the way-weary, groped to your body, our brief wage*
>    *ours for the moment*
> *Before earth's soft hand explored your shape, and the blind*
>    *worms grew fat upon*
>       *Your substance.*

The final version is the dedication in the subscribers' edition.

## THE OXFORD TEXT

In October 1921, from Cairo, he had written to Kennington: "In the leisure of this trip I have read the manuscript of my book; and condemned it. Not good enough to publish because it's not as good as I can make it (unless I deceive myself)."[7] He began this rewriting in the Transjordan. Back in London, once again it was in Herbert Baker's attic room in Westminster that he would work, often far into the night. He may have loved the feeling of utter privacy right in the middle of London where nobody could find him but the garret masterpiece he still yearned to create did not emerge. A letter to Kennington on February 16th 1922 is ominous:

> The real trouble is about my book, which is not good: not good enough to come out. It has grown too long and shapeless, and I haven't the strength to see it all in one piece, or the energy to tackle it properly. After I've got out of the Colonial Office and have been fallow for a time my interest in it will probably come back and then I'll have another go at it: but not at present.

He puts his finger on one of the major problems (too long and shapeless) but was too tired to deal with it. He was paying the price for having taken too long over the project and put it too often aside. His recent trips to the Middle East, far from refiring his enthusiasm and desire to record his experience, merely confirmed in him that the subject matter could no longer inspire him. His interest in the book would not come back and he knew it.

He therefore made a last effort to finish with it. On the 22nd he wrote to Richards of his determination to "put a final end to the millstone, as it now is, of this Arabian book".[8] Despite what he may have written to his mother about the joy of peace and quiet, the same desperate solitary drama was played out in that attic flat as in 1920. On April 10th he wrote to Kennington: "I've had my tenth resignation to Winston rejected, and am sitting in my attic, writing at the never-to-be-presentable-published-or-finished book".[9] And on the 16th to Newcombe, his war comrade: "I spend whole days sitting at a table writing out my *Seven Pillars* straight enough for a printer to read, and after I get too blind to see, stagger out into a street, and get slowly pushed by taxis and buses up Whitehall into the National Gallery ... or down Millbank to the Tate Gallery ... and so to work again."[10]

As he worked through the text again, many more details were added and others deleted or changed. In fact, countless changes were made. But by this time, his aim really was to finish it rather than merely improve it, and he had already begun to send out chapters for printing as he finished them. There were three main problems remaining:

First, to ensure the authority of the book as history. He took great care to ensure that his account did not contradict official documents or histories. To this objective, he later sent out copies of the book to the official historian of the Palestine war, General Wavell, and other leading figures. One thing he did not change was the accusatory tone and content of Chapters 1 and 2. From the historical point of view, he now professed it out of date since the Churchill–Lawrence settlement of 1921 had, he asserted in a footnote, fulfilled our promises "in the letter and in the spirit".[11] But the original statements about broken promises, so important to the impact of the book, he left in. A historian might argue: if there was finally no betrayal, why go on about it? Why not update the text? But that would be to misunderstand Lawrence's purpose. History has justified his "guilty" verdict in *Seven Pillars* and given the book a historical notoriety. Britain has by no means convinced the Middle East that all was put right in the end; ironically, however, this is not *primarily* on account of the Sykes–Picot treaty and the imposition of mandates on Syria and Iraq; the main culprit is Britain's Palestine policy, whose fundamental flaws Lawrence completely failed to predict. Be that as it may, the 'betrayal of promises' has permeated the Arab national consciousness and cast its long and dangerous shadow. So the book has a prophetic justification.

Second, he worked on the style. This meant continuing with the kind of fastidious revision we have already observed in the changes made from one draft to the next. His aim was partly aesthetic, but also to create a greater distance between narrator and reader. He had become disgusted with the intimacy with which he exposed himself. If he now recognised that he would never be an *artist*, he did, however, believe in himself as a *craftsman*, and, as with everything in his life, he worked at the text till he wore his fingers to the bone, "never satisfying myself technically but steadily getting better" as he wrote to Trenchard in that January of 1922. If it could not be a creative masterpiece, it would be a stylistic masterpiece.

Finally, there were the passages of shocking disclosure, especially the Dera' chapter. He wrestled with them but could not satisfy himself. He claims to have redrafted the Dera' chapter nine times, blowing hot and cold between revelation and concealment.

On May 10th the great day arrived. Lawrence pronounced the

*Seven Pillars* finished and went to Pole Hill, his landed property, and ceremoniously burned Text II.[12]

*July 1922*. A crucial month in Lawrence's life, the crisis, the metamorphosis. On the 5th, he had resigned from the Colonial Office. His political career and connections with the Arabs were finished, and he was now without an income. *Seven Pillars* was also finished and he had the proof copies in his hands. He was negotiating with Trenchard to join the RAF as an aircraftman. He was also inventing a secret life with the participation of John Bruce.

However, it is not true to say that he was shot of the "Arab business", much as he yearned to be. This could not be until *Seven Pillars of Wisdom* had been shown to society, and this would be another four years. Until then, he was in a sense bound to his reinvented past.

The letter of resignation from the Colonial Office was published in the *Morning Post* on the 20th. On the very next day, July 21st, Lawrence received the last eight chapters of his book from the *Oxford Times*. There were eight copies, an indication that he had decided to send the text out for comment. It was therefore better to print than type. He persuaded the *Oxford Times* to do eight sets of proof pages printed on one side in double columns in small print. He had begun sending off batches of his draft from the end of January, with the chapters unnumbered and in random order. This may have been for the sake of making it impossible for anyone but himself to assemble the book. As always, the methods of the secret service.

The printing was finished, only the binding remained, and inscriptions in his own hand. The copies were bound elegantly in red and numbered. They were bulky, 330,000 words of text. Eight sets of the Oxford text, which many regard as the authentic untampered-with *Seven Pillars of Wisdom*, were in his hands. He read it in print for the first time, and it confirmed his worst suspicions: "When it came back in a fresh shape I saw that it was no good."

Kennington has given us a fine picture of his friend's state of mind when he brought him a copy of the newly bound Oxford text:

> He actually looked not well, and his still seriousness was frightening. 'It's an evil work. I could not refuse you after receiving the Arab portraits from you. It will not disturb you. Next morning you will start your day's work as usual, but you have an odd brain. It is in compartments. I have not let Robert Graves read it. It can never be published. I could not live if it was loosed abroad.' I began to fight.

It had to be published. It was a grand, immense masterpiece. He looked more tired. 'How could I go on if it was made public? At Stamford Brook I did not know whether I was trying to throw myself under a train, or trying not to. I intended to throw these volumes off the centre of Hammersmith Bridge. I have worked myself out and am finished. Every bone in my body had been broken. My lungs are pierced, my heart is weak.' . . . he began again, gently to prove to me how degraded the book was, and foreseeing defeat in a battle with that brain, I said the book had to be published. He said more gently: 'Give me one good reason – one only.' It seemed the crisis, and I found one reason, and said it was a book on motive, and necessary at this moment of life; the world had lied till it was blind, and had to be re-educated to see its motives. It sounded futile, but he stopped quiet, and after a pause, said undramatically, 'Not bad' – (giggle) – 'Quite good' (many giggles) – 'You win.' Then he laid the book on the table, giggled himself into normality, and backwards out of the room.[13]

## A MYSTERIOUS UNCLE AND LAWRENCE'S ENLISTMENT

It was in July also that Lawrence sent for Bruce again.

> Lawrence met me at the station. He was nervous and dejected, ill at ease; he didn't look kempt, and he was very quiet. We had a cup of tea without much being said and went straight to Barton Street. He told me something terrible had happened to him . . . and that what he was about to say was in the utmost confidence.[14]

Lawrence began by relating his family background and told Bruce that he was illegitimate, something very few people knew at that point in time. He told him he was in debt and unable to repay his creditors without taking out a bank loan; but the bank had asked for a guarantor. Lawrence had asked an uncle who (he said) had inherited most of his father's money. This uncle, whose identity he did not reveal, he referred to as 'The Old Man'. The story, in Bruce's words, continued:

> Lawrence said that at first the Old Man had agreed to be guarantor, but that when he learnt that Lawrence had left the Colonial Office he withdrew the offer and abused him. The Old Man told him he had dragged the family name through the gutters. He had turned his back

on God, had lost an excellent position at the Colonial Office, become involved financially with "the damned Jews", insulted a Bishop, insulted King George at Buckingham Palace; and ruined the life of a great Foreign Minister, referring to Lord Curzon. The Old Man called him a bastard not fit to live amongst decent people. . . . He was told that he had borrowed money from friends under false pretences and would probably land in court . . . thus bringing further disgrace on his family. He was told in no uncertain terms that he would be put away where he could do no more harm. He was not even allowed to speak. He was told to get out of the house and not come back unless he was prepared to place himself in the Old Man's care for as long as he deemed it necessary . . . .

I can see his face now as if he were telling me over again. He kept on saying,"he called me a bastard, and meant it. How he must loathe us for my father's sins".

Lawrence told Bruce that he had decided to agree to the conditions and there was no road back until the conditions were fulfilled to the Old Man's satisfaction, which could take years. He had the option of being sent away or joining the Army as a private soldier. His business affairs would be controlled for him. His discipline would be controlled by the Old Man personally. Any breach of these conditions would prolong the length of time of his Army service. The only friends he was to have in the upper bracket were those connected with his writings. Lawrence's time was to be occupied by soldiering and writing.

He got Bruce into the Union Jack Club for the night and took him again to Barton Street in the morning. He now pressed Bruce for his reactions. Bruce told him he should tell the Old Man to go to hell. "Too late now", said Lawrence, "I've agreed and it must be done. I need help. . . . By agreeing to the Old Man the slate would be clean. But that is not what worries me most. The Old Man has shown his hand . . . I had to agree with him or he would expose the circumstances of my birth. I have my mother to consider and she comes first whatever happens to me."

Lawrence then left for an appointment, leaving Bruce to wonder exactly where he came into this. When he returned, Bruce confronted him but Lawrence made an emotional appeal: "Have I not made it clear to you? I'm on the edge of a precipice crying for help, and you can help, I'm sure of that." "But what is expected of me?" "That depends on what the Old Man has in store for me. He has mentioned that my physique requires attention, and training will be necessary.... Where you fit in depends entirely on him. I was made to swear over a Bible that I would respect the Old Man's every wish and that's how it is going to be. There must be no half measures regarding his instructions. Corporal punishment was mentioned, but that will be resisted."

Bruce said that at that stage he protested. But Lawrence silenced him. He repeated that corporal punishment was part of the Old Man's scheme, but that it would be resisted. He suggested that Bruce should study engineering. "Once I shake off the Old Man's chains, I'll only have need of your friendship.... The *Pillars* should be finished in about two years time and then I shall be in a position to discharge my debts to the Old Man and at the same time discharge myself from the Army."Bruce agreed to do what he could to help. He extended his stay at the Union Jack Club and said he spent most of his time with Lawrence in Barton Street.

That is the story that Bruce told Knightley and Simpson in 1968. They present it as a verbatim account but it is not difficult to see that it must have been tidied. Nonetheless, it has the ring of truth, full of individual detail and chiming with many aspects of Lawrence's psychology and capacities that have been revealed independently. Lawrence's brother, Arnold, although he would have preferred that this had not been published, "believes Bruce has given a true account of what Lawrence told him about the anonymous uncle and the mode of life of this non-existent relative required of him (sic)".[15] Arnold met Bruce two months after TE's death in 1935 and, for the first time, learned this story. "I had no doubt that Bruce believed all this", he wrote Mack in 1968.[16]

The skill with which Bruce was manipulated is masterly. Notice the patience with which Lawrence moves gradually towards his objective, that Bruce should understand that he may have to administer beatings; how the invention of the Old Man absolves Lawrence of all responsibility; the blackmail card, which exploits a real and shameful secret – the fact of his illegitimacy – and at the same time is something that position, fame and influence are powerless against; how the menace of the Old Man is kept before Bruce, getting always closer; above all, the confidence that Lawrence places in Bruce, exploiting his sympathy and making him feel that he is indispensible. Perhaps Lawrence did feel he needed Bruce's companionship at that point, or at least it was a bonus; and the fact of asking Bruce his opinion on these personal matters serves the purpose of binding Bruce closer to him.

Corporal punishment, says Lawrence, "will be resisted". There is a certain truth in this. Lawrence will try hard to resist; but the fact of his having Bruce on standby, and his taking so much trouble over him, suggests that he already knows that resistance is not likely. The entire stratagem suggests that he wishes to avoid the danger of being tempted by more risky encounters that might lead to scandal. He wishes to remain in control.

Apart from manipulator, Lawrence is also actor. How well he feigns to be completely fazed by the Old Man's insults! "He called me a bastard and he meant it", he keeps repeating. Even his unkempt appearance is probably intentional. For he had already shocked Bruce once, and would do so again. He did not display himself unkempt to others.

Lawrence's choice of Bruce, both as confidant and administrator of masochist beatings, reveals a rare degree of psychological acumen. Bruce was young and strong, and not timid about using his strength, in fact he had found work in London as a bouncer. He was as loyal and devoted as any master's dog; revealing none of Lawrence's secrets until many years after his death, when his own poor health and lack of money forced his hand. He was obedient, not over-intelligent, and unimaginative, most necessary qualifications in this case.

What is interesting beyond everything else is the skill with which Lawrence deceives, his manipulation of truth. Like all the best liars, he embeds the fabricated story in a number of indisputable facts. He was indeed a bastard, he *had* resigned from a well-paid job at the Colonial Office, he *had* cooperated with Zionists, he *had* refused to accept a decoration from King George; and so on. He can even use incidents in his life and secret plans as a means of providing proof of the Old Man's presence. For example, when Bruce met him a few months later, after he had been dismissed from the RAF, and was now, unknown to Bruce, trying to get into the Tank Corps, he was able to come back from a meeting with the Old Man and say to Bruce: "It has got to be the Tank Corps, nothing else". And the Tank Corps it was! It was also true that he needed to sell his book in order to make ends meet and would therefore be either writing or soldiering from now on. All these supporting truths make it much easier to live in security with the central lie.[17] Lawrence's habit of discretion in what he told different people, and the constant variations of his stories that he spread around, stood him in good stead when it came to composing and controlling a particular version of the truth. As the secret world well knows, control means control of the truth and the access to it. In this way, it is possible to invent the non-existent man and launch him on a career or, as we shall see, create a non-existent event.

Finally, I wish to draw attention to the boldness of the idea, the invention, since this is of particular relevance to *Seven Pillars of Wisdom*. To invent a non-existent person and to keep him alive, give him a definite character, activities, his own writing style, influence over the lives of others, shows a remarkable ability, and no doubt enjoyment, in mixing fantasy with real life. When Bruce gave this story to the *Sunday Times*, he still believed every word of it; especially did he believe in the reality of the Old Man. This was natural since the Old Man actually wrote to him and answered his letters, paid him for 'dealing with' his disgraceful nephew, sought his opinion on the nephew's progress and how he responded to punishment, and treated him with the utmost respect. And it was not only Bruce, but several other servicemen also, who received letters from the Old Man and never suspected he was a fiction.

Later on, this elaborate fiction will be recalled in order to support interpretations of certain events related in *Seven Pillars*.

Bruce's narrative seeks to convince that Lawrence was close to him, that he knew him well, and that he was indispensible as a moral support; naturally, for he spent several years of his life with Lawrence and he seems to have loved him. That he felt protective towards him, that he took considerable pride in the role of Lawrence's physical guardian, cannot be doubted. And if the young soldier with Lawrence glimpsed by Kennington was indeed Bruce – and everything seems to suggest that – then he wielded a certain moral authority also.

> It was during his tank service [1923–25] that (Lawrence) paid us the most strange visit, as usual without warning, with a soldier on pillion. This time – for the first time – he dropped all defences. There was a wall of pain between him and us. . . . Everything was attacked. Life itself. Marriage, parenthood, work, morality, and especially Hope. Of course we suffered and were unable to cope with the situation. The young tank-man was most positive. He banged his fist on the tea table, and threatened. 'Now, none of that. How often have I told you? Look me straight in the face . . . ' An animal tamer, and T.E. a wild beast that partially obeyed him. Aside, to my wife, the young man revealed his grief at T.E.'s suffering. I don't know who that was, but he had great courage and love for T.E.[18]

Like Lawrence, Bruce had enlisted in the Royal Tank Corps in 1923.

Bruce's role as assigned to him by the Old Man made it inevitable that he would feel responsible for Lawrence. If Bruce is to be believed, T.E. was dependent on him like a wayward child on a severe nanny.

The perspective from Lawrence's end, however, is quite different. It suggests that the emotional role that Bruce believed he played in Lawrence's life was a pathetic illusion. In all their future encounters (except those related by Bruce), and most notably during their service together in Hut 2 of the Royal Tank Corps, Lawrence does not seem to have shown much affection for Bruce (as he did for certain others), only to have used him. We should bear in mind, though, that Bruce belonged to Lawrence's secret world; he would not have wanted to draw attention to any closeness he might have had with Bruce.

Bruce was looked after financially by Lawrence throughout his life, even his mother had an allowance. He was protected, he received much good advice and Lawrence kept faith with him so well that the relationship endured. The beatings seem to have been uncommon, but more frequent in the last months of his service. I would judge that the relationship worked quite well; it still remains rather pathetic and demeaning, as must any relationship based on deceit.

## ENLISTMENT

Not surprisingly, Lawrence was in a poor state when he arrived at Henrietta Street for his interview and medical; he failed both. It is an episode both comic and shameful. The comedy comes out in Lawrence's description in *The Mint*, the more shameful side in an article written much later for the *Sunday Times* by Captain W.E. Johns, the chief interviewing officer:[20] "There was something so off-hand about his manner, almost amounting to insolence, that I took an instinctive dislike to him."

It was all supposed to be secret and he had taken an alias, the name 'John Hulme Ross'. The doctors and interviewing officers had been kept in the dark. Only Trenchard himself and Air Vice-Marshal Swann knew who he was. It backfired at once as his given identity was checked and found not to exist. Lawrence had to admit that his birth certificate was a fake, but came back with an officer with orders to recruit him. When the doctors failed to find him physically fit, a doctor from the Ministry was forced to sign the papers that he was. Lawrence left for the Uxbridge training depot but acknowledged his identity to Johns while waiting for the train. Johns phoned a colleague at Uxbridge to warn him for by this time, wrote Johns, Lawrence was making it clear that he had no time for junior officers. It was an inauspicious beginning. Several people now knew he had influence in high places and was not who he said he was. A spy? His truculent behaviour was just what was not needed. Air Vice-Marshal Swann felt that he was badly used: "I was *ordered* to get him into the R.A.F. I disliked the whole business, with its secrecy and subterfuge; I discouraged communication with him or from him."[21]

However, once a recruit on the training course, Lawrence knuckled down with courage and pulled through the exhausting and sordid trials that he was really too old for. It was a success; he began to feel the tenuous social bond with the 'don't haves' that he sought. After ten weeks, before completing the basic training course at Uxbridge, he was transferred to Farnborough to follow a photographic course. He was much happier there, and began to enthuse about the RAF. He also bought himself a Brough superior, the Rolls Royce of motor cycles. A tad conspicuous, that. As long as he could just behave like any humble serviceman. . . .

CHAPTER

# 5

# LITERARY MENTORS, 1922–24

### THE FIRST READERS

The text of *Seven Pillars*, now seen in cold print, told him that he had failed. His book was no *Karamazov* or *Moby Dick*. The events, the feelings, the state of being it related were dead in him. As a living historical record of himself in the war, the book, like the experience itself, was rapidly receding into unreality. He found no life in it, yet it was supposed to be himself.

But what was it? That was what he had to find out. How did other writers or critics see it? And was it a total failure? Or could it be remedied? Perhaps the book was not as bad as he thought? The meeting described by Kennington shows how unsure he was of himself.

The vast literature of his denigration of his own book begins around this time. The two recurring themes are the general complaint that the book is no good as a work of literature; and its confessional aspect, which in cold print he began to find revolting, even perverse. 'Muck' was the word he often used. To Sydney Cockerell, an admirer, he united both aspects in his self-criticism: "A tremendous masterpiece? . . . No, you are wrong there. It's not a masterpiece, for it lacks form and continuity and colour: . . . and it's not tremendous, for it can be no bigger than my petty self. Hysterical, curious, a human document: those are its proper adjectives."[1] He placed little value on grandiose expressions like 'tremendous masterpiece', 'great book'.

His literary failure, he believed, was lack of "technique", "style", "form", "treatment", "architecture". Lawrence used these words but rarely showed how they applied to his book. In practice, only style obsessed him, and this narrow obsession screened him from facing the real literary problems. There are few writers who have had at their disposal such a talented group of mentors; and equally few who have spoken more and done less about their book.

Now that his book was finished, he had the luxury of being able to discuss it with his readers. For a man so much interested in himself, this was a considerable benefit. He got the same pleasure from it as he got from his portraits: a mirror held up to himself by another. Curiosity was one motive behind the approaches to the perceptive and eminent men of letters, the semi-secret sending out of the eight copies of the text to so many people. Sometimes, in the months ahead, he claimed he did not even have a copy himself. His contacts with the literary world of London were by now extensive. He had met some of the most famous writers: Shaw, Kipling, Conrad, as well as younger writers like Graves, Sassoon, and Edmund Blunden – and they would pass his book on to others. There was almost nobody in London who did not want to know him or read his book.

He was interested in detailed comment, especially if it shed light on himself; but skeptical of advice on how to rework or improve his book. What he also wanted was reassurance, reaction to the more risky passages, and advice on publishing. His situation, as a new recruit in the RAF undergoing basic training, in any case ruled out any serious work on the book. Indeed, the decision to send out the book at this precise moment seems almost perverse. However, the book was written and must now be sent out into the world for judgement. Then he would decide what to do with it.

## EDWARD GARNETT

It was on 17 August 1922 that Lawrence wrote two letters which initiated a new, more hopeful phase in the life of his book. One was to Edward Garnett and the other to Bernard Shaw.

Garnett was not a successful creative writer (although he had written five performed plays) but a critic. Criticism, hard criticism, was precisely what Lawrence thought he wanted. Furthermore, as a publisher's reader, Garnett was well qualified to provide the kind of advice that would make the book look better to a publisher. He was a reader for Cape.

It was another famous Arabian explorer, Charles Doughty, who quite unwittingly caused Lawrence to come into contact with both Cape and Garnett two years previous. Doughty's *Travels in Arabia Deserta*, one of the classics of Arabian travel, was among Lawrence's indispensable books. TE had first written to Doughty as long ago as 1909, seeking advice about his plan to make a tour of Syria in the summer university vacation. Doughty had advised against it. After the war, learning that Doughty was living in straitened circumstances, Lawrence gave much of his time to promoting a new edition of *Arabia Deserta*. He met Jonathan Cape when he approached the Medici Society over the *Arabia Deserta* project. Together with Garnett, who had long been an admirer of Doughty and had written an abridgement of that work, *Wanderings in Arabia*, he persuaded Cape and the Medici Society to re-publish the original work in an expensive edition. Since his name could be guaranteed to at least double the sales, he had agreed to write a preface, and did so.

The success of the new expensive edition of *Arabia Deserta* may have been a factor in persuading Lawrence to go down the same road. In both cases too there was an abridgement by Garnett. But while the Doughty abridgement was published, the MS of the Garnett—Lawrence abridgement of *Seven Pillars* lies little known in the Houghton Library of Harvard University. We shall soon know why.

Naturally, Lawrence had let Garnett know when they had met that summer, at Cape's offices, that he was writing a book about his war experiences. Garnett must have been extremely interested. Here was the famous Colonel Lawrence, man of action and intellectual, who would some day soon write the book that England was waiting for.

※

Garnett was the first person to read *Seven Pillars of Wisdom*. Lawrence had sent the bundle of Oxford Times sheets off to him on August 17th or a day or two after and by the 22nd, he already had Garnett's reply that he had read most of the book. Garnett's reaction was positive and he naturally suggested publication. He discussed the book in some detail and made no secret of his admiration. At the same time, he gave TE to understand that the text needed some improvement and offered to notate it with his suggestions or criticisms. He was quite unaware that Lawrence was about to enlist in a matter of days (August 30th).

No first-time writer could have asked for more. His reply, however, was puzzling, and posed various limitations; first, "Please don't consider the point of publication". He cites "blemishes of style, and while my critical sense doesn't reach as far as subject matter and construction, I judge them equally bad by analogy". A facetious analogy, it has to be said. But also the content is far too personal: "I don't know for whom I wrote it, unless it was for myself", he writes, with a good deal of truth. He is a failure as a writer anyway, he tells Garnett, and describes the extent of the damage:

Hitherto, I've always managed, usually, without trying my hardest, to do anything I wanted in life: and it has bumped me down rather, to have gone wrong in this thing, after three or four years' top-effort.[2]

However, Garnett has won TE's confidence by praising the more personal, confessional passages, and most notably the Dera' incident. 'Severe and serene' he finds it. "The second [epithet] sounds like a quaint failure to get my message across", replies Lawrence, "but I know how you feel".[3] This is cryptic but perhaps he meant this: "Great tragedy plays a *catharsis* and leaves its readers calm at the end. I looked on *The Seven Pillars* as, in essence, tragedy – a victory in which no man could take delight."[4]

We are quickly into an intense correspondence and letters cross. Garnett is aware of a sensitive personality who needs to be encouraged. In fact he is in the role that he has already played with such success, that of encouraging and advising promising authors, and handling them psychologically; here, he must first break down TE's reluctance to publish; it proves far more difficult than he could have imagined.

"Don't call me an artist", Lawrence wrote the next day, "I said I'd like to be, and that book is my essay in the manner of an artist: as my war was a decent imitation of soldiering, and my politics chimed well with the notes of politicians. These are all good frauds . . . "[5] This is not merely self-deprecation; it is a glimpse of a self that can only act to achieve a self-imposed goal but not identify with the social worth of the activity itself, nor value the results. This sense of all action being insincere and hence worthless is a leitmotif of the book.

"I saw that you were shaken", wrote Lawrence on the 26th after their first meeting. In all likelihood, Lawrence told him that he was about to enlist in the RAF (for it is referred to in the letter as known information). It must indeed have bewildered Garnett how a man would send him an unpublished first work which had the makings of a masterpiece at the very same moment that he was signing on as a serviceman. The letter attempts to explain: his enormous ambition in wanting to write "an English fourth" to compare to *The Karamazovs*, *Zarathustra*, and *Moby Dick*, and the failure of his hopes. "When it came back in a fresh shape (from the printers) I saw that it was no good. . . . it is very difficult for me to do nothing, and I've tried soldiering, and science, and politics, and writing: and manual labour seemed the obvious next." We can see what Graves meant when he wrote that Lawrence could not envisage poetry "as a particular mode of living and thinking" but merely as a particular type of technical mastery.

"Confession is in the air", wrote Lawrence in this the first of six letters, some of them very long, written between 26th August and 9th September – at the same moment that he was going through the harrowing first days of his basic training at Uxbridge. Yet they might have been written by someone sitting at his desk by the fire in the study with all the time in the world. The difficult circumstances in which they were written made the discussion that much more enjoyable. They are among the most revealing he has written concerning the motivation behind the *Seven Pillars* and show how much of himself he believed he had put into it. To talk about the book was to talk about himself. So Garnett did not give up.

The fact was that Garnett's praise and comments had set off a chain reaction of pent-up feelings and secrets about the book and was slowly rekindling his hopes. One of Garnett's great strengths was his willingness to listen and his ability to make each writer feel that their work was the most important thing in his mind.[6] A more personal bond was developing. The *Seven Pillars* so exposed the personality of the author, his suffering and his emotional struggles, and his diffidence, that Garnett could hardly avoid seeing the man himself in this light. Indeed, it is the insertion of a personal drama into the narrative of war that Garnett found especially original. He felt strongly that the book was indeed not quite right but that he knew how to remove its flaws – as well he might, given his immense experience and dedication.

At the same time, he could not imagine how a book, or its author, could fulfil their destiny without being published. But he went further; going public was a matter of principle, of duty to oneself. He was well aware that the book was too long to be easily publishable and he also had artistic reasons for wishing it shorter. He felt this would be no difficult task. There was, he believed, a need for a more selective approach to the historical narrative. Within a few days they had agreed on the possibility of an abridgement. Garnett had already abridged Doughty, and Lawrence had already tilted at an abridgement of his own book. He had felt short of money then and he was short of it now. He had widely publicised that this was one of the things that drove him into the RAF. Garnett wanted Lawrence to quit the RAF, which he rightly thought was no suitable place for a writer of such promise, still less for a man of such sensitivity as the author of *Seven Pillars of Wisdom*. The money from the published book would make him independent, probably for the rest of his life.

In spite of these practical considerations, they agreed that the objective was artistic. On 7 September Lawrence wrote: "Isn't there a certain cowardice in publishing for money less than the whole facts I found it needful to put on record? I can understand editing it for artistic reasons: but not for others: and I rather think that should be our standard." That was exactly how Garnett felt. "Yes, that's it", he answered. "The first abridged book if it comes off, must be edited for <u>artistic</u> reasons."

This was the high point of hope. It was the creation of a work of art, rather than the mere production of an abridgement, that Garnett saw as his mission. In order to take this view one has to believe in the potential greatness of the material and of what the writer is trying to express. Garnett did. He perceived in the *Seven Pillars* a "new apprehension of things". For this so experienced critic, who had guided Conrad, Hudson, and D.H. Lawrence, he was the mentor Lawrence needed: "I can help you, I think, because as to <u>effects</u> I really see what a thing is: & I can tell you where you need to be more of an artist."[7]

Garnett believed that Lawrence would eventually be persuaded of the worth of the book. The main sticking point seemed to be his reluctance to expose the revelations of the *Seven Pillars* in published form. Quite apart from that, however, he could see that, although personal revelation was at the centre of *Seven Pillars*, it was inhibited, a lot was being held back. Garnett's persuasion, enthusiastic and sympathetic to a degree, rushes forward in short urgent sentences:

> Don't worry about 'the giving of myself quite away'. We've got to look at it <u>as art</u> here. The complete truth <u>is</u> art. But the point is also, what are meant by 'complete'. If it's <u>essential</u> truth it's great art. It conquers: it leaves everybody else dumb: it replaces everything. It <u>is</u>. It can't be shifted. You've gone very far in that direction, but I can help you to go further.[8]

Art and Truth. The transformation of autobiography into art was at the centre of contemporary literature: Proust, Gide, Joyce, D.H. Lawrence. An artist has a duty to Truth over and above his personal privacy. Garnett will return frequently to this point. He tried to persuade TE that the problem of the personal passages was a matter of treatment, rather than one of self-exposure. "This would be all right if I were writing about a third person,"[9] TE had protested at one point when criticised for covering up. Garnett tended to discuss *Seven Pillars* as if it was a work of fiction.

## THE GARNETT–LAWRENCE ABRIDGEMENT

Although Lawrence was obviously not fully decided about an abridgement, he sent Garnett a copy of the *Seven Pillars*, unbound. Garnett took about ten days to abridge the text. His treatment, apart from cutting out some unnecessary descriptive detail here and there, was to sweep out large sections which do not move the war forward significantly, almost entire books in three cases, a total of 52 chapters out of 139 were cut out, thus increasing the pace of the story and making it into a barely interrupted series of big events, but retaining passages of pathos, dramatic action, or of psychological significance. Summaries, composed first by Garnett and sometimes overwritten by Lawrence, darn the holes in the narrative. He made no alterations to the actual writing but noted passages he thought needed changing. He then sent his copy of the Oxford Times printed sheets back to Lawrence, amended in black ink.

It was not to be. As the abridgement took shape, Lawrence's commitment to artistic integrity was overridden at all points by his unwillingness to make public revelations, either about himself or about others, or about anything sensitive whatever. A study of the cuts made by Lawrence (in red) make it clear that he scanned the pages with no other serious purpose in mind. Each had his separate sphere. Garnett's task was the abridgement of the text, Lawrence's its bowdlerisation.

His actual circumstances at this time could hardly have been less propitious to serious literary work. From the beginning of September he was undergoing basic training at the RAF depot at Uxbridge, square bashing and gym, fire picket, and chores such as emptying the shit-cart. On top of that he was scribbling impressions of the day on pieces of paper from his bed before lights out. Emotionally and physically, he was responding to the tremendous demands of a new life, a new status, a new and disturbing social environment. Even a new name. His letters to Garnett show it: "the difficulty of working in this gust of life is heart-rending" (October 23); "my second self carries on correcting your abridgement under the greatest difficulties. It's nearly hopeless to do it decently in such distractions" (November 6).

On November 7, his basic training came to an abrupt end. At Farnborough he had more leisure and used it to bring the abridgement to a conclusion. "I feel a horrible satisfaction when I'm able to cut a piece out of myself, and draw the edges together", he wrote ominously.[10] He finished the work and posted everything to Garnett on November 20. This included a draft preface. He ends: "I'm rather proud of having achieved any sort of revision, in circumstances as distracting as ever encompassed a writer."

On the 19th he read in his bunk the whole of the Oxford text which, for the first time, excited him. "It is certainly uncommon, and there's power sensible under its peculiarly frigid surface", he wrote the next day.[11]

The final agony for poor Garnett came on November 22 when he felt "excited when I got your letter & the MS, & got down immediately & went through your revision. I felt sulky, – <u>very</u>, when I saw what you've done to the camel charge, & poor Farraj... I feel sulky at your suppression of the <u>best</u> personal passages. 'I gave you up Deraa', I say reproachfully, like a sobbing woman! & now you take Farraj's death from me!"[12] And the next day the rather girlish reproaches continued: "You've revised the camel charge, 'for reasons of self-respect'. Be it so! Keep your self respect & rob English Literature of a passage beautifully spontaneous, <u>Colonel Lawrence!</u>"[13]

Garnett had got caught up in Lawrence's game of hide-and-seek and had paid the price, though one could argue that he was the victim of his own enthusiasm. Lawrence was too indecisive to make it clear that he was not in a position to edit his text to improve it artistically and that, in any case, he would never publish an abridgement that would expose him personally. Typically masochistic, he wanted to have his cake and eat it. Indecision was something he now found quite attractive.

※

The abridgement, if published, would have consisted of seven sections; all but the introduction focus on major initiatives and give a reasonably coherent and varied account of the *Revolt* in Lawrence's terms:

1. The introduction to the book and to the context of the *Revolt*.
2. Lawrence's journey up to Feisal and activity in the Medina–Yenbo–Rabegh area.
3. The journey to and capture of Akaba.
4. The raid on the railway with Lewis and Stokes.
5. The Yarmouk bridge expedition (4 chapters cut) and diversion to Minifir.
6. The battle of Tafileh and snowbound expeditions.
7. The final push: Azrak to Damascus and in Damascus.

This abridgement is half the length of the Oxford text. What we gain is not simply a brisker narrative; but also a sharper impression of the overall chronology and the kind of operation imposed by the stage in the campaign we have reached. Compared to the later abridgement, *Revolt in the Desert*, it is more ruthless in its sweeping away of the less exciting parts of the book.

So it is a sensible abridgement. Obviously, it does not stand up well as a historical memoir; barely 60 per cent of Lawrence's two years with the *Revolt* are accounted for. It also paints a less true picture of what the campaign was really like to those who participated, with all the false starts, changes of plan and failures that were part of the experience and which had that wearying effect that Lawrence so well expresses! To be appreciated it needs to be read for itself, not against other versions. This is difficult since it is still in the cramped two columns a page form of the original Oxford Times printings, with Garnett's and Lawrence's crossings-out, queries and comments![14]

The *Garnett* is less than a tragedy but perhaps deserved a better fate. It overcomes some of the structural problems of the original but its initial serious intention was rubbished by Lawrence. It does not achieve anything original as a piece of literature. With serious cooperation, these bold cuts might have had some artistic merit and freed the text from the tyranny of chronology in such a way as to enable the author to build the development of the personal theme more coherently round the major events, more in the manner of a novel; but with Lawrence's clean-up, the result is too much like a series of instalments from a story of high adventure, the 'boy scout' book that Lawrence called such abridgements. He therefore soon came to despise this one just as he had despised the one he had tried to write in 1920, and would despise *Revolt in the Desert*. In the draft preface to the abridgement[15] he shifts the responsibility onto Garnett for what is his own.

## BERNARD SHAW

Lawrence first met Shaw at the latter's home on March 25th 1922. It was almost purely by chance. Sydney Cockerell, curator of the Fitzwilliam Museum and a friend of GBS, had invited Lawrence to lunch at the Carlton Hotel and happened to mention that he had to go that afternoon to Shaw's London home in Adelphi Terrace, in order to remove a portrait of GBS by Augustus John that had been offered to the Museum by Shaw's wife, Charlotte. He invited his companion to accompany him. Lawrence demurred, but when Cockerell assured him that the Shaws would not be at home, he agreed to come. Cockerell was wrong, the Shaws were at home. "To my astonishment", wrote Shaw, "I recognized in this shy bird Luruns Bey. We hit it off together fairly well."[16]

Lawrence's first letter to Shaw is a classic of Lawrencian letter writing. He asks Shaw to read the book and spends the rest of the letter telling him not to waste his time. Vanity, the fear of being told that his book is not worth much, makes it an orgy of depreciation and pre-emptive criticism. The basic line is that he is a historian, not a writer, and has therefore hopelessly botched the job. "My own disgust with it is so great that I no longer believe it worth trying to improve (or possible to improve)", he warned. But hopefully, Shaw would think otherwise.

Shaw's correspondence with Lawrence shows us the various stages which GBS had to go through in order to understand, as far as he could, what kind of a person he was dealing with. He never quite succeeded in understanding Lawrence's motives. Who could? When Lawrence was already in India, GBS was still writing: "What is your game, really?" Shaw was too sane, and too lacking in introspection, to want to probe the universe in which Lawrence lived and wrote. But he knew the world of books. He therefore took the practical approach.

"To _business_, as if I were your solicitor", he starts off.[17] Unlike Garnett, he is unmoved by Lawrence's affective tone and lengthy self-criticism. As Shaw recognizes, there is no need for his criticism; the book will be published simply because it is by Lawrence of Arabia. He offers his own publisher, Constable. In his second letter, in December, Shaw continues to be practical, although by this time he has sampled the book and his enthusiasm has been kindled. "It is one of the Cheops pyramids of literature and history." High praise indeed. However, he had not yet read the book. Probably, Shaw is referring to size and scope as much as to a general impression of its value. "I estimate the number of words as at least 460,000", he continues.[18] He feels "rather puzzled as to what is to be done with it", but decides to recommend an abridgement "for general circulation". Copies of the original document should be deposited in two or three of the world's great libraries, including the British Museum.[19]

There are also some tentative remarks about what kind of book the abridgement might be; the decision will have to be made about the relative importance of the historical record vis-à-vis the personal experience of war, as the main focus. "Between the two comes the

Thucydidean history, giving the bones of the affair but making them live." In fact, Shaw has already put his finger on the major compositional problem of the book, a problem that Lawrence was deeply conscious of but will be incapable of solving.

We hear no more of this, however, for Lawrence in his reply casually informs him that the book is being abridged by Edward Garnett who Shaw knows is a reader for Jonathan Cape. He omits to acknowledge his own part in the abridgement and disparages its "meanness". This news raises the temperature of the correspondence. GBS, seeing himself as a hardened professional approached by an unsuspecting novice needing protection in the ruthless world of publishing, is now anxious to advise. "With Constables [sic] you would be more comfortable and most respectable. They know your value whereas the ruffians would know only your sales, being incapable of history". He has, he informs Lawrence, told Constable that *Seven Pillars* is "the greatest book in the world".[20]

It is this phrase rather than all the publishing advice that interests the author. "You say that it's a great book. Physically, yes: in subject, yes: . . . but is it good in treatment? Will you let me know your honest opinion as to whether it is well done or not? . . . Isn't it treated wrongly? I mean, shouldn't it be objective, without the first-person-singular? And is there any style in my writing at all? Anything recognisably individual?"[21]

Meanwhile, Charlotte, his wife, has appropriated the book for the moment and it will be she who replies first to these questions. Shaw's next letter, which crosses with Lawrence's, is suddenly and immensely enthusiastic: "I cannot wait to finish the book before giving you my opinion, and giving it strong. THE BOOK MUST BE PUBLISHED IN ITS ENTIRETY, UNABRIDGED."[22]

Why the volte-face? Was it a literary decision, revised now that Shaw was better acquainted with the book? Or purely a publishing matter? Certainly something of both. But the urgency is dictated by the news that Cape are to publish the abridgment. Shaw's urging seems like a possessive desire that the book should be published by Constables, with Shaw himself as advisor. And it so happened that Cape was the bête noire among publishers in the Shaw household. Cape had taken over a small publisher, A.C.Fifield, shortly after Fifield had published a book of selected writings of GBS chosen by Charlotte. She resented the takeover and took up an attitude to Cape as an unreliable and somewhat unscrupulous publisher, and doubtless influenced her husband. She had now read *Seven Pillars* from cover to cover, and been utterly overwhelmed by its power. She would have ridiculed the idea that it should be published as an abridgement. GBS realised that he had made a misjudgement. But to be fair to GBS, there is a great difference between an abridgement written by the author (which was his original idea) and one produced by a publisher's reader.

Shaw now writes: "Later on an abridgment may be considered, though it may take the form of a new book . . . But anyhow you must not for a moment entertain the notion of publishing an abridgment first as no publisher would touch the whole work afterwards."

Three days later, on the last day of 1922, Charlotte wrote herself. Hers is the first reaction to the whole work that we have by an ordinary member of the reading public. It is worth quoting:

> How is it <u>conceivable</u>, <u>imaginable</u>, that a man who could write the *Seven Pillars* can have any doubts about it? If you don't know it is 'a great book' what is the use of anyone telling you so? I have met all kinds of men and women of the kind that are called distinguished; I have read their books and discussed them with them; but I have never read anything like this: I don't believe anything really like this has been written before. When I find in your letter such suggestions as 'should it be without the first person singular?' 'Is there any style in my writing?' 'Anything recognisably individual?' I think – are you laughing at us! Why, foolish man, it <u>could</u> only have been written in the first person singular: it is one of the most amazingly individual documents that has ever been written: there is no 'style' in it because it is above and beyond anything so silly.[23]

But even this unbounded admiration did not break down Lawrence's armour. "Dear Mrs G.B.S", he addressed her, "It's a wonderful letter, that of yours, and I've enjoyed it beyond measure. Though my doubts as to the virtues of the *Seven Pillars* remain." Here Lawrence gets on to a theme of more substance than the nebulous one of style: "It is more of a storehouse than a book – has no unity, is too discursive, dispersed, heterogeneous. I suspect that it's a summary of myself to February 1920, and that people who read it will know me better than I know myself." The advantage of having written an autobiographical book is that one can discuss oneself freely even with complete strangers. This letter also reveals that Lawrence seems to be enjoying himself in the company of "clean and simple men" in the RAF School of Photography at Farnborough and keen to make that known. "There is something here which in my life before I'd never met – had hardly dreamed of".[24]

Meanwhile, Lawrence had replied to GBS telling him he had withdrawn from the uncompleted contract with Cape because the *Daily Express* had revealed that he was in the RAF and that therefore the idea of publishing anything was dead. He also reveals, in a jokey manner, that he has changed his name to Ross. Maddened, Shaw replied by return with a long lecturing letter in an attempt to make him see reason. "Like all heroes, and, I must add, all idiots, you greatly exaggerate your power of moulding the universe to your personal convictions." Shaw has learned at least one important thing, then, about his correspondent. And he correctly predicts: "Lawrence you will be to the end of your days, and thereafter to the end of what we call modern history". He must live with the legend he has created, just as Frankenstein with his monster. "You must make up your mind to do the will of Allah, in whose hand you were only a pen": that is: publish it.

He turns to literature: "As to style, what have you to do with such dilettanti rubbish any more than I have? You have something to say, and you say it as accurately and vividly as you can and when you have done that, you do not go fooling with your statement with the notion that if you do it over five or six times you will do it five or six times better . . . The moment you are conscious of style in your own work, you are quoting or imitating or tomfooling in some way or other. So much for style." Those who prefer the style of the original text to the subscribers' revision may be sorry that Lawrence did not heed this advice.[25]

In sum, Shaw's view of the book is that it should be left as it is and be published. The enormous reputation of Lawrence of Arabia will crush any criticism. Lawrence is just pussyfooting around. There is no point in a confession that nobody else reads.

On February 1st, 1923 Lawrence and the Shaws finally met, in London. If Lawrence was hoping for advice on how to improve the book, or simply a critique, he was disappointed. On the 5th, he wrote to Lady Scott:[26] "He would only say cryptic words, all of commendation. Those are nice, like chocolate eclairs or cream puffs, but not a meal. Mrs Shaw praised even more than he did. . . . My private opinion is that she's read it, and he hasn't: and can't: but is much afraid to shock her by letting on." Lady Scott had also prompted GBS on the book with similarly uninteresting results.

Shaw became the book's leading champion. However, his expressed attitude remained critically uninteresting, he rarely if ever gets beyond superficiality. Given that he gave a great deal of his time to *Seven Pillars* and had some influence on its final form, this might seem rather strange; it is probable that he was indeed influenced by his wife, who had discussed it with him a good deal and read to him from it, and was happy to leave her to provide the detail. Both Shaws were also influenced by a protective attitude to Lawrence himself.

The nearest GBS gets to analysis is his jokey review of *Revolt in the Desert* in the *Spectator* of 12th March, 1927, in which there are frequent references to the original. But this is unconvincing in its overuse of superlatives, its obviously propagandist intention, and its lack of discrimination concerning the book's qualities, especially its historical bias. It does, however, give a general impression of why Shaw, and others among his contemporaries so admired the book: the extraordinary richness of the narrative was self-justifying: its excitement and detail, its intensity, its power as a military chronicle and experience of war, the grandiose landscape and the feeling of its presence, the Olympian display of ethnographic knowledge, and the uniqueness of the writer's omniscient conscience. Its sheer power and magnitude carried all before it and made criticism irrelevant. For both GBS and Charlotte, the calling into question of literary craftsmanship seemed petty-minded.[27] As time went on, however, Shaw seems to have stood less in awe of the book than when he first read it. He found it hard to take the personal aspects of the book as other than posturing

## E.M. FORSTER

He was the last of the literary mentors.

While Garnett had sought to give artistic form to what he recognised as 'a new apprehension of things', and Shaw to give practical advice on how to face up to the real world as a writer, Forster believed he could give Lawrence simple 'tips' on craft, as one writer to another. He was, in this year of 1924, at the height of his powers.

Lawrence had lent Siegfried Sassoon one of the *Oxford Times* copies. On finishing it on a foggy frosty November evening of 1923, he wrote by the warmth of his fire: "Damn you, how long do you expect me to go on reassuring you about your bloody masterpiece? It's a GREAT BOOK, blast you."[28] Looking for support, he asked Lawrence if he might show the book to a writer friend of his, E.M. Forster. Lawrence, who had read *Howards End*, was delighted to learn that its author was still alive!

"Better informed [than Sassoon] in all respects about himself", wrote Forster after Lawrence's death, "I was most careful not to praise the *Seven Pillars* when writing to him. I thought it a masterpiece but to have said so would have been fatal."[29]

Forster made a brilliant start. Unlike many writers, his creative gift as a novelist did not exclude a penetrating and practical critical talent. He also had tact; he could draw a firm line between the personal and the literary, very necessary in a work as personal as the *Seven Pillars*. Unlike Garnett, he never pushed and did not raise moral issues. He sensed what was possible and what was not, and took a strictly pragmatic line, like Lawrence in his political work. And while Garnett wanted to influence TE's mode of self-expression, Forster seems to have wholly sympathised with the autobiographical content. He restricted his criticism to areas where the author had failed to achieve his effect as a story teller or had been obscure. For this he earned TE's gratitude and his friendship within the limits that he could express it.

He had not quite finished reading it when he wrote to TE in February of the new year, 1924. It is a letter on two levels: at first, it reads like a very helpful don's criticism of an undergraduate essay; but beyond that, it is a letter from a sympathetic and deeply impressed fellow writer. For the book had made a profound impression on him.

First, the helpful don. He begins with a fundamental remark about Lawrence's style in the broadest sense which he describes as 'granular' rather than fluid. "You give a series of pictures . . . . there can seldom have been a Movement[30] with so little motion in it"! He praises TE's descriptions of nature. With men, however, it is different: "I find something not very satisfactory in your presentation of the human race . . . all your characters tend to go quiet when the eye is removed, including your own character." He suggests more dialogue. However, the bulk of the letter deals with style. He identifies a 'reflective style' that is "not properly under control" and analyses some passages from the book.

In short Forster gives TE precisely the kind of opinion he had sought from Shaw a year or so earlier, when he got the answer: "As to style, what have you to do with such dilettanti rubbish any more than I have"? Unlike Garnett and Shaw, for whom publishing was a self-evident purpose of writing a book, Forster was cool about a public edition as he realised this would mean cutting, whereas "if anything there ought to be more, as much more about yourself as you'd consent to add; e.g. Some account of your previous time in the East would help one". For in wartime everything is distorted. The *Seven Pillars* responded to something he felt and thought deeply about, especially at just that present moment. He ended: "By the way, your book helped me to finish a book of my own. Seemed to pull me together . . . . . You will never show it to anyone who will like it more than I do."[31]

This new book was *A Passage to India*.

Lawrence replied from Bovington camp with the warmth of gratitude still upon him; the letter had overwhelmed him and his reply is one of the most sincere and touching in his correspondence.[32]

> I've been transferred to B Company: so a man brought your letter over to me two nights ago just after I had gone to bed with bout of malaria: and a miracle happened: the fever left me and I sat up in bed and read it all! This book is my only one, and I have a longing (which I seldom admit) to hear what men say of it. In your case it is wonderful. Writers and painters aren't like other men. The meeting them intoxicates me with a strangeness which shows me how very far from being one of them I am. Of your work I know only *Howards End* & *Siren & Pharos*, but that's enough to put you among the elect . . . and yet you bother to write me whole pages about my effort. No one else has done that for me, and I'm abnormally grateful.

He lays bare to this sympathetic stranger the full agony of the *Seven Pillars*:

> It went through four versions in the four years I struggled with it, and I gave it my nights and days until I was nearly blind and mad. The failure of it was mainly what broke my nerve and sent me into the R.A.F.

Is this last statement the truth? He believed it was. In spite of the precision and length of the criticism – all constructive – Forster had tried to minimise the difference between them, but in vain. Lawrence will not be led into believing that he can belong to a fellowship of Writers.

> Your division of books into the active and passive pleased me. The fluid ones are those written by writers: and the static ones are those (the many more) written by imitators like me . . . . While I was trying to write I analysed most of you and found out, as far as it was within my fineness to see, what were your tricks of effect, the little reserves and omissions which gave you the power to say more than the print says.

There is no invitation to be contradicted. The paragraph, indeed the whole letter, suggests that the situation is irremediable. We are now in 1924 and TE has reached a certain calm in the acceptance that he is not a Writer, a calm which he is loath to disturb. He had, by this time, at last brought himself to agree to a private edition of the book, and the last thing he wanted was to have to look at aspects of the book with a fresh eye and admit the viewpoint of another. Forster's letter pleased him, not because it will help him to improve the *Seven Pillars* but because it thrilled him to have his writing discussed and analysed by a novelist he admired. He was badly in need of this new friend, both stranger and writer (an ideal combination), with whom he could discuss the *Seven Pillars* and literature, and especially his sense of failure as a writer. He thanks Forster for his encouragement . . . "But it is too late. The revise I'm going to give the *Seven Pillars* in the next ten months can be one of detail only: for the adventure is dead in me."

Forster protested at Lawrence's substitution of *active* vs. *passive* for *fluid* vs. *granular*. Otherwise, he must have been rather disappointed that Lawrence showed no inclination to work on his recommendations or to otherwise improve his text. Instead, he took the practical view of helping Lawrence overcome his complex about it. "I can't cheer you up over the book", he replied. "No one could. You have got depressed and muddled over it, and you are quite incapable of seeing how good it is. The only thing is to get rid of it and I should be very happy indeed if I could help you toward doing that. The book is a poem all right, howsoever conceived."[33]

Partly for that purpose, he made a tour in Dorset and stayed at the Black Bear in Wool. He described the meeting to his mother: how, in the evening, he "found a little private soldier awaiting me. This was the romantic Lawrence. He was rather shy and so was I. He had to go at 9.0. Today I went out to his cottage by car. He shares it with two other private soldiers – also little . . . It is all among rhododendrons which have gone wild. We worked for a couple of hours at his book, then had lunch on our knees . . . , very nice and queer; a fine log fire. I like Lawrence though he is of course odd and alarming. . . . I walked back to Wool and got wet crossing 'Egdon Heath'."[34]

The next day he went into Dorchester to call on the Hardys. He had made a good start with Lawrence, Mrs Hardy reported to Cockerell. But in spite of their discussion of the *Seven Pillars*, TE's subsequent letter expresses a certain helplessness:

> Your coming here was a very great pleasure to myself: and a very great profit, I hope, to that difficult book I'm engaged in. You, being by

nature a writer, won't realise how lost I feel in attempting to see whole, & improve what was more an experience than a creation of my own seeking.[35]

Forster stayed several times at Clouds Hill, Lawrence's cottage, and made a real attempt to develop a friendship. He kept up with the Tank Corps friends he had met there, particularly Palmer, known as Posh, a sensitive soul who found life difficult both in and out of the Army. He followed TE's example of giving him books to read. In September TE wrote:

> When he got your book & note (about 9.30 p.m. one evening) he marched out of the hut, & was absent until reveille next morning. By local signs I judge that he sat in Clouds Hill part of the night. The book & the letter are now hidden in his kit. We're quaint little souls, aren't we?

Forster was curious about TE's way of life, which led him away from his middle-class world of Cambridge, Weybridge, and later, Abinger Hammer. He had finished *A Passage to India* and felt free. By September, Lawrence had read it and been dazzled.:

> Oh, it's despairingly well done. The truth is of course that you are a very great writer, & that it's irredeemably weak of me to envy you, even to imagine my following or working by your methods.[36]

In *Friends* EMF writes of TE's "divine jealousy" of other writers:

> (He) felt at the same time pain and joy, for his disgust at his supposed inferiority was inseparable from his delight in the achievement of others. . . . he praised to pacify an inward wound. He was like a god who envies mankind, and for that reason rains blessings upon us instead of shafts of disease . . .[37]

In *A Passage to India* Lawrence recognised a parallel to his own effort in Arabia, Forster's art interpreting Lawrence's experience:

> If the flea may assert a kindred feeling with the lion . . . then let me suggest how my experience (and abandonment) of work in Arabia repeats your history of a situation-with-no-honest-way-out-of-it. You on the large thinking plane, me on the cluttered plane of action . . . and both lost. If excellence of materials meant anything, my book

would have been as good as yours: but it stinks of me: whereas yours is universal.[38]

Forster would never accept this comparison; but he sensed that it was useless to argue. However, Lawrence has raised the big question: is *Seven Pillars* universal, or does it simply 'stink' of Lawrence? Is it merely a case history?

Forster was the best mentor for *Seven Pillars* that TE could have hoped to find. His criticisms were those of a writer: what worked and what did not. He may have understood better than Garnett what motivated the book, and he thought it a masterpiece. As for EMF's criticisms, TE heeded the specific examples he gave of bad style, but that was it. There was no attempt to alter his technique of characterisation or to put in more dialogue. Forster's advice led to no overall simplification of style; on the contrary! He made it more complex and obscure, as Forster later admitted. He remained grateful to him, however: "I found Forster a very helpful and subtle critic, over my *Seven Pillars*. Hardly anybody else . . . said anything that wasn't just useless pap."[39]

# CHAPTER 6

# BOVINGTON CAMP, 1923–25

## OUT OF THE RAF AND INTO THE ROYAL TANK CORPS

When we left John Hume Ross, he had been transferred from the depot at Uxbridge to Farnborough, where he was to undergo training as a photographer, a craft in which he was already skilled. Developing confidence once more, he wrote to Air Vice-Marshal Sir Oliver Swann, who had written the movement order. After saluting him "Dear Swann", our aircraftman second class reminded the Air Vice-Marshal that he had written to him ten days ago and received no reply. He explained that he had arrived too late for the start of the photography course and had been ordered to wait for the next one in two months' time. "This irks me a little because it is a nine months' course anyhow, and it seems a pity to make it eleven." Besides, "I'm already as good as the men passing out". And he warned: " unless I keep working at something I get Bolshie"! Finally, our prospective historian of the RAF wanted to escape the "scrappiness of a training camp" for the real thing. Could he re-muster as an aircraft hand and be posted to an active squadron, home or abroad?[1]

He was tempting the gods and, with that ironic justice they love to administer, they did indeed re-post him – out of the RAF.

A day or two after this letter, the Adjutant was sent for by the C.O. "Air Vice Marshal Swann has just telephoned from the Air Ministry", said the mystified C.O., "he wants to know why AC2 Ross is not engaged in photographic training. Who is this Ross? What is he like?"

Findley, the adjutant, had heard some odd things already about Ross. It wasn't every airman who replied in a foreign language when told off by the Orderly Officer that he was not satisfied with his conduct. Ross was sent for to clean the C.O.'s office in order to be surreptitiously observed. Findley was struck by the blue eyes, the square jaw, the long sensitive fingers. Later:

"Findley! D'you know who I think he is? Lawrence!"
"Lawrence"?
"Yes, Lawrence of Arabia! I saw him once in Cairo early in the war, and this airman looks uncommonly like him".[2]

On December 16th the C.O. informed his superiors that newspapermen, one from the *Daily Mail* and one from the *Daily Express*, had been seen by the gates of the training camp waylaying airmen and asking about Colonel Lawrence.

On December 27th the *Daily Express* broke with:

'UNCROWNED KING' AS PRIVATE SOLDIER
LAWRENCE OF ARABIA
Famous War Hero becomes a Private
SEEKING PEACE
OPPORTUNITY TO WRITE A BOOK

Swann wrote years later that the discovery was due to carelessness at the Colonial Office and Lawrence's "unfortunate love of drawing a veil of mystery about himself". Almost immediately, Lawrence wrote to Cape cancelling the (unsigned) contract for the abridgement. His cover was blown but he thought he might save himself if he avoided further publicity. The cancellation shows where his priorities lay, for with this stroke he ensured that, for the foreseeable future, he was to remain poor; unless he did something else with his book.

By an ironic paradox, the scoop gave birth to the first germ of the idea of a subscribers' edition. On the 6th he got up to London and saw Cape and Garvin, the editor of the *Observer*, who was to have serialised the abridgement, and "made up my mind (is it final? . . . ) not to publish anything whatever".[3] No, of course it was not final. Only a few days afterwards there was renewed correspondence between Lawrence and Cape. Lawrence was having second thoughts and wondering if he had been too hasty. The result was a new proposal. On the 15th Lawrence wrote to Robert Graves that "it may be printed privately, in a limited subscription, next year. A sort of 15 guinea book, almost unprocurable".[4] It was this new idea that finally buried the Garnett abridgement, for with a subscription edition Lawrence would get the best of both worlds: the full story plus the avoidance of public exposure. There will be further hesitations, but from now on this is the version that is making the running.

But that is in the future. For the moment, his precautions were all in vain. It was about January 23rd that he received his dismissal notice from the Air Ministry. Even Trenchard had been unable to save him. On the 30th Lawrence wrote to Shaw as follows: "My mind is like a lump of putty, so that a while later I was sorry to have cancelled it, and began to think of a limited, privately-printed, subscription edition of 2000 copies, illustrated with all the drawings made for me by some twenty of the younger artists. Cape was staggered for the first moment, but then rose to it . . . It took the form of a beautiful contract sent to me to sign: and that very day I got my dismissal from the Air Ministry: and so I've cancelled that too."[5]

So, once more, what now? Not for the first time since the war, Lawrence was footloose in civvy street, "wandering about, rather address-less" as he put it. A totally free man but not willingly so. So for the next month and a half he pulled out all the stops to get back into the services, initially the RAF. But Hoare, the Air Minister, was adamant: the presence of Colonel Lawrence as a ranker was a threat to the discipline of the new force and compromised his superior officers. There was always the Army, which would at least provide mindless discipline, food and shelter, and companionship of the very ordinary kind. The double standard was employed again: to get the very ordinary position of private soldier, the person of General Sir Philip Chetwode, one of Allenby's commanders in Palestine and Syria, was approached by Colonel Alan Dawnay, with the result that Lawrence was accepted into the Tank Corps with effect from 12 March, 1923 and posted to Bovington camp on Salisbury Plain. The old man, Bruce was informed, had insisted on it.

He took another new name: T.E. Shaw. John Hume Ross lives on as the author of *The Mint*, the translator of *Le Gigantesque*,[6] the title of a play by Terence Rattigan, and a signature on one or two cheques in private collections. The new choice of name was pure chance according to Lawrence but Bernard of that name was not amused. GBS now wrote to him as "Dear Aurenshaw". Later, he had to dispel annoying rumours. As late as 1935 Augustus John wrote to Lawrence: "Dear Shaw . . . I hear a report that you are the son of G.B.S. If so, he should have repeated the effort."[7]

## THE ROYAL TANK CORPS

Lawrence must have known that the Tanks would be rather different from the R.A.F, which was a new more exclusive service, but he gives the impression of having been taken by surprise. His notorious nihilistic letters to Lionel Curtis, written between 19th March and 30th

May, 1923 from the Bovington barrack room, show an unprecedented physical and moral disgust at his fellows and at himself. There is an ambiance of degradation and sexual bestiality. There is a whole complex of reasons for this, one of which is simply the onset of middle age (although he still looked very young). He was also conscious of being, perhaps for the first time in his life, where he did not really want to be. He was nostalgic for the RAF where, having taken a great gamble, he had begun to be happy. He had succeeded at Uxbridge in achieving at least a measure of solidarity with ordinary humanity, and at Farnborough he had made deeper friendships with Jock Chambers and R.M. Guy. His frustrated will led him to exalt the RAF and depict the Army as a zoo. Lawrence's brutal distinction between the Air Force and the Tank Corps was later ridiculed by Alec Dixon, who served with Lawrence at Bovington, as "a ripe piece of T.E. humbug".[8] Lawrence himself wrote to Hogarth that "it will be a puzzle for my biographer (if I have one of those unprofitable things) to reconcile my joy in the R.A.F. with my disgust with the Army".[9] Well, I'm trying.

Letters to Guy reveal that there was an affection which went beyond friendship for a hut-mate. There is in it an element of protectiveness, perhaps the beginnings of love. It reminds quite strongly of his non-physical love for Dahoum (also younger and less educated than himself) and seems to have had similar consequences; for while Dahoum was the human symbol of his romantic advocacy of the Arab cause during the war, his feeling for Guy may have been an emotional root of his near-worship of the RAF; and conversely, of his violent disparagement of his mates in the Tank Corps. He wrote Guy:

> My rabbit
> I do no good here. Out upon the army & all its clothes and food & words and works. You in the R.A.F. are as lucky as I thought myself in the old days, & as I used to tell you.[10]

On September 17th he sent him a birthday present and wrote:

> Rabbit, son
> ... My pleasure in the R.A.F. was partly, largely, due to the pleasure I got from your blue and yellow self ... I wish we could meet again: though every R.A.F. Uniform I see makes me heart-sick.[11]

On 18th April he wrote an essay of his experiences with the Handley Page squadron in 1919, in that much interrupted journey to

Cairo.[12] It is a masterpiece of narrative: vivid, full of tense excitement, with unerring choice of detail, concise. It is the actual experience of flight that thrills his imagination. It is raised to a metaphysical level. As he wrote Lionel Curtis: "At Farnborough I grew suddenly on fire with the glory which the air should be, and set to work to make the others vibrate to it like myself."[13]

There is an interesting parallel between a phrase in *Seven Pillars* and one in *The Mint*, his narrative of life at RAF Uxbridge:

> We had "attained a flight-entity which is outside our individualities". (*The Mint*)

> As we moved on, so closely knit in the golden sunlight, we seemed to grow a character, to become an organism, in whose pride each of us was uplifted. (*Seven Pillars*)

The search for solidarity meant the annihilation of the self and he yearned for this feeling, whether with the Arabs, in the RAF or the Tank Corps. Findley wrote of his state of mind: "He appeared to be still trying to shake off something" but "he could not escape the fact of being Lawrence. It was a form of vanity, I think, that made him draw himself apart from his fellows, wrap himself in an aura of mystery...".[14]

Slowly, things got better. As in *Seven Pillars*, the wonder of nature compensates for the all-too-human. By the end of May he could write to Curtis: "For myself there are consolations. The perfect beauty of this place becomes tremendous, by its contrast with the life we lead, and the squalid huts we live in... The nearly intolerable meanness of man is set in a circle of quiet heath, and budding trees, with the firm level bar of the Purbeck hills behind."[15]

This heath, as Forster knew, was Hardy's *Egdon Heath* and, according to Lawrence, Clouds Hill (his cottage on the edge of it) was the house in which lived Eustacia Vye, the dangerous lady of *The Return of the Native*.[16] Lawrence made the acquaintance of Hardy through Robert Graves, very shortly after his arrival in Bovington; it proved to be a valuable friendship for both, and indeed for Hardy's wife, Florence. Lawrence showed once more that special tact and consideration that he reserved for the old. He found peace at Max Gate, Hardy's home:

> I go there as often as I decently can.... Hardy is so pale, so quiet, so refined in essence: and camp is such a hurly-burly. When I come back I feel as if I'd woken from a sleep: not an exciting sleep, but a restful

one. . . . Perhaps that's partly the secret of that strange house hidden behind its thicket of trees. It's because there are no strangers there. Anyone who does pierce through is accepted by Hardy and Mrs Hardy as one whom they have known always and from whom nothing need be hid. . . . Max Gate is a place apart . . . It is strange to pass from the noise and thoughtlessness of sergeants' company into a peace so secure that not even Mrs Hardy's tea-cups rattle on the tray: and from a barrack of hollow senseless bustle to the cheerful calm of T.H. thinking aloud about life to two or three of us. If I were in his place I would never wish to die: or even to wish other men dead. The peace which passeth all understanding; – but it can be felt, and is nearly unbearable. How envious such an old age is.[17]

At the end of June he wrote again to Curtis, in a more self-conciliatory tone:

You've been talking to Hogarth about my discomfort in the Tank Corps: but you know I joined partly to make myself unemployable, or rather impossible, in my old trade: and the burning out of freewill and self-respect and delicacy from a nature as violent as mine is bound to hurt a bit. If I was firmer I wouldn't cry about it.[18]

As if one could burn those things out! In fact life was not that bad. He soon had a fairly cushy job in the stores and had made friends with some of the more articulate, such as Alec Dixon and Arthur Russell. With the famous Brough motor-bike he could get away to the Dorset moorland or wherever. That other social and literary life that his barrack-mates knew nothing about would have had far less zest in it if he had not been able to roar out of camp on the Brough to London, ring highly polished doorbells in Chelsea or Adelphi Terrace, still in uniform and flushed from the speed of the journey, and rush back after a warm welcome and stimulating conversation to the security of camp life. The fact is: he was privileged, but if any of his messmates resented it, they remained silent. From September, apart from Hardy and the Wessex countryside, there was Clouds Hill, near the camp, where he could read, write, or listen to music, alone or with new friends; and from 1924, not only with his mates from Hut 12, but with friends from the world 'out there' like E.M. Forster, Kennington, Bernard Shaw and his wife. Both classes mixed in together. It was a unique experiment in breaking down social barriers and uniting his two worlds.

The June letter to Curtis hints that he had exaggerated his suffering. Indeed, anyone who judges Lawrence only from his letters gets a false picture. He was highly introspective and the letter was the medium for giving it expression. In society, he seems to have been quite different, in early acquaintance being more of a listener than a talker. In his letters to certain close friends – Edward Garnett, Charlotte Shaw, Lionel Curtis – he was quite uninhibited in pouring out his doubts about himself and his philosophical pessimism, it was an absolutely necessary safety valve; but there was a life outside this, varied and not without beauty, and plenty of free time. He had in fact made the compromise that many introspective people do: in his own words, "the sort of job I do doesn't worry me, since the only adventures and interests I have are in my head, and the army leaves you all your thinking-time to yourself. . . . I've found that the way out lay in the freedom of my mind".[19] For the first time he writes of having achieved peace of mind: "I have achieved it in the ranks at the price of stagnancy and beastliness: and I don't know, yet, if it is worth it."[20]

Peace of mind was hardly a permanent state. Alec Dixon, who observed him in camp, wrote that "he never leaned or lounged, and I never saw him relax. He was surely a man with 'ants in his pants' if ever there was one."[21] Dixon doubted whether his service in the Tank Corps helped very much towards restoring his peace of mind. The ghost of Arabia still haunted him. In Dixon's words: "Arabia seemed to cling to him like Sinbad's old man of the sea."

> On one occasion I went to his hut after the last parade of the day and found him in bed. He looked haggard and seemed very depressed. When I sat down he apologised for his state and said that he had a touch of fever. He explained, apropos of nothing, that his visit to the Hejaz in 1921 had been almost too much for him and that the mental strain to which he was subjected during the negotiations had been worse than anything he had known during the campaign.[22]

This has been commented on in Chapter 3. Eric Kennington describes a visit to Clouds Hill in the winter of 1923/24: "I walked into a group of young men. . . . All in Tank Corps uniform, they were very much at their ease, reading, talking, writing. A greater surprise was the condition of T.E. He was possessed of devils, visibly thinner, pale, scared and savage."[23] And there was also that fraught later occasion – probably 1924 – already described, when Lawrence arrived at Kennington's on his Brough with a soldier on pillion. He could put his devils to sleep for a while, but he could not kill them or cast them out.

## CHARLOTTE

In December 1923 the Shaws, who were holidaying in Bournemouth, visited Lawrence at Clouds Hill and took him with them to the Hardys, where they stayed for lunch and tea. Four days later they came themselves to Clouds Hill for tea. It was the seal of a lifetime's personal friendship: between Lawrence and the couple, and between Lawrence and each individual separately.

Although they met many times overall, the friendship between Lawrence and Charlotte Shaw was one of those friendships by letter. Letter writing is the natural medium of the intellectual, of the shy and introspective. It enabled Lawrence to express himself on his own terms and, as Robert Graves observed, pursue "friendships separated by bulkheads".

> Why do wet days usually provoke my writing to you? Is there something in the dash of the rain against the glass which makes me willing to talk confidences? They usually are confidences, you know. I suspect that the rain and the wind give me a shut-away, secret, safe feeling: they warrant one against over-hearing.[24]

From 1924 through 1926 Lawrence wrote about every two weeks – long letters for the most part, on everything under the sun. They are a biography of his life at this time. Her letters, with his usual secretiveness, he destroyed, but the few that survived show that she too was a vivid narrator.

He would write often from Clouds Hill. "Dear Mrs Shaw" (he never addressed her otherwise)

> A perfect afternoon. I rode fifty miles on Boanerges, and have heard the 7th Symphony on the musical box: And Russell and Palmer have made surpassing tea: and the fire is burning well: and I've just read the last of Banba: and replete, I'm going to send you a stodgy word.[25]

Boanerges – the sons of thunder – is his Brough motor-bike; Russell and Palmer his tank corps colleagues; *The Hounds of Banba* probably a book sent to him by Charlotte. She would send him parcels of books regularly from now on. Lawrence showed an interest, of a remarkably unprejudiced kind, in everything she sent him, and gave his thoughts and opinions. He would also pass them round the barrack room and comment on their reception. In fact, his reports on books and theatre visits occupy the largest space in his letters, along with *Seven Pillars* and personal introspection. The one often led to the other. It was not long before, in his typical 'I don't want to but may I?' fashion, he dared to broach the subject of his beating and rape at Dera'a (see Chapter 15 below) and other sensitive subjects, such as his relationship with his mother.

CHAPTER

7

# THE SUBSCRIBERS' EDITION, 1924–26

### A FINE ART EDITION

Not surprisingly, the *Seven Pillars* had been laid aside for some months in the troubled Tank Corps months of 1923; but it was never abandoned. It was during this period that Lawrence collected the feedback from the supposedly secret readers of the Oxford text. Since the first readers in 1922 (including Garnett, Kennington, Vyvyan Richards, the Shaws, Kipling, Hogarth) the six or so copies for circulation had passed to others, usually by urgent request. Shaw was not disposed to take Lawrence's secrecy seriously. He passed the text to Lady Gregory when she visited in May 1923. She found it "enthralling, each sentence rich and complete";[1] and on the next day it was discussed in *The Bull* at Cambridge by a party of five at a lunch ordered by GBS. The purpose of the Shaws' visit to Cambridge had been to present to the Fitzwilliam Museum that portrait of GBS by John that had led to his first meeting with Lawrence. When Cockerell said that the question of Lawrence's book was meant to be hush-hush, Shaw replied loudly that Lawrence was a person who went to hide in a quarry, then put red flags all round it.

Lawrence had also begun to send it out to senior military and civil personnel, especially those who had served in Arabia or in the Palestine campaign (Colonels Wavell and Dawnay, Major Buxton, General Bartholomew, C.E. Wilson). These would vet the historical and military accuracy of the book from the British perspective. When he wrote to Curtis in March, he was anxious to know "what people think of it – not what they are telling me, but what they tell to one another". That we hardly know even now. By the end of 1923 over twenty people had read it and praised it. Only Kipling and Doughty had known serious reservations but they were discreet. Some others would show less enthusiasm later on.

Gradually, he recovered from the disappointment that the book was not a work of art. Deep down he had always believed in it as a personal testimony, and now he began to feel reassured about its literary merit. "Shaw has turned my mind slowly to consider it good", he wrote to Hogarth.[2] But above all it was praise from the gentle and more disinterested Hardy that turned him towards a positive decision.

A letter to Richards[3] from March 1923 shows Lawrence in this more positive and objective frame of mind. As always, the personality of Lawrence's correspondent makes a great difference to his own self-presentation. To Richards, Lawrence did not feel it necessary to be self-deprecatory, nor confessional and emotional as he had been to Garnett and Forster. He sounds a more dispassionate, balanced note.

> Relatively it's a bad book, & gives me no pleasure. That's why your enjoyment of parts or elements of it gratifies me, as a sign that others can find in it something of what I failed to put into it in full measure. Positively I know that it is a good book: in the sense that it's better than most which have been written lately: but this only makes me yet sorrier that it isn't as good as my book should have been.

He has begun to see another side to the matter apart from his own feeling and disappointment. The letter takes the form of comments on underlined phrases copied from Richards' letter. It reads a little like a transcription of a newspaper interview with an author. And the answers seek to build the sort of positive statement typical of such interviews. There are wide-ranging references to other works of both history and literature, yardsticks for his own effort. The conclusion, though full of twisted logic, is defiant:

> I agree that the *Seven Pillars* is too big for me: too big for most writers, I think. It's rather in the Titan class: books written at tiptoe, with a strain that dislocates the writer, & exhausts the reader out of sympathy. Such can't help being failures, because the graceful things are always those within our force: but as you conclude their cracks & imperfections serve an artistic end in themselves: a perfect-picture of a real man would be unreadable.

There is, finally, a feeling of wind in the sails at last: "I'm ambitious after power & want to knock my readers down with it."

Meanwhile, the nihilistic letters to Curtis, and Lawrence's insistence that he had to stay in the services because he was broke, had set his friends worrying. On May 31st GBS wrote to the Prime Minister, Baldwin, about what he called a bad case of Belisarius reduced to begging obols in an ungrateful country.[4] Lawrence should be given a decent pension, he argued. He sent a copy of this letter to Hogarth, who made the famous reply: "He will not work in any sort of harness unless this is padlocked on to him. He enlisted in order to have the padlocks rivetted on to him." He suggested a meeting with Shaw in order to discuss both the man and his book, for he believed that "in some measure the life of letters is best suited to him".[5]

This meeting took place on 6th July and was also attended by Sydney Cockerell and Apsley Cherry-Garrard, the Antarctic explorer who took part in Scott's last expedition, now GBS' neighbour at Ayot St. Lawrence. There was doubtless discussion of what to do with the *Seven Pillars*. Next, Gertrude Bell intervened, asking Lawrence to publish or at least print the book for his friends. Lawrence, showing a renewed interest in the Garnett abridgement as a money spinner (on the back of which he could do an expensive private edition), was in a quandary and wrote to Hogarth: "What am I to do?"[6]

From now on, the hesitant author would be supported and guided by a sort of committee of largely unliterary mentors which included Hogarth, Dawnay, Curtis and Robin Buxton, now Lawrence's banker. Buxton's job was to make the necessary financial calculations for the various schemes discussed and guide the project through, for the committee were well aware of their protégé's contempt for money. They went for the private edition. This solution would pay enough to cover costs (they thought), avoid the impasse of publication, and enable Lawrence to satisfy his craving to produce a beautiful book and get the whole thing off his chest. The Garnett abridgement was finally consigned to oblivion; the coup de grâce came on 13th December, when Lawrence met with Curtis, Dawnay and Hogarth in Oxford. From now on *Seven Pillars* would be an edition for rich subscribers only. In an age of writers for whom Truth meant going public and no taboos, Lawrence had chosen to hide his light under a bushel; at least, that was Garnett's view. But for Lawrence it was the right decision, putting an end to years of uncertainty, by-passing the publishing dilemma, and giving him the opportunity to do what he did so well – manage a project. Unfortunately, due to his extraordinary fussiness over style and lay-out, and his insistence on doing everything himself, he made things far more complicated than he need have done.

Buxton suggested 120 copies at £25 each, which was later modified to 100 at 30 guineas (about £1,500 per copy by today's standards). £3150 in total. The subscribers' edition would be made to the highest standards in the land, each copy individualised, and it would not be difficult to find a hundred subscribers ready to pay this fantastic sum for what was seen as the collector's book of the century. Shaw did not approve of the scheme: "Restricting the book to a hundred copies is nonsense, and you know it as well as I do."[7]

## THE PICTURES

£3150 was a lot of money in 1923. But Lawrence's plans for the book were extravagant, to say the least. He had commissioned a number of different artists to do a large number of portraits – and not only portraits. Kennington, Augustus John and the less well-known William Roberts were first among them, but they also included Rothenstein, William Nicholson, and Sargent for the portraits; Roberts, Kennington, Nash, Colin Gill, Blair Hughes-Stanton, and others, for a miscellany of strange landscapes, stylised action scenes, symbolic treatments; and Kennington again for some humorous drawings. After reading *Seven Pillars* in 1922, Kennington had spontaneously drawn a number of cartoons which had delighted Lawrence. Some of these have appeared in most published editions of the book. They add a sudden touch of humour to a book where it is in fairly short supply. But apart from these, the vast majority of *Seven Pillars* readers have seen only a handful of portraits; only readers of the original subscribers' edition have seen the full collection of art work. To see how these various artists have reacted to the content makes quite a difference as to how the reader may feel, even think, about the book, and also gives it a more definite sense of period; for these works amount to an exhibition of contemporary art. Not all critics agreed with this enrichment: "I know not what outrageous grangerization you are planning with your pictures; but the book is more than self-sufficient as it stands", berated Shaw on 13th May.[8]

It is true that Lawrence lacked confidence over his book. What better way out of the difficulty than beginning a new project, letting the book develop a new dimension from the ideas it suggested to artists? It was a brilliant idea as it pulled Lawrence out of depression with the book and substituted action for unproductive reflection. It helped him to new acquaintances, creative partnerships, active work in a different medium. It enabled him to discuss his own work as something objective and to see it through the eyes of other artists. He was particularly keen to give opportunities to little recognized artists, like Paul Nash. "I think it's going to be great fun", wrote Nash. "Lawrence is of the salt of the earth and I know he's doing much of this simply to help painters who find difficulty in *affording* to paint."[9]

Lawrence had always been interested in the design and production possibilities of the book, and this became a sort of substitute for the long postponed dream of the printing press, even an apotheosis of his lifelong interest in fine printing and illustrated books. No need to hand-print the books of others; his own book would be a unique example of an illustrated book, printed and bound to the highest standards, an immortal creation that married traditional craft and contemporary art. There can be no doubt that this prospect gained Lawrence's support for a subscription edition. It also mitigated in his eyes the inadequacy of the book as literature. "Poor dirt", as he called the writing, "can be hidden by fine clothes".[10]

And do the clothes cover the 'dirt'? That there is a marvellous array of fine illustrations cannot be doubted but are they 'worn' by the text? No set of 'illustrations' (one hesitates to call them so, and indeed Lawrence told his artists he wanted decorations, not illustrations) has ever been so weirdly integrated with their text. Yeomans calls the subscribers' edition of *Seven Pillars of Wisdom* "a unique expression of the period and a marriage of the highest literary and visual achievements".[11] One might agree with the first part, but hardly with the second. If it is a marriage, it is certainly a very unharmonious one. It is in fact one more puzzle for the reader on top of all the others. Most illustrations in a book are supportive in their role. A very fine example is Thesiger's *Arabian Sands*, a travel book which I have compared with *Seven Pillars*.[12] If you look through the photographic illustrations of that book, you already know a great deal about it, its setting, the people in it, and how they live. The pictures in *Seven Pillars* show little of this sort; Kennington's Arabs do, and three straightforward and beautiful works by J.C. Clark: *At a well*, *Stokes gun class* and *At Akaba*. Otherwise, we are in a land of highly individual interpretation, much of it, like Blair Hughes-Stanton's superb woodcuts, introspective and suggestive. But of what? Even Lawrence did not know. The few landscapes are either stylised drawings from photographs (Nash) or atmospheric fantasies (Kennington). There is a possibility that those who like art will become more interested in the 'illustrations' than in the text they were supposed to illustrate. But that was what Lawrence said he wanted; and after all, it's only for 120 rich subscribers.

Illustrations which are works of art in themselves may relate only vaguely to the content; Edmond Dulac's for *The Rubbaiyyat of Omar Khayyam* are an example but they are nevertheless fully in tune with the orientalist mood of the poetry; and they create a unique ambiance, not a pluralistic jumble. In Lawrence, the first question is likely to be: "Why are they here?" Even the Arab portraits, which are the most obviously congruent to the book, contain pictures of Arabs whom the reader cannot place in the story at all. As for the British portraits, they are far too many for the book, going exactly against the impression that Lawrence sought to create in the text: that the Arab Revolt was only minimally dependent on the British; and nothing could be less epic than these urbane statesmen in their suits. Similarly, the almost brutal vorticist style of the most prominent artist, William Roberts, seems utterly inappropriate to the old-fashioned mannerism of Lawrence's writing and the traditional printing format. The one exception is the magnificent *Camel March*, which has been reproduced in published editions. The total freedom given to the artists over interpreting events, landscapes, etc., and the need to place their illustrations as dictated by the page, particularly as tail-pieces, leads to a situation in which the subjects of these pictures are usually quite unrelated to those of the page on which they appear; the reader is therefore doubly unlikely to be able to relate the picture to the book. Finally, there are not enough pages to accommodate 115 illustrations, so many are simply added at the end. The range of different styles from the twenty or so different artists is staggering and this also, in book illustration, gives an impression of the arbitrary (which it is), even the superfluous. The art critic Herbert Read does not mince his words: "I would venture to say that this book is a monstrous exhibition of all that a book should not be."[13] Grosvenor is more positive. However, he admits that "the variety of styles in the decoration hinders the book's overall visual impression" and concludes: "it is the disorientation of the war generation visually presented".[14]

It is only by abandoning the book, and looking at the artwork as an exhibition, that one can really appreciate it. From this perspective we have a very rich collection of art. As Yeomans writes, "A unique cross-section of the best, and in some respects, the most progressive of British art of the post-war period."[15] An exhibition of these pictures was indeed mounted at the Leicester Galleries by Kennington in February, 1927, and later by the National Portrait Gallery in 1988. One cannot help feeling happy for these artists in having their pictures, at which they worked so enthusiastically, exhibited in a decent fashion to a sizeable public.

Kennington was appointed to take charge of all the art work, which was considerable. He had to liaise with Whittingham & Griggs (who were producing colour plates), with the many participating artists, and with the sitters (Lawrence had decided for some reason that the portraits of Arabs that Kennington had done in Transjordan must be matched by portraits of British participants), make judgements on the quality of all the artwork, and liaise with the private printer, Manning Pike.

On the 19th December, 1923, Lawrence wrote a draft of a letter to be sent out to subscribers. It is charmingly frank:

> I'm bound to say that I think the book exceedingly dear ... and I hope no one will decide to get it unless he is in a position to (mis)spend thirty guineas without a regret. ... I much regret the necessity I am under of multiplying the book at all: but I want my illustrations reproduced, and cannot pay the cost of them: and the least evil, in the circumstances, seems to be for my friends to find me a hundred discreet subscribers! I'd be glad if all of them found the book too dull to read, and locked it, forgotten, in cupboards!

To this message he received an appropriate reply from Lady Nancy Astor: "Dear Colonel Lawrence, I am one of the people who are very wealthy and I would like a copy of your book, but I don't promise to read it. However, as that is your wish, you won't mind!"[16]

It was the beginning of a lasting friendship. He also warned subscribers that "you will be lucky to get the finished work in 1924 ... I promise no date". In fact, they waited until the end of 1926. Carried away by the excitement of production and the illustrations, he had not thought through the problems, in particular his ultra-purist printing requirements and his own revision of the text.

He had got over the watershed of worrying about the literary quality of the book and continued to disparage it happily in order to put off unwanted subscribers. He was building up a good head of steam with his plans for the subscribers' edition:

> Whittingham & Griggs are completing the first four chromo-lithos: and Pike (the printer) is preparing me specimen pages.
>
> If necessary we will sell 120 copies. I'm printing 200 ...
>
> Subscribers roll in for my book ...
>
> Some Nashes attached for judgement. Please tell me what you think of them. ...

There's a young cubist artist called Roberts. Very gifted & good. He'll make (your head) look like a problem in Euclid. You'll love it. So'll I. He's in London & will draw you when you can give him two hours.

Dear Robin, I don't like the lady's manner: will you please return her cheques? . . .

I've replied begging him to consider seriously if his bank balance can't be better employed than acquiring luxury books.

Clouds Hill had been furnished with a writing table for the purpose of revising the text. He realised that the book would have to be made shorter, otherwise it would simply be too bulky. He wrote to Hogarth on November 14th: "The book's size is determined by the ready plates (10 x 8, I think it is, a large quarto . . . ). If I can get it down to 250,000 words it will go in one vol. of 450 words a page." Here we have the motive for abridging. When thinking in terms of practicalities like the size of plates, Lawrence felt much more in command of the situation.

250,000 words was exactly the length he did get it to. This represented a total cut of 25 per cent, There were to be "no good cuts or noble changes, no re-writing", he told Garnett, who had hoped there would be, "it will be revised in petto". At the same time, he reassured Shaw, who (the reader will recall) had demanded that the work "MUST BE PUBLISHED IN ITS ENTIRETY, UNABRIDGED", that corrections would be limited to "blemishes of prose".[17] He was so absorbed with the production details that he did not begin revising the book until mid-1924.

### THE SHAWS AND *SEVEN PILLARS*

In 1924, Lawrence remained optimistic that the whole job, including printing and binding, would not take more than eighteen months. He was not this time fighting a lone battle in an unheated attic. The Shaws had promised to help with proof reading and suggestions. Lawrence had an admiration for GBS that became an article of faith; he could take criticism and suggestions from him because of the superman image he had made of him; GBS' mock scolding and ridicule he also liked. Such a tone was infinitely preferable, especially at this stage in the proceedings, to the "heavy father" act of Garnett. Like Kennington's cartoons, it chimed with Lawrence's desire that the book should not be seen to be taken seriously. In any case, Shaw did not see the point in making suggestions of a literary kind, it was a great book and that was that. Charlotte, for whom the book meant more than it did to GBS, had originally offered to look over the proofs and Lawrence was keen to involve her more deeply: "And what form should your corrections take? Any you please. My pleasure is bounded only by your pains. . . . As the hesitant nervous author I'll value most such corrections as affect the manner and matter of the expression of ideas: because they will tend to make the book better, and I dread strangers seeing the thing in its existing unworthy clumsy form."[18]

Charlotte was to take him at his word. By the end of September Lawrence and his printer had got 40 pages in page proof – The Introduction. Lawrence forwarded copies not only to the Shaws, but also to Cockerell and St. John Hornby, Director of the prestigious Ashendene Press, for comments on the printing and lay-out. On October 6th, Charlotte wrote: "G.B.S. has taken to the proofs like a duck to water and is looking at them as if they were his own! I am glad: I am sure it will help you."[19] And on the following day GBS returned the corrected proof, and some suggestions by Charlotte, in the following words:

> My dear Luruns
> Confound you and your book: you are no more to be trusted with a pen than a child with a torpedo.[20]

This refers to several passages that Shaw considered to be libellous. His work had been limited to the rewriting of libellous passages, and to some rather fussy proof-reading. As always, Shaw's main concern was practical and he added, for good measure, some guidelines on libels which are worth printing:

> All criticisms are technically libels; but there is the blow below the belt, the impertinence, the indulgence of dislike, the expression of personal contempt, and of course the imputation of dishonesty or unchastity which are not and should not be privileged, as well as the genuine criticism, the amusing good-humoured banter and (curiously) the 'vulgar abuse' which <u>are</u> privileged.[21]

GBS wrote in the fly-leaf of Charlotte's copy of *Seven Pillars*: "I rewrote these passages for him in terms that were not actionable. He adapted my versions, but, much amused by them, shewed them with his own text to the victims, as first rate jokes." There is no independent testimony of this unlikely and typically Lawrencian story.

Lawrence alleged that "there was scarcely a sentence that GBS did not improve", giving rise to vastly exaggerated claims concerning GBS' contribution. The correspondence with Charlotte Shaw makes it clear that he busied himself seriously only with the first eight chapters; after that, he left it to Charlotte to consult him if she thought it necessary; she rarely did. GBS himself always insisted that, apart from his advice to leave out the first chapter, he had changed very little. He said it to Lady Scott in 1925, and repeated it long after Lawrence's death. It is significant that, throughout the revision process from October 1924 onwards, it was to Charlotte that Lawrence sent the proofs, not to GBS, and that it was with her that he discussed them. In his usual way, he destroyed all data of the suggestions she made along with her letters; but fortunately, the earliest of these notes, those made on the first 40 pages of proof that he sent, were preserved among her papers that she bequeathed to the British Museum.[22]

She objects first to his describing Devon territorials as *clean delightful fellows, full of the power of making women and children glad*.[23] "Clean is a very dangerous word", she writes of this no.1 favourite of Lawrence's vocabulary, "Believe an old woman it is very exceptionally only that men make women glad: do you know the war story: . . . 'This 'ere War's too good to larst, I says. Eighteen shillins a week, and no 'usban giving one at night. My it's 'eaven!'" The criticism might have embarrassed Lawrence, whose meaning had been narrowly interpreted! Charlotte was repelled by sexual intercourse.

She next touches another sensitive area, racial discrimination. She refers to: *I am proudest of my fights in that I did not have any of our own blood shed. All our subject provinces to me were not worth one dead Englishman.* "This implies that you wouldn't mind how much 'black' or 'native' or 'nigger' blood was shed. I don't know if you meant it to. I think the whole para a little . . . young . . . and foolish." This observation, which shows a multi-racial sympathy rare in those days, and even now in our House of Commons when war casualties in overseas interventions are discussed, may seem to rather pull the rug from under Lawrence's feet as a champion of the Arabs. Lawrence is here thinking of the slaughter on the Western Front. He never wasted Arab lives either.

Her strongest comment is the third. After deploring the hypocrisy of British Government and their local representatives in making promises to the Arabs that they had no intention of keeping, Lawrence wrote: *The only thing remaining was to refuse rewards for being a successful trickster, and to prevent this unpleasantness arising I began in my reports to conceal the true stories of things, and to persuade the few Arabs who knew to an equal reticence. In this book, also for the last time, I mean to be my own judge of what to say.* She wrote: "You really must not say that! Are you writing history, or a fairy tale?" The starry-eyed admirer of 1922 has become a lot less timid. If she had written 'fable' rather than 'fairy-tale', it would be a fundamental question on the nature of *Seven Pillars*.

The major contribution made by the Shaws, by far, was their success in persuading Lawrence to drop the first chapter of the book, *How and why I wrote*. As it was GBS who took the responsibility for making this suggestion, it has been credited to him alone. "That it should come out and leave the book to begin with chapter two, which is the real thing and very fine at that, I have no doubt whatever", he wrote.[24] It is certainly true that the literary opinion of GBS weighed more heavily with Lawrence than anyone else's. But it was a recommendation reached by the Shaws jointly. "We both feel that the first chapter is not quite right", Charlotte had written. Also, since Shaw's concerns were usually practical more than literary, it is likely that in reality it was the compromising content of Chapter 1, including Charlotte's third comment above, that he most objected to. For the same reason he objected to a chapter (OX Chapter 92) reporting the aftermath of an act of homosexual intercourse between an English soldier and an Arab of Lawrence's bodyguard, and the relevant pages were omitted.

Some passages from the scrapped Chapter 1 were simply transferred to other relevant parts of the text; I believe that Shaw was right, the true opening of the book is Chapter 2 *Spirit of the Revolt*. One can get the flavour by finding a copy of the first published edition (1935).

## THE REVISION OF THE OXFORD TEXT

There were two ways in which Lawrence sought to improve the text: the first was by reducing the length of the book; the second by improving the style. To begin with, he tried to establish a routine of cutting, aiming at the 10 per cent figure agreed upon with the committee.

He was also by now quite out of sympathy with the subject matter. This made it difficult to decide what was of value and what was not; in this case, he adopted the principle: 'when in doubt, cut it out'. He wrote to Charlotte: "I cut 55% out of the last corrected section of the Oxford text (Book VIII)! So you see I'm getting stronger every day."

If he had not made these substantial cuts in the latter part of the book, one wonders how many people would finish it without getting bored. The books that lost most were those that needed to lose most. But, even here, there are no bold cuts. He cut like a miser. Far from making the book widely different, as he said he would, he has succeeded in making it more narrowly the same.

He believed that he now knew, through diligent application, how to write. As he assured his readers in *Some notes*, "By 1924 I had learned my first lessons in writing, and was often able to combine two or three of my 1921 phrases into one". What this amazingly naive interpretation of 'writing' boils down to is: composing more complex sentences. It therefore involved, across the 334,500 words of the Oxford text, a vast amount of intolerably painstaking revision.

A comparative study across the various drafts and texts of the development of Lawrence's style gives no indication of a sudden revelation, of a change in direction. It moves consistently, from 1919 through the Oxford text to the subscribers' edition, from simplicity to complexity (both lexical and grammatical), from the relaxed to the taut, from the personal to the impersonal, from the immediate to the remote, from the unpretentious to the rhetorical. Of course, in a work as long as this it is not overwhelmingly apparent; the tales of adventure live by the movement of the narrative and the vivid detail of the description. But it was certainly apparent to those who had read the Oxford text, most notably Graves and Forster. The Oxford text, while it is often complex grammatically and rarified in lexis, shows a balance between simplicity and rigour. Lawrence will move towards a rigour that often strains comprehension.

Let us look at some results. They are all examples of his 'reflective style' criticised by E.M. Forster in his first letter to Lawrence.

*1918. Winter in Tafileh.* The Bedu are snowbound and frustrated. Mahmas, a young tribesman of Lawrence's bodyguard, has drawn a dagger against another and been punished by a severe whipping:

What Lawrence originally wrote was this:

> R 495 Now he shrank into a corner showing his teeth, vowing, across his tears, to be through those who hurt him. Arabs did not dissect endurance, their crown of manhood, into material and moral, making allowance for nerves. So Mahmas' crying was called fear, and when loosed, he crept out disgraced into the night ...

This typically subtle Lawrencian distinction is undeniably easier to

> O 563 (Mahmas) was with good reason crying aloud. Arab habit called *such weakness fear, since unlike us* they did not dissect endurance, their crown of manhood, into material and moral *parts*, making allowances for nerves *and spiritual courage*. So when Mahmas was loosed he crept out disgraced into the night . . .

read and understand here. In the revision, Lawrence transposed or deleted vital elements of coherence (shown in italics). The more tenuous the cohesive elements linking ideas, the more the mind has to search for the correct inference.

Here is a passage on Wadi Rumm, lined on either side with huge red perpendicular cliffs.

The sustained yet balanced rhythm takes you right through the

> O 397 The silence and bigness of the valley was like a childish dream, and we looked backward through our minds for its prototype, wondering if or when it had been that we had walked with all the men of earth up between these walls towards that open square where the road seemed to end.

sentence and seems like a written symbol of the long valley itself. But he shortened it.

Perhaps he found the opening 'naive' and replaced it with a state-

> R 360 Landscapes, in childhood's dream, were so vast and silent. We looked backward through our memory for the prototype up which all men had walked between such walls toward such an open square as that in front where this road seemed to end.

ment more grave and rhetorical. But *so* is used in an unexpected sense, he loses the word 'valley' and one cannot walk up a prototype. Above all, the sustained rhythm of the original is obstructed in the revision by awkward syntax, and the sentence stumbles on, losing its power.

From the "Myself" chapter, R 583

The first clause is simple enough and is much quoted; but the rest

> I was a standing court martial on myself, inevitably, because to me the inner springs of action were bare with the knowledge of exploited chance. The creditable must have been thought out beforehand, foreseen, prepared, worked for. The self, knowing the detriment, was forced into depreciation by other's uncritical praise.

is probably incomprehensible to most readers. The Oxford version has been ruthlessly abridged. It is an extreme example of highly idiosyncratic and risky assumptions concerning links between ideas and their linguistic expression. What other writer has written so abstractly, so *remotely*, about himself?

The changes and omissions made by Lawrence have resulted in many passages which are, at best, only marginally coherent.[25] Did he care? "I'm ambitious after power & want to knock my readers down with it," he had told Richards. He had written to his subscribers that he wanted them to buy his book but not read it.

## THE PRODUCTION OF THE BOOK BEAUTIFUL

"This book of mine is too ambitious – I wrote it too hard and big. . . . I've printed it too elaborately: illustrated it too richly. The final effect will be like a scrofulous peacock."[26]

The rewriting and cutting took place between October 1924 and August 1925 – a considerable achievement for a serviceman: that is, the preliminary cutting, for there would be more once the galley proofs had come back from Pike, the printer.

Bored by the largely uncreative revision task, and by the book as literature, he became more and more enthusiastic about the production of the Work of Art. Was he not more of a craftsman than a writer? He certainly knew something about printing and had almost gone down that road with Richards. But he did not have experience, and a little knowledge is a dangerous thing!

He explained to Charlotte the importance he attached to printing:

" . . . Pike (the printer) is an artist of great severity and carefulness, and . . . his pages are made as beautifully as he can compass them. To him the balances of lines and paragraphs and passages are vital: they are the elements of which the physical book is made up. . . . He is fortunate in having found a living author: for it makes his work much easier, often, to leave out a few words, or a few lines, to make a new paragraph begin here or there, to telescope two chapters:- and I've given him carte blanche to cut and change the text as he pleases: this is fair, for words are as elastic as ideas, and type-metal isn't elastic at all".[27]

By now, Lawrence's skill as a writer is, in the final revision at least, in the service of the printer, as a cutter or manipulator of phrases, sentences and paragraphs.But who *is* the printer? Manning Pike himself is in no doubt: "I discovered I was expected to do it his way and from that moment Colonel Lawrence became his own printer and I his paid servant". The wish to be everything at once is a Lawrencian trait observed by others back in his Arab Revolt days. Would he once again wear himself out in this fashion? Or would the hectic activity, which at least involved him with others, be beneficial? It is difficult to decide. It took him another fourteen months to get everything ready, far beyond his expectations. The process was almost absurdly complicated and nearly drove the printer mad. "According to Hodgson (Pike's pressman) Pike 'carried a loaded revolver with which he would sometimes shoot holes in the ceiling'."[28] Lawrence generously paid for a holiday for Pike and his son in Gibraltar; "but how glad I would have been to stay on ship for the rest of my life away from *Pillars of Wisdom*", wrote Pike.[29] So much for the good fortune in having a living author to work with!

The initial setting up, in 14-point, was done, not by Pike, but by the Monotype Corporation, so the Subscribers' edition was not a 100% hand-press job. Pike then ran off a galley proof, which was sent to Lawrence for checking. As the galley proofs of the successive books reached him from Pike, he checked them and sent them off to the Shaws for proof-reading and correction. Then, after deciding on changes suggested by the Shaws, came the miniaturist task of fitting into the frame alterations for the printed page. The rules made by Lawrence were extremely exacting:

(I) Page always 37 lines.
(II) Each page begins with a new paragraph, and a small capital extending over three lines (ornamental and designed especially by Wadsworth).
(III) The last line of each page is solid, i.e. it extends to the right hand margin.
(IV) No word is divided.
(V) Paragraphs end always after the half-way across the line.

The proofs were then returned to the printer who drew page proofs. When Lawrence received these, yet more finicky alterations were made for the better appearance of the printed page. Then came the second page proof, hopefully, but not always, the last.

In spite of what he wrote to Charlotte, the probability is that text changes to meet the criteria for the printed page were almost invariably made by himself, not by his printer. It is not, however, possible to judge whether a change like the one below, or the ones analysed a couple of pages back, have been made to improve the style, to make a paragraph fit a page, or simply to reduce the length of the text.

As a result of all this, different Books were all at different stages in the process simultaneously, making it very trying for everyone. Then there was the very exacting art work, notably the colour prints, supervised by Kennington, and the printing problems they posed. Add to that the enormous problem of building into the text the one hundred and fifteen illustrations in different media: portraits, in oils or pastel or charcoal, line drawings, woodcuts, landscapes in watercolour or pen and wash.

By mid-1924 the costs of production and materials, payments and hand-outs to artists, were mounting rapidly and it was obvious that 120 subscriptions at 30 guineas would come nowhere near to meeting the cost. Lawrence put his land in Epping Forest (Pole Hill) up for sale but then, in the spring of 1925, a very old idea came back again – an abridgement. "Dear Robin", he wrote to Buxton, "I went to Cape & offered him 125000 words of *The Seven Pillars*, with as many of the black & white illustrations as he wants . . . for publication under another title in England & America in the spring of 1927."[30] Cape would pay £1500 on conclusion of contract and another £1500 in six months. So the hut on the hill would be reprieved for the moment.

This would become *Revolt in the Desert*, the bowdlerised book the public would buy, and perhaps read, in their tens of thousands, as the 'real thing'. This abridgement project would succeed where the Garnett abridgement failed. There was all the difference in the world between publishing an abridgement after the complete book, and publishing an abridgement first. He now felt he could easily do it himself, and indeed *Revolt* was the only thing to do with *Seven Pillars* that he did accomplish easily.

Lawrence wrote to Charlotte about the abridgement on 19th March and the Shaws insisted he send them a copy of the draft contract. When he had seen it, GBS wrote at length, beginning:

> My dear Lawrence
> Look here: we really must unmuddle this business. As a private soldier you are not to think; yours but to do and die. As Colonel Lawrence of Damascus you have to make decisions after at least a minimum of preliminary ratiocination.[31]

However, Lawrence did not heed his advice and signed up with Cape at the end of April. The contract contained a clause giving Lawrence the right to terminate the printing of the book once the profits had paid off his debts incurred over the *Seven Pillars*. He used it.

There was, however, a more important result of the abridgement decision. Desperate to avoid the publicity that had led to his dismissal from the RAF last time round, Lawrence decided he would have to leave the country and applied for an overseas posting. By a cruel irony it would be his overseas posting that prompted the second major hullaballoo about him in the press and parliament. But leaving it all behind no doubt appealed to him for more profound reasons also.

## RETURN TO THE RAF THE BOOK IS COMPLETE

In July 1925, Lawrence was finally re-admitted into the RAF. It took a suicide threat to achieve it. One biographer has it that Trenchard told him: "All right, if you insist. But please go into the garden. I don't want my carpets ruined"![32] Shaw wrote a warning letter to Baldwin, once again Prime Minister. At last Baldwin overcame his inertia and the implacable Air Minister, Samuel Hoare, was forced to yield. He would not be the last Air Minister to be riled by Lawrence. He was posted to the Cadet College at Cranwell in Lincolnshire: not as an officer cadet, of course, but as a member of a flight servicing planes used by cadets; nor was he a technician, but a runner-cum-bookkeeper. He was in his "seventh heaven" and celebrated by opening up Boanerges to 108 mph. Quite apart from the change of uniform, there were no bugles or reveille, no guard duty or kitchen chores, no PT, fewer kit and hut inspections and parades. In *The Mint* Lawrence idealises Cranwell. But he missed the visits to Max Gate and many aspects of his former life: "Alas for Clouds Hill, & the Heath, and the people I had learned in the two years of Dorset!", he wrote to Mrs Hardy.

Was the RAF. really going to be a better life than the one he had created in the RTC? A passage like this one, even though it might be somewhat 'composed', makes one wonder:

> Do you know what it is when you see, suddenly, that your life is all a ruin? Tonight it is cold, and the hut is dark and empty, with all the fellows out somewhere. Every day I haunt their company, because the noise stops me thinking. Thinking drives me mad. ... So long as there is breath in my body my strength will be exerted to keep my soul in prison, since nowhere else can it exist in safety. The terror of being run away with in the liberty of power lies at the back of these many renunciations of my later life. I am afraid, of myself. Is this madness?

> The trouble tonight is the reaction against yesterday, when I went mad:- rode down to London, spent the night in a solitary bed, in a furnished bed-room, with an old woman to look after the house about me: and called in the morning on Feisal,[33] whom I found lively, happy to see me, friendly, curious. He was due for lunch at Winterton's (Winterton, with me during the war, is now Under-Secretary of State for India).... Winterton of course had to talk of old times, taking me for a companion of his again, as though we were again advancing on Damascus. And I had to talk back, keeping my end up, as though the R.A.F. clothes were a skin that I could slough off at any time with a laugh. But all the while I knew that I couldn't. I've changed, and the Lawrence who used to go about and be friendly and familiar with that sort of people is dead. He's worse than dead. He is a stranger I once knew.[34]

Only to Charlotte could he make such confessions. The past, especially the Arab past, is still an enemy to his peace.

One big uplift was when harmless acquaintances from Cairo days, Wing Commander Smith and his wife, Clare, arrived at Cranwell; but Clare, like Dixon earlier on, found him nervous: "He was far more restless than when I had met him in Cairo. He would rub his sides with his hands, up and down, up and down, and he would sometimes pass two fingers over his mouth and chin, or rumple up the crest of fair hair which was still unruly and refused to lie down."[35]

If he was further from the Hardys, he was somewhat nearer to the Shaws in Hertfordshire. He grew very close to them and could hardly have continued without their friendship. In his last year he saw them thirteen times, seven times at Ayot St. Lawrence. "I propose, if they [the camp Guard] let me pass through, to kick hard at Boanerges, and rush down the London Road. At Codicote I will give him his head, which will turn to the right, and stop by your front gate." The winter of 1925/26 was a hard one, and in December he had quite a bad accident on the Brough after a visit to E.M. Forster at Cambridge, skidding on a patch of ice in the dark at 55 mph. It was nearly the end of January before he got up to Ayot.

Lawrence knew that he would soon be posted abroad, probably India, and this was confirmed in October. The *Seven Pillars* would have to be ready for publication before his departure. There was a frenetic race to finish but it was only thanks to frequent postponements of the embarkation date that he managed it. He had another mishap in March, breaking his wrist when helping to crank a car. He motorcycled from Lincolnshire to Dorset to visit the Hardys, using

# Lawrence uniformed, 1918 to 1925

**1** 3 October 1918. In Damascus. Painted by James McBey. This is the only painting made of Lawrence during the war. Copyright © Imperial War Museums (Art.IWM ART 2473).

**2** 1919. Paris. A formal portrait of Lawrence in the uniform of a Colonel at the Versailles Peace Conference. Copyright © Imperial War Museums (Q73538).

**3** 1923–25. Bovington. Private T.E. Shaw of the Royal Tank Corps. Copyright © Imperial War Museums (Q83977).

**4** April 1921. Amman, Transjordan. 'The wild ass of the desert' as a civil servant in suit, white collar and Homburg hat. From left: Gertrude Bell, Major Welsh, Lawrence, Sir Herbert Samuel, Emir Abdullah. The person between Samuel and the Emir is probably Subhi al-Umari. Copyright © Imperial War Museums (Q60171).

# Various Arabs of importance

**5** October 1918. Subhi al-Umari, in Bedouin dress, on the outskirts of Aleppo during a truce. This is the photograph widely misidentified as Lawrence, which persuaded Subhi to write his own book, *Lurens kama' areftuhu* (Dar al-Nahar lil Nashr, 1969) from which this image is reproduced.

**6** 1918. Guweira. Emir Zeid (centre) and Nesib al-Bakri holding ceremonial swords. Reproduced from a photograph in *The Memoirs of Emir Zeid: The Jordanian War 1917–18* (ed. Suleiman Moussa), Jordanian Studies Centre, 1990 (Arabic).

**7** Nawaf al-Sha'alan by Eric Kennington. Pastel. One of the Arab portraits made by Kennington during his trip to Amman in the spring of 1921, which were exhibited at the Leicester Galleries. Nawaf was the eldest son of Nuri al-Sha'alan, paramount Sheikh of the Rualla. See Chapter 17. By courtesy of the Trustees of the *Seven Pillars of Wisdom* Trust.

one hand. When he roared off again, Hardy was still in the house and regretted there was no farewell. He would not see Lawrence again.

A trip to Edinburgh, on his bike, to confer with the map makers; then there were the subscription requests still coming in, including one from the King (which Lawrence refused but presented him with the book); every copy had a differently designed binding which Lawrence selected for his friends on an individual basis. Finally, *Revolt in the desert*, which Lawrence also had to prepare for publication before leaving England. He was hurtling up and down the A1 until the closing days.

## GOODBYE TO ALL THAT

One of his last acts was to send or give copies of the book to his friends. To Kennington he presented no less than four copies – "my unexpected fee for art editorship", Kennington called the gift. Amazingly, TE found time to squeeze in six sittings to him for a new portrait, a very fine bust in plaster. To the perpetually hard-up Robert Graves he enclosed a card with the gift copy which said "Please sell when read". Graves got £315 for it. And then EMF: "Lawrence did me proud, devoted a whole day to catching hold of me before his departure for India, and gave me a gorgeous copy of 'The Seven Pillars of Wisdom', with practically all the illustrations. . . . It is a very great work. I am certain."[36] Finally, he said goodbye to the Shaws. As a leaving present, GBS gave him a proof copy of *Saint Joan*, Charlotte the manuscript notebook of her commonplace-book of mystical passages, which, like Lawrence's personal collection of poems, *Minorities*, which he gave to her a year later, had been collected over years. They would continue to correspond much during his absence.

What a rush it had been! Four years earlier, Lawrence had driven himself to the limit to finish the Oxford text before disappearing into the RAF. Now once more, the same hectic race against time before vanishing into the unknown. Only in December 1926 was the last copy ready to be despatched. It was seven years since he lost the first draft at Reading station.

"It is a strangely empty feeling to have finished with it after all these years", he wrote.[37]

Earlier he had written: "You see, if I can clean up the Arab mess, and get it away, behind my mind, . . . the relief it will be, to have the fretting ended." That he had finally achieved and it tells us much about why he wrote *Seven Pillars* as he did. There must be no guilt.

The book must resolve all the guilt. There is no guilt. His hands are clean.

"I can be like the other fellows in the crowd."

※

As the troopship *Derbyshire* moved slowly out of port the small lonely figure in RAF uniform stood at the passenger rail, going out to a future as empty as the barren mountains of Afghanistan beyond the fort where he would end up a year later. Not even 'Boa' would be able to accompany him. Had he made the right decision? He was not at all sure. But as Lawrence had learned in the desert, freedom is necessarily empty. And freedom, whether he knew it or not, was what he was compelled to seek at all costs.

PART
# TWO

# SEVEN PILLARS OF WISDOM

# The Arab Revolt: Participant Accounts

"A man's account of his deeds is already at one remove from the deeds themselves."

Robert Bolt, screenwriter of the film *Lawrence of Arabia*

The book of battle is a large one and each of us sees only his little page."

T.E. Lawrence

CHAPTER

# 8

# LAWRENCE IN THE ARAB REVOLT: A SUMMARY

## SEVEN PILLARS AND OTHER PARTICIPANT ACCOUNTS

The Arab Revolt, launched in the name of the Sherif Hussein of Mecca, began on 10 June, 1916, with the capture of the Holy City from its Turkish garrison. It ended with the armistice of 31 October 1918, by which time Arab regulars assisting the British forces were in Aleppo, far north of Damascus. Lawrence's history covers most, but not all, of the period continuously, from mid-October 1916 to 3 October 1918. From this perspective, the *Seven Pillars* is the most complete account written by a participant.

It seems to have been assumed from the time of the cessation of hostilities that the history of the Arab Revolt would be written by Lawrence. His pre-eminent position in it, his commitment to it, his known desire to write it, and then his fame, left him an open field. It was this identification of Lawrence with the Arab Revolt – by comrades, civil servants and politicians, and then the vast public – that has led to *Seven Pillars of Wisdom* being accorded the status of History.

In Chapter 1 of the Oxford text, Lawrence pleads modesty: "The others have liberty some day to put on record their story, one parallel to mine but not mentioning more of me than I of them, for each of us did his own job by himself and as he pleased, hardly seeing his friends." This last comment is absolutely true of this war, a war of individuals rather than of masses. Others did later (from the thirties) put on record their story: Englishmen, several Frenchmen, and finally (but not until the early sixties) Arabs. Colonel Brémond, Subhi al-Umari, Alec Kirkbride and a few others wrote a book; Hubert Young a large part of a memoir; Ronald Storrs a smaller part of his. And there are numerous shorter memoirs published as articles in journals. Among these, there is none which is anything like Lawrence's experience or his account. Yet each contributes to the historical picture.

Lawrence then continues:

> In these pages is not the history of the Arab movement, but just of what happened to me in it. It is the narrative of what I tried to do in Arabia, and of some of what I saw there. It is a chronicle in the spirit of the old men who marched with Bohemond or Coeur de Lion. It treats of daily life, mean happenings, little people. Here are no lessons for the world, no events to shake peoples. It is filled with trivial things, partly that no one mistake it for history, (it is the bones from which some day a man will make history), and partly for the pleasure it gave me to recall the fellowship of the revolt. (OX 6)

This could not be a clearer statement that this book is a memoir, and nothing more; but it belongs more to the realm of fantasy than fact. This gentle idea of the author as a modern Chrétien de Troyes, travelling unobtrusively with the army and later writing up what he saw of "daily life, mean happenings, little people" is merely an instance of a nostalgia for medieval chronicles. An account that fits better Lawrence's description is Alec Kirkbride's *An Awakening*, which I come to below. Few memoirs are more unlike such a notion than *Seven Pillars*. The book seems to take for granted that the history of the Arab movement is completely covered, not by 'what happened to me in it' but by what he did in it. Nonetheless, in the following chapters I intend to compare his account to those in three other memoirs. In each case the same events are experienced and related by Lawrence and one of the other authors. First, however, I proceed, without specific reference to *Seven Pillars*, to a short and straightforward summary of the Arab Revolt as Lawrence fought it.

## LAWRENCE AND THE ARAB REVOLT

Lawrence made his first important move when, with Ronald Storrs in Jeddah, he persuaded the Emir Abdullah to use his influence with the Sherif and his brother Ali to allow him to travel up-country to the third brother Feisal, who with a few thousand local tribesmen had positioned himself across the probable route of a Turkish advance from Medina to Mecca. He left with Storrs but got off at Rabegh, a miserable fishing port to the north, and waved goodbye from the deserted beach; then turned his face inland to begin his great adventure. Alone. This isolation from other Europeans would be a key characteristic of his rôle, and one of the keys that would open the door to the creation of the heroic legend.

This first trip was a brilliant start. It included his first view of the terrain of the Hejazi interior; he saw at first hand the importance of wells and water pools, tribal territory and desert customs; he had his first experience of camel riding, at which he was to become so expert; and above all, he met Feisal who, though he may have been a lot less ideal than he is painted in *Seven Pillars*, was an effective tribal leader, had an admirable persona, and was, with his weaknesses as well as his strengths, a person Lawrence felt he could work with.

It was purely an intelligence mission but Lawrence's reports give full value to it; indeed, no visit was more exhaustively reported. The army of Feisal is a gold mine in the desert. He recommends maximum support for it. With the luck that comes to those who are determined, he met, on his return, the Commander of the Red Sea fleet, Admiral Wemyss, who invited him to accompany him to Khartoum where he was able to convince General Wingate of his ideas regarding Feisal's importance and of the counter-productivity of large-scale British or French military intervention in Arabia; just a few advisors and experts would be sufficient. This opinion had, as we know, first been mooted by Abdelaziz al-Masri, in opposition to the request of the Grand Sherif and Abdullah (see below). However, it was supported by Lawrence and has now become, deservedly, one of his most quoted principles in discussions about foreign intervention.

The posting of a British–French brigade was strongly urged by the French, in the person of Colonel Edouard Brémond, head of the French mission to the Hejaz, and also, once the effect of Lawrence's persuasion had worn off, by Wingate. In the end, the decision lay with Sherif Hussein who was desperate for it when things were going badly, as after Feisal's defeat in the Wadi Yenbo, but changed his mind when they improved, eventually deciding 'no'. He did not want foreigners in the Hejaz if he could help it. But the truth is that there *was* intervention, albeit of the kind that only once or twice involved putting combatants ashore in the Hejaz; namely, naval intervention, and that was enough to dissuade the advancing Turks. Lawrence wrote that their withdrawal from the searchlights of four British ships one night at Rabegh lost them the war against the Arabs, and no doubt he is right; but would it have been any different if they had attacked Rabegh that night? Probably not. They would have been destroyed crossing the open plain. The Royal Navy not only denied the Turks access to any Red sea ports, but embargoed the landing of supplies, including foodstuffs on occasion, which caused considerable shortages.[1]

In December he was sent back to Feisal and began his new and unbroken partnership with him, officially as liaison officer but more importantly in his advisory role. Feisal, in spite of his fine qualities, was quite hesitant and indecisive and this gave Lawrence the opportunity to advance his own ideas and make himself indispensable. The new role was symbolised by his discarding the khaki in favour of Arab robes. By now, Lawrence had to answer to superior officers on the spot, Colonel Joyce and, later, Major Newcombe. Neither wanted to disturb the close relationship Lawrence had established with Feisal, and Lawrence was already pulling himself away from the British game plan towards one more directly in line with Feisal's ambitions. This involved understanding and exploiting the local means available: i.e. the tribes. The rationale of Lawrence's activity and the sphere of his participation were now set.

He arrived back to witness the chaos, vividly described, of Feisal pitching camp after a rapid retreat, a marvellous instance of his ability never to lose his dignity; then came the retreat to Yenbo, the defence of Rabegh by the British navy, and the failure of the Turkish advance on Mecca. This made it possible for Feisal to pass onto the offensive, moving his army north to Wejh so as to be able to threaten Turkish railway traffic. In this new phase, Lawrence will acquire authority as an expert on the Bedu, and will make his first raids, in line with the new policy. These are described in the account of his solo visit to the camp of Abdullah in Wadi Ais (OX 181-228, R 183-227), which lay not far from the railway line. Lawrence's authority lay not only in his being a British officer with Feisal, but in what he brought with him: explosives, automatic mines. By the time he left Abdullah, he had got valuable practice in demolition. Abdullah, who had recently made a brilliant capture of the Turk Eshref Bey with 20,000 pounds in gold, was rightly feeling neglected by the British in comparison with Feisal, but he did have with him Major Davenport and a number of French Algerian officers, including the brilliant Captain Raho, whose exploits against the railway were probably as daring as those of Lawrence, but who, for the British, is a complete unknown. He was killed assisting Abdullah in his fight against Abdelaziz ibn Saud of the Nejd.[2] By the time Lawrence returns, he has, he claims, formulated his new strategy of mobile war, based on the nature of the terrain and climate, the immobility of the Turks, and the particular fighting talents and deficiencies of the tribesmen. Although he treats us to a most learned essay on military theory and practice, I would agree with Kirkbride that he learnt tactics from the Bedu themselves and made a virtue of necessity. Indeed, as Lawrence wrote, "Our practice was better than our theory". Lawrence was open to unorthodox ideas and could perceive their application, and showed tactical initiative. He also understood the strategic importance of geography and had a flare for exploiting topography.

Feisal's new base was closer to Syria and contact was established with some of the northern tribes, especially the Howeitat, a group of tribes based on Jefer and the Wadi Sirhan. Auda abu Tayi makes his first appearance at Feisal's camp and a plan to put into practice the deployment strategy in the grand manner is discussed and agreed. It results in an expedition to Akaba via the Howeitat tribal area in the Wadi Sirhan, where Auda is confident of recruiting enough followers for a land attack on Akaba. Lawrence accompanies it. He plays an important role in supporting Nasr, the leader of the expedition, to keep everything on course in accordance with his own game plan, and taking charge of demolitions. This expedition, made up entirely of Bedu and Arab mercenaries, took two months to reach its objective. It vindicated Lawrence's strategy, and raised him to a pre-eminent and unique status in Cairo.

From July 1917, with Akaba taken from the land, the whole perspective changes. The Arabs now have a secure base within reach of Syria, and soon Feisal moves up there with his staff, bodyguard, and the small but developing regular Arab army. The Arab success impresses GHQ Cairo and General Allenby decides, with much advocacy from Lawrence, to support the movement on a much greater scale. In fact, the project is mooted of incorporating Feisal's army into the British and of placing Feisal officially under Allenby's command with the rank of Lt. General.

It was to Lawrence that the task fell of persuading Feisal and then King Hussein (as he now was) to go along with this. Lawrence would later complain bitterly in *Seven Pillars* how he had been forced into becoming a 'principal' rather than an innocent participant in the deception of the Arabs; but in reality he was entirely enthusiastic about the alliance. It seemed at that time to be almost the fulfilment of his ambition on behalf of the Arabs: that their political advancement would be guaranteed by the might and good faith of Great Britain. He knew perfectly well of the Sykes–Picot treaty. Perhaps, like some others in the Arab Bureau, he persuaded himself that it could never be implemented. This was no time to be asking questions; this was an opportunity he simply could not let go. So Feisal, and then Hussein, were persuaded to form an official military alliance with Great Britain.

A special unit called 'Hedgehog' was set up in Cairo under the command of Colonel Alan Dawnay. Advisors (nobody could give orders to the Arabs) and weapons and other supplies poured in, and a lot of gold. The Arabs were now Allenby's right wing. This change was momentous, and militarily both sides benefited greatly from it.

The Arabs progressed northwards, but with difficulty. The 3000 Turks garrisoning Ma'an remained there until the end of the war, in spite of the numerous attempts to cut off their supplies by damaging the railway. The exceptionally severe winter of 1917–18 impeded the Arab advance. Only in the very last two weeks of Lawrence's war do the Arabs take off and execute a really worthwhile operation. Nonetheless, Lawrence continues to generate a colossal head of steam. The close relationship with Feisal continues, the visits to Cairo are always crowned with the reward of new supplies, new joint plans; in between, there are damaging raids on the railway and victorious actions against the Turks, notably at Tafileh in January 1918.

After the consolidation of Feisal's army at Akaba, and then further north (Guweira, Abu Lissan) near Ma'an, with the influx of British advisors, and the development of the regular army, the role of the Bedu declined. The Sharifian regulars were playing an ever more important role, seriously waging war against the enemy and his communications, and the British-Indian MMG and French artillery contingents were increasingly in key roles. Lawrence was no longer so successful. The raid on the Yarmouk bridge, the link-up with the British in the Jordan valley after the victory at Tafileh, the proposed joint attack on Salt: they were all failures or non-starters. He became, at times, seriously dispirited. He realized that the projects he agreed with Allenby depended on factors over which he had no control. However, he made a brilliant come-back in the last phase (September 1918), making a supreme effort with Feisal's forces in co-ordinating their railway sabotage with the British advance, his most important field assignment of the war and perhaps the only time he worked successfully with the regulars. Thanks to Allenby's overwhelming success, he was able, with the blessing of the Foreign Office and Allenby, to ensure the rather messy triumph of Feisal in Damascus. He had, I suppose, realised his dream, but dream it was to remain.

# CHAPTER 9

# T.E. LAWRENCE & RONALD STORRS IN JEDDAH

On 16th October 1916, Ronald Storrs, Secretary at the Cairo Residency and the chief negotiator with Sherif Hussein of Mecca, speaking with the authority of the British government, and Captain Lawrence, a highly regarded intelligence officer, arrived off Jeddah by ship. This was Storrs' third trip to the eastern shores of the Red Sea, but for Captain Lawrence it was a new experience, one he had long prepared for and looked forward to. *Seven Pillars* salutes it with appropriate rhetoric:

> The heat of Arabia came out like a drawn sword and smote us speechless. (OX 47)

Storrs' first approach, in June, just before the Arab Revolt was launched, was less sublime. A secret meeting took place on a deserted Arabian shore not far from Jeddah, named Samima. After his cutter had hit the coral reef there, Storrs left his £10,000 bag of gold on a dhow with Hogarth and Cornwallis of the Arab Bureau, was transported towards shore in a canoe full of water, and then carried through the surf, in the traditional manner of the time and place, by two slaves

> who contrived in that short distance to soak me well above the knee. Without looking up I saw Zaid and Shakir slowly advancing upon me. I continued to arrange my clothes so as to bring the two down in front of their guard to welcome on their threshold one who was, after all, representing the High Commissioner. This they did, and shook me warmly by the hand welcoming me in the name of the Grand Sherif and Abdallah.[1]

Zaid, the fourth and youngest son of Hussein, will cross Lawrence's path many times in the Revolt. At this time he was barely nineteen years of age. Yet here he is representing his father, the Grand Sherif, to the British government.

Storrs learned to his delight that the day assigned for the start of the uprising had been put forward, and that it was to take place in four towns simultaneously; and indeed, confounding the traditional British view of Arab unreliability, so it happened. Mecca surrendered on June 13th, Jeddah on the 16th, attacked by land and bombarded by a British vessel; Taif would be captured after a two-month siege. Only Medina, the second of the Holy Cities, would resist, "its troops contained by the Arabs without loss of life on either side".[2]

The expulsion of the Turks from Mecca was important news for the British government and for India, both of whom had been very jittery about the call for a Holy War against Britain, France and Russia by the Turkish Sultan Abdelhamid. Storrs considered it a "fatal blow at the religious prestige of the Turk". However, the Turks still held the second of the holy cities and the fact that, contrary to the advice of General Liman von Sanders, they hung on to it throughout the war, with ten thousand troops locked up there, is testimony to their belief in the importance of the Holy Places and the religious factor. As the provisioning of Medina required the protection and maintenance of the immensely long Hejaz railway, this Turkish stubborness was to provide T.E. Lawrence and others (Garland, Newcombe, Hornby, Raho) with a 1500-kilometre longitudinal target for their adventurous raids. Medina would defy the Arabs and their allies until well after the end of hostilities, surely one of the most extraordinary feats of the war since it lay hundreds of miles from any other Turkish garrison.

After landing with Lawrence in Jeddah, Storrs, with Colonel C.E. Wilson, the Resident at the newly opened Consulate there, was welcomed by the Emir Abdullah, the Grand Sherif's second but most trusted son, in his magnificent tent four miles outside the town.[3] The bitter coffee made Storrs thirsty. He was handed a one-handled silver bowl. "I subsequently found it was the Grand Sharif's own drinking cup, accidently packed by Abdallah's servants".[4] When he had drained it, Abdullah insisted on his keeping it. He had just arrived, fresh from his notable victory over the Turks at Taif, just outside Mecca. The Turkish commander, Ghalib Bey, with two hundred men, had finally surrendered. That was the good news. Otherwise, the situation had changed for the worse. Their first flush of success over, the Arabs became vulnerable to attack in the open. The Turkish commander in Medina, Fakhri, looked ready to march to the Red Sea port of Rabegh, and from there to threaten Mecca. On the other hand, the British, with the panic about the *jihad* now receded, were suddenly chary about spending a lot in money and military hardware on such a doubtful show. The second meeting, in the Consulate, was embarrassing for Storrs, since the British were already breaking promises of help to their new ally:

> It was our privelege to announce to A [Abdullah] that the Brigade, more than once promised by H.M.G., would not be sent; and that the flight of aeroplanes, promised and dispatched to Rabegh, was being withdrawn on the very day that the appearance of Turkish planes was being announced. Individually I had the honour of being instructed that I was to express no opinion at all on military affairs; that in any political request or reply I would not be supported; I was furthermore, not provided with the £10,000 for which A. had made me a personal appeal.[5]

For this October trip with Lawrence, Storrs kept a diary, from which he later published extracts in *Orientations*.[6] The diary was written up on board ship after the days' events as far as possible, so it must be considered a reliable source. To Storrs' relief, Abdallah "took the position like a fine gentleman". But he was not weak. "Pardon me," he replied, "it was your letter and your messages that began this thing with us, and you know it from the beginning, and from before the beginning." Abdallah left the Consulate "leaving us all in a state of admiration for him and disgust with ourselves".[7] Lawrence is mentioned just once in the course of this detailed report of the meeting: to the effect that he understood Abdallah's "beautiful high" Arabic better than Wilson. There was a further meeting the next morning; with the attendance of the two senior military officers serving with the Hashemites, Said Ali Pasha, Minister of War and Commander of the Egyptian artillery, which had made a crucial contribution in the siege of Taif; and Aziz Ali Bey al-Masri, Chief of Staff, both of whom made a favourable impression on Storrs, especially Aziz. "Abdallah began by reading out to us a telegram from Faisal to the effect that two Turkish aeroplanes had begun to operate, to the dismay bordering upon panic of the Arabs.[8] He said that unless these were driven off or in some way checked, the Arabs would disperse. Said Ali corroborated this . . . . Aziz Ali was of the opinion that a [British–French] Brigade [to defend Rabegh] was unnecessary" but the Sherif phoned incessantly from Mecca appealing for both the planes and the Brigade. Although he attended this meeting, Lawrence is not mentioned in Storrs' diary. However, he is mentioned by Colonel Wilson as "a bumptious young ass . . . making himself out to be the only authority on war, engineering, manning H.M's ships and everything else. He put every single person's back up I have met".[9] Wilson will later change this first impression.

Storrs was impressed with Abdullah, the most worldly of the four brothers and his father's right-hand man, and successor-designate. On leaving Jeddah, Storrs wrote in his diary for that day: "He has intelligence, energy and charm, requiring only firm but not too heavy or respectful guidance to prove a valuable asset in future Arabian politics".[10] Storrs was proved right. Abdullah became Emir of the Transjordan and later King of Jordan, which he ruled until 1951. He was ultimately the most successful of the four sons of Hussein, creating a new kingdom out of a desert and a handful of small towns in the West; the only Hashemite entity still in existence and, with the Saud dynasty, one of the only two monarchies left in the Middle East.

Storrs was even more impressed by the Grand Sherif. He had not yet met him but did so on a fourth trip in December. Not in Mecca of course; now that the Pilgrimage season was over, the Sherif had come down to Jeddah on muleback. Storrs wrote in his diary for December 13th:

> The dominating characteristic of the Grand Sharif is a captivating sincerity of utterance, enhanced by a benignant, a noble simplicity of demeanour. I cannot but remember that he has passed a great proportion of his life in Constantinople, where the Ottoman gravity . . . has evolved a tradition of unparalleled dignity of deportment.

One feels, reading his diary or his memoirs, that Storrs was very appreciative of manner, and flattered by a display of culture, Arabic or Turkish or European. Hussein seems to have guessed this. When, some months later, Storrs "without mincing words" protested to him for having assumed the title of King without due consultation with his ally, "he laid his hand on my shoulder and replied by a rhyming Arab proverb":

*Darb al-Habib*
*ka-akl al-zabib*
*wa hajaratu rumman*
"The blows of a friend are as the eating of raisins, and his stones are pomegranates."[11]

On this final visit, Storrs continued by boat to Yenbo and met Feisal there. There is once again no mention of Lawrence, even though he was already there as Feisal's adviser.

## THE MASTER-SPIRIT OF THE REVOLT

Lawrence's impressions, as recorded in *Seven Pillars*, could hardly be more different. First of all, Lawrence's impression of Abdullah; second, his report of the meetings; third, his own role in these meetings; and above all, the role that he had cast for himself in the Arab Revolt.

Abdullah he found pleasure-loving, and self-indulgent: bad traits in the eyes of a puritan. "His eyes had a confirmed twinkle,[12] and although only thirty-five he was already beginning to put on flesh." He was clever all right, but too clever, and "his ambition was patent". This antipathy to Abdullah's character may have contributed to his under-estimating his value. But there is more to it than that. It is quite evident that Abdullah is seen as a *rival*. "His object was of course the winning of Arab independence and the building up of Arab nations, but in these states Abdulla meant to secure the pre-eminence at least of his family, quite possibly of himself. He was watching us and playing subtly for effect all the time. . . . On our part I was doing the same" (OX 48-9, R 67).

That Abdullah was ambitious is no doubt true. However, these extravagant ambitions were harboured by Hussein himself; Abdullah and Feisal shared those ambitions and served them. The irony is that the pre-eminence of the Hashemites was exactly what Lawrence himself promoted and which was perhaps his major political achievement. But it had to be achieved by him and Great Britain and his own Arab protégé:

> My visit was really to see for myself who was the yet unknown master-spirit of the affair, and if he was capable of carrying the revolt to the distance and greatness *I had conceived for it* (my italics): and as our conversation proceeded I became more and more sure that Abdulla was too balanced, too cool, too humorous to be a prophet, especially the armed prophet whom history assured me was the successful type in such circumstances. (OX 49)

His mission is to search for the master-spirit of the Arab Revolt; because, without it, his design for the Revolt lacks an essential element. Furthermore, he must be an armed prophet; why? because History tells us so. We have moved up onto the mythical plane. In the event, the master-spirit and the armed prophet were different people, as this extract is already making clear. The armed prophet (veiled) would be Feisal but the master-spirit was to be Lawrence himself.[13] Here I am writing within the context of the mythical scenario of *Seven Pillars*.

As far the actual discussion is concerned, Lawrence writes as if it was his responsibility to reply to Abdullah, rather than Storrs', and even to "represent his views to Egypt". Lawrence did in fact, on his return, represent views to none other than the Commander-in-Chief of the Hejaz operation, General Wingate; but his own views rather than Abdullah's, for by this time Lawrence was concerned with Feisal's needs. Abdullah is described in *Seven Pillars* as pouring recriminations on the British for the precarious state of affairs, quite unlike Storrs' impression; and while Storrs feels shame at being unable to assist, Lawrence corrects Abdullah with devastating omniscience. *Seven Pillars* also contains a long story designed to illustrate Abdullah's unscrupulousness (O 56-7, R 74). Storrs added a footnote in *Orientations* that he did not agree with Lawrence's estimate of Abdullah but he otherwise let everything pass. He also apologises for giving so little space to Lawrence in his diary account, not knowing that he was in the presence of greatness. That was historically fortunate.

A comparison is difficult since Storrs' account is a narrative, detailed and clear, and naturally has a greater immediacy whereas *Seven Pillars* ranges unthriftily over various topics. Storrs and Abdullah are the centre of interest of the diary account, Lawrence being hardly mentioned; in *Seven Pillars*, Lawrence seems to be the real power. A dismissive atmosphere of ridicule about the Arab situation and its leaders is palpable. He has already made up his mind, he tells us, that his hopes are on Feisal, not here, in clammy exhausted Jeddah. The reader is now primed for the journey into the desert to meet with the armed prophet, which will be one of the great romantic moments.

We should therefore be thankful that Storrs kept a diary. What we learn from him in general is the primitive state of the Revolt, its ad hoc character, and its almost complete lack of resources and money. Lawrence was perhaps right when he diagnosed lack of leadership, but it was not *the* problem, but one among several. On the other hand, we learn of its successes, its hopes, and of the small supporting nucleus: Said Ali, Aziz al-Masri, and Nuri Said, and the various views expressed at the time. The fact that Lawrence sent only telegrams to

Clayton but no full report could be a reason why his account is so much at variance with Storrs'; what he wrote in the telegrams is actually more enlightening and closer to Storrs, especially on Abdullah; what he wrote in *Seven Pillars* is later opinion.

How did Lawrence really see things at this time, 17 October 1916? His mission, as an intelligence officer, was to find out everything he could. That meant going to Rabegh, where was encamped the eldest son Ali, with his little 'army' of tribal supporters, and then inland to Feisal, so that he would have seen the other two 'armies' and their commanders, and the situations on the ground, so a good deal of his energy went into procuring this difficult permission to travel, a Christian, into the interior. From Storrs we would infer that he did not play an important role in the meetings. Did he already have in his head a grand design, with himself in the lead role? That is a little doubtful. Lawrence's Revolt, as he later narrated it, seeks to minimise the element of chance. We shall see a further striking illustration of this in contrasting two accounts of the Battle of Tafileh.

CHAPTER

# 10

# THE BATTLE OF TAFILEH:
# SUBHI AL-UMARI & LAWRENCE

In August 1917, a young Arab officer in the Turkish army named Subhi al-Umari went forward to investigate the situation at one of the forward observation posts at Hisha, over the branch line of the Hejaz railway near Shobek (O374). There had been shooting the night before; however, for Subhi, the investigation of the shooting was merely a cover for a more secret mission. That day he met by arrangement with one of the Sheikhs of the Shobek area, who guided him by routes known only to the local Arabs to Wadi Musa (which lay before the 'rose-red city' of Petra), the Arab 'front line'. There he was greeted by Mauloud Mukhlis, one of the two Sharifian divisional commanders whose forward posts were in this area, and Sherif Abdelma'in, whom Lawrence would later meet on a dark winter evening in the Crusader castle of Montreal (Shobek). On the next day he was taken down to Akaba, met Feisal and Jaafar al-Askari, Commander-in-the-field of the Northern Army, and received his commission as 2nd lieutenant. He was given command of one of the Vickers machine gun sections.

Like most other officers in Feisal's newly formed and embryonic army, Subhi came from Mesopotamia; but most of these men, including their commander, Jaafar al-Askari, had been captured by the British and then taken the option of serving Feisal. Subhi had made his own choice to change sides. Like Lawrence he proved conspicuous for personal bravery. He fought with the regulars right up to Aleppo and was awarded the Military Cross.

## THE BATTLE OF TAFILEH BY SUBHI AL-UMARI[1]

In the severe weather of January 1918, Subhi took part in the successful attack on the station of Jurf al Darawish (O531-3) and then moved north with a regular detachment under the command of the Emir Zeid, with Bedu in support, up to Tafileh, a place of three thousand people, the centre of an arable district. It lay in the first folds of a valley, just under the crest of the great scarp which sheered from the plateau of Western Arabia into the Dead Sea hollow. The town stood on the crest of a spur of land which jutted out from the mountain-side into a deep ravine. To the north, east and south, the distant view was blocked by high mountains but, to the west, the rugged formation opened to give a sight of the depths of the Wadi Arabah and, beyond that, the mountains of Judea.[2] It was a dreary place in winter and, nearly five thousand feet up, bitterly cold. It was occupied by a small Turkish force which, taken by surprise, soon surrendered. Subhi was assigned lodgings near the school but on the way there, "we saw a man in Meccan costume sitting on his abaya which he had spread on the ground. He had pulled off his upper clothing and removed his kuffiya to reveal a body that was pure white. ... We knew at first glance that this was Lawrence, for we had heard that he imitated the Bedu" (183).

This sight of Lawrence gives rise to certain reflections:

> The psychological complex which had formed in us towards them (the English) was made up of contradictory feelings, comprising a hatred of the Turks, nationalist fervour and a fear that the Turkish rule (with which we still had a few links) be exchanged for a foreign colonialism . . . these complex feelings were aroused every time we saw an Englishman or a Frenchman. It was a complex of inferiority which drove us involuntarily to deride foreigners. The sight of this Englishman made us aware that he was making fun of us and considered us children who did not understand what he was about. And the truth was that if we were to ask any soldier or simple Bedu about this Englishman, they would answer exactly as we felt. Lawrence, with his knowledge of the Arabs, was aware that they were not taken in by his imitation; he had undertaken these practices so as to deceive his English comrades, displaying the image of the adventurous hero, and he had become an expert on anything to do with the Bedu to the point of appearing to be one of them. (183)

Only a few days later a large Turkish force of about 1500 men, with 27 machine guns and two field guns, suddenly appeared in Wadi Hesa, a very deep wadi running east–west ten kilometres north of the village. There was a general alarm in Tafileh:

> The news circulated and the exaggerations of the size of the Turkish advance went beyond all sense. Terror and confusion spread over the town and we saw the people packing up their things and carrying them out of town to the west; the most terrified and bewildered were the Armenian refugees. Voices were raised all round us. 'Dubb es-sawt' (literally: 'the start of the noise') – the Bedu name for a general alarm; when danger comes upon any of the tribes, whoever senses it, man or woman, starts shouting at the top of their voice "where are they, where are the horsemen"! It is repeated by all who hear it, and the men take up their weapons and the horsemen mount. The warning passes with the speed of the telegraph from group to group, from clan to clan, from one tribe to another. Those who hear it do not wait to gather, but rush off on their own or with those near them. (185)

The commander at Tafileh, the young Zeid, was still only twenty. He had been sent up to Tafileh by Feisal in furtherance of the new plan to join up with Allenby's troops at the south end of the Dead Sea. However, the detachment was small, only sixty regular infantry under the command of Abdullah el Dleimi (he had arrived the day before to replace Rasim Sardast but they both took part in the coming action) with a few cavalry, four Vickers machine guns and two mountain guns. There were also, according to Subhi, who gives a full list of combatants and weapons, eighty mule-mounted infantry volunteers, probably villagers, and sixty Bedu volunteers (Jazi Howeitat). Later in the day, which was foggy, Zeid ordered most of the force to take up a safe position behind Tafileh, and they were joined by him and his senior officers that night. At dawn the next day, the 24th, Abdullah Dleimi was ordered forward with some cavalry, two machine guns and a mountain gun to recce the situation at the front and to do whatever possible to impede the Turkish advance. The Turks had struck camp in the Wadi Hesa in the night and were now climbing up on to the Tafileh plateau. Abdullah and his contingent, aided by armed villagers, drove the advance unit back to the Wadi, put up a valiant fight and only retired when one of the machine guns broke down. When he returned, he told Zeid that he should move forward since the enemy seemed less formidable than had been thought. Also, there were many armed peasants about, who might be useful if encouraged. So Zeid ordered part of the force forward to a low ridge called Khirbet Nokhi in order to face the enemy. Subhi had command of one of the machine gun sections with two Vickers. From Khirbet Nokhi the Turks, in considerable force, were visible through the intermittent fog on a low hill called Rujom Keraka some three thousand metres distant. Their camp was a good deal further back. Jaafar al Askeri arrived and noted that the enemy was inactive and the number of irregulars increasing. He ordered Rasim Sardast to go with Hamad ibn Jazi and his horsemen (Motalga Bedu) to harass the Turkish left flank. Otherwise, nothing much happened, even when Zeid arrived with the rest. Lawrence was with him.

Then Subhi noticed to his left a quite large group of villagers, many armed with rifles, below the summit of a hill on the Turkish right flank, and their numbers were increasing. It occurred to Subhi that if these villagers could be given some kind of encouragement, they might be able to do something quite unexpected. The ground in front of him sloped gently down to a shallow wadi at the base of the hill at the top of which the Turks had installed themselves. Subhi examined the ground carefully and could see that it should be possible to cross it, at lightning speed, since one would be in dead ground quite some distance before the wadi itself. If he and his section, with the two machine guns, could reach the dead ground they would be safe and he gambled, being himself a machine gunner, that the Turkish machine guns would not have either the correct elevation or the distance and would not have time to set their aim effectively. So they made a dash for it. He was right. The machine guns opened fire en masse but the shooting was haphazard and they all got into dead ground safely.

In the wadi they could see the villagers to their left on their hill, and managed to make contact with them. These came from Aima, a village on that side, and were creeping forward. He had another brainwave: to tell the men of Aima that they were just waiting for a group of infantry; when they arrived they would attack the enemy. When they heard the rattle of machine guns they would know that the attack had started. His unit had, in addition to the two machine guns, two toothed wooden rattles which could be used to imitate the sound of the gun itself! It worked. The villagers, who were now numerous, ran forward when they heard the rattle of the 'guns', and at once the Turks, who were in fact manoeuvering their line to face the threat, appeared to the villagers to be panicking. This sight removed the last doubts of the Aima men and they charged in. The Turks fled in confusion, leaving behind them almost all their machine guns and many rifles.

A boy scout story? Too good to be true? Let us follow the rest before we decide.

Subhi himself forced the surrender of the officer in command there. His name was Kanaan Bey Bejani, who was surprised to learn that the leadership in this battle was not English. Those who captured machine guns ran back with them, throwing them down and demanding that their name be listed for a reward. They would not wait a moment in the chase for booty. In a matter of minutes, there was not an armed Turk on the hill and villagers were now pursuing them from all directions. All became peaceful. "The sun was going down in the west and we remained alone waiting for orders with a great pile of machine guns and their appendages in front of us and about eighty prisoners" (190). The soldiers of the unit began to dance and sing. Then they went back to Tafileh, with the prisoners in single file.

In Tafileh, which they reached in the freezing night, Subhi was summoned to the house of Sheikh Diab al-Auran, where he found Zeid, Jaafar al-Askari, two other Arab commanders, and Lawrence. Jaafar said to him:

> "You know why I refused to transfer you from Headquarters to one of the fighting units when you joined us? Because you looked so young and unsuited to battle, I was sorry for you, but you have proved me wrong".
>
> I replied: "Pasha, it's not a matter of beards and moustaches (at the time I was still hairless), cats also have moustaches".
>
> Everybody laughed and Jaafar, who was laughing too and looking as if he was going to hit me, shouted: 'You damned impudent \_\_\_\_', for Jaafar had a beard too. (191–2)

Lawrence makes a reference to Jaafar, in a letter, to what may be this very occasion (for Jaafar was perhaps only once in Tafileh with Lawrence): "All my memories of the war, whenever he is in the picture, are pleasant ones. You know, he made even Tafileh in wintertime a joke."[3]

## LAWRENCE'S ACCOUNTS[4]

Lawrence wrote a report on the battle immediately after it; naturally, it is largely about what he did and where he was and is quite brief. As far as the events are concerned, it is not very different to Subhi's, except that Lawrence went himself to the ridge where Abdullah Dleimi had confronted the Turks, exposing himself to considerable danger and organising the safe withdrawal of the villagers and Jazi Bedu who were still there under fire. He also makes no mention whatever of Subhi al-Umari and his charge but he does write: "They (the men of Aima) crept down behind the western ridge of the plain without being seen, as we opened across the plain a frontal attack of eighteen men, two Vickers and two large Hotchkiss." It is not clear whether this means firing from the position (the word "opened" suggests 'fire') or whether the eighteen men were actually launching an attack. The sequel: "The ridge was a flint one, and the Turks could not entrench on it... the ricochets were horrible" suggests the former. On the other hand, the numbers fit Subhi's unit, and the Vickers were Subhi's guns. But there is no Subhi initiative, and the men of Aima are paid volunteers sent to their place. Everything is organised. In any case, we never hear anything more about these eighteen men.

An almost constant characteristic of the report, lending it a certain vagueness, is the use of *we*:

*we sent the Aima to our left flank*
*we opened across the plain a frontal attack*
*we sent forward the infantry*

Who are we? Just Lawrence and Zeid or were other officers involved? Or does it mean a 'commander's we', i.e. Lawrence himself? After returning from the west ridge, Lawrence either observed or covertly commanded the battle from the Nokhi ridge; which of the two, the reader must decide for himself. It should be mentioned that Lawrence never commanded Sharifian troops; if he did anything, he would have advised Zeid. In this report he admits to nothing more than persuading Zeid to send forward Abdullah al-Dleimi. Veterans of this battle interviewed by Suleiman Moussa 40-odd years later recalled having seen Lawrence but were not conscious of his having had an important role. Nevertheless, given his fame, and what he wrote later in *Seven Pillars*, nobody seems to have doubted that *we* means himself.

Subhi is convinced that Lawrence deliberately downplayed any contribution made by the regulars in order to highlight his own performance and that of the Bedu. In fact, the activity of the regular detachment – their composition, armament, and officers – are described rather piecemeal, in a disorganised manner. He asks why

Lawrence surnames Abdullah 'Effendi' when he knew quite well that this was Abdullah el Dleimi, the officer second-in-command of the entire detachment. He is identified as "the junior of our two officers" (there were actually more, including Subhi). The other, Rasim Sardast, is mentioned later only by his first name and the reader in Cairo, Brigadier Clayton, is not told who this Rasim is, what his function is or his rank. It is undeniable that the regular detachment is obscured in the report, and credit is given only to the Bedu and the villagers; but the regular detachment was small, too small to have defeated the Turks without the actions of the Bedu horsemen and the villagers. One wonders whether Clayton really believed what he read, or whether he did not care, because it was very good propaganda for the Arab campaign. A DSO was awarded on the basis of the information it contained and Lawrence will comment on that in *Seven Pillars*.

According to Subhi, the real victor was Jaafar al-Askari, who was in command. However, this appears to be a serious error. Jaafar himself, in his memoirs, writes: "I came up to Tafileh *that evening* from Al-Haishah . . . I met Amir Zaid at the home of Dhiyab bin al-'Awran, the Chief of Tafileh."[5] The explanation for Subhi's error is no doubt that he did indeed meet Jaafar in Tafileh at Dhiyab's house the evening after the battle but, nearly fifty years later, he has mixed things up, assuming that Jaafar, his great hero, had been there throughout.

After describing his role in the battle, Subhi also wrote a simple analysis of it. The gist of this is that the victory was due: first, to the external conditions; second, to luck and opportunism. The developments of the battle were not the result of predetermined planning, but grew out of natural impromptu circumstances.

The Turkish force had been hurriedly put together by Hamid Fakhri from three divisions. It passed through Kerak, a market town the other side of the Wadi Hesa. The high plateau of this region, with the steep escarpment to the west, is cut through at intervals by some very deep wadis with walls rising over a thousand feet above them on either side; such is the Wadi Hesa. To cross it with heavy equipment such as guns and machine guns is extremely difficult. As for the valley floor, it is no place for an army to find itself in, in hostile territory in the middle of a severe winter. Sherif Mastur had been sent forward some days earlier with tribesmen to form a screen to hinder enemy progress into Hesa, but it appears that he was unable to organise the Bedu. However, that worked in Tafileh's favour. Unorganised bands of horsemen, including villagers, attacked the flanks of the army from all directions once the Turks were down in the valley, plundering whatever they could. Many clans were passing the winter there as it was warmer than on the heights. But still cold. The Turks were forced to halt in the valley at night but got no sleep. Long before dawn, they were moving on again, making the laborious climb out of the wadi. By the time they were over the crest, they were exhausted, and by the time they had positioned themselves it was already too late to take Tafileh that day. The men from the villages round about, who feared Turkish reprisals, sensed the Turkish weakness and kept close to their flanks. They had the advantage of a close knowledge of the terrain. Furthermore, it was foggy. It was therefore very difficult to see what was going on and these conditions obviously favoured the defenders, and especially the locals, who could move close to the enemy without disorienting themselves.

Kanaan Bey, Subhi's prisoner, told him that, quite by chance, the men of Aima attacked at the moment when he was redeploying to face them. And further, that it took place when many of the unit commanders were not with their units! They had been summoned by Fakhri Bey to be told of the change of plan: that there would be no advance on Tafileh until the next day. Kanaan Bey said that that was the major reason for the Turkish collapse: Fakhri had no respect for his enemy, which he believed was entirely on the defensive, and never imagined they would attack.

To repeat Lawrence, "The book of battle is a large one, and each sees only his little page". Nobody is going to be completely right; but the two accounts are very different. Lawrence gives an account of a logical sequence of actions based on an understanding of how the battle could be won; Subhi of opportunism and profiting from local conditions. I do not wish to show bias but it might be reiterated that Lawrence did have a strong tendency to exaggerate the extent to which everything followed his own plan or inspiration; it is evident in the Storrs section above, and of his essay on military tactics in the desert, and this may well be another instance. Incidentally, his account ignores everything that happened in Wadi Hesa before the battle. Subhi al-Umari's account is very unlikely to be a complete invention but it does suffer from inaccuracies due to having been written fifty years after the event. Let the reader decide!

In *Seven Pillars* Lawrence gives a much longer and more breezy account of the battle. The existence of both the report and a subsequent account provide an opportunity to observe the later psychological and literary overlay to the original report. The account of the battle has not changed in any respect as regards the events and is more entertaining than the report; what is different is that the battle plan is presented as a personal decision and personally executed by himself. It is in fact Lawrence's battle. It has become highly personalised, displaying physical pain, moral dilemmas, strong feelings of contempt, mockery, self-disgust, and 'Olympianism'.

The battle was unnecessary, he writes, and only took place because he lost his self-control. The hopeless stupidity of the Turks, in deciding to attack Tafileh, infuriated him: "I could have won by refusing battle, beat them in manoeuvre.... Bad temper and conceit together made me not content just to know my power, but anxious to display it openly to the Arabs and to the enemy."

In other words, the Battle of Tafileh was fought in order to gratify the will of one all-powerful man. We may not altogether believe that; we might understand rather that, in retrospect, he felt the battle was unnecessary and that he should have advised against it. It merely wasted lives. We might nonetheless wonder what Arab fighters like Subhi or Abdullah Dleimi, or especially Prince Zeid, would think when they read this account. Would they not feel they were being devalued ?

The difference from the report lies in the much less cautious presentation concerning leadership. The reader is left in no doubt that the decision-making power rests with Lawrence alone. Zeid is merely the channel through whom these decisions are translated into orders. Throughout, it is Lawrence who plans and commands the battle.

The action is now presented as a textbook demonstration of the military tactics of the World War I theorists, albeit ironically. He distances himself from them and condemns himself, taking up an anti-'murder war' position and blaming himself for having caused the death of twenty-five Arabs by deciding on a battle. As for the earlier report:

> It was nicely written for effect, full of quaint similies and mock simplicities, and made them [Cairo Intelligence] think me a modest amateur doing his best after the great models, not a leering clown frivolously whoring after them where they, with Foch as bandmaster at their head, went drumming down the old road of effusion of blood into the house of Clausewitz. Like the battle, it was nearly proof-parody of regulation use, and they loved it, and innocently to crown the jest offered me a decoration on the strength of it. We would have

more bright breasts in the Army if each man wrote his own despatch. (O546/R493)

Lawrence's characterisation of his report as 'nearly proof-parody of regulation use' is not convincing. It may have been written for effect but there is no hint of parody. He now disowns that report as a serious account. The last sentence is interesting. Does it mean that Lawrence is admitting the subjectivity of his report and wishes to disown the merit of the DSO he was offered on the strength of it? It seems so. Paradoxically he trivialises his own action, while at the same time aggrandising his role in the battle as commander, master tactician and physical superman (e.g. climbing cliffs barefooted in mid-winter).

Liddell Hart was captivated. "As a military apologia it is a gem. So was the battle that followed, by any 'military' test".[6] Lawrence has his cake and eats it. This feature of negating his own recognized achievement appears frequently in *Seven Pillars*. It has been seen as an expression of modesty; but the mockery and self-denigration that rings out here is hardly just that. What is it that motivates this expression of contempt for the action at Tafileh, and of himself? Towards the end of the book, I will make an assay at explaining these paradoxes.

What we have seen here is a 'trailer' to the next section, titled 'The Drama of the Self', and an example of 'parallel texts': a historical narrative and another personal narrative superimposed on it.

# CHAPTER 11

# KIRKBRIDE'S ACCOUNT

> Thanks to books and films produced by people who had no first-hand knowledge of the events they described, the inhabitants of the western world tend to believe the revolt in the desert to have been a romantic campaign which was started and carried through by Colonel T.E. Lawrence for his personal benefit, with the assistance of a lot of gorgeously robed sheikhs.
>
> *Alec Kirkbride*

### IN TAFILEH

Tafileh was also the place where Lieutenant Alec Kirkbride first met Lawrence. It was just a week or two after the battle and on the same evening or night that Lawrence arrived back from Akaba with bags of gold: February 11th according to Lawrence's reckoning. Kirkbride and his party of a Scottish batman, a Syrian, and a group of Beduin escort had a hard coming of it. Starting from Beersheba, they had crossed the Wadi Araba, below sea level where it was warm, and climbed, in atrocious weather, the 4000-foot escarpment up and over to the grim village. "The slopes were covered with evergreen oaks, pines, and juniper trees, a sight which would have given me pleasure at any other time", wrote Kirkbride.

> We staggered down into Tafileh just as the light began to fail and reported to the garrison of the medieval fort round which the dwelling houses clustered. Considering that no-one had heard of us before, our reception was remarkably cordial and in about an hour's time we had got the camels under cover. . . . Then we were quartered on a hospitable shopkeeper, who produced gallons of scalding sweet tea and laid out rush matting and some dry bedding in his store room. . . . I had to go and see the Commander of the troops and explain who we

were and what we wanted. The Commander was an Iraqi, Colonel Ismail Na'amek.... My story was, apparently, accepted without hesitation and I wondered how a strange Arab would have fared had he suddenly appeared, with a wild looking party of men, and asked for accomodation and food from a British unit in the front line.

Kirkbride had been warned during his briefing by Intelligence staff of "a curious situation" that had arisen in which a certain Major T.E. Lawrence was "acting as if he was independent of local control."

Back at the billet everyone had turned in, in spite of the early hour, and most of them were already asleep. I wriggled into my blankets without delay and faded out also – but not for long. Later that night, I was shaken awake by a small bedraggled figure, dressed in Arab clothes, who asked in English if I was Kirkbride. This was Lawrence, who had got to the town after dark and had been surprised to learn that another British officer was there. He and his followers had had a worse time than my party because, coming from the south, this route had been along the exposed side of the mountains and they had, in consequence, been exposed to the full force of the storm for longer than ourselves. Lawrence stayed with us for the rest of the night while his men joined their friends among the Bedouin bodyguard of the Amir Zeid.

This was the night when Lawrence had got back to Tafileh from Shobek with his camel Wodheiha who had slid down the last hill on her behind with Lawrence desperately hanging on. There had been no mention of any followers. Had they remained in Tafileh when Lawrence went down to Akaba to get the money? He describes Kirkbride as " a taciturn, enduring fellow, only a boy in years (he was 20), but ruthless in action". As we shall see. Two days after this first meeting, Lawrence questioned him on his mission and ended by offering him an attachment to the Arab Army as an Intelligence-cum-Demolition officer. "I jumped at the idea", wrote Kirkbride. The next morning was fine and he was able to walk out and view the magnificent scenery from high-placed Tafileh.

Alec Kirkbride had been brought up and schooled in Egypt and was bilingual in English and Arabic. He had joined up two years previous to these events at age 18 and, given his background and expertise in Arabic, he was now being employed as an intelligence officer. The major reason for his appearance at Tafileh was in fact to discover if it would be possible to supply the Arab army through the Wadi Arabah (the long straight sand valley running from the Dead Sea down to Akaba and Eilat) rather than through the inland mountain country via Abu Lissal and Shobek. It was not, he discovered. There was no way motor vehicles could negotiate the escarpment.

The narrative followed, and frequently quoted, here is that of his memoir *An Awakening*, not published until 1971. In his foreword he explains why, after all these years, he wrote it:

> During the past fifty years much has been written on the revolt by the Arabs against the Turks in the First World War that is either biased, hearsay or even pure invention. Because of this I have decided to write down my own recollections of the period during 1918 when I was attached to the army commanded by the Amir Faisal ibn Hussein. In doing this I have had to rely on my memory supported by a simple record of daily movements, all that is left of a diary I kept. . . .

Sharing this opinion, I dwell on this account in some detail. Unlike Lawrence, Kirkbride did not leave the Middle East when Damascus fell. It so happened that he spent most of the next 30-odd years in this same area, the Transjordan (later the Hashemite Kingdom of Jordan), and Palestine. As a result, his book benefits from a vast experience of the region, of the people who live there, and of the wider implications of the Revolt for all those whom it touched. As far as participant accounts are concerned, it is probably the most even-handed as well as the most knowledgeable.

He stands apart from the other British officers because he spoke native speaker Arabic, had been brought up in the Arab world, and was on a wavelength with all Arabs, regardless of their origin. He neither distanced himself from them, nor did he try to copy them. He had a balanced view towards the Bedouin, including their fighting value. Although he makes a few mistakes concerning events in which he did not himself take part, he is probably the most reliable source, and his experience covers places, people and aspects of the Revolt not found in *Seven Pillars*.

Back in Cairo, Kirkbride found himself recruited secretly, under cover of a lunch party, to the Eastern Mediterranean Special Intelligence Bureau, which he describes as "the most efficient and successful intelligence organisation I have ever known, and later in life my experience in that field was to be quite wide. Its main lines of communication and its agents had been organised by Consular officers in the Turkish Empire long before the commencement of hostilities". His new job was to set up a listening post at the southern end of the Dead Sea and to forward agents, money and instructions to Damascus through the Jebel Druze,[1] where the entry into Turkish-held territory was much easier than across the front in Palestine.

By now Kirkbride is serving two intelligence organisations and, less officially, the Arab army. He duly sailed from Suez in the *Borolos*, down round the tip of the Sinai peninsula and back up the eastern side to Akaba. The experts had found him a Canadian Druze and a Kentish carrier pigeon fancier who would look after the transport of those secret messages. Also on board: Lawrence, and a newcomer to the Arab 'show', Captain Hubert Young, somewhat nervous about his new adventure in what he called "the most desolate country in the world". Lawrence, returning from one of his now numerous trips to Cairo, absorbed himself in *Morte d'Arthur* but found time to solicit the services of Kirkbride, whom he already valued. It was Tafileh again. Lawrence wanted Kirkbride to go back there and find out what was going on. "I was more or less my own master and . . . a suggestion from Lawrence was really impossible to refuse."

The terrible winter was over. We are now in mid-March and the slopes of the escarpment up to Tafileh were covered in wild flowers. "The day was also memorable for the first view I had of Ibex (*capra nubiana*) in their natural state. A large male with magnificent horns, followed by two does, went across the face of a steep hill at a gallop." The slopes were also covered with sheep, goats, overladen donkeys and over-excited men, women and children; all the humans being in a good humour at the prospect of getting back to their homes again. Heavy rains, they said, were falling in the highlands and they had to return there to look after their crops and to benefit from the grazing which would soon grow."

These "unseasonable torrential rains" were ruining the first British offensive across the Jordan, against Amman and Salt some sixty miles to the north. Partly because the Arabs had not succeeded in joining up with his army, Allenby wanted to protect his right flank by getting a foothold on the eastern plateau. The fording of the flooded Jordan delayed the attackers and the supply columns were completely bogged down, giving the enemy time to bring in reinforcements and post their heavy guns on fortified positions. The attackers briefly occupied Salt but had to fall back west of the River Jordan once again. Lawrence, who by this time was not far south of Amman with a group of Beni

Sakhr, already moving west of the Hijaz railway to fulfil the next stage in his plan to link up with Allenby, was very put out and vented his criticism in *Seven Pillars* (OX 594):

> This reverse took us unawares, and so hurt the more. Allenby's plan had seemed to me not merely practicable, but modest: and that he should so fall down before the Arabs was deplorable. It stained our reputation with the Beni Sakhr.... They had never trusted us to do the things which I had foretold to them, and now that we had failed, they returned to their independent thoughts....

In this rare direct criticism of his chief (significantly, the *he* (line 2) of this 1922 text is changed to *we* in the 1926), Lawrence is rightly concerned about his standing with the tribes, who prefer to fight on the winning side; but he seems insensitive to the dangers run by the international force and their casualties, and to the appalling weather conditions.

## THE ARMENIAN GIRL

There was nothing new in the Tafileh area so Kirkbride went on to Shobek.

New orders arrived there telling him to leave at once for the Ghor es Safi at the south end of the Dead Sea, since a new British attack was to take place. He was to gather intelligence of use to the attackers in collaboration with Sherif Abdullah ibn Hamza, the man who had won Lawrence's praise by destroying the Turkish flotilla of lighters on the Dead Sea (OX 547). The pigeons would carry messages to Akaba or Cairo. So Kirkbride and his party descended the escarpment once more. On the way down, he noticed a bundle of rags under a wayside bush which seemed to move:

> There was a girl of about three years of age, lying in a coma but every now and then jerking her limbs spasmodically. I called the others back and made a fire to try to revive her. It was clear that she had been abandoned by the Armenians.... by bathing her face and chafing her wrists and legs, we got her back to semi-consciousness and were able to pour a few spoonfuls of warm diluted milk down her throat. After that she woke up, spoke a few words in Turkish saying that her name was Mary, and then fell fast asleep.

They put her in a saddle bag and took her along. She recovered in a matter of days and quickly picked up Arabic. Her mother and father had both died after they had left home in Cilicia. She travelled in a saddle bag with her head and arms sticking out, and seemed to like it. During halts and at night "she behaved like a tame kitten and was treated as such". The others wanted to keep her as a mascot but Kirkbride had her carried across to Jerusalem to an orphanage kept by the Sisters of the Rosary. She was rebaptised as Mary Kirkbride. She grew up in the convent but, unfortunately, having already taken her vows, she died of tuberculosis at the age of twenty-five.

### THE ARAB OFFICERS

On June 12th, by which time the weather was stifling at the Dead Sea, Kirkbride was moved back to Abu Lissan, now Feisal's base. There was a change of plan at GHQ to the effect that news from east of the Jordan was no longer a high priority. After a second attack against Salt had also failed, Allenby would make his thrust elsewhere and the east would be used to make the enemy believe that the next attack would, once again, be there.

Kirkbride saw that he would pick up more interesting information at the front line with the Army than at Feisal's HQ and, fortunately for readers of his book, persuaded his chiefs to let him be based at Waheidah, messing with the officers there. They were about thirty in number, mainly from Iraq, a few Syrian. They had all served in the Turkish army and the majority, but not all, were captured by the British, who had given them the option to serve with the Arab army. They formed a distinct, very exclusive group of their own. It was a remarkable achievement to be welcomed by these officers, since "it was noticeably rare for any of the British Staff from Abu Lisal to appear at Waheidah and, when I remarked on this fact, it was explained that the Arab commanders were quick to resent anything which could possibly be taken as 'inspections' by British officers".[2]

Lawrence also avoided the Arab officers socially, and was therefore obliged to cross-question Kirkbride about the political attitudes of his messmates as well as their conduct of the war. One reason why the role of the regular army is so inconspicuous in *Seven Pillars* is because Lawrence had little contact with it up to the very last days of the campaign, and was on friendly terms with only the commanders, This lack of socialisation did nothing to dispel an atmosphere of mutual suspicion between the allies that never really went away, and was exacerbated still further by the post-war neo-colonialist political settlements. Also, Lawrence's self-portrayal and his version of the Arab Revolt in *Seven Pillars* had unfortunate long-term effects on Arab attitudes to Lawrence himself, which often came as a surprise to Englishmen who visited the region. Kirkbride, writing at the beginning of the seventies:

> In contrast with his fame in the West, very few Arabs remember Lawrence's name except, perhaps, as that of a legendary figure for whom the Americans and the British claim a glory not due to him but to others. (118)

This was very much Subhi al-Umari's view and his book was written to show it. These officers were "intensely politically minded"; most of the more senior among them had been members of one or other of the secret societies, especially *Ahd*, a 'covenant' of Arab officers serving in the Turkish army which had been formed before the war in Syria and Iraq to work for Arab independence. Its founder was the same Ali Abdelaziz al-Masri whom Storrs and Lawrence had encountered in Jeddah. They now felt that there was a real possibility of achieving independence, in spite of the difficulties which lay ahead. This aim set them apart from the British, towards whom they had an ambivalent attitude made up of admiration on the one hand and suspicion on the other. Also, they were Arabs of a new class that "had lost the customs and traditions of a tribal society and instead had acquired from the Turks a quasi-European culture which seemed to create a secret inferiority complex".[3] This confirms the words I quoted from the book of Subhi al-Umari.

This is why Lawrence felt uneasy with them. They had "eastern minds" but "habits moulded after ours. My spirit, more sensitive to manner than to character, dared not mix with theirs for long" (OX 566).[4] Both Englishmen were more at ease with Bedu, who did not question their own culture. Kirkbride contrasts the two different mentalities. "The beduin with whom I had worked until then were proud of being Arabs and approved, in a general sort of way, the idea of winning national independence, but fundamentally, they were more interested in their personal freedom and in what profit they could make out of the situation without running too many risks. It is not that they were less courageous than the others, but it was a matter of outlook."[5]

In his romantic chapter *The spirit of the revolt* Lawrence wrote: "We had ropes about our necks, and on our heads prices which showed that the enemy intended hideous tortures for us if we were caught." Lawrence may or may not have had a price on his head (I have found no testimony of it that does not originate from Lawrence himself), but he would no doubt have been honourably treated if caught, unless perhaps caught spying in disguise. The people who were running the risk were the Hashemite family and the Arab officers: "These men were well aware that if they fell into Turkish hands they would be executed as traitors. I would not have liked to serve under such a threat. . . . In many instances, the families of the Arab regular officers were living in territory which was still under Turkish control and they were therefore targets for reprisals."[6] The father of one of the Syrians, Subhi Halim, was a full Colonel in the Turkish service and commanded a unit of the garrison of Damascus. This is what makes it so remarkable that Kirkbide (who was employed by two British intelligence agencies, one of them top secret!) was able to win their confidence. "I discovered that some of the brigade staff suspected that I had been planted in their midst in order to spy on them. I never completely overcame that belief although, in fact, I never reported on what they were saying or doing."

The only other European who seemed to have the run of their mess was the ebullient Captain Pisani, Commander of the French contingent, a Corsican, who would roll in from time to time to play cards, drink Scotch, or relate bawdy tales. "My shortcomings in the art of playing cards were made good when Pisani came to visit the brigade: he knew all the tricks."[7]

On July 20th, Kirkbride took part in an attack on the railway station of Jerdun, which was done in the grand manner, with Nuri Said's regular brigade, Beduin led by Sherif Nasr (these two forces charging separately from four different directions simultaneously), six guns, of which two were the new French 65 mm and four 'Arab' (i.e. archaic), explosives and Very lights. The event was graced by the presence of Amir Feisal himself. The signal for battle to commence was a salvo from an isolated distant gun in an attempt to draw the fire from the Krupps artillery in the station. In spite of a total lack of artillery experience, it was Kirkbride who had been accorded this honour. The gun was one of "my very old friends the 2.9 Nordenfeldts", i.e. an antique. The event was spectacularly successful. Only a goods train got away by managing to cross a complete gap in the track on its double bogies. There were casualties on both sides "including some Turks who were shot by tribesmen after they had surrendered".

One of the Arab wounded was a young Palestinian of Algerian origin who had worked with Kirkbride. Tall, fair-haired and blue-eyed, he must have looked more like Peter O'Toole than an Arab; perhaps he came from the Kabylie. In 1937, when District Commissioner for Galilee, Kirkbride walked into a prison and found himself face-to-face with this man who, along with other Arab notables, had been interned for 'sedition' against the mandatory power. "I tried to obtain his release in return for his promise to abstain from political activities but he declined to surrender his freedom of action."[8] His name was Subhi al Khadra.

Kirkbride stayed there for nearly two months (not eight, as Lawrence wrote). The stay with the brigade was an ideal practical course for a young officer who would later become an administrator and diplomat in the Middle East. "These men and their descendants", he wrote, "belonged to a class that was to dominate the Arab political world after the passage of a few decades. . . . Between the two World Wars, and after 1945, the tide of events in the Arab countries was to set against hereditary rule and, as one dynasty after another toppled over, power was to be seized by men such as my messmates at Waheidah."[9] However, this needs qualification; many of his more senior companions, though "republicans at heart . . . were constrained by the absence of other leaders" to remain faithful to the traditional order. After the war many of the Iraqi officers stayed with Feisal in Syria until the French drove him out, and it was in large measure due to Lawrence's intervention with Lord Curzon that they were allowed back into British-ruled Iraq (1920), then in revolt. It was a typical Lawrencian move, both generous and politically astute. For under Feisal's kingship in Iraq, Jaafar, Nuri, Ali Jawdat, Mauloud Mukhlis, and Jamil el Madpai were all at one time or another Prime Ministers; and others also played leading roles in supporting the Churchill–Lawrence Hashemite Iraq. Later, however, the narrow social base of Iraq's political elite led to instability, resentment, and finally, revolution, and some of these patriots paid the price.

In the last few years, another immense convulsion has shaken the Arab world, as the rulers from the post-monarchist regimes are in their turn swept from power, with the Western powers once again deeply implicated.

※

## THE GREAT RAID

In July, Dawnay and Lawrence had been briefed by Allenby on his plan for a September offensive. The plan was to break through the

Turkish line near the coast with an infantry attack and then send the cavalry through. These would fan out across the communication lines of the Turkish seventh and eighth armies, driving towards the north and east into Syria. There was also the Turkish Fourth Army, under Mehmet Jemal Pasha, east of the Jordan river, to be at least contained by General Chaytor. The jugular vein of Turkish railway communications was Dera', a junction garrisoned by two thousand men. The lines from Palestine (Haifa) and from southern Syria and the Hejaz joined there the main line up to Damascus. This was a settled country of many villages, the Hauran.

The Arabs were given a task particularly suited to their abilities. They were to move behind the Fourth Army and from the east disable the use of all three railways around Dera'a on an exact date just before the launch of the offensive. This would cripple Turkish communications and prevent reinforcements from Damascus. It would also, in the event of a successful offensive, cut off the means of retreat and create chaos. But if the offensive failed, the Arab task force could find itself in a critical situation, several hundred kilometres from its base. The regular force would be five hundred camel-mounted infantry, well armed and well supported by, inter alia, armoured cars with mounted machine guns, demolition units, and four 65 mm mountain guns of the French detachment commanded by Pisani.

The forward base and gathering point for the "Great Raid", as Hubert Young called it, was Azrak, six days' camel trek from Abul Lisal. On September 12th the main body moved out of Azrak and on the 15th the first attack against the railway was made.

Kirkbride remained close to Nuri Said, the commander of the regulars. He had a brush with Lawrence at the Nisib bridge, which Lawrence demolished after the Turks had been driven out of the station and the redoubt. In Lawrence's very long account (OX 738-44, R 626-9), which emphasised the need for a massive amount of gelatine, there is no mention of Kirkbride, leaving one to wonder whether he was there at all. Lawrence had ordered him and his party to destroy any useful objects left in the abandoned railway station while he dealt with the bridge just to the north of the buildings.

> Knowing his (Lawrence's) habit of using unnecessarily large amounts of explosives, I asked him to give me plenty of notice so that I could fire my charges and get my men away to safety before he blew up the bridge. He was quite stuffy with me and said, 'Oh, all right, all right, don't fuss!' I was still busy when there was a terrific detonation and chunks of the bridge showered down around us from the sky. It was

only by the grace of God that no-one of us was hurt. As soon as my work was done, I went over to speak to him. I was tired, hungry and boiling with rage. I probably spoke as no subaltern should speak to a senior officer but all he did was to sit on a boulder and laugh at me. The realisation that my anger amused him brought me up all standing and I walked off and left him.

(Later) Lawrence sent over one of his men to invite me to take coffee with them after supper. This was a great honour, as he did not normally offer to entertain British personnel. I squatted down with him in the ring of colourful members of his bodyguard, and forced myself to stay awake as the little cups of aromatic bitter coffee were circulated ceremoniously. The bodyguard were carefully picked and most of them belonged to sheikhly families; their manners were excellent by Arab standards, and the conversation witty and interesting. Lawrence was most pleasant to me and never mentioned the incident of the bridge either then or later. I suppose that was his idea of making amends. He did give me an intermittent lecture on the Hauran and on the ancient buildings which stand on the various sites of towns.[10]

All of this passage (little though it is) is precious since it is rare to get a glimpse into Lawrence's social behaviour, a different perspective to that of *Seven Pillars*. A person of many qualities is revealed just by these three paragraphs. That the bodyguard came from the families of tribal chiefs and engaged in witty and interesting conversation is hardly to be reconciled with *Seven Pillars*, where the tough image is the prevailing one. The scriptwriter of *Lawrence of Arabia* was evidently wide off the mark when he had Ali al Harithi (Omar Sharif) express disgust as Lawrence's 'band of brigands' gather in Wadi Rumm. But this was no doubt needed to precharge the atmosphere before the screening of the violence at Tafas.

With the destruction of the bridge at Nisib, the Arab detachment had now met all its objectives, having put all three railways out of use and some officers, notably Hubert Young, thought that enough was enough. Kirkbride was to write: "Up to this point, the exercise had been conducted in an orderly manner but, after the successful termination of the raid, so many different non-military elements joined in that affairs on the Arab side could no longer be described as under proper control."[11] Groups of Beduin roamed and ravaged the countryside, attacking not only fleeing Turks, but pillaging villagers and townsmen. In *Seven Pillars* this is encapsulated in the Tafas incident, for which Lawrence himself takes responsibility.

Kirkbride crossed the railway with the main group, led by Lawrence, to Sheikh Saad. It was the 26th September. Allenby had attacked on the 19th, and by this time the Turkish armies had ceased to be coherent units. Chaytor had captured Amman to the south and the Fourth Army was a mass of fugitives, mostly unarmed, pouring along the road north, watched on either side by the Arabs. However, a large detachment of retreating Turks had occupied the village of Tafas, which Nuri Said was now advancing on. Kirkbride, who with Young had joined Nuri Said in his command post near there, describes what happened next:

> With so many irregulars dashing about in every direction it was difficult to keep a clear picture of what was happening: the first inkling we got of the tragedy which had taken place was the sight of a single horseman dashing towards the Turks until he fell from the saddle riddled with bullets. . . . It had looked like an incredible scene in a melodramatic desert war film. . . . Young came running back with blazing eyes and shouted to me, 'Come along, Kirk, and help me. They are going to kill the prisoners'. A lad had escaped from Tafas to say that a score of women and girls had been killed in a most abominable manner. We had great difficulty in persuading Nuri Said and his colleagues to prevent their troops from butchering the several hundred prisoners who had been collected before the advance on Tafas, and who could not be held responsible for what had happened. Soon afterwards most of the Turks who had committed the atrocity were captured by the regulars as they tried to break away towards Damascus and they were killed out of hand by the villagers and by the beduin, whose blood lust was now aroused. I had no sympathy for the actual perpetrators of the murder of the women but it was not a nice thing to see unarmed men done to death in such a manner. . . . By the time dusk fell, only stragglers were coming up and, throughout the night, which we spent on our ridge, I could hear the rifle-shots as these miserable men were shot down in cold blood by the menfolk of women and girls who had died.

He comments: "(The Bedu) are capable of bloody deeds in the heat of passion but acts of vicious cruelty, such as that at Tafas, are foreign to their nature as a rule."[12]

This account is similar to Lawrence's in *Seven Pillars* on three specific points: the abominable way in which the women and children of Tafas were killed, the dramatic lone charge of Talal al-Hareidhin, and the revenge slaughter of unarmed Turks. Lawrence himself is not in view. Kirkbride's account is important for two reasons: the first is that it shows that the scenario that Lawrence developed in his own manner did indeed exist; secondly, it makes more understandable the killings of wounded Turks at Dera' later that night and the following day that so shocked General Barrow (see below).

## DAMASCUS

By October 1st, all forces were close to Damascus. "Just as the order to march was given, we were surprised to hear the noise of a car, driving at speed, coming from the rear. There were very few of them about. The source of the noise, a Rolls Royce tender, dashed past us containing only Lawrence and a driver. I waved, but Lawrence did not look round; he was staring ahead in the fixed way which I had noticed a few days before."[13]

Kirkbride rode into Damascus on a camel lent him by Nuri Said, for whom only the best would do; with the camel was included a sword with a golden hilt and scabbard reputed to be worth three hundred golden guineas, the gift of the Amir Feisal. His party was the first to reach the Meidan (the old city centre). "People shouted greetings from their shops . . . (but) there were no cheers or other signs of joy, which one might have expected from a population supposed to be in the process of liberation." A shopkeeper warned him to be watchful of his sword. Lawrence, who arrived a little later, understandably gives a more emotional description:

> Quite quietly we drove in, up the long street to the government buildings, on the bank of the (river) Barada. All the way was packed with people, lined solid on the side-walks, in the road itself, at the windows of their houses, and on their balconies and roof-tops. Many of them were crying, a few of them cheered faintly, some of the bolder ones cried my name[14] aloud: but mostly they just looked and looked, joy in this deliverance, almost too great to be credible, shining in their eyes. A movement like a breath, in a long sigh from gate to heart of the city, marked our course. (OX 793)[15]

'We' denote Major Stirling, himself, and his driver in the Rolls Royce tender.

Kirkbride had written earlier in his narrative that the breakdown in law and order following the Turkish collapse was going to create a lot of trouble in the city, and so it did. Once again presenting a picture different to Lawrence, he writes: "There had been an almost unnatural calm in Damascus during the morning of its occupation, but the situation deteriorated with progressive rapidity as the afternoon wore on. There were thousands of Bedouin in the city with nobody in charge of them, and a great number of Druze. The local population were brutal to those Turks that were still in evidence. There was killing and looting. Shops were closed and barricaded, and people stayed indoors." That is Kirkbride's version. Lawrence wrote of later that Day:

> Every man, woman and child in this city of a quarter-million souls was out on the streets: and as the miracle of victory was at last confirmed, they waited only the spark of our appearance to unchain their spirits. Damascus went mad with joy. The men tossed up their tarbushes to cheer, the women tore off their veils.

Australian troops had moved into the western barracks next door to the military hospital, but they, and all other British and Dominion forces, were ordered not to intervene in internal affairs. It had been decided to let the Arabs manage their own affairs for the moment of heat and triumph. When things sobered down, Allenby would arrive. Kirkbride believes that it suited the British to let the Arabs do the dirty work first. This makes understandable Lawrence's disgust with General Chauvel (OX 796-7) and the Australians for standing aside.

In the evening, Lawrence, "with his extraordinary habit of wanting to do everything himself", insisted on going out onto the streets to see what was going on. He took Kirkbride who acted as a bodyguard, having failed to persuade Lawrence to take a proper escort. He had to shoot two people who turned aggressive. "Lawrence seemed to be really shocked at my shooting and told me not to be so bloody-minded."[16]

The next morning Lawrence, Sherif Nasser and Nuri Said sent the regulars out on to the streets to restore order. It had to be a fairly ruthless operation. Druze and Bedouin, who were sworn enemies, fought battles against one another and against the citizens. Kirkbride, who was again involved, shot four Bedouin horsemen of the same group out of their saddles, and Subhi al-Umari, still head of the machine gun section, reported killing twenty-two. Most of the disorder was due to the comparative anarchy that all these armed strangers had brought into the city.

One unpleasant surprise had been to find that the Al-Djezairi brothers, Damascus notables of Algerian extraction, Said and

Abdelkader, had declared an Arab government in the name of King Hussein. This was the last thing Lawrence wanted. These Algerians were deeply suspicious of Feisal, whom they regarded (with a good deal of justification) as a kind of Trojan Horse for a British takeover. Lawrence now set about neutralising the Al-Jezairi brothers. Abdelkader, who drew a knife on Lawrence at the town hall, was placed under house arrest. After Lawrence had left Damascus, he was killed by Feisal's police.

The final unpleasant task was the Turkish military hospital. Lawrence describes this notorious scene as if he had gone there alone but this is not so. The tough Kirkbride had once again accompanied him throughout.[17] "A doctor and a sanitary squad would have been a better combination to deal with the mess at the hospital", was his dry comment.

"'Hullo, Mecca, how are tricks'?" came from an Australian trooper looking over the wall of the adjacent barracks. "My reply, 'Bloody awful'!' seemed to take him aback,"[18] wrote Kirkbride. The Australian had not imagined that a British officer would be digging a trench for Turkish corpses. Australians were much easier in fraternising with Arabs than either the British or the Indians. But they did not help with the hospital.

At last Allenby arrived. He at once sent for Feisal, who had been intending to make a triumphant entry the same day. As it was, he galloped in by horse, having refused to sit in the car sent for him by the British Commander-in-Chief. Kirkbride was too junior to be at that meeting but his friend, Tahseen Qadri, Nuri's aide-de-camp, told him that it had not gone well. Little else was to go well for a long time to come.

For Kirkbride, "Lawrence left the Middle East feeling that he had failed in his mission". But in *Seven Pillars* he would justifiably celebrate the meeting as symbol of the victory which he had enabled, the bridge uniting East and West. "It was fitting that the two chiefs should meet for the first time in the heart of their greatest victory; with myself still the interpreter between them." (OX 810)

※

If we are to compare Kirkbride with Lawrence as a war memorialist, I would conclude that Kirkbride gives a better picture of the wider reality of a small war like this: its impact on non-combatants, the danger posed by irregulars, its cruelty, but also its humorous side and its odd surprises; as I wrote earlier, what Lawrence wrote about his own account applies much more truly to Kirkbride: "It treats of daily life, mean happenings, little people". His lens has a wider focus. He is also more balanced and less prejudiced in his assessments, and he is always clear. After *Seven Pillars*, there is something reassuring, even restful, about his account. He does not mystify or mythologise, exaggerate or personalise; he carries less emotional lumber around with him, he is in less of a hurry, the style is less strained. Lawrence's strengths lie in his narrative and descriptive power, and the very detailed and lively account of an operation that he can provide. The manner in which he lays before us the whole experience is something of a tour de force. Some of Kirkbride's own common sense conclusions are worth mentioning:

## Regulars and Bedu

Kirkbride is in no doubt that the most important group in Feisal's army were the trained Arab officers and soldiers. "Without them the revolt would have been ineffective and would probably have collapsed before long." This is a view that must astonish those who take their history from *Seven Pillars of Wisdom*. However, it is supported by Hubert Young also. As for the irregulars:

> The tribal formations were of two types of men . . . . The most useful were groups of mercenary camelry, recruited mainly from the nomads of the Hejaz and the Nejd, who only went back to see their families at intervals of months. These men were paid far more than their worth, in gold. The others were levies of local tribesmen who turned out for a specific operation and then went home again. Their sheikhs were given hand-outs of gold after the actions were over and left to settle accounts with their individual followers. The value of the tribesmen in battle was limited; they did not lack courage but they were without discipline or military training. They were good at tip-and-run tactics of their kind but they disliked having to stand and fight if circumstances were unfavourable. Their principal virtue was their ability to fend for themselves in the desert, for weeks on end, with little food and water. They were also very picturesque.
>
> These tribesmen did, however, make one important contribution to the war effort, though possibly without realising that they had done so. They taught Lawrence desert strategy and tactics. He applied the lessons and by so doing earned praise, as a natural military genius, from some members of the higher command in Cairo. Perhaps it was a touch of genius on his part to recognise that advice from his followers might be of more practical value than the dogma of staff college graduates.

## Lawrence

He was, in a sense, lucky to find himself sent to a sphere of the war where an extraordinary man was permitted to do extraordinary things and to become famous in the process. Although a film has depicted him as wallowing in blood, his views were that war should be avoided if possible; and, if inevitable, be waged and won with as little damage to either side as could be managed.

His will-power was greater than the average and he used it to drive himself and others to feats of endurance which circumstances did not always require. He had a flair for flamboyancy in his acts which appealed to the mentality of the tribesmen . . . He made no secret of the fact that he loved fame and it was, no doubt, this longing for notoriety that led him to exaggerate and embroider his version of the happenings in which he played a part.

# The Drama of the Self

"I aimed at providing a meal for the fellow-seekers with myself. For this the whole experience, and emanations and surroundings (background and foreground) of a man are necessary."

*T.E. Lawrence*

# CHAPTER 12

# THE OUTSIDER (1)

The Drama of the Self: either parallel to or integrated with the narrative of the Arab Revolt there is a drama drawn out of it, which leads up to a climax; the subject of this parallel climax is himself; it is a psychological drama of change and self-discovery brought about by the experience of Arabia, the Arabs, the Arab Revolt and above all himself. The change is from action to paralysis, from belief to nihilism, from innocence to guilt.

In a sense, the entire book is a drama of the self. We have already seen, in the previous section, plenty of evidence that the Arab Revolt is not narrated objectively. It is not presented as an independent event in which the author is one of the participants but as his brainchild, which is planned and controlled in accordance with a personal vision or will. But we are talking here about Lawrence's own personal destiny, about passages that are autobiography, not history.

The difference between *Seven Pillars* and *Revolt in the Desert* is that this drama has been largely obliterated from *Revolt*. It was not difficult because the drama of the self and the story of the Revolt are largely independent of one another. They are parallel texts and are motivated by different objectives, and have different origins. One is a day-to-day narrative based on notebooks, reports and memory; the other is composed mainly out of retrospective reflection, which may include experience that is outside the space-time of the Arabian adventure. The parallel texts work against each other; the nearer the Arab Revolt gets to its objective, the closer the narrator gets to mental breakdown. As Forster wrote: "To the attentive reader something has gone wrong here, the analysis has reached one conclusion, the text keeps implying another." [1] Readers of *Seven Pillars* tend to 'see' one of these texts but rarely both: the heroic extrovert text or the pathologically introspective one.

In this chapter I trace the development of the introspective drama,[2] as far as the Dera' incident of November 1917, which is dealt with in the chapter following. Chapter 14 takes us through to the Damascus climax. Finally, Chapter 15 looks at the biographical background and to the aftermath of the war.

## CHAPTERS 1 AND 2[3]

The personal is stamped upon the book from the start. The first two chapters establish once and for all the force and complexity of the personality. Both are infused with moral doubts and are highly judgemental. Otherwise the chapters have a different orientation: the first, while it includes a miscellany of information about the book, its purpose, origins, inclusiveness, and style – is essentially political in orientation, and is accusatory; the second is private and existential.

The personal tone of the introductory chapter cannot fail to surprise. Not for Lawrence the modest low-key guidance comments of the average introduction. The battle between himself and what opposed him is engaged at once. He takes up a number of positions that are implicitly or explicitly anti-establishment: first, he presents himself as anti-war and anti-colonial, particularly anti the kind of warfare that had been waged in the British 1916 invasion of Mesopotamia:

> (And) we were casting them [English soldiers] by thousands into the fire, to the worst of deaths, not to win the war, but that the corn and rice of Mesopotamia might be ours. . . . All the subject provinces of the Empire to me were not worth one dead English boy. (OX 7, R 23)

Next, he sees himself as an enlightened visionary striving for universal brotherhood through the mediation of a new benevolent commonwealth. The high rhetoric of this passage might be a model for an American president on a re-election platform. Lawrence articulates that Olympian tone that so impressed Charlotte Shaw:

> If I have restored to the East some self-respect, a goal, ideals: if I have made the standard of rule of white over red more exigent, I have fitted those peoples in a degree for the new commonwealth in which the dominant races will forget their brute achievements, and white and red and yellow and brown and black will stand up together without side-glances in the service of the world. (OX 7)

They are indeed claims for which he can justly take some credit. They are also attitudes or achievements that at that time marked him as modern and which in this time mark him as a person from whom we can still learn something.

He then presents himself as a man betrayed by the politicians of Whitehall and Paris:

> The Cabinet raised the Arabs to fight for us by definite promises of self-government afterwards. The Arabs believed in persons, not in institutions. They saw in me a free agent of the British Government, and demanded from me an endorsement of our written promises. So I had to join the conspiracy, and, for what my word was worth, assured my men of their reward. . . . but of course, instead of being proud of what we did together, I was continually and bitterly ashamed.[4]

This is aggressive language for an introduction to a historical narrative and could scarcely have been written by a man who was not already famous and revered. This theme, *fraud & betrayal*, is elaborated at some length and repeated ad nauseam. It plays the key role in the unfolding of the drama of the self. The way it is presented here already shows clearly the link between the politics of the Arab business and the author's personal feelings during the war. Kirkbride offers an explanation based on Lawrence's sense of honour and responsibility:

> The Arabs there [he is referring to those who fought for Feisal] had come to believe in the individual British officers with whom they had worked and who had encouraged them to set up an administration. Lawrence had not been in any way responsible for the text of the controversial MacMahon letters, but he had encouraged the Amir Faisal and he felt a deep sense of blame for having allowed his associates to take up a position in Syria from which they had to be driven by a French army. It was this feeling of personal involvement that made his reaction so strong.[5]

His failure to act when this happened, as he had threatened to do before his King, stoked his bitterness, anger and sense of guilt to white heat in that summer of 1920. All three excerpts reveal a desire for self-justification and the definition of an idea of virtue that opposes him to 'them'. As Tabachnik observed, "Lawrence defines himself against the outside world".[6]

There is one side of his mind that is wilful and outsider-motivated, instinctively oppositional, which expresses itself in *Seven Pillars* as pro-Arab and anti-British; and another that made him in practice intensely loyal, as patriotic and England-loving as Rupert Brooke, unwilling to leave a stone unturned in order to be well thought of. In the truthful and intriguing words of the *Myself* chapter: "The falsity of the Arab position had cured me of crude ambition: while it left me my craving for good repute among men. This craving made me profoundly suspect my truthfulness to myself" (R 579).

In the development of this theme of divided loyalties, betrayal and guilt, Lawrence anticipates a genre that will later be fully exploited in fiction, by Graham Greene and John Le Carré among others.

The curtain opens on the desert scene:

> For years we lived anyhow with one another in the naked desert, under the indifferent heaven.

The first part of the chapter *The Spirit of the Revolt* is a description, or rather poetic evocation, of his experience in the desert with the Arabs. Life under the stars, companionship in suffering for the ideal of freedom, contempt of the body, sexual indulgence, the agony of self-alienation. It is an image at once poetic and mysterious, one the reader will take with him through the book. In form, it is partly idyll, partly confession, partly self-analysis; a powerfully emotional self-examination by a troubled moral conscience. We seem here to get at once to the heart of the matter; it is an opening of immense promise of a deeply revealing personal drama to follow, intimately married to the Arab experience.

A kind of prologue, it gives the reader the impression that this was the life he led during the Arab war. It is also a summary of the moral consequences of living with the Bedu. The pronoun *we*, that dominates in the first part of this chapter, creates a feeling of fellowship, as if he and the Bedu were one social organism. Here there are no individuals, all is anonymous. This fellowship with the Bedu he must have felt – and for an outsider a thrilling feeling it must have been. Later in this chapter he will dismiss it as an illusion: "I was not of them".

> We were a self-centred army, without parade or gesture, devoted to freedom, the second of man's creeds, a purpose so ravenous that it

devoured all our strength, a hope so transcendent that our earlier ambitions faded in its glare.

The idea of freedom, and that the Arabs fought for that, is a central assumption. When Lawrence first wrote this chapter the issue of Arab independence was still open. But I doubt whether that is really the point. It was the regular officers of Feisal's army, like Mukhlis or Subhi al-Umari, who were motivated by the idea of independence; this took the form of anti-imperialism. But as Lawrence spent little time with them, and did not welcome their political mistrust of Great Britain, they get little notice in the *Seven Pillars*, and their ideology is never addressed. What Kirkbride wrote about above happened after the war and washed back into the *Seven Pillars* as overpowering guilt. The Bedu were not politicised; the idea that freedom was 'a purpose so ravenous that it devoured all their strength' is simply a poetic invention. Freedom, as Lawrence admits and elaborates in many places, was not something the Bedu strove for; they already had it. And that, surely, is the whole point. The freedom evoked here is something other than mere political independence, but what one could hardly define. It is mystical, and for Lawrence it is more than a yearning, it is a need transcendent and absolute. Not just here, always.

The chapter now takes a surprising turn. The yearning for freedom is a kind of tyranny, and entails a sado-masochistic scenario of subjugation, physical pain and moral surrender.

> We had sold ourselves into its slavery, manacled ourselves together in its chain-gang, bowed ourselves to serve its holiness with all our good and ill content. The mentality of human slaves is terrible – they have lost the world – and we had surrendered, not body alone, but soul to the overmastering greed of victory.

From here, Lawrence moves on to sex. The development is carefully prepared. There was a separation of body and soul. The body was "abandoned ... as rubbish" by minds so exalted by the extremes of grief and ecstacy, that it escapes all moral restraint.

> We were young and sturdy; and hot flesh and blood unconsciously claimed rights in us and tormented our bellies with strange longings.

This is the original (1919–20) version. In later versions he dissociates himself at this point from his companions; the *we/us/our* is replaced by *the men/them/their*.[7] The sexual confession includes descriptions of homosexual intimacy on three levels: pure physical release; passion; and finally degrading forms of sado-masochistic sex. In order to show the progression, I have separated out consecutive sentences of a single paragraph: In my second paragraph, the italics refer to the more sensual wording of the early draft, later replaced by the forms between square brackets:

> In horror of such sordid commerce (sex with prostitutes) our youths began indifferently to slake one another's few needs in their own clean bodies – a cold convenience that, by comparison, seemed sexless and even pure.
>
> Later, some began to justify this sterile process, and swore that friends quivering together *naked* in the yielding sand *writhing* [with intimate] hot *intimate limb with limb* [limbs] in supreme embrace, found there hidden in the darkness a sensual co-efficient of *that* [the] mental passion which was welding our souls and spirits in one flaming effort.
>
> Several, thirsting to punish appetites they could not wholly prevent, took a savage pride in degrading the body, and offered themselves fiercely in any habit which promised physical pain and filth.

Lawrence uses quantifiers, such as *some* or *several* in order to limit responsibility for the content, but that does not convince that this a truthful account. The idea of desert Arabs gravely discussing sex in the sand as a sensual co-efficient of mental passion is rather unlikely, even if one could imagine what they actually said. The language, the thought, the entire construction of this paragraph plus what we know of Lawrence's nature and post-war behaviour, suggests that this passage is motivated by a desire to express diverse sexual longings in his own nature, to create a scenario where the physical and mental are united, in a setting where these longings are romanticised. It is a blend of veiled confession and fantasy, or perhaps pure fantasy.

My interpretation does not mean that he witnessed no sex at all. He may well have done. But that is hardly the point. The carefully developed scene he evokes, and its metaphysical implications, are retrospective mental constructions. In this chapter Lawrence wants to speak for truth; but only in the abstract and under the alias of the desert Arab. It is in fact the first of several passages in the book in which Lawrence deals with the relation between the body and the soul. A vision of sex as an ideal fusion of mental and physical passion is no doubt meaningful for Lawrence. More usually, however, the body is seen and treated with contempt,[8] but mental and physical always live very close together in Lawrence and are constantly at war.

It is worth pointing out that love among male Arabs is usually described as clean ("their own clean bodies", we read here) and idealistic, pure-hearted; Daud and Farraj, the 'Arcadian love pair', embody it. By contrast, the Turks are shown as depraved (venereal disease, lust, etc.).

This memorable chapter is not just about solidarity with Arabs. He suddenly distances himself from them: "I was sent to these Arabs as a stranger, unable to think their thoughts or subscribe their beliefs . . . ". No longer solidarity, but solitude. In this part the essay becomes more purely analytical and introspective, a type of discourse in which Lawrence excels and which he privileges. The *we* gives way to the *I*. In its final form it expresses the dualism of his nature, in which one part of his mind is at the opposite pole to the other. These lines express as well as any the devastating consequence of being tempted by an alien culture; the temptation of the outsider.

> In my case, the effort for these years to live in the dress of Arabs, and to imitate their mental foundation, quitted me of my English self, and let me look at the West and its conventions with new eyes: they destroyed it all for me. . . . I had dropped one form and not taken on the other . . . with a resultant feeling of intense loneliness in life, and a contempt, not for other men, but for all they do.

This rich and sensational evocation of the 'spirit of the revolt' raises the reader's expectations. But it is a prologue to a play that will never be performed. Never will we *see* these relationships, this companionship, this passion; what is related here may have a basis in reality but, whatever that reality was, it is here incorporated into the Lawrencian dream. Its value is autobiographical in the widest sense. It seems to be a statement of the importance of fantasy, as well as reality, as part of experience. An important component of the Drama of the Self is imaginary.

## FROM WEJH TO AZRAK

Lawrence gives us an early revelation of his ambivalent role and the personal insecurity it provokes as early as January 1917 after he reports a difference of opinion with Major Vickery, another British officer seconded to the Revolt, during a stop on his ride to Wejh. This keenly felt difference between himself and British and Indian Army regular officers will be the cause of many outbursts of quite aggressive resentment. Behind it lies a passionate defence of his 'outsider' position and mentality: individual initiative *versus* Discipline. In the Oxford edition, Vickery, Murray, Young, Barrow, Chauvel follow one another as targets of his acid pen. Three of these are Generals. Many are those who have used their memoirs to settle scores, and Lawrence is not the least The antagonism is less evident in the 1926 text, due in part to the intervention of Bernard Shaw. Thus, the allegation that Vickery, a guest in Feisal's tent, "pulled out a great flask of whisky and mixed himself a hearty drink" (OX 137) is omitted, even though it is true. He does not tell us that Captain Boyle of the Royal Navy was also present. Boyle wrote that Feisal merely laughed and that the whisky was very welcome.[9] We then learn that Vickery humiliated Lawrence in Feisal's tent, and afterwards condemned him as "a braggart and a visionary" to another officer. Lawrence had said that in a year we would be tapping on the gates of Damascus. He defends himself and the visionary genius:

> ... though the (my) outburst was foolish, as I saw when I had made it, yet it was not an impossible dream, for five months later I was in Damascus, and a year after that I was its governor. ... The Arabs nearly made shipwreck through this blindness of European advisers, who would not see that rebellion was not war: indeed, was more of the nature of peace – a national strike perhaps. The conjunction of Semites, an idea, and an armed prophet held illimitable possibilities: in skilled hands it would have been, not Damascus, but Constantinople which was reached in 1918.

But the passage that follows is purely a judgement on himself.

> My only assets for the position in the Arab movement that I at last unwillingly assumed were goodwill and an open mind, and hope. I had no sense of command, no instinct for tactics, no mastery of Arabic: and at every step, and glaringly in every crisis, my raw methods made our progress hesitant and dangerous. I knew it (the self-knowledge itself unfitted me for leadership) and again and again I tried to find a master from among the qualified: but they would not lend themselves, and so the adventure had to suffer. It had been my fault always to hold places for which I was ten years too young, and the penalty of youth was heavy. In myself I paid it cheerfully, but in this war the Arabs paid

it for me. . . . Vickery had the age of me and beside him I felt miserably wrong. It was difficult to resist the man with the strong point of view who showed his belief that he was right. (OX 139)

But it is Lawrence who is right and of course we know that. He suffers because he is right. And yet, more profoundly, we hear the message 'I am wrong because I am an amateur, an outsider'.

The reality is that Lawrence resented any military intrusion into the world he had created, both because he thought it would wreck the movement and the aims he was now designing for it, and at a more personal level, because it would disturb the special relationship with Feisal, which enabled him to believe in and pursue the possibilities of realising his great idea, and maintaining the freedom of his life among the tribesmen. He is not sincere in claiming that he had not sought the position he held, nor in claiming that he would have liked to have a "master from among the qualified" in his place; he wrote to his mother in the same month regretting that he would shortly have to hand over to Col. Newcombe and return to Cairo.[10] There were, however, moments when he doubted himself.

To professional and moral insecurity, Lawrence added brutalisation, mental stress and physical pain in the build-up to burn-out. It begins in March 1917 during the journey to Wadi Ais, where Emir Abdullah is camped (OX 181-90, R 183-92). At first, this is nothing more than another journey through the desert hills, a group of Arabs journeying slowly through rough country of astonishing beauty and variety, to the eye that observes it, the pen that records it. Lawrence, already in pain and fever, has to formally execute a Moroccan who has shot dead a tribesman, in order to prevent a blood feud from developing. The execution is described in excruciating detail. The effect is repellent and we can only feel pity for Lawrence, though scarcely for the victim owing to his abject cowardice. To his contemporaries, such descriptions must have been shocking, Lawrence was in the avant garde of realism in descriptions of killing and physical horror. What he wishes to show here is the effect on himself. Yet he makes no introspective comment on how he felt. Like Hemingway after him, he allows the description to speak for itself. More is the pity, given his descriptive powers, that he did not stick to this rule (OX 185, R 187).

Book VI, one of his best, describes the long expedition to the Yarmuk gorge; the mood darkens. Where in the Akaba expedition all had been positive, with the Arab tribes lending their enthusiastic support, now the same tribes were absent. The expedition was under the leadership of Ali ibn Hussein el-Harithi, a Hejazi Sherif, but the decisions were made finally by Lawrence, who had organised the expedition at the request of General Allenby. Ali, in spite of his considerable prestige, had a good deal less clout in the north than Nasir and Auda abu Tayi. Auda himself, and his brilliant desert commander Zaal refused to join. It became necessary to recruit for this very risky expedition men from the untried Serahin. He relates the dismal failure of the raid on the bridge in the rain and cold – how different to the Akaba expedition of the previous summer!

The expedition retreats to Azrak, a famous oasis where stands an old Arab castle of black basalt, cold and barely fit to be lived in in winter. The Bedu went home, leaving Ali, Lawrence and the Indian machine gunners, who suffered badly from the cold. In this miserable atmosphere, Lawrence goes out to explore the town of Dera' and meets with the most terrible experience of the book: his capture, flogging and sexual abuse by Turks.

A whole chapter is devoted to this incident. It is obviously intended as a watershed and raises the Drama of the Self to a climax where the Arab Revolt retreats into the background.

CHAPTER

# 13

# THE CLIMAX AT DERA'

Does it make any sense to display one's suffering, shame, and punishment to the surrounding world? ... Most of us certainly prefer to hide shame or punishment. It must have a meaning or even a number of meanings if the masochist directs the attention of his environment to his misery unconsciously, if he exposes the punishment or the degradation inflicted on him with such obtrusiveness. Does he want to show something? Or does he wish to hide something by doing so?

*Theodor Reik*

Since the triumph of Akaba (Book IV) the growing alienation of the narrator from the campaign is a theme of the book. However, we are still in the rough-and-tumble of a campaign that is essentially an adventure, if less amusing than before. Then suddenly he decides to relate an experience, one might say, for its own sake. Until now, however much Lawrence might have shoved his own plaintive oar into the current of the historical narrative, his personal life has not been narrated nakedly for its own sake. Here, in the happening at Dera' on 21 November 1917, it is. For there is no historical reason whatever why this incident should be included. It had no consequences, no significance in the campaign. And no witnesses have ever attested to it. It can easily be detached from *Seven Pillars* without anything appearing to be missing.[1] Its effect on Lawrence was never commented on at the time by any one of his colleagues and does not appear to have in any way affected his performance. If he had decided to keep silent, the much discussed 'Dera' would never have existed. The relevant chapters are OX 87 'Being taught', and R LXXX in the revised edition.

The manner of the description, which is by far the most striking aspect, is of a different nature to anything else in the book. It is a wholly independent composition and its significance is entirely autobiographical. The fact that he included in both editions such a deeply shocking and yet historically unnecessary incident, and caused himself so much agony over it, points to deep and compelling personal motives. These will be looked at in some detail. However, it is important first to reach a position concerning the truth of the incident. For if it is not historical truth, it throws into question its raison d'etre, and the nature of truth itself as far as *Seven Pillars* is concerned. What is the provenance of the story? What are the circumstances as described? What is the evidence from the text? And outside the text? But that is not all. The analysis must be fully explanatory: can we answer the last two questions asked by Theodor Reik above?

It will not be simple and we will be led into domains of psychology, notably masochism, that may be unfamiliar. No biographer can altogether ignore it; but half-baked or evasive responses will certainly not do in a book about *Seven Pillars* itself. In my case, a detailed explanation has been inevitable because it can be seen to form an entirely coherent part of Lawrence's psychopathology, of what he wanted his book to show, and how we are to avoid misunderstanding his later life. For these reasons I shall explore in the next chapter but one the whole biographical background, before and after the war and his later treatment of the incident.

## LAWRENCE'S STORY

There are some significant differences between the 1922 text and the 1926 revision. The earlier text, more explicit, is closer to representing what Lawrence wanted to write rather than what he later allowed his restricted readership to see. The changes made later are important.

From Azrak, which was to function as a northern base from which to gather support and intelligence, Lawrence, with the Sheikh of Tafas, Talal al-Hareidhin, set out to reconnoitre Dera', a key railway junction and Turkish headquarters of the Governorate of the Hauran, a large arable area of southern Syria. This adventure ended in a personal disaster to which many commentators have attributed the breakdown of his will, self-esteem and motivation to act after the war. It is, however, a moot point as to whether this incident ever took place.

On entering Dera' disguised as an Arab and accompanied by a local tribesman (but not Talal, who pleaded that he would be recognised inside the town) Lawrence is apprehended by a Turkish sergeant with the words "The Bey wants you". He tries to pass himself off as a Circassian; Circassians are often fair and have blue eyes. The Turkish soldiers in the guard-room tell him that he cannot be freed until he has "fulfilled the Bey's pleasure this evening". He remains in the guard room until evening. He is then taken to the Bey's house.

> They took me upstairs to the Bey's room, which I was astonished to see was his bedroom. He was another bulky man, a Circassian perhaps, sitting on his bed in a night-gown trembling and sweating as though with fever.

This scenario of the Governor of the Hauran sitting there trembling in a night-gown on his bed, to receive a street Arab he had never set eyes on, was understandably rejected by David Lean, the director of *Lawrence of Arabia*, who took the liberty of changing this first meeting to an inspection by the Governor of the 'prisoners' taken that day. Lawrence's Governor is an altogether pathetic and loathsome character, sadistic, and totally mastered by his lust. There is just one moment in which the Bey manages to stop behaving like a rather babyish sex maniac:

> (He) controlled his voice with an effort and said significantly, 'You must understand that I know about you, and it will be much easier if you do as I wish'.

Lawrence decided that "it was evidently a chance shot, by which he himself did not, or would not, mean what I feared". In this classic example of ambiguity and inexplicitness, Lawrence the writer leaves open the possibility that he was recognised by the Bey as an Englishman spying, and even perhaps as the man he actually was, and was being blackmailed. This is the sensible conclusion taken by Lean and Bolt and it is very subtly performed. Peter O'Toole resembled his original in that neither could have been taken for anything but a European. Given that the Governor of Dera' was only too aware that he was fighting British as well as Arabs just to the south, he would obviously have taken Lawrence for an Englishman, not a Circassian. The superficial similarity of fair hair and blue eyes is not good enough. Kirkbride, who had met countless Circassians, rubs in the point in his other book, *A Crackle of Thorns*, and he is followed by the Arab historian, George Antonius, who met Lawrence in 1921:

One of the myths that grew up about Lawrence was that he could pass himself off as an Arab. This was not so. He spoke Arabic imperfectly and his blue eyes and ruddy countenance were entirely European. Even if his appearance had not been enough to show that he was no Arab, he betrayed his origin the moment he spoke.[2]

> Neither his accent nor his use of words – to say nothing of his appearance – could have deceived anyone in Arabia for long; and an episode in *Seven Pillars of Wisdom*, in which he tried to pass for an Arab under the scrutiny and cross-examination of a suspicious stranger, shows the lengths to which he could go in deluding himself.[3]

The soldiers would have been Turk or Arab conscripts and the place was full of Arab civilians and Circassians. This is made clear in an intelligence report written by Colonel Joyce in 1918.[4] Given normal Arab inquisitiveness and Lawrence's long waiting time in the guard-room, it is inconceivable there were not suspicions – I should say certainty rather – that this was no local Circassian; there would have been a great deal of gossip afterwards, enough to keep the town busy for days. A final example (among many) is the way he was treated by the soldiers. What the Bey had ordered, after Lawrence had violently repelled his advances, was that they should "teach me until I prayed to be brought back". Presumably, this meant persuasive torture, not by any means unknown in Turkish prisons. Instead, he was beaten almost unconscious and then apparently buggered, before being dragged up before the Bey once more.

> (Hajim) now threw me off fastidiously, cursing them for their stupidity in thinking he needed a bedfellow streaming with blood and water, striped and fouled from face to heel. They had laid into me, no doubt much as usual: but my indoor skin had torn more than an Arab's.

The soldiers knew very well what they were supposed to do and that they would incur the displeasure of their commander if they disobeyed; which in a Turkish garrison in wartime would be harsh punishment. Is it possible that they would serve up a prisoner in that condition for the pleasure of the commanding officer? The treatment meted out had nothing to do with persuasion, everything to do with sadistic punishment, even sexual gratification. Lawrence's explanation about torn skin is unconvincing; neither Arabs nor Circassians have skins of leather.

Lawrence's desire to relate a maximally violent flogging experience makes it hard for him to create plausible environmental details. This, then, is a badly put together story. Judging from my experience and research, no Arab who has read it believes it. It can only persuade those who are unable to imagine the reactions of the participants because they have no familiarity with the social world in which it purports to have taken place.

The main body of the story, the beating and rape, does not read as if it is authentic either. Its sensational nature makes it thoroughly readable and many have found it gripping. Nonetheless, it is stereotypical. In real life, especially in unpredictable or unique situations, odd things happen, arbitrary details intrude, and people do things that are individually characteristic and often appear strange. This is not the case here. This part is very carefully composed, vivid, and uses a rich vocabulary. Nonetheless, it reads like fiction, the kind of fantasy fiction that carries you through a progression of stereotypical incidents and behaviour of mounting violence. The Bey also is a stereotype; he is characterised without variation as the worst and most despicable type of Turkish officer: cruel, venal, and stupid; thereby repeating Lawrence's portrayal of Turks throughout the book. It also applies to the escape, which is worthy of a boys' adventure story: the whispered hint from a Druze soldier "that the door into the next room was not locked", the suit of clothes left hanging on a door, the open window. And to cap it all, the discovery of a hidden valley on the way out of town, ideal cover for a secret raid on the town. Lawrence's gift for invention was more subtly applied in the real world than in fiction.

### *The Bey of Dera'*

In the 1926 text, unlike in the Oxford, Lawrence uses a fictional name both for the Bey, and for his original Arab companions – with the exception of Talal al-Hareidhin, who was killed in the war. No named witnesses, therefore. However, the Governor was indeed named correctly in the Oxford text as Hajim, or in Turkish: Hacim Muhittim Bey. The first biographers who thought of searching out the Bey were Colin Simpson and Philip Knightley in 1968 but they were three years too late; the Bey had died in 1965. However, they did some very thorough research among his family, friends and acquaintances, and examined his diaries. First of all, the Bey was known to be an aggressive heterosexual; this appeared to be confirmed by entries in his diary when he was Governor in Dera'. Not one respondent who had known him – friend or enemy – accepted the possibility of his being a homosexual. But what is much more important, the Bey was a clever and patriotic official of authority, highly competent. In short he was, in the words of Knightley and Simpson, "in every respect unlike Lawrence's description of him".[5]

## THE LETTER TO STIRLING

The first person to be told about the Dera' incident was Major Stirling. He owed this distinction to being Deputy Chief Political Officer in Cairo in the summer of 1919. Lawrence, also in Cairo after the Handley Page odyssey from Paris, sent him a letter from the Grand Continental Hotel on June 28th.[6] It was semi-official, being addressed to D.C.P.O., not to Stirling personally. But Stirling was a great admirer of Lawrence, and had been his subordinate and closest collaborator in Damascus. He was therefore the ideal recipient. Lawrence, for once, threw caution to the winds.

The entire letter is a catalogue of the alleged crimes and despicable character of the Al-Djazairi brothers, Abdelkader and Mohammed Said, whom we have had occasion to mention already as the 'Arab government' that Lawrence had to overthrow when he entered Damascus nine months previously. Abdelkader had also accompanied Lawrence on his ill-fated expedition to the Yarmouk in November 1917 but had unaccountably disappeared, presumably into Syria, when the expedition was at Azrak.[7] According to this letter, Abdelkader betrayed the expedition to the Turks in Dera', but how did Lawrence know this? Here's how:

> I went to Deraa in disguise to spy out the defences, was caught, and identified by Hajim Bey the Governor by virtue of Abd el Kadir's descriptions of me. (I learnt all about his treachery from Hajim's conversation, and from my guards.) Hajim was an ardent paederast and took a fancy to me. So he kept me under guard till night, and then tried to have me. I was unwilling, and prevailed after some difficulty. Hajim sent me to the hospital, and I escaped before dawn, being not as hurt as he thought. He was so ashamed of the muddle he had made that he hushed the whole thing up, and never reported my capture & escape.

In this, the original edition of the Dera' incident, certain unlikelihoods of the *Seven Pillars* version are missing; but these original details are no more credible than the later ones. According to the letter he was indeed recognized as that Englishman whom any Turkish governor would have considered a gift from heaven to have in his power (again one wonders in what language this "conversation" with Hajim took place). From what we now know of Hacim Muhittim Bey, his sending such an important prisoner to a Turkish hospital without an adequate guard stretches one's credulity. And the chances of such a matter being hushed up, when Lawrence was evidently known to his guards as a special prisoner and seen by others in the hospital, can be discounted. Nobody who knows the Arab world could believe it, of a small town the size of Dera'. Yet not so much as a whisper ever escaped. The reason given by Lawrence for the Bey's silence is feeble in its predictability.

Two questions now raise themselves: why did Lawrence choose to make this revelation to Stirling? And why did he not report his knowledge of Abdelkader's treachery at the time since it was obviously vital to the security of the campaign? The ostensible reason for the first is that he wanted to convince Stirling that Abdelkader had been a Turkish agent, a traitor to the Arab cause. Abdelkader was already dead. But the knowledge that he, Lawrence, had learned direct from the horse's mouth that he was a traitor was part of the scenario of the wicked brothers. "If ever two people deserved hanging or shooting in Syria they were these two brothers", wrote Lawrence. It would, he hoped, persuade Stirling to move against his brother also. For Mohammed Said, a man of considerable influence in Damascus, was still favoured by the French as their 'protégé', a counterweight to Feisal, more amenable to themselves. So the Dera' incident appears to have first seen the light of day for political reasons. As for the second question, there is no satisfactory answer to it which does not incriminate Lawrence.

In June 1919, nothing had yet been finally decided concerning Syria, which was still under the ultimate military authority of the British. Nonetheless, Lawrence was by this time in a pretty desperate state, knowing that the French were winning the diplomatic battle for Syria. In fact, the letter found its mark: whether Stirling naively believed what Lawrence wrote or not, he used it as justification for having the Algerian arrested on August 15th in Beirut, inside the French zone, to the fury of the French, whose Ambassador in London protested to the Foreign Office. *The Times* wrote a report on the incident on September 11th, obediently repeating many of the accusations made by Lawrence.[8] This shows, incidentally, the secret power that Lawrence wielded at this time, for he held no position of authority in this matter whatever. But as Reginald Wingate had recently discovered to his cost in Cairo, the official hierarchy could be, and frequently was, overridden by Lawrence.[9]

Whether or not the letter was inspired by an urgent political request, and even if Lawrence's account were true, the only important detail for Stirling concerning Abdelkader was his treachery. So there was no reason to mention the sexual assault. There was doubtless another more secret reason. By this date Lawrence had begun working seriously on *Seven Pillars*. He himself has insisted that the Dera' chapter was one of the first to be written. Once the idea of the story came to him, it is quite possible that Lawrence chose to mention it in the letter to Stirling in order to give it an official birth and legitimacy in the historical context: in other words, to transpose it from the realm of fantasy into fact. It is parallel to the method Lawrence used with John Bruce.

What is interesting here, in this first version of the story, is the coupling of the incident with the treachery of Abdelkader; in the *Seven Pillars* versions Abdelkader is not mentioned, and so there is no political context. The story has generated an independent momentum.

### *A masochistic text?*

I now return to *Seven Pillars* in order to examine once more the text itself; not, this time, to point out the circumstantial improbabilities, but as a literary creation. The first thing that must strike the reader is the highly dramatised presentation. This is particularly evident in the beating scene. The detail of the narrative is remarkable. For example, the instrument of punishment, and its effect:

> a Circassian riding whip, of the sort which gendarmes carried. They were single thongs of supple black hide, rounded, and tapering from the thickness of a thumb at the grip (which was wrapped in silver, with a knob inlaid in black designs) down to a point much finer than a pencil.

> ... a hard white mark like a railway, darkening slowly into crimson, leaped over my skin , and a bead of blood welled up wherever two ridges crossed.

The very precise detail of these descriptions, as well as the phenomena themselves, are typical of masochistic fantasy. In the masochistic context one might use terms like 'loving detail' or 'obsessive detail'. Lawrence uses all his linguistic resources to describe the appalling pain of the torture and each stage, in a complete tour of the realm of pain, is dealt with in similar detail. In a brief pause, lying on the dirty floor, he feels "a delicious warmth, probably sexual, was flowing through me". There is an escalation of both pace and intensity until the climax:

> A roaring was in my head and my eyes went black, while within me the core of life seemed to be heaving slowly up through the rending nerves, expelled from its body by this last and indescribable pang.

A sense of completion. But of what? Is this a description, real or imaginary, of pain-driven orgasm? The power of the scene is created by two levers: the first is the variety and escalation of pain; the second is the unmitigated sadism of the soldiers. The description is virtually restricted to these stereotypes of masochistic fantasy. The final scene hints that he was forced to submit to sodomy, or an attempt at sodomy, by one or more of the soldiers. Suggestive, not explicit. At the very end of the chapter there is an important difference between the Oxford text and the subscribers'. He excised from the latter the following very important lines:

> Probably it had been the breaking of the spirit by that frenzied nerve-shattering pain which had degraded me to beast-level when it made me grovel to it; and which had journeyed with me since, a fascination and terror and morbid desire, lascivious and vicious perhaps, but like the striving of a moth towards its flame. (OX 501-2)

The meaning is now explicit (but only in the Oxford text) that the experience has revealed to him a perverted sexuality; and beyond that, the spirit no longer rules, his body has betrayed him. He is, from now on, dependent on bodily pleasure-in-pain. In the revised edition he ends with these words: "In Dera' that night the citadel of my integrity had been irretrievably lost". He means bodily and spiritual integrity. Note the word "irretrievably".

## MASOCHISM

The point we have now reached I summarise as follows:

- The circumstances in which Lawrence places this happening, and the roles of the participants, are unsupported by evidence and are implausible in a large number of respects.
- Different versions of the incident are incompatible.

- The narrative shows typical characteristics of fiction, and particularly of masochistic fantasy.

However, we still face the question posed by Reik: what is the meaning of displaying one's suffering, shame and punishment to the surrounding world? Is he showing something or hiding something?

The story could be interpreted, as it already has been, as essentially a literary idea: it is the climax, and a very successful one, of the Drama of the Self. The active gives way to the passive. It is the final annihilation of the bright idealism, the emergence of a 'lost' personality wrecked by violence and humiliation. It prepares the development of the broken triumph that the Arab Revolt now becomes for Lawrence. He himself spoke of it in these terms to Garnett, and Garnett thoroughly approved.

All this is true and important. But it still leaves an awful lot unexplained: in the manner of the telling, the sexual orientation of the revelation, the sheer disgusting nature of the humiliation. It is far too provocative to have a purely literary aim; and this would need explaining whether the story is true or whether it is not. I believe that the only interpretation that meets the case is masochistic, that is: that the behaviour of the writer of this passage can be understood through our knowledge of masochistic behaviour – and in no other way, because masochistic behaviour is characterised, indeed explained, by ambiguity, opaqueness, and, especially, obliquity. Nothing is straightforward.

One of the most exhaustive and best known works on the subject is Theodor Reik's *Masochism in Modern Man* (1941). The usefulness of Reik's approach is its breadth. He writes: "I use the word 'masochism' in that general sense as a peculiar attitude to life. Why men unconsciously strive for physical and psychic pain, voluntarily submitting to privations, deliberately accepting sacrifices, shame, humiliation, and disgrace." He also shows, systematically, how various symptoms of masochistic behaviour derive from this "peculiar attitude to life". Rathbone, sixty years later, has written: "His findings... may be peripherally modified, but are unlikely to be invalidated since they are deadly accurate."[10]

Rathbone's own *Anatomy of Masochism* (2001) I have already referred to. This not only provides a good summary of Reik's theory (1939, 1941)[11] and those of others, but above all, it includes a very readable and insightful discussion of T.E. Lawrence himself, surely[12] one of the most interesting cases of masochism of all time!

That Lawrence enjoyed pain is evident to any reader of *Seven*

*Pillars*; he went out of his way to hurt himself, driving his body to the limit and exulting in it, taking no or few precautions to safeguard his body from injury, openly despising it, describing it as 'lumber' and so on. However, his fellow officers, with very few exceptions, and nearly all his post-war admirers, regarded him as a daredevil, motivated solely by high idealism or love of adventure; he incurred pain as a result, they thought. One of the few to disagree was Lieutenant Kirkbride: Lawrence loved suffering, he wrote, and took unnecessary risks. It is not surprising then that his colleagues, as well as his civilian friends, were unaware of anything unhealthy, that they took the Dera' torture to be literal truth, or that the later revelation of Lawrence's flagellation rituals caused a good deal of astonishment. In truth, however:

> (Masochistic behaviour) is the effect of an unconscious desire for punishment. . . . The people involved neither know it nor would they confess to it. Nevertheless, its effects are obvious in their acts and in their thoughts. . . . Unconsciously these people inflict punishment on themselves to which an inner court has sentenced them.[13]

What Reik repeatedly stresses here is the *unconscious* character of masochism. For this reason it is practically incurable, for how can one cure what one is not conscious of, or even solicit help? It is not a mental injury sustained in the course of a normal life, like post-traumatic stress disorder; it is an injury sustained in the very distant past, possibly before consciously accessible memory. Masochistic behaviour is often, perhaps always, in the last resort *compulsive*, the fulfilling of a punishment "to which an inner court has sentenced them". Trying to cure oneself is like Sysiphus in Hades pushing his stone towards the top of the incline but never over the top because what the 'patient' is trying to cure is never the thing itself, merely conscious manifestations of behaviour whose origin lies in the unconscious.

Therefore (if we accept that the Dera' narrative was motivated by Lawrence's masochism), we cannot expect to fully interpret it; there will always remain a last line of darkness. However, a great deal of work has been done since Freud first worked on it, so we can get quite far. There is, using Freud's terminology, 'sexual masochism' and 'moral masochism'. Probably, most people associate the term 'masochism' with the former: a sexual deviation involving whips, bondage, master and slave, the acting of prescribed rituals, pain and orgasm. In 1968, Lawrence's sexual rituals (beginning not later than

1923) were sensationally revealed to the world by the *Sunday Times*. However, among the many who exhibit masochistic symptoms, comparatively few will enter into the rituals of sexual masochism.[14] Dera' supposedly describes the precise moment at which Lawrence passes from one to the other. There he learns that a flogging leads to pleasure, that he is sexually perverted. He learns, in fact, what he is. Whether real or imagined, that is (at the first level) the autobiographical importance of the Dera' chapter.

## ESSENTIAL FEATURES OF MASOCHISM

I now turn to two essential features of masochism (Reik) and examine Lawrence's description in the light of these. They provide an entirely coherent basis for an interpretation.[15]

### 1. Fantasy

Fantasy is absolutely fundamental to masochism. "Phantasy is its source, and at the beginning there is nothing but masochistic phantasy."[16] All masochistic rituals that lead to orgasm are dependent on fantasies and are inhibited without them. The fantasy is not spontaneous and an exact and well-tried sequence must be followed, maximising sexual tension and leading to a climax (of pain and anticipation) that is a trigger for orgasm. Rathbone, summarising Reik, describes the masochistic perversion as "a realization of imagined situations with which the person has long concerned himself, the staging of a drama".[17]

> The mere sight of a dog whip may be sufficient to produce sexual excitement in a masochist, but this is only when there has been a long phantasy preparation since the distant past. The material has been gone over so often that everything is prepared, and the glimpse of a whip can precipitate it at any moment, like the first notes of a familiar melody.[18]

Pain, and its increase, is intimately linked to anticipation of pleasure, but only through fantasy: in a beating, for instance:

> the *phantasied anticipation* helps to bear the suffering and the humiliation. Does it merely help them? No, the phantasy welcomes the discomfort and its increase, for the acme of the discomfort is the signal

for the approaching pleasure. When the blow is felt most distinctly, ... the climactic point of orgasm is reached.[19]

These descriptions cannot but remind of details in the Dera' narrative: the obsessively detailed description of the whip on the one hand, the climax on the other. A narrative in which images become increasingly pain-inducing or debasing, and end in orgasm, is absolutely typical of masochistic fantasy. The stereotypical nature of this narrative suggests that it is a construct, a simulation of a fantasy of an erotogenic-narcissistic kind.

A final point is simply the difficulty of believing that a man of nearly 30 who was so acutely self-aware and so obviously masochistic in character had had until then no personal experience of the relation between pain and sexual pleasure.

### 2. The demonstrative feature

I have already suggested that there was no need for the Dera'a incident to be recorded at all. It exists in a bubble of its own. And even if he had to include it, why relate it in this very provocative form? We have been amply informed of the prolonged psychological battle that Lawrence waged with himself over the inclusion, and exact wording, of this narrative. And yet he would not withdraw it. There can be few more extraordinary insertions into a historical narrative than this. Even the Tafas incident (see below), with all its bloodlust and sadism, stands within the canon of vital action and war. But at Dera'a the hero is shown as a helpless victim, passive, degraded.

The term *demonstrative feature* was coined by Reik to explain a behavioural phenomenon which, he shows, is not merely common but one of the distinctive features of masochism. "In no case of masochism can the fact be overlooked that the suffering, discomfort, humiliation, and disgrace are being shown and so to speak put on display."[20] Display is a *sine qua non* of masochistic behaviour, whether sexual or non-sexual. The most famous, and even frequent, examples in literature are probably from Dostoevski's novels, an author Lawrence enormously admired (but not primarily for these reasons). Suffering without demonstrative intention is not masochistic suffering. The masochist needs witnesses. Many writers have taken Lawrence's efforts with this chapter to have been a source of suffering and a courageous demonstration of openness; but they do not explain why he had to include it at all. Some have suggested that it was a necessary therapy or catharsis (Lawrence himself apparently suggested that to Garnett) but then why is it necessary to achieve this catharsis in public, before an entire readership, whatever the risk to his self-respect? The answer is: because he was a masochist. Ultimately, the compulsion to come clean in a public display is mysterious; but it is stage-managed, hence controlled, by the masochist. If the incident had actually happened, I believe he would never have publicly recorded it.

A more simple example of this feature is the incident on the journey to Wadi Ais when an ill and exhausted Lawrence is pissed on by a camel (OX 187). With another writer, it might be good for a laugh but there is no humour. It is a humiliation. Why mention it then? Yet the fact is that the masochist 'enjoys' this kind of shameful display. Descriptions of being pissed on are common in masochism.

### 3. Demonstrative concealment

If the masochist's suffering, or shame, goes unnoticed, it loses its enjoyable character; however, it is not so simple as that. At the same time, masochists do feel that their exposure is shameful and wish to hide it. There lies the tension and the vacillation. "The most frequent result is a compromise between display and concealment", continues Reik. Bernard Shaw put it beautifully: "Lawrence is a person who goes to hide in a quarry, then puts red flags all round it." It also fits exactly the Dera' confession and Lawrence's future references to it. Reik insists on the term *'demonstrative concealment'*.[21] The two urges are in a relationship of mutual and dynamic dependence and competition. It is partly this vacillation that gives to the Dera' narrative its odd feel. Here is a person confessing the unpublishable in lurid fashion, and yet leaving key facts signalled behind a veil. It is not difficult to understand why he rewrote parts of the text several times (nine, he told Charlotte in a letter dated 30 July 1925). The creation of ambiguity was for Lawrence one of the hallmarks of concealment and mystery, and the Dera' chapter is perhaps his most carefully worked masterpiece as a writer, but he was even more skilful in life.

## THE ORIGIN OF THE DISPLAY

We have gone some way to answering the question *why?* by introducing the compulsion to fantasise and the compulsion to 'demonstrate'. Masochists wish not only to confess, but to display their disgrace in the most *provocative* manner possible. "The demonstrative feature has the primary and essential goal, *often unconscious*, of provoking definite reactions in the environment."[22] This Lawrence undoubtedly succeeded in doing, via *Seven Pillars* initially, and as a follow-up, through his treating the experience as a social reality (see Chapter 15).

All this presupposes that there is some disgrace, suffering, or humiliation, real or imaginary, that must be displayed. It is also characteristic of masochistic display, in that what is shown is usually not what actually triggered it; the original experience has been displaced and/or transmuted. If the argument is accepted that Lawrence is describing an experience that revealed his masochism, but that this did not happen at Dera', then either there was another incident at another time, earlier or later, which has been transposed to Dera' 1917, or there was no such incident at all, in which case the Dera' story is a fantasy rooted in experience of a more general kind.

**Was there another incident?**
What evidence is there for the first possibility ? There are the intriguing words, casually let drop towards the end of the narrative:

> I struggled to my feet, and rocked unsteadily for a moment, wondering that it was not all a dream, and myself back five years ago in the hospital at Khalfati, where something of the sort had happened to me. (OX 500)

A perfect example of demonstrative concealment: something is revealed and something more, the crucial element, is hidden. Similarly in the 1926 edition, where the information has been changed:

> ... and myself back five years ago, a timid recruit at Khalfati, where something less staining of the sort had happened. (R 455)

But for masochistic theory, it would be difficult to understand why Lawrence wanted to reveal these gratuitous pieces of half-baked information.

Khalfati is a village in what was in 1912 the Ottoman Empire, in northern Syria east of Aleppo. From 1911 to 1914 Lawrence had worked more or less continuously excavating the Hittite mound at Carchemish in the same region. Instead of going home in the holidays, he made tours of the region, usually alone but sometimes with his Arab friend, Dahoum. In a report dated 20 August, 1917 René Doynel de St. Quentin, the French military attaché in Cairo during the war, who quickly became an admirer and close friend of Lawrence, wrote:

"He travelled throughout Syria and Palestine, sometimes on horseback or by motorbike but more usually on foot dressed in Bedouin costume, so well disguised that one day he was picked up by some Turkish recruiters and did three weeks of service at Urfa before managing to escape." The source of this story is not given but since a large part of this report is devoted to Lawrence and his life at Carchemish, the source is clearly Lawrence himself.[23]

Urfa, the former Edessa of the Crusaders, is not far from Khalfati and both places were visited by Lawrence. He kept a diary of one journey, made in the summer of 1911, which has been published with photographs he took.[24] Lawrence gave a further version under questioning by Liddell Hart in 1933, in which he reported that he was wearing Arab dress, and that he and an unnamed workman had both been kicked downstairs into a dungeon but released the next day through a bribe. Lawrence would evidently have us believe (in the Dera' hints) that at Khalfati he received some severe corporal punishment. If that did happen, it could well have been the source for the Dera' incident; if nothing of the sort, it would, in Lockman's words, "be even more consistent with a perverse urge in Lawrence to invent such fantasies".[25] I entirely agree.

Another similar incident is related by S.C. Rolls, Lawrence's driver in the last months of the desert war. Rolls recounts that, while at Azrak with Lawrence, he was shown a well or cellar. "Once I was kept a prisoner in that dungeon for months", Lawrence told him, and showed some scratchings as 'evidence'.[26] Both the St. Quentin report and the story related by Rolls date to before the end of the war, and the former is pre-Dera'. That is evidence that fantasies of the Dera' type were in Lawrence's mind around this period. With Dera', that makes three imprisonment stories relating to different places; there is no evidence for any one of them.

## THE OBLIQUE CONFESSION

The second hypothesis is that no incident like Dera' ever happened anywhere. It is in that case a coded statement of a masochistic perversion, expressed as an involuntary experience but narrated as a masochistic fantasy including elements of punishment, flagellation, pain, pleasure, and degradation. The perversion of masochism engendered in Lawrence deep feelings of guilt, which could not be directly confessed, and at the same time could not be buried. The half-true, half-hidden confession we have here, a story in which he was forced to confront a masochism of which he had not been aware, was as far as he was willing to go.

Once again, Reik is able to provide revelatory insight from his own clinical observations. The need to display one's shame and humiliation serves the more overt purpose of the *demonstrative feature*; but this display has another more subtle and more practical purpose, one well known to conjurors, and indeed to spies and counterespionage experts:

> If something which otherwise would be concealed is put on the surface, it is a good guess that something else is meant to be hidden at the same time. The conspicuousness of the one side is meant to effect a concealment on the other side.[27]

This is the secret meaning of the public display and it takes us a step further because it reveals an intention to hide something even behind something normally regarded as highly confidential. This is precisely the major characteristic of the story Lawrence invented to Bruce (*see* Chapter 4). There, the secret element put on the surface was the shame of his illegitimacy; the hidden element was the perversion which, like the beating in Dera', is presented as a punishment forced on him, in this case by the threat of blackmail by a sadistic uncle. The ostensible, but secondary motive is to win Bruce's sympathy and co-operation in getting him out of a hole; the hidden, but primary objective is to persuade him to co-operate in beating rituals.

In the Dera'a situation it is even clearer. What is put on the surface, in the most alarming and convincing manner possible, is a shaming but involuntary experience, evoking pity, that reveals to him and his readers that beating was a route to sexual pleasure. What is hidden is his previous knowledge of this condition (probably of long standing) and his existing dependence, not necessarily in 1917, but certainly by the time at which this chapter was written in this form, i.e. between mid-1919 up to mid-1922, when the need for flagellation was becoming increasingly irresistible.

## CONCLUSION

To explain the display in purely rational terms is necessarily speculative. The punishment that he underwent has earned him the sympathy of an entire world, of several generations. A compulsion to come clean after the war and all the destruction of innocence that had gone with it, to seize the unique opportunity of his autobiography to show that something crucial in his life had changed, that nothing was ever going to be the same again, underlies this insurpassable display of masochistic fantasy. He needed the freedom it would give him. I do not see it as a description of a traumatic experience, but as a dramatised presentation of a *moral* breakdown or disorientation. I do not mean 'morals' in the narrow sense, I mean the very puritan values that had underpinned his life, motivation, and action. In Lawrence's psyche, Dera', like its sadistic counterpart at Tafas, was symbolically true and therefore autobiographically valid.

# CHAPTER 14

# THE OUTSIDER (2)

Back in Azraq Lawrence was summoned to Jerusalem to take part in General Allenby's ceremonial entry into the city that had fallen after nearly 400 years of Turkish overlordship. It was an honour to be invited and the trip no doubt revived him and restored his motivation. From now on, with Allenby's HQ at Beersheba, the British are nearer, while the Arabs seem to be further away. Lawrence's role is increasingly a liaison between Allenby and the Arab army, meaning not only Feisal but the British officers with him. In fact, the Arab adventure is entering its final stage. He picks a substantial bodyguard from among the Ageyl and messes with them. They are his paid servants and they constantly escort him. He is like a Sheikh, a desert condottiero. It means he can go anywhere he wants without needing any other assistance. But at the same time it isolates him. His raids against the railway continue but are now increasingly mechanised and he enjoys the company of British officers, mechanics, drivers, and engineers, and the wild races across the hard sands in Rolls Royce tenders and Talbots. Fighting deluxe, as he called it.

Little by little, his sense of solidarity with the Arabs begins to crumble. He is obsessed with the notion of fraud. There is still the direct fraud of the Sykes–Picot treaty, but more generally now the fraud of being there at all, an alien among Arabs. (I was) "conscious always of my strangeness, and of the fraudulence of an alien's preaching others' liberty" (OX 503). In Tafileh, whither he followed the Arabs with his bodyguard, Subhi al-Umari sees him as if alone, as if he belongs nowhere. Snowbound there with his bodyguard, in lice-ridden village rooms, he escapes down to Akaba and returns with gold; long journeys through mud, snow, sleat and ice. After this merciless self-punishment, he quarrels with Emir Zeid over the misuse of funds. He has reached a point of moral and physical exhaustion and decides to resign: "My will had gone and I feared to be alone, lest the winds of circumstance, or power, or lust, blow my empty soul away."

By this time he was not alone so much as lonely. He shunned the British officers socially; he was tired of the Arabs. As he informed us in Chapter 2, "I had dropped one form and not taken on the other . . . with a resultant feeling of intense loneliness in life and a contempt, not for other men, but for all that they do. Such detachment came to a man exhausted by physical effort and isolation." In a fine chapter describing the ICC with the Bedouin in Wadi Rum (OX Chapter 113), "homesickness came over me, reminding me vividly of my outcast life among these Arabs" and like a refrain at the end of each paragraph, he reminds himself also of the fraud he is committing for his beloved England (OX 572, R 514).

The second and final climax of *Seven Pillars* is Book X, comprising the 'Great Raid' on the railways out of Dera'a, the capture of Damascus and three days of Lawrencian rule there. The key manifestations in Book X are the first encounters with the Allied Army on the one hand and the bloodbath of the Turkish retreat on the other; finally, the transitory triumph in Damascus and, at the personal level, the glory of achievement, then emptiness and solitude.

From Chapter OX 133/R 116 the final phase begins as the united Arab force – the Bedouin leaders and the regular detachment under Nuri Said – cross the Hejaz railway and the Damascus road to await the retreating Turks. Allenby has sent a message to Feisal: "Thanks to our combined efforts, the Turkish Army is defeated and is everywhere in full retreat . . . it rests upon us now, by the redoubled energy of our attack, to turn defeat into destruction".[1]

> It was a glorious fresh morning. We had not passed the crest before we met Nasir and Nuri Shaalan and Talal. . . . Our joined forces marched with a heady breeze in the teeth northward across these rich plough-lands, between Saida and Gharija: fat, happy villages. Over the harvested fields, whose straw had been rather plucked than reaped, grew thistles, tall as a child, but now yellow and dried and dead. The wind snapped the more hollow ones off, short at the root, and they fell pitch-polling on their branchy tops, along the level ground, thistle blowing against thistle, and interlocking their spines till a huge matted ball of them careered merrily across the fallows.

This is Lawrence at his descriptive best. We are in the cultivated region of the Hauran, near Dera'. Note the amazingly fine detail. And there is a note of happiness that becomes one of dawning triumph:

> Men rode up every minute from both sides and joined us, while by each village the adventurous young ran out on foot, and joined our ranks. As we moved on, so closely knit in the golden sunlight, we seemed to grow a character, to become an organism, in whose pride each of us was uplifted. . . . it was something exterior we had created, a work of art. (OX 769)

The narrative now gathers pace and maintains it to the end. It is a fine achievement: a hectic jostling of movements and happenings. The first part centres on the Turkish retreat and the Arab pursuit. The climax of this, as far as *Seven Pillars* is concerned, is the massacre at Tafas (OX 775-9; R 652-55).

## TAFAS

Tafas is the village in the Hauran near Dera' where Kirkbride witnessed a massacre by Turks and revenge killings by villagers and Bedu. Lawrence's account follows to a large extent the details given by him in a report published in the *Arab Bulletin* on 22 October 1918, entitled 'The Destruction of the Fourth Army'.[2]

There are three scenes: what he saw in the village; the death of the Sheikh of the village, Talal al-Hareidhin; and the two subsequent massacres of Turks, the second the mowing down by machine gun of a largely unarmed body of two hundred men already made prisoner.

In the first scene, we are made to witness the last pathetic moments of a little girl about to die from a savage wound; and "the body of a woman folded across [a low wall], bottom upwards, nailed there by a saw bayonet whose haft stuck hideously into the air from between her naked legs. She had been pregnant, and about her lay others, perhaps twenty in all, variously killed, but set out in accord with an obscene taste". . . . I said: "The best of you brings me the most Turkish dead" (OX 776).

In the second scene, we witness the lone charge of Talal, superbly narrated, both heroic and agonising. Then the Arab massacres. "By my orders we took no prisoners, for the only time in our war."

> There lay on us a madness born of the horror of Tafas or of its story, so that we killed and killed, even blowing in the heads of the fallen and of the animals; as though their death and running blood could slake the agony in our brains.

The final episode to this bloodbath is a repetition, in revenge for an Arab found pinned to the ground with bayonets run through him "like a collected insect" by a group of Turkish prisoners, who are duly shot en masse until "at last their heap ceased moving".

To get a detailed idea of how Lawrence composed a narrative of such a brutal nature it is useful to compare it with the *Arab Bulletin* report. This report is long and the Tafas incident is only a part of it. It is written for the most part in an appropriately objective style (the last ride of Talal is given some colour, however) and this is in part carried over into the book. However, there is in the report one sentence justifying the order "We ordered no prisoners and the men obeyed" as follows:

> The common delusion that the Turk is a clean and merciful fighter led some of the British troops to criticise Arab methods a little later – but they had not entered Turaa or Tafas or watched the Turks swing their wounded by the hands and feet into a burning railway truck, as had been the lot of the Arab army at Jerdun.[3]

This justification (the criticism very likely refers mainly to that of General Barrow – see below) is omitted from *Seven Pillars*. There, as in the killing in Wadi Kitan, he does not spare us the most naturalistic details. He pulls out all the stops to shock his readers and prepare them for the terrible and bloody revenge: the death of the child is excruciatingly pathetic, the charge of Talal superbly heroic, the Arabs hysterical. Yet, as in all his scenes of extreme brutality, except those for which Turks are responsible, he essays a manner that is coldly objective and eschews any justification – a striking contrast, to say the least. "I do not say that this is good or bad", he seems to tell us, "I say that this is how it was. If you want to judge, judge without my help. I am indifferent."[4]

### *Lawrence of Arabia*, 1962

What happens when an enigmatic book "not written to be read", with a very particular idea of autobiographical Truth, is translated into a film epic for all the people of the world? In 1962 the film *Lawrence of Arabia* was praised as one of the greatest epic pictures of all time and it still maintains this reputation fifty years on, a remarkable feat. There was just one minus: the scene at Tafas that shows Lawrence wallowing in blood, after ordering "no prisoners", raised a storm of protest, creating an international notoriety. In the van of the protest were, not surprisingly, those who had known him:

his brother Arnold, his biographer Liddell Hart, F.G. Peake of the Arab Legion and Alec Kirkbride. These individuals attacked the film for sensationalising the scene and Lawrence's role in it, and proceeded to present their evidence. There are two separate issues: first, did he give the order to kill prisoners (which he admits to in both the report and the book)? Second, and chiefly, did he participate in the blood-lust, as he claims in the notorious paragraph quoted above?

There were quite a few British and Arab officers about, though not actually with Lawrence (Young, Kirkbride, Ali Jawdat, Peake), all of whom insist that Lawrence did no such thing; on the contrary, they claim, he did everything he could to stop the Bedu from killing the prisoners. Peake's account is convincing.[5] They are not, however, able to tell us why in that case he said that he *did* give the order, still less why he wrote that he took part in the slaughter, but some have tried. One suggestion has been that he considered himself responsible for the Bedu and therefore nobly accepted the blame for what he could not stop them from doing; thereby also in some way excusing them. This is Liddell Hart's view, and Peake's. This is a weak argument as it stands; one feels there must be more to it than that. And quite possibly there is. It is worth reading carefully Barrow's account of his utter disgust with the Bedu in Dera' (below), Lawrence's attempt to defend them and his very strong contempt of Barrow that is evident in the account in *Seven Pillars*, in order to suspect that Lawrence's defence of the Bedu is a retrospective answer to Barrow. There is also some belief in the legitimacy of revenge, as Lawrence himself argued forcefully in the report. His brother stated that he believed that TE gave the order "but makes plain, I should have thought, that he did so because he shared the ungovernable fury of every Arab".[6] Mack tentatively suggests an unconscious desire for revenge as a possible motive, related to the brutality of his treatment at Dera'. None of these suggestions adequately excuse the massacre of unarmed prisoners by a British officer. Whatever Lawrence meant, he disdained to explain.

In the *Iliad*, Achilles, avenging the death of Patroclus, wallows in Trojan blood, and then, after killing Hector, strips him of his armour and drags the body round the walls of Troy in front of his widow. The Bedouin also believed in bloody revenge. Homer's Greeks stripped their victims of their arms and possessions; at Dera' (see below) the Arabs did likewise; Lawrence told General Barrow: "This is their idea of war". He was well aware of parallels between his idealised Bedouin and Homer's idealised Greeks.

The strength and scope of the protest led the screenplay writer, Robert Bolt, to write an 'apologia'. To start with, Bolt makes it crystal clear that (for the entire film) "*Seven Pillars of Wisdom* was my prime, almost my only source for the screenplay".[7] Peake wrote: "It is to be regretted that a film showing Lawrence of Arabia should give the impression that he was a callous person or rather enjoyed seeing such horrible scenes. It would have been no less interesting and far more truthful had he been shown rushing about on foot trying to persuade the Sheikhs to call back their men." Far more truthful? To an observer, no doubt. But Bolt was not an observer, he was a reader of *Seven Pillars*. What is Lawrence's idea of truth there? Against Peake and Liddell Hart, Bolt argues that "if they are right . . . they are calling Lawence's veracity into question at a crucial – I would say *the* crucial passage of his book. . . . if we are to doubt his veracity here, why not elsewhere? I could not decently accept as truth whatever was suitable to a screen hero and reject as falsehood whatever wasn't. That, to my mind, really would have been a belittlement."[8] It is a valid argument.

Lean and Bolt were perfectly aware that not everything in *Seven Pillars* is literally true but they were also aware that this was the truth that Lawrence meant to show. And they showed it. It should come as no surprise, for *Seven Pillars of Wisdom* is the story on which the colossal success of the film was built. *Lawrence of Arabia* shows Lawrence largely as he portrays himself in the scenes extracted from it; and the film is essentially a series of scenes (as are all films of its type): the meeting with Feisal, the rescue of Gasim, his execution of an Arab to prevent a blood feud, the triumph at Akaba, the raids on the railway, the meetings with Allenby; Dera' and Tafas; the 'end of the affair' in Damascus. Lawrence has a great sense of the dramatic; naturally, it is this aspect of the book that Lean and Bolt have taken by the scruff of the neck and exploited for all that it is worth. As a whole, the film is nothing like the book. Its aims are different. The book reveals itself as a creative autobiography; the film as a historical drama. In the latter, the hero's dream is frustrated by historical circumstances; in the book it is far more complex. The Tafas scene does not really 'gel' in the film; the sudden plunge into an unexplained sadism seems arbitrary. That is one reason why it went down so badly with so many people; it is too brutal a jolt from the romantic and noble image that lies at the heart of the film. In *Seven Pillars* the incident is also quite unexpected, but we have been surprised already several times by "strange free disclosures", and we look for reasons beyond the obvious.

"Many of the events in it are . . . morally shocking or psychologically weird", Bolt writes. We are now talking about the second issue: did Lawrence take part in the wanton killing? Bolt gives a strong description of what happens when you translate words into film:

> If the film was to be half-way honest then, the massacre had to be shown. Consider that. "Others' lives became toys to break and throw away" is a statement, but a poeticised statement; it is all metaphor. To put it on the screen you have to uncover what it means in terms of concrete action (men kill other men, wantonly, foolishly, as children break toys), take a picture of that, and show it; the comforting blanket of metaphor has gone. It looks quite different and arouses a different response.[9]

Lawrence also wrote: "We killed and killed, even blowing in the heads of the fallen and of the animals." There is nothing metaphorical about that. Nonetheless, even that is not as powerful as the visual image. Nobody ever protested about this passage until 1962.

For Bolt, a deservedly famous writer of plays of some psychological depth, "the massacre at Tafas could not be presented merely as one incident among others. A man must have supped full indeed of horrors if he could match it elsewhere in his life. It must be crucial. The seeds of it must have been in him from his past." Here, we are getting nearer to the truth. But Bolt evidently did not consider that Lawrence's insertion of himself into the killing was a fantasy trip. This is introspective fantasy-autobiography. To repeat Lawrence:

> I aimed at providing a meal for the fellow-seekers with myself. For this the whole experience, and emanations and surroundings (background and foreground) of a man are necessary . . .

### WITH BARROW IN DERA'

As in war, the narrative does not digest its horrors; it rushes on, leaving Tafas behind and carrying its legacy unseen and unheard. He orders a Rualla leader to gather the tribesmen and sets off after midnight for Dera', taking Kirkbride with him, whose camel is broken by Lawrence's urgent pace in the night. The speed of the uninterrupted narrative seems to be saying: 'Do not think about it'. He arrives at dawn and there is met by more trouble.

Dera' had been evacuated by the Turks who left behind many wounded. The Rualla, who had occupied the town the night before, had plundered all night and were in a state of frenzy. Lawrence and

Nasir had arrived at dawn and, with the indefatigable Kirkbride and a detachment of Nuri Said's regulars who arrived shortly afterwards, they established what they considered some degree of order. General Barrow arrived at 9.30. Barrow's cavalry division, a force composed of both Indian and British troops, was in the van of Allenby's lightning advance. This was the first meeting of the war between Allenby's regulars and Arabs (excepting the short organized visit to Feisal's camp of the Imperial Camel Corps) and it was not cordial. Lawrence's account is quite exceptionally hostile to Barrow. It bears many of the same features that characterise his 'bad' meetings with other adversaries: continuous self-justification, accusation, belittlement of character, sarcasm, and the rubbishing of his opponent's outlook as against his own.

Barrow, *Seven Pillars* narrates, had not expected to find Arabs in possession of Dera' and was displeased, if not shocked. Lawrence draws his fire by forcing him to be a 'guest' of the occupiers, showing him that he was not needed because everything was thoroughly organized, and persuading him to salute the Sharifian flag. In a forceful passage, Lawrence opposes his ideals to those of the disciplinarian, personified by Barrow (or Captain Bligh of the Bounty):

> I had studied Barrow and was ready for him, from the day of his being ordered to cross Jordan. Years before, he had published his confession of faith in Fear as the main motive of moral activity in war and peace. Now I found Fear an over-rated motive . . . . In my view, war and government could only be maintained by people whose fear had been conquered – or rather transmuted. Instead of making them afraid, I tried to make them eager for some remote, unintelligible, unearthly ideal (in this Arab instance Freedom was what we called it). . . . Therefore Barrow and I could never have worked together, as I could have no alliance with his pedant belief of scaring men into heaven: it was better that we part at once. (OX 782)

According to Hubert Young,[10] who had arrived with the Sherifian regulars, Barrow "entered Deraa to find it in an appalling state owing to the excesses of the Bedouin. Until the Sherifian detachment arrived, there was no sign of any organised Arab force, and he naturally hesitated to leave at the mercy of what he regarded as a pack of ragamuffins a town which had been evacuated by the Turks as a result of his own advance". Barrow seems to have severely berated Lawrence, who defended himself with "a mixture of schoolboy cheek" and "an assumption of omniscience and of being in General

Allenby's confidence which Barrrow found extremely trying". Barrow claimed in his memoirs, in a scene that is like a preview of the Turkish Barracks scene in Book X, that the place was full of dead, dying and still living Turks who begged for mercy and water, which he ordered to be given them. In the railway station he found Bedouin going through a train full of sick Turks, whom the Arabs were stripping of their clothes and whatever else they could find and then cutting their throats. "A revolting scene . . . far exceeding in its savagery anything that has been known in the conflicts between nations in the past 120 years" is Barrow's comment. He continues:

> I asked Lawrence to remove the Arabs. He said he couldn't 'as it was their idea of war'. I replied 'It is not our idea of war, and if you can't remove them, I will.' He said 'if you attempt to do that, I shall take no responsibility for what happens.' I answered 'That's all right. I will take the responsibility', and at once gave orders for our men to clear the station. This was done and nothing untoward happened. All the Arabs were turned off the train and it was picquetted by our sentries. I then went with Foster to the Sherifian headquarters and arranged with the Arab commander, Muni (sic. i.e. Nuri) Bey, that during the march to Damascus we should remain west of the railway and his forces should keep east of it. He agreed. Lawrence was present but took no part in the conversation.[11]

I have quoted this because, if it is true, it would explain, at least in part, the bitter resentment that Lawrence gives vent to in his account. He would have felt humiliated, something he never forgave. He is shown unable to control his own Arabs and then sidelined. One might wonder if there is not some connection between this scene and his assumption of solidarity with the Bedouin at Tafas and their 'idea of war'. Barrow's account is itself self-justificatory but probably less distorted than Lawrence's. Young's account attempts to be impartial, but on the evidence he gives it favours Barrow's version. Himself an Indian Army officer but attached to the Sharifian army, Young harboured feelings of some contempt for the Bedouin.

Whatever the truth, in *Seven Pillars* this scene confirms Lawrence's consciousness of his outsider position. "Barrow and I could never have worked together." He compares the Indian rank and file in Dera' with his Bedu and takes a swipe at their officers:

> The Indians round it (Deraa station) had angered me by their out-of-placeness. The essence of the desert was the lonely moving individual,

> the son of the road, apart from the world as in a grave. These troopers, in flocks like slow sheep, looked not worthy of the privelege of space. ... The manner of the British officers towards their men struck horror into my bodyguard.

The British regular officer, especially Indian Army, offends everything he has worked for himself: their easy self-assurance, the assumption of being the ruling class, that is the outcome of the public school education that he never had, the recourse to a system of hierarchical discipline to preserve their ascendancy. In this chapter, written with such vehemence, he defines himself against them through his support for the Bedouin, symbol of individuality and freedom. It is the climactic scene in a process of conflict that began with Vickery, but we have come a long way. While at that time Lawrence pleaded his lack of professionalism and unfittedness for leadership, here he contrasts two irreconcilable codes of behaviour, attitudes to life.

Lawrence's is a vivid narrative, but, from the literary standpoint, it might be seen as a missed opportunity. The entire story is distorted in order to put him in the right, and Barrow in the wrong; whereas at Tafas, he does not excuse himself and leaves us to draw our own conclusions. What the two accounts have in common is that behind each lies something unacknowledged. If his aim in *Seven Pillars* was to recount a tragedy, would it not have been much more effective here to simply relate what really happened. The material is there all right: his lack of control over the Bedouin, coinciding with the fatal arrival of the British-Indian army under the commander who personifies an everlasting opponent who must always win in the end; his humiliation and solitude. Instead he created yet another exemplary story of a personal victory.

The final scene in Damascus, at the Turkish barracks 'hospital', when another stereotypical British regular officer, in the Medical corps this time, turns up and berates Lawrence over the conditions there, will be remembered by those who have seen the film *Lawrence of Arabia*.

> 'Scandalous, disgraceful, outrageous, ought to be shot ... ' ... he smacked me over the face and stalked off, leaving me more ashamed than angry, for in my heart I felt that he was right, and that anyone who pushed through to success a rebellion of the weak against their masters must come out of it so stained that nothing in the world would make him clean.

There is no tragedy, no catharsis. There cannot be that, for a man who feels guilty for having espoused the cause he did. This is the last round in the drama of the Self. It ends in self denial. When all is done, his task completed, he hears the alien cry of the Muezzin. And goes home.

CHAPTER

# 15

# THE BIOGRAPHICAL ENVIRONMENT AND SEQUEL

We have now finished with the direct focus on events, of one sort or another, narrated by Lawrence in *Seven Pillars*. In this final chapter of Section 2, I turn to what we can learn about Lawrence's state of mind, social attitudes and morale, before, during and after the war in Arabia. The aim is to discover what the Arabian experience did to him and why his life changed so radically after it. For that, we need to begin at the beginning, before Arabia. There is also a more specific thesis, which opposes that held by Mack and J.M. Wilson, among many others; it is that Lawrence's post-war behaviour does not depend on the theory of a single traumatic event (the beating and rape at Dera') in order to be understood.

### THE ORIGINS OF EMOTIONAL ISOLATION

Looked at with retrospective wisdom, 2 Polstead Road seems to have offered a promising environment for a narcissistic-masochistic development: the narrow puritan upbringing, the dominating mother, the son's desire to at once defy her and please her, the beatings received from her, apparently on his bare buttocks. Is this sufficient explanation? I somehow doubt it. Was there something else, some devastating blow to a personality as yet unformed, beyond conscious memory? We will never know.

We do know that, from an early age, he was showing character traits that he would become famous for and which we judge positive: ambition, will, the desire to achieve, to master and be in control of his environment, self-reliance. He liked to show off, exaggerate his achievements, set himself ambitious targets, test himself physically and mentally. He was very much a self-starter and, although he enjoyed the company of his peers, he did not depend on it. He was not afraid of taking risks and he liked adventure. He was fascinated by the past, especially the medieval past: pottery, brasses, military architecture and armour, literature.

At school he was not unfriendly or standoffish but he did not reveal emotional needs and did not seek friendship that involved the sharing of emotion. Even at that time, it was noticed that he did not seek physical contact, though he was happy to take part in informal wrestling matches. He had his own agenda, and his friendships were totally centred on his interests. "Our acquaintance ripened under his desire to share with others an already masterly appreciation of the treasures of Oxford", wrote his schoolfriend C.F.C. Beeston. It was the same with Vyvyan Richards several years later when an Oxford undergraduate. With or without companions, we have the development of a super-ambitious programme of activities which are directed both towards knowledge and excellence but, in human terms, are entirely self-centred. They manifest continually the importance of achievement and mastery, including the mastery of his own body. Mack wrote: "There was no discernible transition from early childhood to adolescence, as we understand adolescence, with its frequent rebellious storms and the development of sexual interests. Lawrence had, in my opinion, no real adolescence at all." And he goes on to quote Bernard Shaw: "His great abilities and interests were those of a highly gifted boy."[1] There must come a time for friendship (for its own sake), for sharing of emotion and the fragility of the self, if not for sexual love. Wilson claims that the idea of sexual relations became abhorrent as a result of the Dera' experience. But in what state were they before? It is important to remember that he was already twenty-nine years old by then but he had had only one experience with another human being which could perhaps be called love, that with the young Dahoum in Carchemish. It involved no sex, and we do not know whether there was any emotion on Dahoum's side, though there was certainly warm friendship and admiration. If there was, nobody noticed it. Lawrence's feeling for Dahoum is also difficult to know, partly because of his secretiveness, partly because of his compulsion to retrospectively romanticise. The absence of an emotional life led, in his quiet moments, to romantic yearning when the war separated them. As with all romantics, the greater the distance from the beloved, the more he is longed for. It was not only *physical* distance; he was attracted to Arabs because they were different to us.

One must avoid being wise in retrospect. To show a passionate interest in certain aspects of the world you live in, to shun the banalities of social intercourse, to be single-minded, to pursue the ideal of self-reliance does not lead necessarily to a sexual narcissism. Lawrence was not anti-social. He had plenty of friends and he enjoyed having them. We have all met adolescents, young men, who are self-contained and socially undemonstrative, who can only be reached through their interests. Was Lawrence so very different? It has been argued, by Mack, that while there may have been a masochistic latency – and there obviously was, a perverted sexuality was not inevitable. He would agree, however, that one is much more vulnerable to the vicissitudes of life and to stress if one lacks the ability to share eventual emotional or sexual needs. One ignores nature at one's peril. At university his greatest friend was Richards. But it seemed to Richards, who wrote after Lawrence's death that he had been in love with him, that Lawrence was asexual, innocent of any sexual feeling whatever. But of course he meant: the expression of sexual feelings towards others. Lawrence's proposal to Janet Laurie, an old friend of the family, made when he was still an undergraduate, and attempted without the slightest semblance of any courtship, so sudden that she could not help laughing, demonstrated his complete lack of savoir-faire and ardour. One can understand the shyness, but there is something half-hearted about this episode, an absence of passion, tenderness or enthusiasm, as if it was a duty to himself that he had to get out of the way, or as if somebody had suggested it. It was never repeated, to Janet or to anybody else. Mack recounts fascinating interviews with both Janet in 1965 and a childhood friend, Midge Hall. He concludes on good evidence that Lawrence, who had known her from childhood, loved her "but he was unable to share his emotions".[2]

## THE ORDEAL OF WAR IN ARABIA-SYRIA

What happened in Arabia? He gave himself. It all fell apart. Why did he not come back and continue with archaeology or hand-print books with his friend? His home, Oxford? Why was there nothing to fall back on?

It is certainly tempting to blame the Dera' incident. Up to the point of his departure for Arabia, Lawrence's psychological development can be studied in the same way as anyone else's, i.e. from his behaviour, from reminiscences, from his letters. But thanks to *Seven Pillars of Wisdom* everything now becomes a blur. Or to put it another way,

Lawrence creates a double. We only have to read the opening chapters of the Oxford text to be confronted by a writer who is living in different worlds, in which the imagination and the passion for self-justification are mythologising reality. And yet this is the book that has guided, if not dictated, our perception of T.E. Lawrence during the war, and afterwards; and finally in the film *Lawrence of Arabia*, almost totally. Let us remember that there is absolutely no evidence whatever for the Dera' incident. It is a story told by Lawrence in *Seven Pillars*.

'What was it (the war) *really* like', one asks oneself. *Seven Pillars* abounds with observations on Lawrence but they all come from Lawrence himself. The book contains scarcely a single *personal* observation on him made by anyone else; this is part of the loneliness, opaqueness, and oppressive sameness of the book; he seems to move in a cloud that makes him untouchable, separates him off from what are called human relations (always excepting the momentary solidarity of action). The Arabs are shadowy figures, there and yet somehow not quite there.

Fortunately, there are the letters; few, but precious. The highly perceptive French orientalist Louis Massignon, who met Lawrence during the war, wrote: "His letters are infinitely more true than his books". Throughout the war TE continued to write to his parents. There are a few other letters to friends. There are also the memoirs of his colleagues, but it has to be said that these rarely tell us much about the inner Lawrence. Accurate, though usually very brief, observations, such as those recorded by the undeferential: Young, Kirkbride, Massignon, and Matte help one to build up a picture of sorts but they are a series of fragments; not enough to get any reliable impression of the link between the inner and the outer man.

The letters to his parents, faithfully gathered together and published by the eldest brother Bob, are admirable, even moving. One might call them models of the letter parents back home would hope to get from their son on a war front. They are calm, conscientious, considerate, always ready to give news of mutual acquaintances, showing interest in other members of the family and offering advice, especially to the youngest, Arnie. They seem to illustrate that his parents meant more to him than has been realised, as a unit. Some, like the one below, are full of news. There is no sign here of the emotional tension or self-pity of *Seven Pillars*. Yet he does not conceal his state of mind. Taking the letters as a whole, the two most striking characteristics are the comparative cheerfulness and the lack of any sudden change in their tone; noticeably, the absence of any sudden change after the Dera' incident. The first post-Dera' letter was written from Cairo on December 14th (1917). I reproduce about half of it; it is interesting enough in itself, and in its vivid contrast to the closed world of *Seven Pillars*. It is so much more human.

> Well here I am in Cairo again, for two nights, coming from Akaba via Jerusalem. I was in fortune, getting to Jerusalem just in time for the official entry of General Allenby.[3] It was impressive in its way – no show, but an accompaniment of machine gun & anti-aircraft fire, with aeroplanes circling over us continually. Jerusalem has not been taken for so long: nor has it ever fallen so tamely before. These modern wars of large armies and long-range weapons are quite unfitted for the historic battlefields.
>
> I wrote to you last from Azrak, about the time we blew up Jemal Pasha and let him slip away from us.[4] After that I stayed for ten days or so there, and then rode down to Akaba in three days:[5] good going, tell Arnie: none of his old horses would do as much as my old camel. Tomorrow I go off again to Akaba, for a run towards Jauf, if you know where that is. Mother will be amused to learn that they are going to send me to England for a few days in the spring, if all works well till then: so this is my last trip possibly. Don't bank on it, as the situation out here is so full of surprise turns, and my finger is one of those helping to mix the pie. An odd life, but it pleases me, on the whole.
>
> . . . Many thanks to Father for investing that cheque of mine. When I stay out in Arabia for months on end I spend comparatively little, for the Government buys my camels, & the Sherif pays the men. I have only clothes (cheap things Arab clothes) and personal presents to pay for. On the other hand, when I get to Cairo I have many commissions, from Arab sheikhs, for things they want – and if they have been useful, or will be useful, they get them free of charge! My acquaintances are legion, or the whole population from Rabegh to Deraa. . . .
>
> The French Government has stuck another medal on to me: a croix de guerre this time. I wish they would not bother, but they never consult one before doing these things. . . .
>
> This letter should get to you about Christmas time, I suppose, as few mails have been sunk of late. That will mean that you are getting at least fortnightly letters from me, which should put off any anxiety you may otherwise feel. Mr Hogarth[6] of course hears from me every few days, so that his information is much fuller than anything I can ever give you.

I'm in the proud position of having kept a diary all the year 1917 to date. It is rather a brief one, consisting only of the place where I sleep the night of each day: and the best thing about it is the disclosure that ten successive nights in one place is the maximum stop in the 12 months, and the roll of places slept in is about 200.[7] This makes it not astonishing that my Arabic is nomadic!

I hope Arnie is getting on with his army subjects. It would be a useful thing to know how to drive a car, but judging from the papers there must be fewer cars in Oxford than in Akaba. . . . I'm (also) sending you a sheet of Hejaz 1 piastre stamps.[8] You said that you had not received any of this value. These are of course 1st edition, and are worth a good deal more than you would expect! Lady Wingate[9] gave them to me, for of course it is impossible to find them anywhere for sale.

Here endeth this letter,                      N [for Ned]

Certainly, this is not the letter one would expect from a man who, just three weeks before, was beaten without mercy, raped, and suffered a life-long psychological trauma. The name of Dera' comes up perfectly naturally; and life 'pleases him on the whole'. Of course, one can lie, conceal; and it is part of my thesis that Lawrence was highly skilful at it. But this letter is so outward-looking, so interested in the small details of life, so calm, so expansive, and indeed so like his letters of past years from France and Carchemish, that it is hard to believe that he has just gone through an experience that has broken him.

The evidence suggests that we have to do with a matter of gradual exhaustion and disillusionment, the second partly the result of the first. He pushed himself for a long period beyond all sense, losing contact with any kind of normal life. He had not sold himself to Freedom, but to Success. This can be dated roughly between October 1917 and March 1918. At the end of October, Hogarth wrote: "He is not well and talks rather hopelessly about an Arab future he once believed in."[10] After the capture of Akaba and the assignment of the Arab forces to Allenby's command, Lawrence is placed in a position of extraordinary responsibility. The demands on him are ever more complex, there is much more at stake. More and more British officers arrive. He sets himself apart from them and lives close to his Bedouin bodyguard. On the one hand, he is determined to stick with the Bedouin, to make them count, to raid with them; indeed, this is necessary for his well-being: "Am very fit and cheerful enough when things are not too hectic. Going up country is always a relief, because then there is only one thing at a time to do", he wrote in September,[11] in a first sign of overstrain. On the other hand, he is the slave of Allenby, determined to meet the objectives he has been asked to pursue (and which he has agreed to), to show that he and the Arabs can deliver the goods. He seems fatally motivated by the fear of failure. After the exhausting failure at the Yarmouk bridge in November (a commission he received direct from the Commander-in-Chief), his heroic efforts in the north, around Tafileh, in the middle of the exceptionally harsh winter, do indeed also fail (in spite of the victory at Tafileh itself). He drives his camel to Akaba through rain and snow, then back again, apparently alone carrying a fortune in gold sovereigns. A sign of growing desperation? More than one former army officer has commented that he lacked the ability to delegate responsibility.

The crux came in Tafileh on February 22nd, 1918, when he discovers that the money he has so bravely carried through the mountains has been spent by Prince Zeid, not on priming the tribes for the coming campaign, but on rewarding those who fought in the last one. The advance that was to join up with Allenby at the northern end of the Dead Sea must grind to a halt. Lawrence decides to ask to be relieved of his post. At the time, it was doubtless the professional failure that loomed largest; he had failed Allenby again. He found he did not command the respect he needed among the Arabs. But it was also a case of the straw that broke the camel's back. The loneliness of living cheek by jowl with Arabs in the flea-infested stone hovels of Tafileh cut off by snow was too much of a strain, but how else could he carry out Allenby's instructions? The constant disappointment and endless problems of working with Arabs was also too much. The ambivalence of his status, now flouted, the exhaustion and the pain ... suddenly, for the first (and last) time his belief in the whole enterprise collapses; and also his belief in himself. He now feels that by imitating the Arabs he has betrayed his own integrity.

It is the contact with the British that saves him. Allenby and Hogarth tell him how indispensible he is in the coming offensive, patch up his self-esteem, and send him back repaired; it is a more disillusioned, a less boyish Lawrence. In the coming months the support of Allenby is an immense psychological bulwark. On the other hand, although he continued to be here, there and everywhere with Arabs, journeying, reconnoitring, liaising, the 'dream' was in reality over.

Six months before he had been able to write: "It's the maddest campaign ever run, . . . and if it ever works out to a conclusion will be imperishable fun to look back upon." A month after the money fiasco he wrote again to his parents; rarely, if ever, had he written so negatively to them: "It will be a great comfort when one can lie down & sleep without having to think about things; and speak without having one's every word reported in half a hundred camps. This is a job too big for me."[12]

There is fortunately one last letter which casts a unique pool of light onto his mentality just before the end of the war. It was written to Richards on 15th August 1918, in Cairo on one of his longer stays: it is one of the finest letters that he ever wrote and certainly one of the most detached, and truthful.[13] It reminds one of those speeches from the last act of a play when all the illusions are gone. The consciousness of the *cumulative* effect of the war, and his detached perspective on it, is clearly demonstrated. Richards' letter must have spoken of pre-war, and the post-war future, a return. But this letter holds out little hope for the fine printing of books on Pole Hill:

Well, it was wonderful to see your writing again, and very difficult to read it. . . .

It always seemed to me that your eyes would prevent service for you, and that in consequence you might preserve your continuity. For myself I have been so violently uprooted and plunged into a job too big for me, that everything feels unreal. I have dropped all I ever did, and live only as a thief of opportunity, snatching chances of the moment when and where I see them. . . . it's a kind of foreign stage, on which one plays day and night, in fancy dress, in a strange language with the price of failure on one's head if the part is not well filled. . . .

This is a very long porch to explain why I'm always trying to blow up Railway trains and bridges instead of looking for the well at the world's end. Anyway these years of detachment have cured me of any desire ever to do anything for myself. When they untie my bonds I will not find in me any spur to action. Though actually one never thinks of afterwards: the time from the beginning is like one of those dreams, seeming to last for aeons, out of which you wake up with a start, and find that it has left nothing in the mind. Only the different thing about this dream is that so many people do not wake up in life again.

I cannot imagine what my people can have told you. Until now we have only been preparing the groundwork and bases of our Revolt. and do not yet stand on the brink of action. Whether we are going to win or lose, when we do strike, I cannot ever persuade myself. The whole thing is such a play, and one cannot put conviction into one's day-dreams. . . . Achievement, if it comes, will be a great disillusionment, but not great enough to wake one up.

Your mind has evidently moved far since 1914. That is a privelege you have won by being kept out of the mist for so long. You'll find the rest of us aged undergraduates, possibly still not conscious of our unfitting grey hair. For that reason I cannot follow or return your steps. A house with no action entailed upon one, quiet, and liberty to think and abstain as one wills, yes. I think abstention, the leaving everything alone and watching the others still going past, is what I would choose today, if they ceased driving me. This may be only the reaction from four years opportunism, and is not worth trying to resolve into terms of geography and employment.

Of course the ideal is that of the lords who are still certainly expected,[14] but the certainty is not for us, I'm afraid. Also for very few would the joy be so perfect as to be silent. Those words peace, silence, rest, take on a vividness amid noise and worry and weariness, like a lighted window in the dark. Yet what on earth is the good of a lighted window? . . . Probably I'm only a sensitised film, turned black or white by the objects projected on me: and if so what hope is there that next week or year, or tomorrow, can be prepared for today? . . .

Very many thanks for writing. It has opened a very precious casement.

I cannot help being sorry that he was not able to write like this in *Seven Pillars*.

### AFTER THE WAR

But when his war ended, there was no peace, silence, or rest. Paris was a failure, disastrous for his self-esteem. Once so influential, he lost the support of the political milieu and found himself a mistrusted outsider on both sides, British and Arab; never mind the French! Nor did he achieve anything for Feisal, in fact he left him in a hopeless situation. There was now only the book, the titanic 'English fourth' he set out to write. Then came the difficulties with that: the 'loss' of the first draft, the frantic rewriting, the interminable revision, the dawning realisation that he had not written a masterpiece, that he was not a great writer. The cost to him should not be under-estimated; it was another heavy blow to his self-esteem. "Hitherto", he explained to Garnett, "I've always managed, usually without trying my hardest, to do anything I wanted in life; and it has bumped me down, rather, to have gone wrong in this thing, after three or four years top effort." A friend later remarked: "He could never say to himself 'I have done my best' and accept that part which was human failure."[15] The last route out of the maze was barred to him. He was moreover very conscious of having achieved everything possible at a very young age. What was left?

The lone achiever, who has cut himself free from the need of others, is living over a void. For those the day must never come when there is nothing achievable or to be achieved. He achieved at Oxford; he achieved at Carchemish; he achieved in Cairo; and the summit of his achievement was the desert war. But then it seemed to elude him. There was a last moment of political success in 1921 but by then it was too late. By then, achievement was what he wanted to escape from.

Undoubtedly, we must also count the effect of the war, and the supercharged level of activity that he had risen to. Kirkbride had said that he was, in a sense, lucky to be sent to a sphere of the war where an extraordinary man was permitted to do extraordinary things and become famous in the process. But from another perspective he was not lucky. It was a climax to which there could be no sequel. "To act when there is a call for action is one thing; to act when there is none is a more difficult matter," wrote William Rothenstein, who added: "Returning tired and disillusioned after a long period of unnatural strain, no wonder he was unable to find himself at home in a distracted world."[16]

Reik writes of "the high and even exorbitant demands that the masochistic character makes on himself. The resulting deficit must fill him with discontent. He cannot achieve those great aims, he cannot get rid of his shortcomings and weaknesses. The comparison of the actual ego with the ego-ideal he has set up for himself nearly always goes against the person and causes guilt- and inferiority- feelings."[17] Reik believes that these high and exorbitant demands on the self can be traced to unconscious feelings of inferiority.

## CREATIVITY: LETTERS FROM THE OLD MAN

The beatings began, as far as we know, in 1923, when Lawrence, after another bitter disappointment (his dismissal from the RAF), had been admitted to the Tank Corps as a private soldier. They continued intermittently, with long gaps, possibly years rather than months, until his death in 1935. The chief administrator of punishment throughout was John Bruce. The arrangements were of course secret and were planned in meticulous detail and with creative flare.

In the extraordinarily elaborate and carefully planned invention of the 'Old Man', this threatening father figure who signed himself 'R' would communicate with 'Hills' (Bruce), and also with a very few other observers (fellow-servicemen) about the punishment administered by Hills. The sole intermediary was 'Ted', the name used by R to refer to his 'nephew' (Lawrence). The letters would not of course have been opened. Those to Bruce would explain in fine detail how the punishment was to be administered, what kind of whip was to be used, etc. Those to the observer would ask for details of Ted's reaction to the birching, mention various misdemeanors committed by Ted that justified punishment, and discuss Ted's 'progress'. As all this is difficult to envisage, here are short excerpts from letters found at Clouds Hill after Lawrence's death, from the 'Old Man' to an anonymous observer. These letters are from the end of his life and we cannot be sure that the procedure was not a little different when the beatings started.

26 Oct. 1934
Dear Sir,
I am very much obliged to you for the long and careful report you have sent me on your visit to Scotland with Ted; and for your kindness in agreeing to go there with the lad and look after him while he got his deserts. I am enclosing a fee of three pounds which I hope you will accept as some compensation for your trouble and inconvenience. . . . Please take any chance his friendship for you gives, to impress upon him how wrong it is for him, at his age and standing, to force us to use these schoolboy measures against him. He should be ashamed to hold his head up amongst his fellows, knowing that he had suffered so humiliating and undignified a punishment.

After being loosed, did Ted stand quite steadily, or did he show any signs of trembling on his way from the club-room to the cafe or the train? . . . Hills reports that after the birching Ted cried out quite loudly, and begged for mercy. Can you confirm this, and do you recollect in what terms his plea was made? . . . Does he take his whipping as something he has earned? Is he sorry after it? Does he feel justly treated? . . .

Believe me
Yours very sincerely   R

And this to another:

16 November 1934
... Ted's punishment at X had proved not enough, due to the inadequacy of a belt for use upon a grown lad, and not through any fault of yours or your friend's. Unfortunately you could not arrange another dose at the time, and while we were thinking about it Ted allowed himself to give offense upon quite another subject. It was with this second offence that Hills dealt last month. Ted still owes us (as he very well knows) proper payment for his very mean action in trying to steal money in transit from me to you.

John Mack concludes: "The Old Man fantasy is characteristic of Lawrence's inventiveness and creativity. His elaborate imagination and rich fantasy life is welded as usual with action. . . . Childhood and adult elements, the medieval flagellation rituals with which he became familiar in his youth, and his own complex psychological conflicts and inventiveness were all drawn together by Lawrence in his creative psychopathology." Given this insight, it is quite surprising that Mack never saw even a hypothetical connection between the Dera' narrative and this 'elaborate imagination and rich fantasy life', this 'creative psychopathology'.

Those who doubted Lawrence's literary ability to invent the Dera' narrative have confused different meanings of the term 'creative'. 'Creative writer', as it might be applied to Dostoevski, is one thing; the creation of sexual fantasies is another, and the substitution of non-existent people and events for reality itself is a further extension, a very special talent requiring precision and daring. They are all forms of creativity.

## THE CREATION OF A SOCIAL REALITY

Without losing sight of the Old Man, or the comment of Mack, I now come to the final barrier defending the 'truth' of the Dera' incident: Lawrence's own later references to it – possibly the most intriguing element in the entire puzzle.

After the letter to Stirling of June 1919, the Dera' incident was, obviously, not mentioned at all until Lawrence circulated copies of the Oxford text in August 1922. We do not know what any of them might have written to him about it but, in all likelihood, it was generally passed over in a polite silence with some regret that Lawrence exposed himself in such a fashion. Edward Garnett, however, took it up enthusiastically and this is Lawrence's reply:

> If that Deraa incident whose treatment you call severe and serene (the second sounds like a quaint failure to get my message across, but I know what you feel) had happened to yourself you would not have recorded it. I have a face of brass perhaps, but I put it into print very reluctantly, last of all the manuscript: because I could not tell the story face to face with anyone, and I think I'll feel sorry, when I next meet you, that you know it. The sort of man I have always mixed with doesn't so give himself away.

How could anyone, reading this, believe that it refers to something that never happened? Thanks to Garnett's comments, and Lawrence's reply, the Deraa incident was now a *social fact*.

A few years after this André Malraux wrote *La condition humaine*, a novel about an insurgency which Lawrence himself might have wished he could write. Among the characters is one Baron Clappique, an eccentric who can only live by creating around him a world of fantasy with the stories he tells. At one point, in a bar, after having betrayed a friend, he wins the sympathy of a woman by telling her that he must kill himself:

> When he said that he would kill himself, he did not believe himself: but because she believed him, he entered a world in which the truth no longer existed. It was neither true nor false, but lived.

The belief of others gives reality to one's invention. The more one can talk or write about it, the more lived it becomes. It might even become possible for the inventor of a fictitious event to believe that it really did happen.[18] Lawrence was discreet about the Dera' chapter, but by no means loath to comment to loyal friends, introducing the topic on his own initiative as part of his autobiography. These included Garnett, E.M. Forster, Robert Graves, Jock Chambers, and especially Charlotte Shaw. In the course of a discussion in a previous letter of her husband's new play, *St Joan*, concerning the portrayal of pain and horror on stage, Lawrence had made a contrast between the heroine's death off-stage, and "the plain narrative of my mishaps in Deraa." Charlotte had evidently made a comment about that in her reply and here is Lawrence's reply to that:

You instance my night at Deraa. Well, I'm always afraid of being hurt: and to me, while I live, the force of that night will lie in the agony which broke me, and made me surrender. It's the individual view. You can't share it. About that night I shouldn't tell you, because decent men don't talk about such things. I wanted to put it plain in the book, wrestled for days with my self-respect ... which wouldn't, hasn't let me. For fear of being hurt, or rather to earn five minutes respite from a pain which drove me mad, I gave away the only possession we are born into the world with, our bodily integrity. It's an unforgiveable matter, an irrecoverable position: and it's that which has made me forswear decent living, and the exercise of my not-contemptible wits and talents.[19]

He is seeking her reaction to the story, testing her belief and wooing her acceptance of the entire argument – for an argument it is. Hence the insistence on absolutes: 'unforgivable matter', 'irrecoverable position'. He writes: "You instance my night at Deraa"; but it was he who instanced it, not her. The reader will also notice that once again, in similar language to that he used to Garnett, he writes "Decent men don't talk about such things". Yet that is exactly what he proceeds to do. He thus creates the impression that he is reluctant to discuss it, whereas in fact it is he who has introduced the topic. What is going on here, as in the paragraph to Garnett, is the creation of a social biography for the Dera' incident. It is being clothed with biographical facts, mixing the actual details of the experience with their effect on his present behaviour. It is neither true nor false, but lived. One wonders whether this explanation (of his present way of life, his withdrawal into the ranks) convinced Charlotte. Later she would call him a liar.

I do not at all agree (with Mack) that there are no significant differences between this passage and the narratives in *Seven Pillars*. Lawrence specifically states that he is here confessing things that he could not in the book. The major emphasis there is on the beating, the pain, and the revelation of pleasure through it, a masochistic experience. And, more important, on the breaking of the *spirit*, insisting on the body's betrayal. Here, it is the homosexual rape, and *shame*; he writes of himself as if he were a fallen woman. A yet more important difference is that here we are given to understand that he gave in to sodomy because he could not stand the pain; whereas in *Seven Pillars* the pain occasioned, finally, sexual pleasure. So it is all very Lawrencianly puzzling.

Possibly, the fact that Charlotte refused from the start of her marriage to have sexual relations with her husband leads Lawrence to put so much emphasis on the value of bodily integrity. She would understand the psychological impact of a rape, but whether she understood why he felt so guilty is another matter. Later, perhaps much later, Lawrence confesses that his account of the affair is not true. This confession was made to Bernard Shaw, who considered it sufficiently important to record it on the fly-leaf of his wife's copy of the Oxford text before he deposited it in the New York Public Library. This is the text:

> Even my wife, always friendly and a help to him said to me, when, after his unusually long absence from our house, I asked whether there was any quarrel – any unpleasantness: "No, no quarrel, no unpleasantness. But he is such an INFERNAL liar!" He was not a liar. He was an actor. But I must add that neither was he a model of veracity. One of his chapters (LXXXI) tells of a revolting sequel to his capture by the Turks and his attraction for a Turkish officer. He told me that his account of the affair is not true. I forebore to ask him what actually happened.

Possibly Charlotte already disbelieved him. To call someone you know that well an infernal liar cannot be argued away easily; but Shaw elegantly does his best. Some critics have minimised this confession as simply another potential variant. It is much more likely that here, at last, to the man who became something like a father to him, he wanted to make, for the first and last time, a more radical confession of truth. But Shaw spared him the shame, and us the knowledge.

## THE ENCODED TRUTH

In 1924 Lawrence wrote to Robert Graves about the book as follows:

> Its sincerity, I fancy (is) absolute, except once where I funked the distinct truth, and wrote it obliquely. I was afraid of saying something, even to myself. The thing was not written for anyone to read. Only as I get further from the strain of that moment, confession seems a relief rather than a risk.[20]

It is, I believe, significant that Lawrence had not given Graves access to the Oxford text and so knew that he had not read it. The tantalisingly veiled reference to something he had not been allowed to see must have maddened Graves. However, it could scarcely be clearer that he is alluding to the Dera' chapter. "*I wrote it obliquely. I was afraid of saying something, even to myself.*" It chimes with what Thomas Mann wrote of Dostoevski:

> In every man's memory there are things which he does not reveal to everyone, but only to his friends. There are also things which he does not reveal to his friends, but at best to himself and only under a pledge of secrecy. And finally there are things which a man hesitates to reveal even to himself.[21]

The encoded meaning of Dera' is the transposing of guilt feelings about his masochism on to circumstances in which he was blameless. It was motivated by a compulsion to confess a perverted sexuality, a desire, conscious or unconscious, for spiritual cleansing and freedom from guilt and falsehood. It is the core of his "apology for my first thirty years, and the explanation of the renunciation that followed on them".

*Between Myth and Reality*

# CHAPTER 16

# THE ARAB MIRAGE

> The "Seven Pillars" is ... a profound epitome of all that the Arabs mean to the world ... forever it will reveal all that is most characteristic of the Arab race. ...
>
> *Winston Churchill*

> Nation, race, class – any abstraction which designates a human collectivity, once it is charged with a destiny, becomes a myth: his Arabia was a myth.[1]
>
> *André Malraux*

### THE ARABS IN *SEVEN PILLARS*

The image of Arab society we are shown is a traditional one that had scarcely changed for centuries, except that rifles have largely but not entirely replaced swords and daggers. Much of the time, Lawrence and his companions live in tents; most of them were born in one. Their society is tribal and their allegiance is to the family, clan, tribe. The notion of allegiance, loyalty, is so fundamental as to be almost instinctive. They are nomadic or semi-nomadic Bedu, like the Juheineh, Howeitat or Beni Atiyeh. There are also the Ageyl, the mercenaries who made up Feisal's bodyguard and also Lawrence's. Lawrence is very punctilious about the naming of tribes, and, in the case of large tribes like the Howeitat or Beni Sakhr, their clans. He is slightly less conscientious about the Ageyl. In fact, he depended a good deal on the Ageyl, as did Feisal, for the simple reason that they were more dependable, especially as groomers of camels. They were used to service and their service could be bought.

It needs to be made clear from the start that the desert Arab represented even at this time a very small proportion of the Arab race, probably not more than five per cent. When Lawrence uses the term

'Arab' he may be referring only to this number, or to the wider concept, as the case may be. His imaginative Chapter 4 *The nomadic phase* argues with breath-taking convincingness that nomadism is a universal feature of the Arab ancestral experience in the peninsula.

It is not, however, a typical situation. These Arabs have been recruited to serve a revolt against Turks. Their overlord is the Grand Sherif of Mecca; this, for the tribes of the Hejaz, had been the case before the revolt also, but now they have taken an oath of loyalty. Their leader in the field, in the case of those whom Lawrence moved with, is Feisal. So the stars that make up the constellation of the Arab image in *Seven Pillars* are *Desert—Bedu—Sherif*. This suited Lawrence's literary purpose since the essential elements of an epic composition are already present: a Sherif is of noble lineage,[2] and the Bedu are portrayed as a people naturally warlike and courageous. Raiding on camels or, more rarely, on horseback, was a part of their way of life. The traditional epic poetry of the Arabs makes use of just these elements. In *Seven Pillars* it is Arabs on raids, Arabs as escort, or Arabs in the retinue of Feisal or Abdullah that dominate; with the exception of the short stay at the tents of the Howeitat in Wadi Sirhan, we see little of the normal everyday life of the Arabs in this book.

The Arabs are always there. The long historical narrative is peopled by hundreds of different Arabs, mainly tribesmen, appearing for a brief moment in Lawrence's history, then disappearing. This is inevitable since the Revolt moved through one tribal area to another, and because the narrative is strictly chronological. There is Shakir's dance by the fire in Wadi Ais; there are the Ageyl, advancing in formation on Wejh; there is Sheikh Motlog, falling off the top of a box-Ford and apologising: "I have not learnt to ride these things". There are countless incidents of one sort or another. Some Arabs reappear several times, like Mohammed al Dheilan and Zaal of the Howeitat, ibn Dgeithir, Sherif Shakir, the Zaagi, the young Rahail, Awad the Sherari. But few readers will remember them by the time they put down the book. It is so very long; and, as Forster had noticed, they rarely speak, and they only live at the moment they are acting.

"You give a series of pictures . . . there can seldom have been a Movement with so little motion in it!" He praises TE's descriptions of nature. With men, however, it is different: "I find something not very satisfactory in your presentation of the human race . . . all your characters tend to go <u>quiet</u> when the eye is removed, including your own character."[3] He suggests more dialogue.

Nothing interrupts the chronological sequence; the amount of detail is enormous and it is as if filmed by a greedy video camera that films unstoppably here, there and everywhere; the video camera is being held always by Lawrence himself, focussing on the scene for a couple of paragraphs before being turned somewhere else. Nobody breaks free to show us who he really is, independent of Lawrence's vision. The Arabs fare best in the accounts of raids, probably because there Lawrence's attention is concentrated on a single object, and individual and group actions count for much and have a special vividness.

Cumulatively, on the other hand, we learn a good deal about this people: their dress and appearance; their tribal organisation and leaders; their loyalty and inter-tribal enmity; their sense of independence; their unreliability and quarrelsomeness and capacity for treachery; their skills in the desert; their fighting spirit and their caution; their love of booty and occasional bloodlust; their endurance. We learn about raiding, ceremonial banquets, camel grooming, camel riding and racing, tribal jealousies and blood feuds, ownership of wells, and much more. All this we pick up, higgledy piggledy, in the course of Lawrence's story.

Important Arabs we will remember and, perhaps, put a face or figure or attributes to, like Sherif Nasr, Emir Zeid, Nuri Sha'alan. They appear more or less throughout the story but remain undeveloped as characters. What, for instance, do we learn about Zeid that would help us to judge the likelihood of his misusing funds at Tafileh? Hubert Young's handful of lines on Feisal in his tent, or Zeid watching the Turkish engine driver, actually provide more lasting and valid images of *character* than all the mentions of Feisal in *Seven Pillars* or the forty-two of Zeid; here is that latter glimpse:

Young, when up-country, finds the Emir Zeid sitting on a high hill overlooking the station of Abu Jerdun which the Arabs are attacking. Zeid, as Feisal's brother, is nominally in charge of things. He watches as a daring Turkish engine driver pushes some trucks right into the station under attack, from which Turkish reinforcements pour out and save the day.

> "I fear we shall not take Abu Jerdun today," said Zeid. "I am sorry."
> "Yes, indeed," said I, "it is a great pity."
> "Do you know why I am sorry?" he went on. "I should like to have taken that engine driver and given him a medal!"[4]

Kennington's portraits of Arabs as they appear in the subscribers' edition illustrate the point. They are very fine portraits. But who are these people? Most of them do appear in the book but who remembers where, or what they did? Of them, only Auda, Ali ibn el-Hussein and the Amir Abdullah are significant personages in the book. Seen in the Leicester Gallery, apart, they were a sensation and presented a unique and penetrating look at a certain society, unknown to the vast majority of visitors. But as portraits of characters in the book, they are mainly superfluous. What they show us is a vast potential that was never touched; the dangerous greed that speaks out of the portrait of Nawaf Sha'lan is a story waiting to be written. Rather than to illustrate what is in *Seven Pillars*, their value is to illustrate what is not in *Seven Pillars*. Lawrence freely admitted this and was glad of it. Both collectively and individually these portraits have vitality, and psychological interest; they make individual statements that are strange to us.

The film *Lawrence of Arabia* scores more points on characterisation for the simple reason that the Arabs are acted by living people. They may sometimes be totally unlike their originals in physique (Auda and Ali) and in some cases in character (Ali), but they do *have* character and we can identify with them.

## EPIC. THE PROPHET AND THE HEROES

> I saw standing framed between the ports of a black doorway, a white figure waiting tensely for me. This was Feisal and I felt at the glance that now I had found the man whom I had come to Arabia to seek, the leader alone needed to make the Arab Revolt win through to a success. He looked very tall and pillar-like, very slender, dressed in long white silk robes and a brown headcloth bound with a brilliant scarlet and gold cord. His eyes were dropped, and his close black beard and colourless face were like a mask against the strange still watchfulness of his body. His hands were loosely crossed in front of him on his dagger. (OX 76, R 92)

White is the colour of the prophet (the colour chosen by Lawrence himself). It denotes above all the immaculate, and also an apartness from others. It is surely significant that Jesus Christ, the prophet of Lawrence's childhood and adolescence, is usually portrayed by the painters in white. No portrait of Feisal could be more idealised but, to give Lawrence his due, it is similar to a photograph taken of Feisal at Wejh in March 1917; with the vital exception that his *abaya* is brown, not white; Lawrence adds an element of mystery. This Feisal is a prophet. A spontaneous impression gives a very different result. Not long after coming ashore in Akaba in March 1918, Hubert Young was introduced to Feisal. This is how he describes him:

> He was simply dressed in a long brown zibun, rather like a cassock, and an embroidered kerchief was loosely knotted round his head, without any head-rope. The whole time he was talking his long slim fingers were busy with an amber rosary, chasing the beads nervously round the thread. As he leant eagerly forward and waited for Lawrence to translate Dawnay's carefully chosen sentences, he reminded me of some beautiful thoroughbred quivering at the starting-gate.[5]

Young's portraits show an eye for significant detail. This Feisal is young, nervous and alive.

In epic poetry, too much individuality would compromise the epic stature. Feisal is presented as the archetype of the desert prince, the "prophet who if veiled would give cogent form to the idea behind the Arab Revolt". Veiled he was. Many of the descriptions of Feisal emphasise the desert culture that supports his regality. It is a representation of character that concentrates on externals, as Feisal, we are told, did himself: dignified bearing, perfect manners, outward self-control.

The two most important Arabs in the book are Emir Feisal and the tribal leader Auda abu Tayi. Auda's entrance on stage is another epic moment:

> Suleiman the guest-master hurried in and whispered to Feisal, who turned to me with shining eyes, trying to be calm, and said, 'Auda is here.' I shouted 'Auda Abu Tayi' and at that moment the tent-flap was drawn back and a deep voice boomed salutations to our lord, the Commander of the Faithful: and there entered a tall strong figure with a haggard face, passionate and tragic. This was Auda.... Feisal had sprung to his feet. Auda caught his hand, and kissed it warmly, and they drew aside a pace or two, and looked at each other: a splendid pair, as unlike as possible, but typical of much that was best in Arabia, Feisal the prophet, and Auda the warrior... (OX 229; SP 228)

But Auda also has his comic side; the same evening, at supper:

> Suddenly Auda scrambled to his feet with a loud 'God forbid!', and flung from the tent. We stared at one another and there came a noise

of hammering outside. I went after him to learn what it meant, and there was Auda bent over a great rock pounding his false teeth to fragments with a stone. 'I had forgotten,' he explained, 'Jemal Pasha had these made for me. I was eating my Lord's bread with Turkish teeth!' (OX 230, SP 229)

Even this has an epic character, even though it is a parody of it, as is Lawrence's mimicry of Auda's story-telling style. Auda appears many times and his appearances can be guaranteed to revive any flagging interest. With his exaggerated zest and comic simplicity, he is Lawrence's best characterisation. The veiled Feisal, on the other hand, is the image par excellence of the noble Arab, and really nothing more. This is rather unsatisfactory because Feisal is the most important historical figure; we need to know his real motives, his ambitions, his politics.

Ali ibn Hussein al-Harithi comes nearest to the Homeric hero; he is physically beautiful, perfect in movement, a masterful rider, an accomplished and courageous warrior, imperious, noble, yet fiery, wild and childlike also. His role, however, is much less important. The 'Arcadian love pair', Daud and Farraj, also have a place in the epic conception. They are alone in achieving that fluidity of being that Forster found wanting. They are invested with a living something that is still with them the next time we see them.

## THE MEANING OF THE DESERT ARAB

The meaning of the desert Arab for Lawrence may be summed up in the famous words of Dahoum and his companions when, having guided Lawrence round a desert castle (Ibn Wardani) in northern Syria whose rooms all gave out a different scent, they breathe in the air at an empty window socket facing east, and say: 'This is the best: it has no taste'. He adds: "My Arabs were turning their backs on perfumes and luxuries, and looking out towards the wilderness, *choosing the things in which mankind had had no share or part*" (my italics).

> The Bedouin of the desert had been born and grown up in it, and had embraced this nakedness too harsh for volunteers with all his soul, for the reason felt but inarticulate that there he found himself indubitably free. He lost all material ties, all comforts, all superfluities or complications to achieve the personal liberty which haunted starvation and

death. He saw no virtue in poverty herself: he enjoyed the little vices and luxuries – coffee, fresh water, women – which he could still preserve. In his life he had air and winds, sun and light, open spaces and great emptiness. There was no human effort, no fecundity in nature: just the heaven above and the unspotted earth beneath. There unconsciously he came near to God. (OX 20, R 38-9)

It is a state of freedom and spiritual purity. The first cannot exist without the second. This is one of the most fundamental of all Lawrence's beliefs and the meaning of the Arabian experience. Sterility of nature is one with human non-creation *and absolute material simplicity* as conditions of spiritual knowledge, coming near to God. The context here is religious, it is from the chapter on semitic monotheism (OX 5). This description of the desert Arab is at one and the same time the explanation of their attraction to him. It is a fusion of Lawrence's perception of the Arabs, and of his own ideal.

It is interesting to compare this description of the Bedu with Wilfred Thesiger's, who wrote of the Bedu of the Empty Quarter in the 1940s:

On the oil-fields the Bedu could find the money of which they dreamt. They could earn large sums by sitting in the shade and guarding a dump, or by doing work which was certainly easier than watering thirsty camels on a nearly dry well in the middle of summer. There was plenty of good food, abundant sweet water, and long hours for sleep. They had seldom had these things before, and now they were being paid into the bargain. Their love of freedom and the restlessness that was in their blood drew most of them back into the desert . . .

Tonight while I was warm in my sleeping-bag the others would shiver under the cold north wind. They were Bedu, and these open spaces where there was neither shade nor shelter were their homelands. Any of them could have worked in the gardens around Salala; all of them would have scorned this easier life of lesser men. Among the Bedu only the broken are stranded among the cultivations on the desert's shore.[6]

Thesiger agrees with Lawrence on the notion of freedom, the willing foregoing of material comforts, the contempt of an easier life. But the perspective is different. They accept their hard lot because it is in their nature as Bedu, because the desert life is an integral part of their identity. Like a species, they meet the conditions of their territorial habitat; if they are removed, they are 'stranded', they are lost because they are not with the tribe, in their homelands. Thesiger's perspective is socio-anthropological, Lawrence's spiritual.

Lawrence's actual experience was different to that of Thesiger or Doughty. Certainly he had a great deal of experience of Bedu; he accompanied them, he fought with them, he organised them, he ate and slept with them on the march. But apart from a few days with the Howeitat, he never lived with a tribe (and even the Howeitat would hardly be Bedu by Thesiger's standards).[7] Those he got to know best were the Ageyl from whom was formed his bodyguard, who were not nomads, but came from Nejdi towns or villages. Dahoum, because he was, apparently, the only Arab he was ever close to, became the embodiment of the Arab ideal; however, he was no Bedawi, but a villager of the north Syrian plains. What Lawrence attributes to his companions is influenced by his imagination as well as by his experience. It is the *idea* of Bedu that counts, and what they stood for: simplicity, freedom from material cares, instinctive hospitality, no care for the future; courage, faith, indolence, disinterestedness, solitude; the 'incomparable style' of those who had always been hunters, never known the curse of Adam; and the Sherifs, rulers by birth, descendants of the Prophet.

Lawrence, like Thesiger, did not much like Arabs as a whole; indeed, the mere contrast between the Europeanised Levantines and the Arab of the desert inspired him with antipathy. To him, the former were decadents, spoilt by civilization. It is doubtful whether he even considered Lebanese or Egyptians to be 'Arabs' at all. An Arab for him was tribal, of the desert or steppe of the Arabian peninsula. This explains something about his often puzzling political attitudes during and after the war and his early post-war disinterestedness.

Lawrence's rationale of the Bedu and his identification with them is more important – and true – in relation to himself than in relation to them. The Bedu represent a stepping-stone on the way to spiritual self-conquest, a necessary encounter on a spiritual pilgrimage.

## THE UNSHARED CONFLICT OF BODY AND SPIRIT

The chapter *Spirit of the Revolt*, already examined above, is Lawrence's most powerful and intimate evocation of the Arabian idyll, what he shared with the Arabs, and then, what he did not share with them. The pronoun *we*, that dominates in the first part of that chapter, creates a feeling of fellowship as if he and the Bedu were one social organism, sharing an ideal of freedom to which they were enslaved and for which they were prepared to sacrifice their lives and suffer any hardship. Later in the chapter the tone changes; the feeling of intimate solidarity is replaced by a lecture-cum-apologia on the danger of mixing with the natives, getting stuck between two cultures.

I have shown how he used his Arab companions as a kind of shield to make possible confessions that he would otherwise have been shy of making, either imputing them to the Arabs themselves, or including himself with them. Here below, I pursue this theme, showing how he co-opted the Arabs throughout the book as sharers of his masochistic attitudes and practices.

In Chapter 5 *Monotheism*, he writes of the desert-dweller:

> His sterile experience robbed him of compassion and perverted his human kindness to the image of the waste in which he hid. Accordingly, he hurt himself, not merely to be free, but to please himself. There followed a delight in pain, a cruelty which was more to him than goods. The desert Arab found no joy like the joy of voluntarily holding back. He found luxury in abnegation, renunciation, self-restraint. He made nakedness of the mind as sensuous as nakedness of the body. (OX 21)

Whether there is truth in the first sentence I cannot judge, but what follows is an idealisation of himself. This is a description that rings true of sophisticated Western man; the Bedu had their hands full dealing with the harshness of existence and natural catastrophes, without cultivating "the joy of voluntarily holding back", a thoroughly masochistic trait. Elsewhere he contradicted himself:

> He enjoyed the little vices and luxuries – coffee, fresh water, women – which he could still preserve.

Or here:

> They were absolute slaves of their appetite, with no stamina of mind, drunkards for coffee, milk, or water, gluttons for stewed meat, shameless beggars of tobacco. A cigarette went round four men in a tent before it was finished, and it would have been intolerable manners to have smoked a whole one through. They dreamed for weeks before and after their rare sexual exercises, and spent the intervening days titillating themselves and their hearers with bawdy tales. Had the circumstances of their lives given them greater resources or opportu-

nity they would have been just sensualists. Their strength was the strength of men geographically beyond temptation: the poverty of Arabia made them simple, continent, enduring. (OX 227)

This, somewhat closer to Doughty, seems the exact denial of the previous paragraph, and it betrays the subjectivity of his starting point. Some readers might wonder whether Lawrence knows what he is talking about but the truth is that he left the reader to make sense of his inconsistencies – or not – as they wished. To be fair, he does emphasise that the extremes of sensuality and self-denial live together in the Arab soul: "The Semite havered between lust and self-denial". (OX 22, R 40). But he does not make his case.

The description of his bodyguard mixes elements of what might be truth with an insistence on masochistic qualities: the 'antithesis between body and spirit', and an ideal of freedom that is related to pain: these are two of Lawrence's central tenets on the Semite nature:

> (They) seemed to be fascinated by their physical suffering. Servitude in the East was based, like other conduct, on their obsession with the antithesis between body and spirit, and these took pleasure in subordination, in the utter degrading of the body, to throw more into relief the freedom and equality of mind . . . Servants were afraid of the sword of justice, and of the whip, . . . because these were the symbols and the means to which their obedience was vowed. They had a gladness of abasement, a freedom of consent to yield to their masters the last service and degree of their flesh and blood, because their spirits were equal and the contract voluntary . . . . Pain was to them a solvent, a cathartic, almost a decoration to be fairly worn, so long as they suvived it. (OX 525, R 475).

This is purified, spiritualised masochism. Physical abasement to a master is married to an assumption of spiritual equality with that same person because "the contract [is] voluntary".

And here:

> While we rode we were disembodied, all unconscious of physical needs and feelings: and when at an interval this excitement faded and we did see our bodies it was with hostility, with a contemptuous sense that they had reached their purpose, not as instruments of the spirit, but when, dissolved, their elements served to manure a field.

The Bedu did live close to physical pain, they did know and tolerate deprivation, their code of punishment was no doubt crude and physical; they did value personal freedom and often put it before material comforts. But their values were not those of masochists, nor their behaviour.

These passages are distortions of ethnological truth.

## ORIENTALISM

*Monotheism* is a most extraordinary chapter, a masterful exposition of the Arab nature and condition. When I write 'masterful' I do not mean truth, but the power and self-confidence of the analysis, the impressive display of heterogeneous knowledge, the brilliance of individual insights and images, the rhetorical strength of the prose, the sweeping statements. The new practical orientalists – Hogarth, Bell, Lawrence – inherit and internalise a mode of discourse appropriate to generalisation and evaluation. Lawence's Chapter 5 is a brilliant example; indeed, it is really too brilliant, verging on parody. Here are some generalisations, mainly from passages in this chapter:

Their inert intellects lay fallow in incurious resignation.

When you had Arabs and an idea you could sway them as on a cord.

Servitude in the East was based, like other conduct, on their obsession with the antithesis between body and spirit.

The desert Arab found no joy like the joy of voluntarily holding back.

They were absolute slaves of their appetite, with no stamina of mind.

The Semitic mind was strange and dark, full of depressions and exaltations.

In broad terms, the analysis includes all Semites. Lawrence sways between Semite and Arab as if they were almost synonymous in terms of the ideas he is discussing, for the generalisations made are underpinned by an orientalist body of knowledge of essentially racial classification.

Edward Said, a Palestinian, comments ironically on the obsession with racial typology and generalisation. "We are to assume that if an Arab feels joy, if he is sad at the death of his child or parent, if he has a sense of the injustices of political tyranny, then those experiences are necessarily subordinate to the sheer, unadorned, and persistent fact of his being an Arab."[8] Generalisation is a major characteristic, almost an obsession, of *Seven Pillars*, not only in the expository essay, but also throughout the narrative. The strength of his Arab stereotyping contrasts with the weakness of individual characterisation. I have given examples to show how less scholastic writers, like Kirkbride or Young, bring out rather than stifle individuality. They do also generalise; no human being in a foreign land can understand his environment or explain it without doing so; similarly, in Thesiger, notwithstanding his knowledge of tribal behaviour, his Bedu companions each have their individual character. It is precisely these differences in character which give such a rich portrayal of the Bedu in *Arabian Sands*. When Churchill writes that *Seven Pillars* is "a profound epitome of all that the Arabs mean to the world", does this not mean that we like our Arabs still to be mythical beings acting on a mythical stage? Noble, picturesque, conservative, unchanging, unthreatening.

While the Semites are uncreative and unproductive, their "inert intellects" can, like a volcano, be active after a long period dormant; but even this is merely the active phase of an unchanging cycle of behaviour:

> When you had Arabs and an idea you could sway them as on a cord . . . they were incorrigibly children of the idea, feckless and colour-blind, for whom body and spirit were for ever and inevitably opposed . . . since the dawn of life in successive waves they had been dashing themselves against the coasts of the flesh. . . . One such wave (and not the least) I raised and rolled before the breath of an idea, till it reached its crest, and toppled over and fell at Damascus. The wash of that wave, thrown back by the resistance of vested things, will provide the matter for the following wave, when in fullness of time it shall be raised once more. (OX 22)

The reader cannot but react: either, like Charlotte Shaw, we are carried away by the cosmic grandeur of this Man of Destiny; or must feel embarrassment at such megalomaniac imagery.

At this point on the time-map of Arab history, in the years 1916–18, a sudden spiritual awakening, the latest of an 'eternal recurrence' of such awakenings since 'the dawn of life', generates a terrific energy that gravitates round the figure of the new prophet. "Lawrence *was*, in a manner of speaking, the Arab Revolt", wrote Robert Graves.

"The Arab Revolt acquires meaning only as Lawrence designs meaning for it", adds Said.[9]

※

Lawrence was one of a new kind of orientalist: orientalist-*cum*-imperial agent. The others Said names include Hogarth, Gertrude Bell, Storrs, St. John Philby – all friends of Lawrence. The orientalist of the previous generation had been concerned with gathering and classifying information about the Orient. Of course, this was not innocent: Knowledge is Power in any circumstances; but the band of intelligence officers who gathered in Cairo under Gilbert Clayton in 1914–15, code-named the 'Intrusives', were far more ambitious, as Lawrence himself explains: "We meant to break in to the accepted halls of English foreign policy, and build a new people in the East" (OX 38). This more aggressive, creative attitude was occasioned by the expectation that the eastern Ottoman empire was about to be up for grabs. The task of the intrusives was prepare a new East under the aegis of Great Britain, and not that of France or other Western power.

*Seven Pillars* was for Said the ultimate literary expression of modern orientalism. It incorporates the idea of *control*, in which the movement of *history* – which is unpredictable, unstable, even chaotic – is subordinated to *vision*, the expert vision of a Westerner who assumes the role of master-spirit and leader.

> The great drama of Lawrence's work is that it symbolizes the struggle, first, to stimulate the Orient (lifeless, timeless, forceless) into movement; second, to impose upon that movement an essentially Western shape; third, to contain the new and aroused Orient in a personal vision, whose *retrospective mode* (my italics) includes a powerful sense of failure and betrayal.

For the 'unchanging Orient' now appears unstable, problematic. "Instability suggests that history, with its disruptive detail, its currents of change, its tendency towards growth, decline, or dramatic movement, is possible in the Orient and for the Orient. History and the narrative by which history is represented argue that vision is insufficient."[10] Nothing could be more true of the Arab East since 1918 and the failure of British policy there.

There can be no doubt that Lawrence has had an enormous influence on our image of 'the Arabs'. The already time-honoured theme of the desert Arab as the true Arab reached its apogee in the legend of Lawrence of Arabia and flowed like a precious ichor through the ideology of our political settlements in the Middle East. The lectures with lantern slides that Lowell Thomas presented at Covent Garden and the Royal Albert Hall were attended by over a million people. When Oscar Wilde wrote: "The important thing in a man's life is not what he does, but the legend that grows up around him", he did not err. After Lowell Thomas, *Revolt in the Desert* (1927) and then *Seven Pillars of Wisdom* (1935) formed a palimpsest of legend, each new layer poured successively over the existing stratum. Finally, the magnificent film *Lawrence of Arabia*, based on the *Seven Pillars*, revived the image of the noble Arab in his exotic background for another half century. "You must never destroy legends", ends the Wilde dictum. *Can* you destroy them?

## THE SEVEN PILLARED WORTHY HOUSE VERSUS NEO-IMPERIALISM

Flowing from another spring, those intimations of freedom, spirit versus matter, asceticism, non-existence – those ideas that seem to be haunted by Arabia itself and its inhabitants and to have no solid reality without them – are more profound *to him* than his orientalism. They have everything to do with Lawrence himself, with that obscure meeting ground between the spiritual and the psychological, and they had a profound influence on the rest of his life.

They express the yearning of Lawrence's hidden soul. They are the guiding principles of a kind of quest for lucidity that assumes more and more prominence within his narrative of the Arab Revolt. The key is the association of *Arab* with these other ideas, with himself. It is a psychological strategy which gives him a chance to explain the otherwise unexplainable.

"He had not discovered Arabia", wrote Malraux, "he had recognized it".[11] The ideas that drove the Arabian adventure and the spiritual 'marriage' with the Bedu germinated much earlier; they developed in northern Syria during his three and a half years at Carchemish, even earlier on that first Syrian journey of 1909. It was here that he saw with his own eyes the value of simplicity of living, the habit of bareness of materials that married with his very puritan nature and upbringing; it was at Carchemish that he met the Arab who is the symbol of his striving in the Revolt; and here also that he thrilled to the emptiness of the landscape, which in Arabia became a symbol of the sublimity of non-matter, non-existence – "There was no fecundity in nature: just the heaven above and the unspotted earth beneath". The desert was the only theatre in which the idea of freedom, Lawrence's freedom, could be meaningfully fought for, and articulated. His literary idea was to invest the story of the Revolt with the idea of a spiritual quest, in the manner of Arthurian legend. Political freedom is vaguely fused with freedom of the spirit.

> In every society not chosen by himself, he felt – he knew – himself a stranger. To be totally a stranger then, to have the right to be one, to have become the passer-by, the traveller – that restored his equilibrium. And more than equilibrium; joy. The right he sought in the Orient, whether he knew it or not, was the right of asylum. There, to be a foreigner was legitimate. And he was not bound to a hierarchy. The Orient had become for him a sort of homeland because that was the place where he felt himself free.[12]

This writer sees Lawrence's 'Arab identity' as no mere pose, but as the only possible solution to an existing psychological alienation from his own society. But it could not withstand the stress of war.

Looking at Christopher Matheson's *Images of Lawrence* the other day, I could not help remarking that the only photographs in which Lawrence looks happy and relaxed are those from Arabia.

What then of orientalism, of the language of generalisation, of power, of manipulation? There is, once more, no unexplainable contradiction. Throughout *Seven Pillars*, the two personalities alternate; at one moment we are in the midst of a Western cultural mind-set, centred on solidarity with the intrusives, at another the pendulum swings violently to the other side, to the need to protect his adopted homeland, the children of the desert, even against the imperialist ambitions of his own country. What is striking throughout *Seven Pillars* is how solidarity with the group is sought in both directions. There are the passages evoking companionship with the Arabs – with Feisal, with Ali, with his bodyguard; but also solidarity with his British colleagues, with Clayton, Lloyd, Joyce, Newcombe, Wilson, which is expressed by a different style of discourse: a certain tone of voice, humour, turns of phrase, the 'Oxfordisms' of Forster – all marked features of his book.

Finally, his view of Arab politics. He writes much and mystically about Arab freedom, but he knew very well that, politically, the Arabs of the desert were only slightly touched by Turkish tyranny. They fought for Feisal, or Abdullah, or Hussein, because these men were the overlords of the Hejaz and the descendants of the Prophet, because it was an honourable cause, because the fighting happened to be at a particular moment in their tribal lands, and because it was profitable to them and worth the not excessive risk. They were not permanently committed to anything. Did they see the British as liberators? Nothing is more doubtful.

The historical reality concerning Lawrence himself, his wartime role, is very different. Lawrence was the best servant of Great Britain's war aims in the Arabian peninsula and the guarantor that the Arabs would give no trouble at the end of the war. For Great Britain, there was never any question of the great Arab kingdom that the Arabs – some of them – thought they were fighting for. He himself was well aware that the Turkish eastern empire would be divided into individual political entities under the tutelage – to say the least – of the victorious powers. The question that mightily exercised him was: which one? He did not believe that the Arabs were capable of managing political freedom on their own. In a 1916 report he wrote:

> Their (the tribesmen's) idea of nationality is the independence of tribes and parishes, and their idea of national union is episodic, combined, resistance to an intruder. Constructive politics, an organized state, and an extensive empire, are not only beyond their capacity, but anathema to their instincts. They are fighting to get rid of empire, not to win it, and the only unity that is possible is one to which they are forced by foreign influence, or control. Unless we, or our allies, make an efficient Arab empire, there will never be more than a discordant mosaic of provincial administrations.[13]

This remarkable analysis is a perfect example of the type of discourse dear to the 'intrusives'. It is at once very astute, and overgeneralised. He is reporting on the nationalism of the desert tribes, not of the Arabs as a whole, but he seems by the end to have conflated the two. But how true was this of Syria, Palestine, Iraq?[14] What about Arab nationalism? Lawrence had convinced himself that there was no conflict between Arab autonomy and British hegemony, which he always saw as fundamentally benevolent. In this spirit, even after Churchill's settlement of 1921, which was a very pale shadow of the Hashemites' and his own aspirations in the Revolt, he claimed that his hands were clean. Meanwhile, frustrated Arab nationalism grumbled on, turned in on itself.[15]

# CHAPTER 17

# THE PRESENTATION OF HISTORY

> In regard to so elusive a mind as Lawrence's, no simple distinction can be enforced between action and response, what "really" happened and what he made of it in memory.
>
> *Irving Howe*

### THE EPIC

When Lawrence wrote Richards that "the story I have to tell is one of the most splendid ever given a man for writing" he saw it as an epic. An epic needs a hero (or heroes), a vast canvas, a distant and difficult goal, and plenty of action, preferably the glory of war. These elements were present. And, to frame it, a magnificent setting, and an army of warriors who still practised hand-to-hand combat. Add to this a chivalric element.

The traditional epic requires simplicity. The war is drastically simplified and usually limited to a number of distinctive incidents which move the action forward and are crucial for the completion of the heroic ordeal or quest. In the *Iliad* we are shown only the climactic events of a ten-year war, which finally opposes the two heroes, Achilles and Hector, in mortal combat. The story is narrated in a long series of set pieces, dominated by battle, camp scenes and individual feats of arms, but including much else. *Seven Pillars* does not greatly resemble this structure, but the film *Lawrence of Arabia* does up to a point. It also is structured as a series of scenes of epic character, chosen from *Seven Pillars* itself, each of which moves the action forward; so also is the 1920 abridgement, consisting of eight discrete scenes of which six are battles or raids, one a camp scene. But this is a fragment.

Lawrence was certainly partial to the classical epic, and above all the *Iliad*. Of the large number of historical authors that he had read, those he was most familiar with were classical. He discusses the question of history with Richards:

> Written history is inevitably long & must be judged by the standard of epic rather than lyric. The *Iliad* has only a fictitious unity. Gibbon at least as much. I suppose the *Peloponnesian War* has more unity than the average drama. Only perhaps you'd call it not true. I'll admit that modern history has seldom been 'composed' in the artistic sense. Trevelyan's Italian efforts perhaps. But modern history tries to be a science, not an art.[1]

He does not declare a bias here but he is clearly opposing the values of past historians, especially the ancients, to those of the modern historian, who relies not on the values of literature but of science to compose a history. We assume that he wants to see his history as an artistic composition. Lawrence had a much freer attitude to history than the modern 'scientific' academics, some of whom were later to criticise him. He was well aware that past historians had written in order to present history as a contribution to universal knowledge, or to moral philosophy, or as a contribution to the national heritage or national identity; to persuade, to philosophise, to propagandise, to entertain; finally, if written by the makers of that history, to justify or advertise oneself. They were not obsessed by 'historical truth'. He cites the name of G.M. Trevelyan, who had written his Garibaldi Trilogy just a decade earlier. Trevelyan happily confessed that it was "reeking with bias" and explained: "Without bias I should never have written them (the three books) at all. For I was moved to write them by a poetical sympathy for the Italian patriots of the period, which I retrospectively shared".[2]

If one substituted '*Arab*' for 'Italian' and '*at the time*' for 'retrospectively', this might have been written by Lawrence about *Seven Pillars*. Otherwise, the two are rather different; for while Trevelyan placed the Italian patriots right in the foreground, as does Homer the Greek heroes, Lawrence takes pole position himself. As Tabachnik observes: "His dual role as Homer and Achilles caused problems unknown to Homer himself, who wrote fiction and not autobiography".[3] The epic is a third person genre. The praise and admiration that is due to the epic hero can only be lavished by a bard, a narrator. The self-centredness of *Seven Pillars* is awkward in the epic mode. This is one (of many) reasons why Trevelyan's trilogy is much more clearly in the tradition of the historical epic than is *Seven Pillars*. It is one of the last great epics in this tradition.

Lawrence's idea as to the structure of his account was simple: he would relate everything that he did, his history would be a personal narrative which partly through his own heroic actions, partly by his Olympian manner of presentation, and above all through the sheer magnificence of the scenery, and exoticism of the desert warrior and mode of war would achieve the stature of an epic, and thus satisfy his craving to create out of a historical memoir a work of literature. He created simple personalities of grandeur and nobility. The characters are seen and described in action, from the outside. Auda, Ali, do they have thoughts? Feisal, is not his discourse copied from Elizabethan historical drama?

History was on Lawrence's side. It is created by men, until then it has no existence. The history of the Arab Revolt was waiting to be written – by him! It is no exaggeration to say that, in the West, he created the history of the Arab Revolt as surely as did Homer the history of the Trojan war. The antagonists, Arabs and Turks, could be treated as symbolically as the armies before Troy; in the world of western literature, the noble Arab was already the stuff of legend, and a stereotype of western literature. Lawrence himself was also a legend. Lawrence's Arab Revolt has a mythical status that could have put it beyond such banal considerations as historical truth. Through his own desire, it did not work out that way.

## MEMOIR AS HISTORY

Lawrence's own inclination – natural flamboyance and need to romanticise himself and his deeds – made him strive for the epic. However, he was a man whose mental nature accomodated diffuse and incompatible motives, but did not tolerate sacrifice, concession, compromise. He had to satisfy both impulses, however contradictory.

This other motivation was simple and obvious: to write *the* contemporary *history* of the Arab Revolt. It was the public raison d'être of the book. After all, he had taken part in it, invested in it two years of enormous effort, and he wished to provide a full record, not an artful selection. Everybody was expecting it. He definitely wanted to have full control over the entire history.

As it happened, the story of the Arab Revolt, thanks to Lawrence's achievement, divides itself into two very distinct parts: the first part ends with the capture of Akaba in July 1917; the second with the capture of Damascus on 1st October 1918. The first part was perfectly suited to the epic treatment, the second much less so. To a British reader, a British campaign, which the account later almost became, featuring British and Indian Army officers, rather dissipated the epic character of the Revolt. Secondly, the increase in complexity makes the narrative less purposeful, more fragmented; and on top of this, it is very very long.

The historical problem that now emerges is that this whole thing does not really add up to much. 'Was that all it was, then?' ('N'était-ce donc que cela?') was the title of Malraux' critique of *Seven Pillars*. From a certain distance, Lawrence's Revolt does appear more and more as an over-inflated side-show, being directed by the British, largely for their own sake. Historians have little to say about the revival of a people, a national movement in Hijazi Arabia. In Syria, Egypt, Iraq, yes, but in the Hijaz? Lawrence speaks much of it but where is this national movement? It was indeed a side-show but for the author it was the moment where an external event, a rebellion, is met by a consciousness that entirely embraces it. He invested in it an imaginative grandeur in the same way as a child can create out of the molehills of a small garden an imaginary Himalaya, or a test match out of a school cricket game. The agrandisement of the Arab Revolt is achieved because the narrative relates nothing outside it, it has no measure but its own; and because of the grandeur and persuasive rhetoric of the protagonist/author himself. It is in fact a kind of unmediated dictatorship. The narrator and creator are one. All the historical generalisations are underpinned and justified by the narrative, which is itself the author's own autobiography.

From the literary standpoint, simplification of the messy reality of history is a *sine qua non* of the epic. One does not narrate every event simply because it happened. The film *Lawrence of Arabia* maintains the epic perspective right through because it selects just those events that evoke it, and presents each as a scene. *Seven Pillars*, however, is a chronological continuum. It seems to say: nothing happened in which I did not participate so here is my report on what I did.

The method has little literary or historical merit. Many of the larger issues of an uprising are ignored. The memoir as history enables Lawrence to keep control over the supposed history of the Revolt. He moved much with Bedu; so the Bedu seem to play a big part in the Revolt; Feisal's contacts with the Arab world are almost unmentioned. "I mean to be my own judge of what to say", he wrote in the introductory chapter. It is important to remember that Lawrence had much more justification than Trevelyan for bias. As he wrote, the issue of the political future of the Middle East, the fate of King Hussein, Feisal and the Arabs, still hung in the balance, though failure seemed almost inevitable. His book had to be both a justification of the Arab cause and an indictment of broken promises, fraud and betrayal. And then, on top of that, the effect of all this on himself. To all of this we shall now turn our attention.

## THE PRESENTATION OF HISTORY: AN EXAMPLE – THE CRISIS AT NEBK

Lawrence's treatment of the historical is already problematic. The main danger is his assumption of the roles of both actor and author, which would lead, in the latter part of the book, to the notion of an 'introspective epic'. The personal looms very large, and I propose to illustrate that through a major incident, a turning point.

In May 1917, he had set out on his long journey from Wejh with Auda abu Tayi, Sherif Nasir and their bodyguards and followers. The first objective was the Wadi Sirhan, far to the north-east, nearby to the tents of Auda's Howeitat, and where, at Nebk, they made pause for two weeks, recruiting tribesmen for the second stage, the assault on Akaba . It was in the tribal area of the Rualla, the great tribal confederation that spread over the northern desert into Syria. The paramount Sheikh was Nuri al-Sha'alan, who also had a tent pitched, at Ageila, not far away but empty. It is at this remote spot that the theme of bad faith becomes a part of the story. Why here?

In line with the dominant idea of the *Seven Pillars* that the Arab Revolt was executed according to his plan, Lawrence gives the impression that the second stage of the expedition – to turn back west to Akaba – was a pre-ordained continuation of the first. In fact, however, Feisal, who veered constantly between a desire to rely on the British and a feeling that he must be more independent, had another more general strategy, which was no mere Plan B: to prepare his own move north to gather support in Syria itself. Key elements were the attitude of Nuri Sha'alan towards the Revolt, and the situation in the Jebel Druze, the abutments of Syria to the north-west, where lived a warlike rebellious people protected by a mountainous terrain, who had twice rebelled against the Turks in the recent past, whom Feisal hoped to make use of.[4] Feisal's eyes were no longer on the Turks in the Hejaz, but on Syria. What Feisal wanted was to make his presence known as forcefully as possible in the north, and to gather support for actions in Syria aimed at getting control of the railway, using the Druze and the northern tribes. Feisal was very worried about French intentions in Syria. However, there is no evidence of an immediate intention to foment a large-scale rebellion, as Lawrence claimed. The Akaba plan was new and tempting to Feisal but there was no certainty it would be carried out.

Although nothing has been clarified as to what really happened at Nebk in June 1917, the final decision to launch an expedition against Akaba seems to have been contested. *Seven Pillars* lengthily describes a struggle for influence between him and a Syrian nationalist, Nesib al-Bakri, who had accompanied the expedition from Wejh. Nesib al-Bakri, a Syrian notable close to Feisal (Feisal preferred to stay at his house when in Damascus), of considerable influence in Syria, landowner in the Jebel Druze, and going there on Feisal's business with a considerable allocation of gold, was an opponent. The career of Nesib al-Bakri and its political implications are described in Appendix 2 entitled: 'Nesib al-Bakri and the Syrian Alternative'. He was, in fact, the man designated to implement Feisal's plan. The mutual distrust between Lawrence and Nesib, who was well-informed, had political insight, and believed that pan-Arab nationalism would be better served by promoting revolt in Syria, must have been acute. On Nesib's side there was doubtless a suspicion, perhaps a conviction, that Lawrence was an agent influencing the Arab Revolt for British imperialist ends. He had good reason for such a suspicion even if it was unduly simplistic.[5] That there was a public difference of opinion is clear. The time Lawrence takes in *Seven Pillars* to ridicule Nesib's arguments and to justify his own, the prosecuting tone, the rubbishing of his personality, the misrepresentation and trivialisation of his aims, and the contemptuously complete victory over Nesib that he records are Lawrencian signs that his leadership or judgement has been seriously challenged. He was in a vulnerable position, the only Englishman among Arabs, completely cut off from friends and moral support on an expedition on which he had an anomalous status. He had joined it of his own volition and yet he had now begun trying to exert his influence and power, financial and political (as a representative of Great Britain or of Feisal, who could know which?).[6] At this point, begins the saga of Lawrence's mysterious 'journey to the north'. Perhaps to get relief from further conflict, perhaps for reconnaissance objectives, perhaps to make contacts, Lawrence wrote that he left camp for ten days and made an extraordinarily daring solo journey by camel well north of Damascus. It would in any case have been uncharacteristic for Lawrence to sit around in camp doing nothing while the recruitment of tribesmen proceeded. He makes rather a point of giving no information about this alleged ride in *Seven Pillars*.

During the long journey from Wejh he had convinced himself that "I was the only person engaged in the field of the Arab adventure who could dispose it to be at once a handmaid to the British Army of Egypt, and also at the same time the author of its own success." The Akaba objective would be the key move in this process. But he was well aware of what this meant, both for himself and for the Arabs: for the latter, a greater dependence on Great Britain; for himself a greater responsibility, not only for command, but also for policy. In spite of the brilliant plan which he sees only himself fit to carry out, he repeats that he is not suited to the position he is in: "So many men craved action, detested thinking: it was an irony I should fill one of their places unwillingly." He has said this before. There would be no happy solution to this conflict.

But there is worse. He carried the knowledge that the Arabs may eventually get very little for their pains. Only just before leaving Wejh, he had met with Major Mark Sykes, the dangerous amateur of the Sykes–Picot treaty, which had reminded him again of the awful muddle of conflicting promises made by Great Britain. If people like Nesib al-Bakri got to know of this – and maybe he already suspected something – he could be put in a very difficult position, and the Akaba plan endangered.

The treatment that he prescribed for himself evidently worked and the cloud passed. When he got back to Auda's tents at Nebk, Nesib was either no longer there or left a day or two later. Sufficient tribesmen had been recruited from both Howeitat and Rualla. "Nothing hindered the start. The freshness of the adventure in hand consoled us for everything.". The crisis had passed and did not return in earnest for several months. They set out towards Akaba.

※

The decision implemented at Nebk (to go for Akaba) marked the watershed of the Arab Revolt. As for Lawrence, he became, as he said, a 'principal' of the Revolt because the move on Akaba, if successful, would give him a political role. Akaba was his idea. The view represented by Nesib was that the Arabs should concentrate on preparing for action in Syria, not bother about Akaba, which he saw as of no possible use to such an aim (as a port on the Red Sea it is decisive for linking up with the British, but far out of the way for land operations against Syria and contacting its human resources there) and which would increase Arab dependence on the British, whom he mistrusted.

Nesib al-Bakri, within the *Seven Pillars* mythology, is an alien, a representative of an Arab political class which opposed the vision of the Revolt of its master-spirit. We therefore hear next-to-nothing about him and his relationship with Feisal. The conflict between these men represented an irrevocable parting of the ways, where Nesib went up into Syria to prepare a Revolt that never happened, and Lawrence towards a British-Arab alliance and, as an ironic consequence, the facilitation of the Sykes–Picot arrangements for Syria after the war, the French mandate. Nesib had been right.

### The wider political background

The Sherif of Mecca had taken, in June 1916, the risky step of rebellion against the Ottoman empire, after having assured himself of British military and financial assistance. The chief British negotiator was Henry McMahon, High Commissioner in Cairo. Negotiations were by letters carried by messengers. The failure of the Gallipoli landings against Turkey in 1915 led Great Britain to the point where, in order to persuade Hussein to revolt against Turkey, she was ready not only to help with arms, money, naval bombardment and transport, but to make lavish promises of British support to the Sherif for independent Arab rule in most areas of the Arabian peninsula if Turkey were defeated. These areas included most of greater Syria without excluding the area known as Palestine. There was, by October, a desperate sense of urgency in Whitehall over the Turkish threat to the Suez canal now that an allied withdrawal from Gallipoli was inevitable, magnified by the frightening spectre of a pan-Islamic movement, which might include Muslims in British dominions such as India, against the enemies of Islamic Turkey. The following telegrams give an idea of just how anxious were top-ranking British policy makers to make an alliance with Hussein of Mecca:

*From Lord Kitchener to General Maxwell, GOC Egypt, 11 Oct. 1915*
The Government are most anxious to deal with the Arab question in a manner that would be satisfactory to the Arabs . . . You must do your best to prevent any alienation of the traditional loyalty of the Arabs to England.

*From General Maxwell to Kitchener, 16 Oct. 1915*
Unless we make a definite and agreeable proposal to the Shereef at once, we may have a united Islam against us.

*From Sir Edward Grey, Foreign Secretary, to McMahon, 20 Oct. 1915*
The important thing is to give our assurances that will prevent the Arabs from being alienated, and I must leave you discretion in the matter as it is urgent. . . .[7]

Given the extremely difficult circumstances, McMahon's 'pledge' to Mecca (24 October) by letter concerning those areas where Britain would support Arab independence after the war was a masterpiece of diplomacy – subtly ambiguous here, evasive there, and vaguely conditional overall on "the interests of our ally, France". Hussein, though himself a cunning negotiator, seems to have been duped by it into believing that he had been promised Syria and Palestine. That he should not disbelieve it was indeed the intention. Lawrence, like Hussein, took a positive view of the pledge, but it had been sabotaged by a "treaty" (long kept secret from McMahon, and therefore from the Sherif).

### The meeting with Nuri Sha'alan

The abyss opened suddenly before me one night upon this ride, when in his tent old Nuri Shaalan bringing out his documents asked me bluntly which of the British promises were to be believed. I saw that with my answer I would gain or lose him: and in him the outcome of the Arab Movement: and by my advice that he should trust the latest in date of contradictory pledges, I passed definitely into the class of principal. (OX295-6).

The meeting with Nuri Sha'alan was the first meeting between a British officer and the greatest tribal leader in northern Arabia. Yet the meeting is mentioned with a studied vagueness which is not satisfactorily clarified in any report, including the secret one to Clayton (see below). We know not where it took place, when, or who Lawrence was with. An aisled tent materialises somewhere in the deep desert with a man inside who has on file the texts or reports of secret agreements. The Sykes–Picot agreement (which Lawrence must be referring to) was secret and King Hussein certainly did not know of it. Obviously, there would have been rumours and questions circulating all over the area concerning British intentions but the British presence in the area was still discreet. Not until the Bolsheviks came to power in October 1917 and published these imperialist plots, did the Arabs learn of Sykes–Picot. So Lawrence must be referring to a later meeting (perhaps that in August 1918 when he accompanied Feisal at Jefer – it would have been much more likely for Nuri to have raised questions then as he was about to commit himself to Feisal); otherwise, he was simply being over-imaginative in order to enhance the drama. A final intriguing possibility is that he is transposing onto Nuri the concerns about British intentions raised by Nesib. Such transpositions are not unusual with Lawrence. Nuri's policy at this earlier time was to retain his neutrality, to remain friendly with both sides, British and Turk, and await developments.

Doynel de St Quentin, the French military attaché in Cairo, already mentioned as being a close friend of Lawrence, who was well sourced with agents, has a different but not necessarily accurate version of events. According to him, Nuri Sha'alan and Nawaf, his brother, "had already moved back along Wadi Sirhan towards the north-west in the direction of Kaf. Lawrence and Nasir followed them there".[9] Nuri welcomed them as emissaries of Feisal but maintained his neutrality. Nonetheless, he allowed 150 of his men, led by Benaiah ibn Dughmi, to join the column to Akaba. Nuri and Nawaf then left Kaf but Lawrence and Nasir remained there. This report at least provides some substance to the alleged meeting but no other new information.

### The ride to the north

Lawrence gave a secret report to Clayton (dated 10 July) on his northern journey, which encloses a map of his itinerary, stating that he met with Nuri and Nawaf at Azrak on his return from the north.[10] The report is a list of place names and the chiefs he met there, with a few notes. The journey has caused a good deal of controversy because of the very evasive way in which Lawrence subsequently referred to it here in *Seven Pillars* and elsewhere, and, perhaps, because the report came very close to winning Lawrence a V.C. because of the incredible audacity of the journey and what he achieved on it. There is no reliable independent confirmation by a witness of any part of it (and this is why the recommendation for the V.C. had to be dropped); this is surprising since he allegedly met many people in many different places and even blew up a bridge with dynamite with a party of 35 Arabs. Even without this, it was not every day that a lone English military officer (whether dressed as an Arab or in khakhi) with an escort was seen in such remote places. News travels fast in the desert and tribesmen have sharp eyes, sharp ears, and very long memories.[11]

There has been no confirmation from those he claimed to have met, and flat denials from their descendants or acquaintances. In the early sixties, an Arab historian interviewed tribesmen who had either had contact with the expedition to the Sirhan themselves or whose fathers or uncles had. Nobody knew anything about Lawrence's trip.[12]

St Quentin also mentions a trip north, stating that during this period Lawrence headed north to Azrak to meet another (named) tribal leader but missed him there and had to turn back (Azrak was the place where he claimed in the secret report to Clayton to have met Nuri and Nawaf, with Hussein al-Atrash, a Druze leader). This is the only source I have come across that provides a different version of Lawrence's ride to the north, albeit far less ambitious than the one he claimed in his report to Clayton. One cannot exclude the possibility that St. Quentin's source was, once again, Lawrence (during his long stay in Cairo after Akaba), especially as the report is the same one that reported the highly unlikely story of his recruitment by the Turks before the war (*see* above). If that were so, it would indicate that he provided different versions of the ride to St. Quentin and to Clayton.

Later, Lawrence was indiscreet. Lowell Thomas picked up a garbled version about the journey, either while at Akaba in 1918 or later, and it found its way into his book.[13] Robert Graves, when researching for his biography on Lawrence in 1927, asked him about it. In a very long reply, TE ended as follows:

> You may make public if you like the fact that my reticence upon this northward ride is deliberate, and based on private reasons: and record your opinion that I have found mystification, and perhaps statements deliberately misleading or contradictory, the best way to hide the truth of what really occurred, if anything did occur.

There is a brazen patrician honesty in this confession of possible dishonesty. It does not prove that the report to Clayton is false but it is hardly reassuring! It is an important comment because the method suggested for hiding the truth, indeed his notion of responsibility towards expressing the truth, is not limited to this one instance; it is an admirably frank admission of how he has several times dealt with mysterious incidents or references from *Seven Pillars*, of which the identity of S.A., and the Dera' incident are further examples. In fact, it is reasonable to assert that this strategy is habitual. Later in this letter, Lawrence also casts doubt on the validity of his secret report to Clayton. In particular, he hints that he never attacked a bridge at Ras Baalbek, which was undoubtedly the most extraordinary feat of the reported trip. He urges Graves to hide the truth, if any, as follows: "He must have ridden light, and demolition work cannot have been in his programme, though an intercepted enemy report of this date mentions a bridge being damaged near Ras Baalbek, south of Hama, considerably beyond Damascus and Baalbek, the furthest points associated by rumour with his journey. The destruction of this bridge was probably a coincidence."[14] In this manner he completely rewrites Graves' first account[15] and demonstrates his desire to have absolute control over what passes for the truth.

My object is not to prove that the entire story is untrue (which is impossible), or that this is true but that is not; but to show how it cannot pass as history – there is simply no reason why one should believe it. In this muddle I agree with Barr that "what matters is that his colleagues believed him" (see Chapter 15).[16] For that created a new reality. 'It was neither true nor false, but lived'. The story itself, by Lawrence's own treatment of it, is the ride of a phantom.

## THE PERSONALISATION OF HISTORY

There are considerable differences between the Oxford text (OX 295-6) and the 1926 revision (R 282-4). The former does not lose sight of the narrative and is therefore limited in its introspection. The later version expands the crisis of confidence into a thoroughgoing analysis of the betrayal and an orgy of guilt-ridden language: There are few passages in which an author of a historical narrative uses so much emotional language, so much self-justification, and takes such a personal attitude towards the reader. In four paragraphs on page 283 [R], I picked up the following expressions:

> *false pretences* . . . . . . *fraud* . . . . . . *agony of mind* . . . . . .
> *disingenuous answer* . . . . . . *chief confidence-man* . . . . . . *in revenge*
> . . . . . . *I vowed* . . . . . . *I had no leave* . . . . . . *in resentment* . . . . . .
> *false place*

What is Lawrence trying to persuade us of here? The driving idea seems to be that, owing to British deceit at the political level his own position has become untenable; this is because the Arabs themselves have been betrayed, and those sent out to help them compromised. There must be countless good men, honest colonial administrators or advisers who in the last century felt let down by their government. Joyce and Newcombe, the two senior officers with the Arabs, and Colonel C.E. Wilson, British Representative in Jeddah, knew about the treaty and it worried them. Wilson went so far as to threaten resignation rather than deceive King Hussein. However, they did not let it change their behaviour. Lawrence, as Kirkbride has shown, did. Taking the oppositional view that the exploited Arabs now have to look after themselves, he appoints himself their champion in the fight to beat the British to the winning-post.

The very personal language I have extracted signals a concentrated display of accusation and self-accusation, exposing the raw vein of guilt, confessing and massaging it, a procedure of lucidity and self-restitution.

*A priori*, there is no call for him to feel responsible, he is a mere Captain doing his job, but that is not the narrative of *Seven Pillars*. He is a stakeholder in the Revolt. One might almost say that he *is* the Revolt. Him, not Nasser, not Auda, not Feisal. "I had no leave to engage the Arabs, unknowing, in a gamble of life and death". This is the myth. The child-like Arabs have no will of their own. He should send them home. As for guilt, he clearly wants to participate in it, even though it is not really his fault. Or is it? How can one know? As the vocabulary in italics demonstrates, he seems more concerned with the effect of the British deceit on *himself* than on the Arab movement. The drama of fraud and guilt has been personalised to the extent of placing it before history.

What is quite clear is that we are in retrospective mode. When he wrote this he knew that the Arabs would get nothing, had got nothing. The third paragraph takes us to Versailles. Once this is understood it becomes more clear why he makes here such an issue of the Sykes–Picot treaty. For by the time this text was written he had indeed taken upon himself political responsibility for the Arabs and had supped full with guilt-inducing compromises.

Now there is a reason for this time warp and its name is Bernard and Charlotte Shaw. It was they who persuaded Lawrence to withdraw Chapter 1 How and Why I wrote. Lawrence did not want to jettison some of his best passages, so he found what he thought an appropriate place for them within the narrative at Nebk. Here is an extract from Chapter 1:

> It was evident from the beginning that if we won the war these promises would be dead paper, and had I been an honest adviser of the Arabs I would have told them to go home and not risk their lives fighting for such stuff: but I salved myself with the hope that by leading these Arabs madly in the final victory I would establish them, with arms in their hands, in a position so assured that expediency

would counsel to the Great Powers a fair settlement of their claims. It is not yet clear if I succeeded: but it is clear that I had no shadow of leave to engage them unknowing in such a hazard. . . . I risked being made a fraud, on my conviction that . . . better we win and break our word than lose. (OX 8)

If the reader now reads the four paragraphs on page 283 of the standard edition (I regret that, due to USA copyright, I cannot print them), he/she will see that it is full of the expressions used above, and it is this which accounts for (1) the very accusatory and self-justificatory style, and (2) the sense of time warp

## THE QUESTION OF LAWRENCE'S HISTORICAL RESPONSIBILITY

We need some perspective on this much-discussed subject in order to be able to judge the background to *Seven Pillars* and his guilt-loaded attitude there. Clearly this can be nothing more than a sketch.

French sources confirm the very close relations he had formed with Feisal and accuse him of egging Feisal on, fanning his ambition. Father Jaussen, a Dominican priest, one of the best informed westerners in Arabia whose reports were highly valued by the French, had met Lawrence at Wejh with Feisal on 2 March, 1917. He noted how close the two already were: "The English Captain Lawrence has an intimate relationship with Feisal, the son of the Sherif, who seems to place great store on his friendship. He has a real influence over him", he wrote in a despatch.[17] He soon understood that Lawrence wanted to take Damascus in order to prevent the French, criticising him for both sharing and encouraging Feisal's antipathy to foreigners in Arabia. Auguste Lamotte, who commanded the French detachment at Wejh from February 1917 to July 1918 and knew Feisal well, goes further: "Everyone knew that Lawrence and Feisal were in league together to gain Syria" and "Lawrence was to be the instrument of (his) ascent to a sceptre and crown".[18] How much credence to put on Lamotte's strong views is difficult to know but Jaussen was an astute and accurate observer, fluent in Arabic. It does appear that, at the very least, Lawrence was encouraging Feisal beyond the call of duty.

As a highly influential member of the Intelligence staff in Cairo, he undoubtedly knew all about the Hussein—McMahon correspondence and at least the broad lines of the Sykes–Picot treaty before he even set foot in Arabia. Hogarth wrote later that Lawrence had been a moving spirit in the negotiations leading to an Arab revolt. As for the treaty, it was approved by the British government in February 1916 and was discussed in Cairo from April onwards. He may not have known all the details but he knew of the treaty and what it meant. He thus knew that there was no guarantee whatever that the British would back Arab claims after the war, whether the Arabs contributed to the victory or not. It was a gamble. The other 'intrusives' were gambling on the non-implementation of the treaty too; but it was no skin off their noses one way or the other. Lawrence had engaged his heart and his honour.

In May 1917, just before Lawrence's departure for the Sirhan, Mark Sykes, the British negotiator, arrived in the Hejaz, and gave his carefully doctored version of the treaty to Feisal in Wejh. He also met Lawrence tête-à-tête and it is not to be believed that he, Sykes, was allowed to conceal much.

On the strength of the passage unquoted from *Seven Pillars*, we have a man who did not know about the treaty but who nevertheless takes upon himself the guilt and responsibility; an attitude that is noble: I am innocent *in fact* but I am guilty *in spirit*. But since he did know, and had encouraged a Feisal who presumably did not (unless we assume Feisal chose to keep his own father in the dark and watch him being made a fool of by Sykes and Picot in Jeddah), he does indeed bear some moral responsibility. But not all; Feisal was a politician, he knew of French ambitions in Syria, he was prepared to take the risk. It was *after* the war that Feisal was let down. This is passed over in complete silence. There can be little doubt that later feelings of resentment and guilt have been transposed to Lawrence's book.

Contrary to the general view, I am persuaded that the Sykes–Picot fraud narrative is unreliable, because to an unknown extent retrospective, fall-out from the British withdrawal of support for the Arabs at Versailles, and the French annexation of Syria, fed emotionally by his sense of failure and his masochism; otherwise, there is a credibility gap between what he writes and what he did or did not do. On July 29th, just after the capture of Akaba, Lawrence had had two long private conversations with the Grand Sharif in Jeddah in which Hussein, in upbeat mood, demonstrates how completely he had been deceived by Sykes and Picot, in a visit from them in May, into believing the opposite of the truth concerning French intentions in Syria. Yet Lawrence's long report about it[19] expressed no anxiety at this fatal misunderstanding. There is, it is true, no reason why Lawrence should be anything than strictly objective in a report to Cairo. Nonetheless, C.E. Wilson, Newcombe, and Joyce all showed a good deal more public concern at the dishonesty of the procedure and the possible consequences of deceit.[20] His anxiety at Nebk was real, but I suspect it had more to do with the risk he was taking, and the challenge posed by Nesib to his authority than with the shame of dishonesty. That, I believe, was later.

Of course, the entire notion of trading future promises of Arab independence in exchange for Arab engagement against a common enemy was a risky venture, and Lawrence encouraged this engagement to the limit. He, with eyes wide open, committed himself to the idea that Arab and British objectives should be pursued as one and the same, since, he believed, that gave the Arabs the best chance of being among the victors and of being recognised as such when the war was over. He may have been sincere in binding the fate of King Hussein and Feisal to the political will of Great Britain, and ignoring or even discouraging other sources of support for the Arab movement, but by doing so he facilitated precisely the results he had wanted to avoid: the implementation of the treaty, then the brutal expulsion of Feisal and the French seizure of the whole of Syria.

Lawrence's assumption of total responsibility justifies Edward Said's remark: "(Lawrence) is unconscious of anything in the Orient that history, after all, is history and that even without him the Arabs would finally attend to their quarrel with the Turks."[21] The influence of *Seven Pillars* has hindered the British public from imagining any alternative scenario for the Arab movement – the *larger* Arab movement, that is; and, as Antonius argues immediately below, from appreciating what was happening in other parts of the Arab world. Was it necessarily true that a tiny armed insurrection, entirely dependent on its British paymasters and suppliers, led by a religious family with anachronistic ideas, ruling a backward and sparsely populated province without resources, with little political influence (except the prestige of the Sherif) in the greater Arab world, was the ideal or only possible vehicle to which to harness the Arab movement for independence? For the British perhaps, but for the Arabs?

## HISTORIANS: NARRATIVE HISTORY VERSUS CREATIVITY

The historians of the past have not given *Seven Pillars* a good press:

GEORGE ANTONIUS: "His knowledge as revealed in his book was in some important respects faulty, and his conception of the play of forces in the background of the revolt palpably defective . . . . It seems as though Lawrence, with his aptitude to see life as a succession of images, had felt the need to connect and rationalise his experiences into a pattern; and in so doing, had allowed sensations to impinge upon facts, and predilections to colour both. This hankering after a pattern seems to have been a dominant trait and one which governed his vision more masterfully in thought than in action, and perhaps most masterfully of all when the time came for him to narrate his experiences in a form dictated by his craving for literary creativeness."[22]

ELIE KEDOURIE: "As history it is riddled with falsehoods" and "in making popular and attractive the confusion between the public world of politics and the private dramas of the self, I judge it to be profoundly corrupting."[23]

ALBERT HOURANI: "One of the traits which the two men [Lawrence and Massignon] shared was a powerful imagination, which could impose its own order on the remembered events of their lives."[24]

EDWARD SAID: "In his work we can see most clearly the conflict between narrative history and vision."[25]

CHAPTER

# 18

# THE PROBLEM OF AUTOBIOGRAPHY

For both reader and writer, the autobiographical aspect of *Seven Pillars* is the most difficult of the book, the most elusive, the most fragmentary; yet also the most pervasive.

### MEMOIR & AUTOBIOGRAPHY

It was a memoir of the Revolt, he wrote, a chronicle of "myself in it". Characteristically, this was very thoroughly remembered. His own movements, exactness in place names and the names of those with him (when not deliberately changed or suppressed), exhaustive accounts of his major actions, his more important meetings in Cairo and what was discussed. Every incident of every day is clothed in its special characteristics, beginning with the unique topographical scenario. Furthermore, there is a huge contribution of well-informed comment and argument: plans, the military backgound to the events and campaigns, strategy and tactics, the geographical, topographical and geological characteristics, notes on tribes, participants, etc. Too much, some would say.[1]

All this fills the place of autobiography. There is such a superfluity of detail, and impulse to comment on anything and everything, that autobiography in the usual sense hardly gets a look in. What there is of it is all on the level of immediate action, immediate sensation, immediate effect. He is a doer. Heroes are the sum of their acts. Social relations are almost a blank; he spurns the luxury of a social life. He is reticent towards himself most of the time and even more reticent towards his companions; and discreet. Who led the Akaba expedition? Was it really Lawrence? Was it Naser? Was it Auda? Who can tell? The style is distant, full of understatement. When somebody is about to shoot him, he is "sorry". Nothing more. The ideal, he tells us, is to be "an unseen presence". His job is to record.

As for autobiographical history, it does not exist. There is no Before and there is no After. At the other extreme, he wrote in letters: "It's an apology for my first thirty years, and the explanation that followed on them". Or: "the book is a summary of what I've thought and done and made of myself in these first thirty years". And again, in the *myself* chapter, "taking stock of where I stood mentally at this moment of my thirtieth birthday" (16th August 1918). Clearly, therefore, there is also present within these pages a far-reaching autobiographical intention, independent of the Revolt.

In his essay on Lawrence and Louis Massignon, Albert Hourani wrote: "The Arab East was the place of some experience so deep and challenging as to have revealed their true selves and the orientation of their lives".[2] It is more clear-cut in the case of Massignon, who experienced what might be termed a Pauline vision. Hourani suggests that for Lawrence the symbolic expression of this deep and challenging experience was the 'citadel of my integrity'. This was Lawrence's phrase for what he lost at Dera'. Hourani is shy of giving any opinion of the veracity of that event; but he adheres to the phrase 'citadel of my integrity' which was lost "if not at Dera'a, then elsewhere."

It is not difficult to see in the Drama of the Self a life-changing experience. In 1916 he was still innocent, on the threshold of putting his great vision to the test; in 1918 it was over and a huge personal failure was staring him in the face. What the Arabian experience had taught him was the limits of power, and that power was dangerous, to others as well as to himself; the meaning of responsibility, and that he could not live with it; that to aspire to two cultures at the same time is fraudulent and makes you an alien in both; that dreams are vain things and become corrupted in their contact with reality; and that, in the end, outsiders never win. All these revelations were checks. The confident assumptions on which he had based his usefulness, his dynamism, his sense of purpose, his success, were overturned, invalidated. He was *morally* rather than psychologically disoriented. "From now onwards", continued Hourani, this was the summons to find some kind of order in the chaos of life. . . . Lawrence . . . ardently wished for "that vision of the wholeness of life" which was "not a visitor to me, but always there." "The revelation of this tragic disharmony between will and purpose is what his Eastern adventure ultimately meant to him."[3]

Internal equilibrium is a condition of free life. The lucidity he seeks in his narrative-cum-analysis would, he hoped, provide a mental and moral foundation for turning the page, beginning a new life. There is no doubt that the Arabian experience was not simply something to be narrated like an ordinary memoir. It was deeply troubling. Many times, he tells one or other of his correspondents that he has to get 'the Arab business' behind him. The Drama of the Self is his attempt to put this together as a story, a story which will arrive and end at a point at which the adventure is 'washed out', so to speak, at point zero. The revelation that Hourani defines, as being the mismatch between will and purpose is perfectly evident.

Inevitably, given these concerns, the analysis is retrospective. The man whose voice we are hearing is not always the man of 1917/18 but the writer of 1920 or later. This is reflected in many ways, perhaps most insistently in the ethical perspective. As we have seen in the previous chapter, one may doubt whether he felt quite so concerned by the ethics, the morality of his position, at the time. What we learn is how he feels about it now, but we may not realise this, since he conceals it. This 'other' biography creates a time warp, a man living in two time zones simultaneously.

Nonetheless, it is also perfectly evident why this revelation had to be here, in the desert, primeval and empty, and not (for example) at 2 Polstead Road, Oxford. For Lawrence, it had an enormous literary potential and he had hoped to give it a tragic significance. He failed largely because he was mightily distracted by another question, also coming from his post-war self:

"Am I guilty?" This other question gets in the way all the time and exhausts his energy. The Speech for the Defense. He had to put his demons to rest: convince himself that he was not guilty. It was an uphill road all the way; an obsessive anxiety-laden exploration of his motives, a plea for condonation which struggles against his self-contempt and often ends in mystification. And yet it was not possible for him to face certain facts of his behaviour head-on, so what we learn, like so much else, has to be deciphered.

## THE INTROSPECTVE EPIC

The literary idea was to base his introspective epic on his perception of what had happened to him in Arabia, thereby making it one with the narrative. But this was after he had chosen to build his book round the strong backbone of the day-to-day narrative of his part in the

Revolt; because this was him, what he knew, what he had written down. By this design he had barred the way to truly integrating an intimate autobiography. He could only add digressions, make collages, or run a parallel text. When one reads of the extent of his literary ambition, and of his disappointment at the result, one wonders why he did not modify his structural plan. Perhaps he knew, or he found out, that it was beyond him. His perception of himself was too fragmentary, too uncertain. This is where Garnett was so keen to help. But Lawrence would not be persuaded. It is clear that the taut busy pauseless narrative, with its 'blade-like tension', was what he wanted. It was a refuge. It was solid. Lawrence had a weak sense of social identity. His predilection for solitude, for the lone adventure, his idea of himself as a being apart, meant that his identity could be known only in his acts. The revelations about himself in the course of his acts are those that make up a hero: his courage, his skill, his tactical genius, his endurance, his useful heterogeneous knowledge, his care for his companions.

## *1. Comment*

He tried various techniques: the most common method is introspective comment, such as his rationale of the quarrel with Vickery, or the conflict of loyalties at Nebk, or the introductory chapter, and these passages are often shadowed by guilt, self-justification, self-accusation, or are themselves accusatory; we should add to these longer passages many of the countless sentence-level comments on what he observes, or reflects on, which are all part of the search for identity, for lucidity.

## *2. Stories*

Another technique, much more daring and original, was simply the invention of an incident. That at least is my conviction, but I have no proof; this is inevitable; for if an incident never happened, there won't be any evidence. Four events which seem to be improbable, either wholly or in part, are:

> Lawrence's execution of a Moor in Wadi Kitan.
> The first incident at Dera'.
> The death of Farraj (OX 597-8).
> The slaughter of Turkish prisoners and fugitives by
>   Tafas (OX 775-8).

All these passages are about death or degradation and three of them involve killing by his own hand. All of them are milestones on the road towards a psychological burn-out, a moral annihilation. They are all controversial: are they fact or fiction?

If one believes in Lawrence's intention to create an adequately powerful psychological drama in a text parallel to the historical one, it is tempting to believe that these passages are invented. They seem to be imaginative solutions to the problem of expressing a drama that never really happened as shown, but of which, in a less dramatic way, he believed himself the victim and the effects of which he was actually suffering. He believed in the truth of fiction from the pen of masters like Conrad or E.M. Forster. I believe he liked to use his imagination to break the bonds of constraint. The arguments against his execution of a Moor in Wadi Kitan, or against a deliberate slaughter of Turkish prisoners at Tafas, are similar to one another: circumstantial improbability, lack of evidence, stereotypical description, the common ground of sado-masochistic fantasy.

### 3. *Self-analysis*

At the opposite pole to these lurid incidents, we have, near the end of the book, recourse to emotionally disciplined self-analysis: the *Myself* chapter, what Garnett called a "strange free disclosure". It is a brilliant analysis of the complexity of his nature. Of all the chapters in the book, this is the one that is most obviously free of the time and space of the Revolt. Hence Garnett's term for it. It does not grow out of the story and is largely irrelevant to it. It could be as he said – because it coincides with his thirtieth birthday. Its ruthless honesty and detail shows by contrast how little of himself the *Seven Pillars* does actually reveal and how little of it has that open clarity that we find here. The complexity of his character, as he expresses it here, makes it easy to understand how difficult it would have been to use any other method of presentation but analysis to explain himself. "I was very conscious of the bundled powers and entities within me; it was their character that hid."

The fragmentary nature of his book reflects the fragmentary nature of his personality. He knew it. The Myself chapter, for all its remarkable self-insight, struck Garnett as a cop-out, a throwing in of the towel. 'I cannot reveal myself in actions or situations', it seems to say, 'only through self-analysis'.

### 4. *A superstructure of ideas*

In the latter part of the book, in the midst of a scene with the Arabs, we may suddenly find ourselves in a landscape of abstract ideas, metaphysical speculation and complex analysis. The 'sermon' to the

Serahin, the discourse on his bodyguard, his meditations in the tents of the Rualla (OX 653-662) on vicarious suffering: they focus on different ideas but, cumulatively, they are meditations on behaviour whose gist, to use the Nietzschean term, is a revaluation of values: questioning the value of action, putting failure above success, presenting sacrifice and the redeeming of others as an ego trip, glorifying punishment and pain.

Once more, there are problems of insertion. The reflections are tied to what are presented as historical incidents. For example, the 'sermon to the Serahin', in Book VI, is presented as an incident in which Lawrence himself, and Ali ibn Hussein, successfully persuaded men from the Serahin tribe to join their risky expedition to the Yarmuk gorge. At first, they had no stomach for it. Far into the night, Lawrence and Ali seek to persuade them. The 'midnight sermon' to the Serahin, Lawrence's sole recorded effort at preaching, is one of the most interesting – and improbable – discourses in the *Seven Pillars*.

> We put it to them, not abstractedly, but concretely, for their case, how life in the desert was sensual only, to be lived and loved just in its extremity. There could be no rest-houses for us, no dividend of joy paid out. Its spirit was accretive, to endure as far as the senses would endure, and to use each such advance made good as a base for further adventure, deeper privation, sharper pain.
>
> To be of the desert was to wage unending battle with an enemy who was not of the world, nor life, nor anything, but just hope itself; and failure seemed God's freedom to mankind. We might only exercise this our freedom by not doing what it lay within our power to do, for then life would belong to us, and we should have mastered it by holding it cheap. Death would seem best of all our works, the last liberty within our grasp, our final leisure ...
>
> To the clear-sighted, failure was the only goal to seek. We must believe, through and through, that there was no victory except to go down into death fighting and crying for failure itself. (OX 462-3)

Note the threefold repetition of failure as the only goal. Rathbone asks: "Could he have made a clearer statement of that cornerstone of the masochist's philosophy which may be summed up as 'victory through defeat'?"[4] The insistence on *failure* as an important element is striking. It is the necessary antidote to what hitherto had absolutely dominated his life: determination to succeed; and the slavery to the

Will that success presupposes. But, as Hourani asks: "By an effort of will, how could he escape from the tyranny of will?"[5] In its insistence on violent struggle, pain and privation, and mastery over an imaginary enemy, the passage is masochistic throughout.

The desert mise en scène of self-deprivation and sterility wonderfully contextualises the argument; but once again there is an absurd clash of genre. There is an obvious incongruity in trying to insert this quintessentially Lawrencian passage on moral philosophy into the historical narrative of speech-making to a desert tribe. Even if they understood a word of what he and Ali were talking about, it is inconceivable that a group of simple life-loving Bedu be persuaded to risk their lives by such arguments, however concretely they may have been put – and how *does* one put such arguments concretely? The Serahin were no doubt recruited by gold sovereigns, and by a call upon their valour and prestige. The fact that so few (if any) Western critics have found anything absurd about it is interesting, in that it shows how little readers are conscious of an Arab reality in this book independent of the author.

These abstract discourses are an oblique form of autobiography in the retrospective mode. "What I was trying to do, I suppose, was to build a superstructure of ideas upon or above anything I made", wrote Lawrence years later.[6] They are an attempt to directly link the Arab experience with a philosophy of living that is better understood as a result of it, and in essence the antithesis of that he lived by in Arabia.

### NEW LEGENDS FOR OLD

Lawrence knew that 'Lawrence of Arabia' had never existed. His mission was to show its falsity. Instead of the unreal 'perfect hero', which he detested, he would show us a human being: a vulnerable man, a sensitive man forced to kill twice in cold blood, a man almost always in pain, often humiliated, once flogged and buggered, a man tormented by guilt, unsure of what he believed in, exhausted finally and completely disillusioned, after ordering the massacre of 200 Turkish prisoners. All this amounts to a confession of some magnitude.

Yet, in spite of all that, all those differences from the pure Lowell Thomas legend, he did not shed the mantle of the mythical hero. On the contrary. He wove himself a more splendid one than before. The personality was more complex perhaps, but not less heroic. By doing so he effectively adulterated the search for the man he believed he had become after thirty years. He did not even rub out the 'Lawrence of

Arabia' title. Is he not still that today? He undoubtedly deepened the image, gave it a more human, a more wounded persona, and of more relevance to the post-war *Zeitgeist*, but he did not abolish it. As Bernard Shaw correctly prophesied, when Lawrence wrote him that he wanted to wash out his name: "Lawrence you will be to the end of your days, and thereafter to the end of what we call modern history."[7] In writing this, Shaw shows his awareness of the enormous power of legend, a parallel insight to that of his fellow-countryman, Wilde. The implication of Shaw's observation is that the re-creation of a 'plain man', stripped of his legend by that same man, is impossible. Especially is it impossible in a book which deals with the very events and background that created the legend in the first place. Lawrence sincerely wanted to show the inner self; but for one reason and another he could not let go of the 'other'.

The legend it was that drove him to ask himself, obsessively, who he *really* was. Why did he go five times to see himself portrayed by Lowell Thomas at Covent Garden? Why this obsession to be portrayed by artists and then spend long minutes looking at himself? Is it possible to imagine this man or his book without 'Lawrence of Arabia'? I myself could not envisage it. Instead of beginning his book with an out-of-hand rejection of his image from the word 'Go' (the only way to succeed), he made use of it. From A to Z *Seven Pillars* is a book written by a man who is a legend and who knows it. Any reader who did not know this in advance would be mystified, or even think that he was in the presence of a writer with a megalomaniac pathology. The legendary image is promoted not only by his deeds and the trials he undergoes, but at least as much by a perspective totally dominated by the self, and most of all by the awesomely self-distancing, Olympian style, "the sense of the mystic, immeasurable personality lying behind it".

In presenting the Revolt as his own creation we are no longer on the plane of history, but of myth. It is impossible from then onwards to present oneself as merely an all-too-human sufferer. The contrast is too grotesque, even revolting. It was necessary for himself that he should glorify the Revolt; and necessary for the Revolt that he should aggrandise himself.

Lawrence was obsessed with control. Nobody can control reality (at the time) but we can control its interpretation. It is the desire for control, especially the categorical imperative of guilt management, that not only impels him to impose patterns on events, but always holds him back from the brink of confession, from crossing that threshold into genuine confessional literature. The reader might speculate, but he could not *know*. Lawrence alone holds the keys to the castle. The secret self was the only self worth showing, he believed; this was the raison d'etre of autobiography. Yet that was exactly what he could not do, except in disguise.

*Seven Pillars* was the recreation of the heroic legend. It is the story of the triumph *and* failure of the outsider. But this failure is itself heroic, is part of the triumph. In 1962, the book would be reopened and the image recast as the definitive legend of our time: *Lawrence of Arabia*, signed David Lean and Robert Bolt, who wrote: "*Seven Pillars of Wisdom* was my prime, almost my only source for the screenplay." I wonder what Lawrence would have thought of it.

## GARNETT'S VERDICT

Edward Garnett had the courage to criticise. In a moving letter written on 18 July, 1927, after reading the final version of *Seven Pillars*, he tries very hard to reassure Lawrence, who was anxiously bullying him to agree that the 1926 edition was better than the 1922, that he had written a masterpiece. He does agree, and he lavishes praise, but the comfort he knows Lawrence must receive is hedged about with reservations and a veiled disappointment. Here are some excerpts:

> I have criticized you severely in the past for your self-consciousness, for your hiding of your own emotions, for your subtle evasions & omissions,- & for the elaborate tricks you play & for the 'Peccavi' thrown at us in the abrupt section 'Myself'.

> I take this back in recognizing that you are built that way, & that the whole character of the book reflects and is governed by the laws of your own character. One cant quarrel with the individuality that has made 'the S P' what it is – a masterpiece of narrative. Your instinct of keeping yourself and your emotions, so much down & under is justified by the result, & even the glaring beam you suddenly throw on yourself in 'Myself', fits into its place, now, much better than I thought was possible. 'The Seven Pillars' is <u>extraordinarily individual</u>. It holds one firmly from first to last: it is a very big yet exceedingly complex picture, both broad in the mass, & minute in the details – a just sympathetic and impartial chronicle & <u>extraordinarily truthful</u>. In its own way it is a real work of art, as much of a work of art as was possible in such an historical-chronicle, following your plan of keeping your

emotions so much out of sight. . . . but a bigger man than you would have been much more explicit & much more careless about giving himself away. And these sudden breaks and strange free disclosures would have lifted us out of ourselves, & produced a richer, more variegated effect – something incalculable. The version you have preferred is so to say the version of the official you which might have been supplemented by the revelations of the unofficial you, thereby attaining a richer range of colouring. . . .

You are a born writer, fearfully handicapped by fixed ideas & all sorts of complexes . . . That you have cut off the public from 'The S P' is bad enough. For the book is now a valuable curiosity for the Cabinets of rich men, Collectors who <u>never</u> let their books be read for fear of spoiling their 'condition' . . . I remember what you said about your ambition to write something artistically great. Dostoevsky emptied <u>himself</u> out in 'The Karamazov Brothers'.

This reaction, with its emphasis on what is missing, may be compared to that in the Epilogue.

## THE STRUGGLE WITH MASOCHISM

One can of course attempt to interpret his book without mentioning the word. Nonetheless, I feel quite certain that reference to a universal phenomenon that has been deeply researched makes it easier to interpret some of the stranger and more persistent features of the book, to be aware of a certain unity among those features, and to see Lawrence's decisions and baffling contradictions (as a writer) as symptoms of this same phenomenon (that we call masochism) and hence as something that can be related to human experience as a whole.

*Seven Pillars* is a story of a massive struggle; this is one of its most evident, and heroic, and inspiring characteristics. It provides a good deal of the force and tension of the narrative. There is the political and military struggle, but this, in the final analysis, is dwarfed by the personal. It portrays the triumph, against all the odds, of the disadvantaged outsider, it is an extreme expression of romantic individualism. Lawrence is at war with himself. His presentation of himself is saturated with the imprint of masochism. Guilt, pain, punishment, injured self-esteem, the sense of failure, defiance and contempt, self-justification, grandiosity alternating with self-deprecation, a fierce solitariness, he is victor and vanquished. *Seven Pillars* is "a kind of flagellation", wrote V.S. Pritchett.[8]

Lawrence called the book "everything I have made of myself in these thirty years". Masochism reaches very far back in time, to some kind of irreparable injury. It is, therefore, ultimately, *unconscious*. There is no more conscious book than *Seven Pillars,* and it is also a search for yet more lucidity. But there is a level of consciousness below which not even Lawrence can penetrate. It may be more understandable to speak of compulsion; one may imagine that one is writing by free choice but, in truth, there is no choice. It means that we do not really know to what extent he was conscious of what motivated him to write what he did. There is an unsettling element of compulsion in *Seven Pillars*. This is most evident in the almost grotesque alternation of passages of immense grandiosity with others expressing helplessness and self-pity.[9] This may explain why, when he read the whole thing through, he was at first disgusted with it. It is as if he had not been aware of what he had written.

In *The Economic Problem of Masochism* (1924) Freud distinguished three forms of masochism: *erotogenic, feminine,* and *moral*. The Dera' narrative is evidently a simulation of an erotogenic experience which, I have suggested, points to an existing erotogenic masochism. And there are other hints in the book of an interest in sexual masochism. Here, however, I am concerned with the moral masochism that is exhibited throughout the book and very obviously conditions the autobiography. Freud defines moral masochism as a "norm of behaviour" which is governed by "a sense of guilt which is mostly unconscious."[10] He concedes, however, that, while the idea is true, its expression is counter-intuitive for the sufferer, who is always conscious of guilt feelings. He then prefers the expression "a need for punishment".

We therefore have two related themes: Guilt and Punishment. There is no doubt that these are two major obsessions in *Seven Pillars*. We should also note that the need is unconscious.

Most of us believe that we feel guilty for a reason which has to do with our concept of ethics, or right and wrong. To read *Seven Pillars* is to wonder whether this is here the case or whether there is discernible an *insistence* on feeling guilty. Freud confirms that the consciousness of guilt pre-exists the deed to which it is ascribed by the sufferer. It is necessary for the masochist to feel guilt, and, however guiltless he is according to the ethical code, he will find a reason for feeling guilty and displaying his guilt. For without it, there is no motive for punishment. Another nuance of guilt in masochism is that the factor to which the sufferer ascribes his guilt is often not the real one, but a substitute. There are indications of these features of guilt in previous chapters, at Dera' and, probably, in the arguments displayed in his account of the Nebk crisis.

We have to bear in mind constantly that there is a deep wound that is felt, unconsciously perhaps, as a rejection and loss of self-esteem. Fantasy serves the need for the restitution of injured self-esteem. Life is a permanent struggle to regain that self-esteem. *Seven Pillars* is a plea for appreciation. It is only a difference of style and cunning that divides it from all those pre-war letters home from France and Syria with their long narratives of his achievements and prowess. Reik puts it strongly indeed: "There is nothing a masochistic character craves more than appreciation and admiration. For these he will go to any extreme. It is doubtful if masochism would exist without the decisive co-operation of impulses originating in wounded pride."[11] Hence the irresistability of creating an exemplary persona, the impossibility of losing to an opponent, and the temptation of self-aggrandisement.

Self-esteem can only be won back on the masochist's own terms, in opposition to society, not within it. Lawrence defines himself almost always in opposition. Most masochists never succeed in gaining much of a foothold on the ladder of self-esteem, but Lawrence, because of his prodigious will, his intelligence and cunning, his physical and mental strength, his trained body and self-control, and war (where, as Kirkbride so rightly says, "An extraordinary man was permitted to do extraordinary things") he succeeds *in* the world in spite *of* the world. Is it not this incredible rarity that makes him so special? To be recognised as successful and worthy of appreciation, but also to be able to despise oneself for that very success, thus despising that world from which one has (one feels) been alienated, and its values.[12] He describes a textbook victory, at Tafileh, and then proceeds to despise himself for having achieved it. He achieves the double aim of recognition and rejecting that recognition. There is a poisonous pleasure in rejecting earned praise. Even then, alas, the masochist does not really gain anything permanent because what he hopes to achieve has a meaning only for himself and, once achieved, has no value. The capture of Akaba produces the following reaction:

> Now we had achieved the end, and we despised a little the life which had bestowed so much effort on an object whose attainment changed nothing either in our minds or in our bodies.

The entire masochistic process is presented by Lawrence as a sort of discovery of the self. It is an immense struggle that ends in defeat because the victory, finally achieved, is solitary and leads only to loneliness. This is brilliantly symbolised by the final evening call of the muezzin in Damascus, and words which only he, the architect of the victory, cannot share (R 674). The belief in the Arabs, in the Revolt, dies with the achievement. "Set free" is the caption to the last page of the book.

In the 'discourse to the Serahin', this negative part is explicit; there is no longer any desire to succeed at any level. Failure is the only goal, the negative principle is absolute.

The need, for admiration, is universally evident in *Seven Pillars*; also the need for condonation, which is more obviously related to guilt.[13] If *Seven Pillars* is a 'speech for the defense', then there must be an accuser, and indeed there is; it is the superego, or in everyday language, the ethical conscience (though this does not capture the unconscious nature of the process). The tyranny of the superego can be excessive and it is connected to the excessive demands that masochists place upon themselves. They cannot "accept that part which was human failure".

It is the superego that acts as judge and rectifier of reality, and as censor. Lawrence wrote to Forster: "I let myself go in *The S.P.* It was an orgy of exhibitionism."[14] That may have been how he felt it but it cannot be more than half true. Even the moments of 'free disclosure' are carefully stage-managed. The aim of the masochist is, we have said, to be always in control, in particular, in control of the truth. He was a *control-freak*. The price paid for this is heavy: it is to be imprisoned in thought, unable ever to escape from it or, precisely, to let oneself go. A great deal of the mystification in *Seven Pillars*, the ambiguities and veiled confessions, the strange omissions, the unwillingness to identify individuals, the obsessive use of the unidentified *we*, and the complete monopoly of story telling, opinion, analysis and perspective, are all part of being in control. Even the self-blame is part of it, since it pre-empts blame from anyone else.

His autobiography is written to the music of masochism.

## CONCLUSION

What makes *Seven Pillars* permanently accessible is the mystery of Lawrence himself, the conviction that there is self-knowledge or knowledge of 'our disorder' to be found within its pages. From this point of view the book is a case history of our time whose significance is enormously magnified and dramatised both by heroic legend and the historico-geographical stage on which it is played. Whether the self-portrait is unique, whether it contains universal truth, or whether its significance is "no bigger than my petty self",[15] readers must decide for themselves.

Lawrence sought to express a quite particular idea of truth, which in the last resort is mysterious. That he chose to do this in a historical narrative has led to misunderstanding and confusion. The row over the Tafas depiction in the film is a direct result. There is no doubt that Lawrence did not lay about him slaughtering Turks like a wild beast; what the events of Tafas gave him was an opportunity to reveal unseen truths about himself: "the unseen cargo of the ship". There was a "panther" down there in the cargo, he wrote, ready to spring and "feed upon the kill. So meshed in nerves and hesitation, it could not be a beast to be afraid of: and yet it was a real panther, and this book its mangy skin, dried, stuffed with sawdust, set up squarely for men to look at" (OX 681, R 581). It could hardly be clearer. He did not want to show simply what he had done, but what he imagined himself doing, what he felt himself wanting to do: that is, what he was, stripped of his inhibitions. For a man as inhibited as Lawrence it is not surprising that he felt this way, so much of his nature he had had to suppress. The incidents at Tafas and at Dera' may not have been literally true but they show aspects of him that were extremely real to himself. His early life had been devoted to the creed that Man is the sum of his acts; but he had learned that Man is much more complicated than that.

In the Epilogue at the end, he reveals that "my strongest motive had been a personal one, omitted from the body of the book, but not absent, I think, from my mind, waking or sleeping, for an hour in all those years". This has been taken to be a reference to his love for Dahoum and, with the dedicatory poem, it may represent the symbolic front- and end-covers of the book. Malraux accuses Lawrence of "suppressing", by his silence over Dahoum, a crucial aspect of his biography. This strange after-the-event revelation in the Epilogue carries the message that personal motives, though usually hidden, are more fundamental than those that history pays lip service to.

# Epilogue

## *Was that all it was, then?*

### A commentary on an essay by André Malraux

There are few books more seldom appraised in any comprehensive way than Lawrence's. As 'For Only Those Deserve the Name' developed, I became more and more sure that any formal assessment by me would be futile and repetitive. For a book as idiosyncratic as *Seven Pillars*, and as perverse (Lawrence himself used this term), what would be the criteria for appraisal? As Lawrence commented sadly, there are no absolutes for judging his book, or, so he thought, any book. There are few books which have drawn, and still draw, such a vastly heterogeneous array of responses; as for Lawrence's friends, their appraisals were distinguished by timidity and discretion. My 'literary mentors' – Forster, Shaw, Graves, Garnett – contributed nothing significant after the appearance of the subscribers' edition. "In the end the reader finds himself alone: he has to decide for himself, to make up his own mind", wrote Lawrence's first negative critic, Herbert Read, in 1927. I could not agree more with this opinion. If there is one thing all readers should be able to agree on, it is that.

If, however, there was a man who did believe in absolutes, in a firm commitment to the vocation of writer, who had thought through the human condition to arrive at certain supreme values on which to base one's life and art, and – extraordinary coincidence – discovered in Lawrence a kindred spirit, an alter ego, then one should find that belief and understanding which can inform a certainty of judgement and appraisal. That man was André Malraux.

It is interesting because he was a Frenchman, wrote about Lawrence 75 years ago, and is probably the most highly regarded writer, in Europe, to have written on Lawrence and the *Seven Pillars*. And yet this remarkable essay is relatively little known or appreciated. Where Englishmen took the book for granted as something in a class by itself, a mythical artefact, beyond such silly things as criticism (to paraphrase Charlotte Shaw), or for the "purification of the legend", and even if they did not like it, thought it futile or unwise to get involved, Malraux had quite other reasons for being interested in it and had no inhibitions about judging it as a literary creation.

The essay we are talking about is not unknown and has been three times translated into English, twice by anonymous translators for English-speaking periodicals. What is more, the French text, together with all three translations, was published sentence by sentence in a special edition of *T.E. Notes* in 2003 with an introduction by the foremost expert on Malraux-and-Lawrence, Maurice Larès. The effect of seeing each sentence placed with its translations, as a unit and not in paragraph form, brings out Malraux's trenchantly aphoristic style, in which an idea, a complete thought, is encapsulated in a single sentence. It is this density of style that enables him to write a comprehensive evaluation in just fourteen pages.

Malraux's essay was not originally conceived, or written, as an independent creation but as part of a book, unfinished, with the title of *Le Démon de l'Absolu* (*The Demon of the Absolute*). This was not published until 1996 (after a monumental editing task by Larès) and that is certainly a major reason why this deeply insightful work is not well known and has never been translated and published in English. The one chapter that Malraux pulled out and published as a separate essay was Chapter 35, the critique of *Seven Pillars*, to which he gave the title: "N'était-ce donc que cela?" "Was that all it was, then?". More complete details of the history are detailed in the note.[1]

A few words about André Malraux, up to the time he wrote *Le Démon de l'Absolu*. He was born in 1901 in Paris, thirteen years after Lawrence. He quickly became dedicated to literature but was also attracted to the big world of international events and politics. He travelled widely, especially in the Far East. In 1927, he witnessed the Communist revolution in Shanghai. This was the subject of his first novel and, in 1933, of the one that brought him enduring fame, *La condition humaine*. He became a communist. In 1934, he met Trotsky and addressed the first Congress of Soviet Writers in Moscow. He met Gorky and Pasternak, and the famous Russian film director Eisenstein who wanted to make a film of *La condition humaine* but Stalin vetoed it. He became a prominent opponent of anti-Semitism and, as President of the World committee against War and Fascism, of Hitler. In 1936, he travelled to Spain and joined the Republicans against the Fascists, heading an international air squadron. He claimed to have flown on sixty-five missions and been twice wounded. In 1937, he wrote *L'Espoir* (*Hope*), a factual and searchingly explanatory novel about the Spanish civil war. In June 1940, when the Germans invaded, he was captured in France with his tank unit but escaped to the free zone five months later.

There, from 1941 to 1943, in a period of comparative calm, in a villa on the Côte d'Azur, he began to make notes for a book on Lawrence, using a 1936 translation of *Seven Pillars* by Charles Mauron and a few other sources including *The Letters of T.E. Lawrence* edited by David Garnett, which he had studied carefully. His English is reported to have been limited but his book demonstrates a perfect understanding of his English sources. He also had the help of the English wife of a friend, Dorothy Bussy, who was the first translator of *N'était-ce donc que cela?*

Thus what follows is a true Epilogue in that it excerpts an appraisal by a man who was Lawrence's contemporary, and who, a few years after Lawrence's death, sets *Seven Pillars* into a European context of contemporary literary ideas. Malraux's essay deserves to be better known and my excerpted commentary is an attempt to give it context and significance, and show clearly its relevance of his judgements to the work you have just read.

Malraux felt a deep affinity with Lawrence. He shared with him the secret of being both a man of action and a contemplative, and other important traits. Larès writes: "It was without doubt the relative similarity in their personalities that made possible such comprehensive understanding and intuition."[2] Malraux sees him as a man who faced the same existentialist predicament of the age: the knowledge that, in a world without God, life is absurd, without any sense except to exist. "To be or not to be, that is the *only* question", wrote Camus. Against that, the world is not neutral, it implies evil. In such a situation, "To give a meaning to one's life is to submit it to a value which one accepts oneself without question" and whose "object is to change the order of the world."[3] For him as for many others at that time, especially in France, Lawrence was a living exemplar of the existentialist struggle: 'l'angoisse de vivre', the struggle against 'the demon of the absurd', the search for an Absolute; like Hemingway, like Saint-Exupéry, like Malraux himself, he had chosen action. "Lawrence appears like a precursor of Malraux's own vision of the Tragic, of Man's fight against his destiny, and of his efforts to transcend himself", wrote Denis Boak.[4] This background places Lawrence firmly in a literary movement (even if he may not have known it! – a movement which, incidentally, scarcely existed in

England). Malraux's own experiences of war and revolution are translated into books that explore their meaning, and glorify action and solidarity. It is difficult to imagine anybody better placed to write his biography. The more he discovered Lawrence, the more he perceived him as an *alter ego*. What he had in common with him above all was the idea that a man is what he makes of himself. This shared background gives the essay a powerful sense of struggle against fate.

## PROLOGUE IN BARTON STREET

*July 1922.* The curtain goes up on Lawrence in the ordeal chamber of the Barton Street flat in Westminster. Now free of the Colonial Office, he sits in front of the proofs he has just received from the *Oxford Times*:

> He felt even more involved in this intellectual adventure than he had been in the Arabian one – imprisoned as he was with this book for his decisive wrestle with the angel, more a prey to himself through the decomposition of everything to which he had hitherto been attached than he had been by the fear of defeat at the Peace Conference and by Feisal's flight.[5] He hoped to recover from these proofs that freshness of sight and judgement which his manuscript could no longer give him . . . and the implacable evidence that these agonized days forced on him, when he read the printed book as if it were the work of someone else, was that the book was not a work of art.

That Malraux was a novelist one can already sense from the extract above, with its narrative form, its sense of the drama of the actual moment, its attempt to see inside the mind of its character. Malraux writes that his essay is not a critique, but "an analysis of the author's feelings in the presence of his book." In fact, it is both simultaneously. Lawrence own disappointment with the result justifies the critique. By using Lawrence's own reaction to the book as a starting point, Malraux makes him a participant in the narrative, and also ensures that the book will be judged "as if it were the work of someone else." There are no bonus points for being Lawrence of Arabia. Malraux is able to put himself in Lawrence's position as a man *trying to write* a book, as an author struggling for lucidity and coherence. We return more than once to Barton Street. Malraux discerns the way the book develops and the various and sometimes contradictory themes. The flashbacks to Barton Street enable him to suggest a progression.

The essay is presented as seamless but one can discern four main sections: the Arab Revolt; the book as a story or memoir; the book as autobiography; and a final discussion of Lawrence's idea of the Great Personality. This takes us outside *Seven Pillars* into the literary and spiritual world of the writers Lawrence had wanted to be worthy of: Nietzsche and Dostoevski. Malraux's experience of these writers (he virtually ignores Melville, the third of Lawrence's icons), allied to his psychological insight into Lawrence, makes this analysis of Lawrence's feelings for each of them a tour de force of knowledge and intuition.

I hope to show here the movement of Malraux's thought, the reasons for his negative judgement, the manner of his expression. We need to understand that Malraux, while a very open-minded critic, was deeply committed to the mission of the writer and, like Garnett, to the transcendence of art. There is no doubt of the significance of the *Seven Pillars* for Malraux. But after the almost iconic presentation of Lawrence as a superior being in *Le Démon de l'Absolu*, he is disappointed. Lawrence's efforts, whether set against the great literary works or not, score few positive points. It is, he believes, a series of missed opportunities in the midst of conflicting aims and powerful inhibitions, a failure to say what he had really wanted to say.

## THE STORY OF THE REVOLT

Malraux begins with a discussion of the epic presentation. This man, who had written his most famous book on the Communist rising in Shanghai of 1927 and fought in the Spanish civil war against Franco[6] and written a book about that also, was sympathetic to the idealistic presentation of the Revolt: "Lawrence knew that his reader, whoever he might be, would demand purity from a national movement." The fact that the truth was very different – that the Arab tribes were undependable and sometimes disloyal, that there was seldom any real sense of unity, that their cooperation had to be bought with gold, that political independence in the modern sense was an idea they scarcely understood – did not matter since, writes Malraux, no national movement can be presented as other than a noble crusade. The history of revolts, national or social, likewise requires exemplary actions from its leader. So far, so good. However, "an artist's gifts, alas! are not always those which he most needs. . . . The reader must feel himself carried away by one of those exalting epics of generosity which make one believe that a few inspired days can hold all the beauty of the world. Lyricism alone could do it . . . that transfiguring lyricism that lives by what it brings with it."

An exalting epic of generosity presupposes somewhere a generous spirit, a genuine experience of solidarity with one's fellows, an unclouded belief in a just cause, above all, a spirit of self-sacrifice. "To the eyes of a European, every national movement is first of all brotherhood." This is how he shows the republicans of the Spanish civil war or the communist insurgents in Shanghai. Lyricism is inspired by that brotherhood. In Malraux, the glory came from the self-sacrifice of the insurgents; he was disappointed by the lack of that element in *Seven Pillars*. "What was worthy of admiration in the Revolt was not that imaginary cavalcade by which the Arabs were to renew the birth of the Islamic epic; it was that men, alternately courageous and cowardly, greedy and generous, heroic and venal, like most men, more than most men, should have reconquered their historic capital, in spite of so many weaknesses."

He finds it puzzling that Lawrence's narrative gives so much attention to a long succession of rather trivial incidents, instead of showing us how the Revolt actually developed. He takes the example of the discovery of Feisal's negotiations with the Turks being given less space than Abdelkader's treachery. "Whence the singular perspective of his story, in which all the help that enabled Allenby to make the breakthrough which forced the Turks to ask for an armistice is given less space than an attack on two trains – Lawrence discovered now that a detailed account of his acts was far from being the best means of expressing his action."

We learn little about the Sharifian army who were, after all, the people who were moved by ideals of political freedom, essentially similar to those of Malraux's fighters, and who sustained almost all the casualties. In *L'Espoir*, which may be a novel, but which is in reality as close to being a factual account as Lawrence's, Malraux gives a far more comprehensive picture of an irregular war than does Lawrence, because of the multiple perspectives that he presents, not only through widely different scenes, but also through the characters, the roles they play, their leaders' perceptions of the war, their disagreements, their different backgrounds, outside influences. He creates a credible picture of a social world. Of course, the Spanish civil war was a far bigger affair than the Arab Revolt. Nevertheless, he must have noticed that there is precious little about a national movement. Malraux was a believer in proletarian revolution and a believer in Lawrence; that Lawrence had done his utmost to gain freedom for the Arabs, without side-glances, he did not doubt. He accepted that Lawrence was the master spirit of the Revolt. He was unable to explain why Lawrence "had chosen to be, if not discreet, at least cursory." But we will get an answer to that later.

He had wanted to bear witness to the resurrection of a people, and he sometimes seemed to be re-reading the memoirs of a dynamiter. So much so that, having written his book for the sake of bestowing greatness on a confused and legendary insurrection, he wondered whether the reader's first question as to the Revolt so precisely detailed, would not be: "Was that all it was, then?"

The reader knows there was in truth very little, and that, far from playing down the importance of the Revolt, Lawrence exaggerated it. But what Malraux means is that Lawrence does not invest the Revolt with any significant content or spirit; the continuous narration of day-to-day adventures in preference to the action of the Revolt as a liberation *movement* – trivialises the whole story. So much for history. "He did not believe in history", concludes Malraux, "but he believed in art."

## THE ART OF STORY WRITING

The rest of Malraux's essay, except for the last section, is in one way or another concerned with *Seven Pillars* as a work of art. He begins with the art of narration. He regards the linear form of the narrative as inimical to artistic creation; it is not only a historical but also an artistic failure. "His book was not a great story, the absence of premeditated perspective, the submissive following of his diary had resulted in the absence of artistic perspective, in an action evolving on a single plane." He then proceeds to give a lesson in the art of story telling, using both fiction and memoir as his points of reference. The key point is the art of representation. He calls the history of narrative technique "the search for a third dimension; for that which, in the novel, *eludes narration*; for that which makes it possible not to narrate but to represent, to make present. Narration expresses a past whose total effect – scene by scene – is that of a present."

One cannot accuse Lawrence of painting no scenes. *Seven Pillars* is full of scenes: telling stories round the fire in Azrak castle in winter; the she-camel mourning over her lost foal; the march across the railway in the Hauran on a pristine September morning. But these scenes, often vivid and beautifully described, are random because they are subject to the chronology of the narrative. Altogether, they equal the content of the Arabian experience; individually, one after the other, they are swallowed up in the endless narrative. What difference would it make if this one or that one were cut out? They are not scenes in the sense meant by Malraux, or shown by Lean. However, there are a very few that are; most notoriously, the episodes at Dera' (November 1917) and Tafas (September 1918). These episodes certainly 'make present' and make one feel at the end that there is nothing more to follow but silence. But they stand out as exceptions and are at least partly fiction. They are not merely recorded, but created.

The example chosen by Malraux himself is the awkward cohabitation of Lawrence with his bodyguard in a lice-ridden stone house in snow-bound Tafileh (R 494-6).

The savagery of discipline amongst his bodyguard, these men showing scars always fresh from flogging, who moved about him as he sat and read *Morte d'Arthur*, and never ceasing to glaringly contradict everything most pure in his desire for victory, his resolution not to let a single man be killed in vain – that whole background of evil which, obsessively contradicting every ideal, would have expressed so well that presence of the absurd that Lawrence felt so acutely; he could make of it nothing more than a picturesque blood-soaked fragment.

Malraux evidently sees something here which the author does not. A better example would surely have been the massacre at Tafas. This episode does express powerfully the presence of the absurd and the evil of the world. The images speak out strongly, and, in terms of the protagonist's psychological degradation, it moves the action forward. The absurdity lies not only in the presence of a man who wanted "to change the order of the world" being caught up in a spiral of evil revenge and bloodlust but, beyond that, succumbing to a dark side of his own nature. It is more powerful than Malraux's example.

Ignoring the more obvious conclusion that Lawrence did not think in scenes because his real aim was to write a highly self-centred record, or because he did not have the mind of the creative writer, Malraux connects it to his confused and highly personal feelings towards his subject:

He had known ever since he had begun his narrative that the Revolt inspired him with feelings so contradictory that he had only overcome them by starting his book *as a speech for the defence.* The only way not to be paralysed by this was to avoid giving his book any pre-imposed architecture.

To plan the form of a book, to decide what is significant and what is not, and to select before beginning to compose, demands a certain tranquillity of mind and a firm idea of what you want to say. The only way he could avoid 'paralysis' was by following the easiest and most uncreative course: copying the day-to-day narrative out of notes or relying on memory. This is a highly plausible theory. The phrase 'speech for the defense' (*'plaidoirie'*) is well chosen and it recurs two or three times. It reflects Lawrence's whole guilt-laden perception of his role in the Revolt. This need to prove something also affects his approach to characterisation, which is therefore not free.

> This book might have revealed in its personages the mystery that obsessed its author. What existence had he given them? The portraits of the Arabs were never more than picturesque, of the English nothing but sketches. What reader, once he had shut the book, would 'recognize' Joyce, Young, Clayton? The most characterised person, Feisal, is he not a sort of official portrait? The mystery of human beings cannot be elucidated in a speech for the defence. Those beings he had seen in action he had instinctively brought within the limits of their definition and confined them in the meaning that action had so often imposed upon them. Not one of them seemed to carry within him the germs of his future destiny. . . . To what part of the chevalier Auda did his dealings with the Turks relate? And to what part of Feisal ..his negotiations for a separate peace?

As for the abominable Abdelkader, "no doubt (his) soul was unintelligible, and the reader would only accept it because he knew that Lawrence related facts. In a fiction the Algerian would never have passed." A perceptive remark. The same might be said of the Bey of Dera'a. But what if Lawrence was *not* relating facts? Malraux never voices this possibility.

### THE FAILED AUTOBIOGRAPHY

We now reach a major turning-point. The personal narrative moves centre-stage. It is this part of the analysis that is the heart of the matter for Malraux. He would have recognised at once in that vague region where life and literature overlap the unique constellation of circumstances which cried out for a creation in the genre of action literature and personal struggle, his own field and that of Hemingway and Saint-Exupéry. Some might say that *Seven Pillars* is very much about this; but we will have to read on. Lawrence had written to Vyvyan Richards: "The story I have to tell is one of the most splendid ever given a man for writing." Malraux obviously agreed.

He goes back to the start, to that day in February 1919 when Lawrence began writing the book immediately after Feisal's appeal for an Arab nation to the Versailles Council of Ten. He claims that the purpose of the book was "an *apparent* appeal to history against injustice, and a *real* appeal to art against the absurd" (my italics). The first part is obvious. The second is the statement of an article of faith. The absurdity of the world, of one's own life and action, of the human condition, can be transcended (to use Boak's term) through Art, and sometimes, as Lawrence believed here, only through Art. In Malraux this view of Art is fully articulated in philosophical terms; in Lawrence perhaps not, but was Malraux wrong to interpret his struggle as a struggle against the absurdity of life? And his book as an attempt to redeem it? I think not. Lawrence knew that it is redeemable only by unquestioning commitment to a great value, like freedom or religious faith, or Art. By the time the Handley Page aircraft lifted Lawrence above the sordid deals of Paris in May, he no longer believed in action. Nor in revolution, nor in God. If he was not a Writer, he thought, he was nothing. Malraux now addresses the autobiographical problem head on:

> It was not only the Revolt he wanted to save from absurdity, but his own action, his own destiny.... Gradually, without its frame being altered, the picture of the Revolt had passed from the foreground to the background. In its place had arisen the absurdity of life for a man who had been reduced to solitude by an irreducible difference and by the meditation to which it condemned him. The subject of the book he believed he was writing had become the struggle of a being lashed without mercy by the contempt he felt for certain appeals of his own nature, by a fatality experienced, with terrible humiliation, as a permanent failure of his will, – against the vehement determination of this same being to kill his demon by force of conquests and lucidity.

The last phrase presumably means: conquests of the body by near-impossible feats and through pain and self-punishment; lucidity (also achieved through pain) is the fruit of his constant self-analysis and soul-searching.

Was he wrong to believe such a struggle worthy of the Karamazov?

Here we come to the first of those three writers who had inspired Lawrence with their spiritual power and whose example, Malraux believed, were indispensable. He would have answered his own question "No". Such a story would surely have thrilled Dostoievski. There are no aspects of a man that are not part of his fate, which are not part of the struggle against the Absurd. Malraux believed very strongly in the literary potential of Lawrence's predicament; but, in spite of the boldness of the Dera' chapter (R 549-557), which he refers to as "a fatality experienced with terrible humiliation," Lawrence did not write this English *Karamazov*. Was it a problem of lack of the artistic gift, a simple case of naive ambition outstripping talent and experience? Malraux does not think so. The problem lay not in the writer, but deeper, in the Man.

The opening chapter in *Seven Pillars* had promised much.

There, he had said in clear – though abstract – language what he wanted to say. 'I was carried away first by the call of freedom: I was so committed to it that I ceased to exist: I lived under the constant threat of torture: my life was ceaselessly crossed by "strange longings fanned by privations and dangers"; I was not able to subscribe to the beliefs I was stirring up to serve the ends of my country at war; we had experienced the need to degrade ourselves; I had ceased to believe in my own civilisation or in any other, until I was aware of nothing but an intense solitude at the edge of madness; and what I remember most is the agony, the terrors and the mistakes'.[7]i

But where, he asks, in the 700 pages that follow, is all this portrayed? "What were these terrors, these mistakes, this degradation?" One might wonder why Malraux mentions degradation, given the Dera' incident; however, he is partly justified because Lawrence is referring in Chapter One to a degradation shared (according with Malraux) with his companions (R 28).

Every priest knows that a confession in the abstract costs little. The concrete confession here would have consisted in picturing himself during the mistake; in embodying himself in the phantom which said I.

Edward Garnett had already reproached Lawrence for concealing and had reminded him of Dostoevski.[8] For Malraux, it is a fundamental cause of the artistic failure, if not *the* fundamental cause. He failed in effect to express the real Self; because of his puritanism, his sense of guilt, his fear of exposure or ridicule, or whatever. He failed as a writer because he failed as a human being.

The introduction (he means this same Chapter One) was an introduction to his secret memoirs rather than to his book; his drama, his portrait, were written in its margins. The embodiment of this portrait alone into the *Seven Pillars* would have made of it, not a historical fresco, but a book of the order, if not the genius, of the *Brothers Karamazov* and of *Zarathustra*, the great accusatory work of which he had dreamed.... But to say "Behold the Man" is an expression of the human mystery only in as much as the confession he utters is free from reticence.[9]

He suggests that the 'Myself' chapter (R 579-84), which is the only chapter in the book in which he describes himself (albeit in abstract discourse), occurs so late and is so different to every other chapter because he realised later that he had completely masked himself.

He now comes to Nietzsche, the second of Lawrence's spiritual heroes. Malraux would have wished that Lawrence, his admired precursor and *alter ego*, had shown his suffering, his knowledge of the absurdity of his condition, the 'moral dishonesty' of public life, the stifling of freedom, as an indictment of the conditions of existence itself, as did (in his own completely different way) Nietzsche.

The whole end of *Seven Pillars* Malraux qualifies as an anticlimax. Disillusionment and despair. But even here all is not lost:

But a Melville, even a Conrad, would have found, beyond the atmosphere which Lawrence had perhaps achieved, the supreme source of poetry which makes of disillusion and despair not paralysis but tragedy. Solitude and inward failure, the futility of epics, are also powerful means of art.

If Lawrence's aim in *Seven Pillars*, like Conrad's in *Nostromo*, was to show a personal tragedy evolving within a wider historical drama, as he said *Seven Pillars* was, would it not have been more effective to simply relate what really happened – never mind any literary pretension – to *show*, without comment, the impossibility of his position, of the outsider dream, of identifying with one 'barbaric' culture while depending on another far mightier one, of struggling against the order of the world? There are hints of this at Tafas but it is too confused. He could have exploited the unfortunate meeting at Dera' with General Barrow (R 656-9).

In truth, he had no intention of exploiting tragic potential. Lawrence saw the 'introspective epic' as ending in hopeless passivity, a man who has lost his faith and hence his moral justification.

I felt that anyone who pushed through to success a rebellion of the weak against their masters must come out of it so stained that nothing in the world would make him clean again. (OX 809)

Is this the voice of a man who has submitted his life to a value whose object is to change the order of the world? Instead of: "I wrote this to show what a man can do", wrote Malraux, he ended up with: "I wrote this in order to show what the gods can make of us." Not tragedy, but paralysis.

"Was that all it was, then"?

Was the paralysis because of this "fatality" in his nature for which he could not forgive himself? Was Malraux aware of this link? He is surely aware of what this 'fatality' was; he observes Lawrence's love of self-degradation, and self-humiliation; the description of homosexual practices in the desert in Chapter One leads him to ask: "Do they hide a deeper and more painful solitude?" Whatever he means, he does not name it. He finds it hard to accept why this flaw should be so completely disabling: "No man, even among the sanest, can found his life on a spiritual basis if he does not seize the right moment for escaping his meditations and letting himself go once in a while."

## THE RECREATION OF THE LEGEND

The last return to Barton Street:

A subtler poison was still emanating from these pages which were decomposing between his fingers. There were in this book, as in all memoirs, two personae: the one who said *I* and the author. What Lawrence had done was embodied in the person who acted: what he was, in the rectifier and judge of this other – in the writer. It was the writer (not as artist but as judge) who was to enable Lawrence to subordinate his legend to himself instead of remaining subordinated to it, who on the spiritual plane was to serve the exemplary Lawrence, just as on the moral plane he had been served by his refusal to make any profit.

Malraux shows a perspicacity that has eluded the vast majority of his successors: the prodigious influence of the later persona on the earlier, and the ostensible reason for it: the legend, the "purification" of the legend, as Liddell Hart has it. In effect, what this creates is a book that exists in two different time zones: a remembered past and a present that wishes to judge and rectify that remembered past in order to create an exemplary legendary persona. Lawrence's description of what happened at Dera' with General Barrow (R 656-9) is a good example of this purification. Ignoring the uncontrolled Bedouin, the Turks dying in the streets, the chaos, we have a portrayal of an exemplary Lawrence, calm and completely in command of the situation, putting Barrow firmly in his place and having him salute the Arab flag.

It was no longer a question of literary talent; but of being, of human density.

"A Tolstoy would have drawn from the death of the humblest Arab soldier the grand and bitter significance of the Revolt. Because he had Tolstoy's talent, but primarily because he was Leo Nikolayevich." Because he was Leo Nikolayevich! And here is the crux of the problem: the man who writes "I" in *Seven Pillars* is not the real Thomas Edward Lawrence. Let us recall first the words of Bowhay, Kennington's friend:

Reading this book has made me suffer. The writer is infinitely the greatest man I have known, but he is terribly wrong. He is not himself. He has found an *I* but it is not his true *I*, so I tremble to think of what may happen. He is never alive in what he does. He is only a pipe through which life flows.

Malraux's damning but brilliant conclusion is remarkably similar to Bowhey's. But Bowhey's lifeless narrator is here an 'exemplary persona', driven by the need to achieve his own legend.

Lawrence's book was in the highest sense of the word a test. And here the demon of the absurd appears in his cruellest form – if Lawrence had not expressed the man he believed he was, was it not simply because he was not that man? And if he was not that man, he was nothing. But that man he judged himself *guilty* for not being, what was he? Merely the matrix of the exemplary persona that the legend was driving Lawrence to substitute, if only for his own sake, for Lawrence of Arabia.

## *The Great Personality*

At the end Malraux goes back to the beginning or before the beginning: the meaning of the 'great writer'. Here we have a brilliant insight into why the idea of the great writer so obsessed Lawrence. Malraux may have added this conclusion because it is partly autobiographical. His extraordinarily intuitive speculation of the influence on Lawrence of Dostoievski and Nietzsche may be some sort of a projection of his own experience, for these two writers also had a great influence on him.

Malraux sees the confusion of the heroic image in a lack of definition of the 'great personality'. There are two models: the first, the man who has accomplished great things, is no longer paramount because "history seems to us less and less a guarantee of greatness". Lawrence knew that the heroic image bestowed upon him by history was fraudulent. The second model "derives entirely from the domain to which Lawrence owed his formation and his dreams: Literature."

> To his imagination, as to ours, Nietzsche was not a professor whom his mother called Fritz and who elsewhere wrote great, unrecognized books; Dostoievski was not a Russian man of letters who had bad health and gambled. Each of them was in the first place the mythical personage born of all the works he had written, as a character in a novel proceeds from all the remarks given him by the author. In our dreams of such personalities, we give them an imaginary aptitude for answering, with the very words they wrote, the questions put to them by life and men. . . . A great personality is a man who, in that rather hazy region where art and thought meet, has expressed an essential truth. The great personality such as Lawrence dimly conceived it – such as many of us dimly conceive it – was a truth incarnated, come to life: Nietzsche become Zarathustra.

Was this the illusion which prompted, in a man of spiritual inspiration but prone to illusions of grandeur, the ambition to write "an English fourth" alongside the works of an American, a German and a Russian? "My great passion for living books snared me into the hopelessness of trying to create."[11] Malraux had written of human density. Here at last he explains fully what he means:

> It was not of prestige that he dreamt but of the possession of his (Nietzsche–Zarathustra's) plenitude: what he longed for most ardently in the world and what lay furthest from him. He had always been profoundly at odds with himself. "I was very conscious of the bundled powers and entities within me: it was their character ('le personnage central') which hid" (R 563). And this dislocation was not one of the least elements of his strength when it flung him into action. Outside of action, it was merely suffering. What fascinated him, without his fully realising it, was the existence of this centre, whose absence was intolerable to him – this invincible density which Dostoievski had expressed above all in his *staretz* Zossima, (the Holy Man of the monastery in *The Brothers Karamazov*). This profound and complete self-identity of being obsessed him, because he knew it capable of what he had

demanded successively of action and of art: of overcoming man's feeling of dependence.... Zossima is invulnerable.

"When I'm forced to describe *The Karamazov* in a word", wrote Lawrence, I say 'A fifth gospel'. It is that intense preoccupation with supra-moral goodness, Christ-like-ness, which marks him [Dostoievski] so strongly.[12]

According to Lawrence's conception, a great personality is a saint or a prophet – minus God.

This is not a paradox: Nietzsche saw himself as a prophet but he preached that God is dead. Christ was a great prophet but not, for Lawrence, the Son of God. Malraux calls Lawrence "one of the most religious spirits of his time, if one defines a religious spirit as one who experiences the anguish (*'angoisse'*) of being a man to the depths of his being". And yet he refused Christianity: "It was only from his own self that he sought the remission of his sins". Hence the desperate need for self-justification that runs through the *Seven Pillars*. He realized no doubt that Zossima is invulnerable because he has surrendered the Self. That Lawrence wanted to achieve this is made evident in *Seven Pillars* and in his letters. In *Seven Pillars* he sought its annihilation through breaking through a pain threshold in his desert journeys.

He looked not for an assuagement but a victory, a peace by force of conquest.

It is not the way to a surrender of the Self. In a person as vulnerable as Lawrence, the only alternative to that impossible surrender was complete control. *Seven Pillars* is a demonstration of that control: control of history, control of image, control of truth. But what was created was "not his true *I*", "merely the matrix of an exemplary persona".

Less than a year before his fatal accident, he had written to Kennington: "There is an ideal standard somewhere and only that matters: and I cannot find it. Hence this aimlessness."[13]

Malraux translated 'ideal standard' as 'Absolute'. He defines it here as follows:

The Absolute is the last resort of the tragic man, the only solace, because it alone can consume – even if the whole man is consumed with it – that deepest feeling of dependence, remorse at being oneself.

We do not know why Malraux never finished the book on which he had devoted so much effort. Perhaps it was the war that interrupted a period of comparative calm never to return (Malraux played a heroic role in the Ardennes), perhaps he had too much hero-worshipped Lawrence at first, and closer acquaintance and the passing of time had disillusioned him, perhaps his obsession with Lawrence bothered him and he saw no issue to it. He claimed that his manuscript had been lost, or in other versions, destroyed by the Gestapo. Not so, but a very Lawrencian story.[14]

# APPENDICES

## APPENDIX 1
### CHRONOLOGY OF TEXT 1: FOUR VERSIONS

Lawrence gave four short accounts of the chronology of the writing of what he calls 'the first draft', 'the first edition', or 'Text 1'.

Essential information for the reader: The 1922 Oxford text has eleven parts: an encyclopaedic Introduction of 16,673 words (Chapters 1–9) and ten Books.

The 1926 subscribers' edition also has the Introduction and ten Books. The Introduction is reduced to seven chapters.

1. The first in time of these accounts is in the page of notes that he attached to the MS of the Oxford text when he presented it to the Bodleian Library in Oxford in 1923. Here he states that the *First edition* was begun on 10 January 1919 and finished on 25 July "flying to Egypt". He also states that "Chapter 2" of this text was written in the Handley Page between Paris and Lyons and that only the "Introduction" survived the Reading mishap. In fact, Lawrence was not flying to Egypt in late July, but between mid-May and June 28th. He was back in Paris by mid-July. But the finishing date of July 25th is plausible.
2. 'Some notes on the writing of the Seven Pillars of Wisdom by T.E. Shaw', composed in 1927 and distributed to subscribers of the 1926 private edition separately, is more than a little different. He wrote:

Text I
I wrote Books 2,3,4,5,6,7 and 10 in Paris between February and June of 1919. The Introduction was written between Paris and Egypt on my way out to Cairo by Handley-Page in July and August 1919. Afterwards in England I wrote Book I: and then lost all but the Introduction and drafts of Books 9 and 10 at Reading Station, while changing trains. This was about Christmas, 1919.

This tells us that only seven books were completed in Paris. An Introduction was added on the journey to Cairo (dates are again different, and wrong) and another Book (Book I) not written until he returned to England in August. Book 8 is not mentioned. He mentions Book 9 in draft but does not say when or where he wrote it.

The clue to one apparent difference in the versions so far is almost certainly that the original *Seven Pillars* had seven books, as intended, so Version 2 is merely asserting that a first draft was completed in Paris. Why then does he not write Books 1–7 ? The reason is clearly that, here, the numbering is according to the design of the 1926 version and is based on the content of that version. This means that the content of the book was already being expanded when the loss at Reading station occurred. What he lost then, it seems, was the original Paris MS and the draft of the new Book I.

It would have helped the reader if Lawrence had explained that he had completed a draft of seven books in Paris and had decided to expand it, adding other books to 10, when he returned to England. But Lawrence did not necessarily believe in making things easy for the reader by giving explanations. Why in any case give all this completely redundant detail about a lost draft ?

> 3. A 'Private Record' dated 1927. It is briefer: "Written in Paris 1919 (Feb-June). Introduction completed on way out to Egypt. July-Aug 1919. All but the 1st 9 chapters of this lost at Reading." The first nine chapters comprised the Introduction in the Oxford text. It thus agrees with the 1923 version in the Bodleian except for the still later dates given for the trip to Egypt.

Versions 1 and 3 differ from 2 in that they make no mention of the rewriting completed or being done at the time of the loss, all of which Lawrence describes as "Text 1", "First edition" or "First draft".

> 4. Interview with Basil Liddell Hart in 1933. He answered questions about the original version and the reader will not need to be told that his account is different to the other three. Here, according to Liddell Hart's interview notes, he said he had "only sketched out" the book before flying to Cairo, that he wrote the "introduction" flying down the Rhone valley and that he "moved to Arab Delegation headquarters in Paris [on his return on July 15th] and wrote there. Was complete in

Paris." He also says something about the manner of composition during the last phase in the Arab Delegation HQ.[1]

This account, in spite of being later and verbal, fits best the constraints of circumstances during the Versailles period. The key points are that the first draft was little more than a sketch before his trip to Cairo, and that he must therefore have worked intensively on it on his return to Paris, with the aid of the documentation he had brought back. This seems to me to be very likely because he had little to do otherwise, Feisal being in Syria; and with the documentation retrieved from Cairo in his hands, he would have been keen to use it at once. It fits the finishing date of July 25th given in the Bodleian Library note. But typically, he creates yet more confusion by using the term 'introduction' to refer only to Chapter 2 rather than Chapters 1–9 (This confusion will be perpetuated by others, such as Graves and Malraux). Even Lawrence could not have written the nine chapters of the Introduction (over 16,000 words) between Paris and Lyon in an aeroplane!

The variables, ambiguities and uncertainties that Lawrence deploys are several:

the dates of the trip to Egypt;
whether or not the text was worked on after his return from Egypt;
whether Text I was a complete or incomplete text;
whether by 'introduction' he means just what became Chapters 1 and 2, or the whole Introduction;
whether the terms 'Text 1' and 'first draft' are equivalent;
whether Text 1 was supposed to contain only seven books or ten.

The dates of the trip to Egypt are wrong in each account where they are mentioned; otherwise, by manipulating these variables, one can claim that any one of the four accounts is the truth.

None of this supports assertions that there is proof that the early fragment (Curtis draft) is copied from the original draft of Text 1 that was lost at Reading Station in December 1919.

## APPENDIX 2
### NESIB AL-BAKRI AND THE SYRIAN ALTERNATIVE

Nesib al-Bakri was certainly not the ineffectual and feeble character that appears in *Seven Pillars*. He played a conspicuous, effective and courageous part in the Great Syrian Revolt against the French imperial power, especially at its outset (1925). Among Damascene nationalists, Nesib was clearly the most respected by Druze leaders and it was these who would give the French so much trouble during the Revolt. He belonged to an aristocratic family that claimed descent from the first Caliph, Abu Bakr, and owned a lot of land in the Jebel Druze. One immediate cause of the Revolt was the razing to the ground of a village called Jarmana by Circassian troops under French orders. This village belonged to Nesib and he immediately gathered a force which, as part of a co-ordinated attack (only part of which materialised), he led right into the city centre of Damascus, provoking French panic and indiscrimate shelling of the centre which killed nearly 1500 people and caused great consternation among the European population. The plea for a ceasefire by some prominent Damascus notables, including Lawrence's other Syrian bugbear, Said al-Jezairi, brought the shelling to a halt. Said was praised for protecting 'defenceless residents from rebels and bandits' and his 'chivalry' was praised by British residents, local Christians, and even nationalist leaders. This is the man described by Lawrence in his letter to Stirling of June 1919 as an insane murderer. Throughout the Revolt Nesib was the main line of contact between the Druze leader Sultan al-Atrash and the nationalist politicians in Damascus. "Sultan's call to arms was clearly the result of this collaboration," writes Patrick Seale, "The rebel council he had formed, and which consisted of fomer Ottoman officers and of men engaged in the Hauran grain trade, had been one of the most effective command centres of the Revolution." After the Revolt had been finally overcome (over 6000 French soldiers were killed – most of them 'colonial troops'), Nesib was sent into exile but was pardoned less than a year later (March, 1928). He and his brother, Fawzi, received a hero's welcome in Damascus. He remained an important member of the nationalist bloc until 1937, and when at last a treaty was signed with the French he became governor of the Jebel Druze. According to Philip Khoury, "The Great Revolt of 1925–27 was a major watershed in the history of modern Syria and in the national independence struggle against the French." See Khoury (1987), Seale (2010).

As far as our story is concerned, all of this demonstrates that the idea of Nesib al-Bakri's sounding out the possibility of an eventual anti-Turkish revolt in the Jebel Druze, with Feisal's approval, was not a silly pipe-dream; it could have given Feisal a second string to his bow and reduced, however slightly, his dependence on the British. It was this that Lawrence was determined to prevent. The potential of

Syria was neglected throughout the campaign, which ended with Feisal fatally weak politically. In the event, Nesib did make contact with Sultan al-Atrash but there was no revolt in the Jebel Druze, which led Lawrence to write scornfully that the Syrians deserved nothing since they had done nothing to help themselves. It was, however, a jejune remark since Lawrence himself and the British did nothing to encourage a rising in Syria, rather the contrary; British policy was to respect French claims in Syria, under the terms of the Sykes–Picot agreement. The Syrians waited for assurances that never arrived that they would get British support for a rising against the Turks but once Feisal had placed himself under the command of Allenby there was no doubt little that Nesib could do. It was probably just as well they did not act alone. All that seems to have happened was that Druze cavalry invaded the Hauran just ahead of the British-French-Arab army, doing little good there or in Damascus, where they were treated by the Hashemite forces as enemy and driven out. However, the link established between Nesib and Sultan al-Atrash would later have momentous consequences for French imperialist ambitions in Syria.

Nesib was too close to Feisal for Lawrence's liking. When Feisal was sent to Damascus by his father in May 1915, he stayed with the Bakris. One thing that was less well known is that King Hussein had fallen out with Feisal in May 1918, stung by information from Hogarth and presumably originating from Lawrence, that Feisal was putting too much confidence in the Bakris (in Damascus) and wasting money on them. Now this was going on at the same moment during which Feisal, independently of Lawrence, was in touch with the Commander of the Turkish Fourth Army over terms for a ceasefire.[2] The Sykes–Picot treaty was by this time published and Syrian nationalists, with every justification, were deeply suspicious of British intentions. In Feisal's first government in Damascus immediately after the capture of the city, Nesib was his Chief Secretary, a clear indication that the Emir continued to trust him.

In *Seven Pillars*, almost everything concerning Feisal's thoughts about 'the Syrian alternative', the Arab nationalist movement, and how he thought of using his contacts there, is suppressed. So much is this so, that the reader cannot appreciate why Nesib is with Feisal at all, still less the close relationship between them.

One nice irony of the Druze Revolt might be mentioned. Looking for scapegoats for the murderous anti-French revolt of 1925–27, the French General Andréa accused the British of being involved – in the person of that old enemy of Nesib (and of themselves), T.E. Lawrence!

(*see* Larès (1980), 285, & Villars, 289, quoting Général Andréa: *La Révolte druze et l'insurrection de Damas*. Payot, 1937).

## APPENDIX 3
### THE DEMONISATION OF ABDELKADER

In order to understand Lawrence's hatred of Abdelkader al-Djazairi, we need only remind ourselves of what happened in the Town Hall at Damascus, when Abdelkader drew a knife on Lawrence. He and his brother were in fact Lawrence's main rivals in Damascus, seeking to wield power in the name of King Hussein, but not in the name of Feisal, whom several Damascus notables considered to be too close to the British for the good of Arab independence.

Abdelkader first appears during the ill-fated expedition to the Yarmouk gorge (Book VI). He accompanied this expedition as far as Azrak. There are close parallels between this account in *Seven Pillars* and that concerning that other Syrian, Nesib al-Bakri, who had accompanied the expedition to Nebk six months before. Both wielded political influence in Syria, both were accompanying an expedition largely for their own security in order to bring them near their Syrian destination (in both cases the Jebel Druze), both had been given commissions by Feisal, and in Abdelkader's case by King Hussein, to raise support for the Arab Revolt in Syria. The importance of both men was played down in *Seven Pillars* and both of them, because they were working to an agenda independent of the British, were held in deep misgiving by Lawrence. In both cases, the forced close companionship of a long march created almost unbearable strains. Abdelkader quitted the expedition at Azrak, without telling either Lawrence or the leader Ali ibn Hussein. This is how Lawrence reported it to Joyce on November 13th, in a letter from Azrak after the expedition had returned there:[3]

> Emir Abd el Kadu (sic) came with us to Azrak, where we made the plan of attack on the bridge at Tell el Shehab. He said he would come with us, and we had no idea anything was wrong, but the same day he rode off (without warning either Ali or myself or the Arabs with us) to Salkhad, where he is still sitting. Tell Feisul I think he was afraid: much talk, and little doing, in his way. Neither Ali nor myself gave him any offence.

It is not clear from this letter whether or not the original intention of Abdelkader had been to take part in the assault on the bridge or not; merely that he had said at Azrak that he would do so. The likelihood is No. His mission was to raise support for Feisal in Syria. It is nonetheless very understandable that Lawrence and Ali were shaken by his sudden desertion northwards, for this was Turkish-ruled territory and the possibility of their plans becoming known was only too possible if Abdelkader was intercepted by a Turkish patrol. Abdelkader's loyalty was not taken for granted by Colonel Edouard Brémond, Head of the French Mission. But there is nothing in this letter about treachery or even the fear of it; Abdelkader was simply "afraid". If, as the letter claims, he went to Salkhad (in the Jebel Druze) and was still there, then Lawrence would have no fear of treachery. This letter is in fundamental contradiction of the story that Abdelkader went to Dera' *before* the attempt on the Yarmouk bridge had taken place. Another discrepancy is over the bridges: the original target was the Hamma bridge below Um Qais, already reconnoitred by Lawrence during his secret journey in July. However, that had to be abandoned due to intelligence of a large number of Turkish soldiers in the region. The account in *Seven Pillars* states that the expedition had then intended to attack a bridge further up the gorge because the villages on the further bank (Wadi Khalid) were a fiefdom of Abdelkader; and only *after* Abdelkader's desertion was the decision made to attack the Tell el Shehab bridge instead. However, it is clear from the letter that Tell el Shehab had been chosen *before* the desertion; there is no mention of bridges at Wadi Khalid.

Lawrence enclosed a report to his Cairo chief, Clayton, with the letter to Joyce. This was published in the *Arab Bulletin* on 16 December. It states that, once the el-Hemmi (Hamma) bridge had been ruled out, (this) "left Tell el-Shehab the only approachable bridge in the Yarmouk valley". Wadi Khalid is not mentioned. Nor is Abdelkader. The treachery story has nothing to support it.

In the *Oxford* text, Abdelkader's desertion is presented as presumed treachery, and when Lawrence gets back to Azrak after the Dera' incident later that month, this is confirmed. In a clumsy attempt to give credence to the treachery story, we hear how the Druze chieftain Hussein al Atrash, on a visit to Azrak, relates how he had met Abdelkader in Salkhad and how, after a display of rowdy and arrogant behaviour, Abdelkader had ridden down to Dera'. But, in Lawrence's words, "the Turks knew his madness of old and left him to play. They disbelieved even his yarn that Ali and I would try the Yarmouk bridge that night" (OX 502, R 457). This invites us to believe that they therefore took no special precautions. Only the very credulous could believe that Hacim Muhattim Bey and his lieutenants would ignore first-hand and highly detailed intelligence of a large party of well-armed raiders, led by an Arab Sherif and an English officer, actually in the area at that very moment, even more so if it were Major Lawrence, for whom they were offering a £20,000 reward![4] In the 1926 revision Lawrence changed Hussein al Atrash into 'Xury, the Druse Emir of Salkhad'. In the same way, he will change the name of the Bey and of his companions on the Dera' reconnaissance, a sign that the 1922 accounts are either unreliable or fictitious.

## APPENDIX 4
### ABBREVIATED REFERENCES

| | |
|---|---|
| B:LH | T.E. Lawrence to his biographer Liddell Hart. London, Cassell. 1963. |
| BR | T.E. Lawrence papers, Bodleian Library, Oxford. |
| B:RG | T.E. Lawrence to his Biographer Robert Graves. London, Cassell. 1963. |
| BL | British Library |
| DG | D. Garnett (ed.). The Letters of T.E. Lawrence. London, Jonathan Cape. 1938. |
| F.O. or FO | Foreign Office |
| Friends | A.W. Lawrence (ed.). T.E. Lawrence by his Friends. London, Jonathan Cape. 1937. |
| GBS/CFS | J.W. & N. Wilson (eds.). T.E. Lawrence. Correspondence with Bernard and Charlotte Shaw: Vols I to III, 1922–1926, 1927–1928, 1928. Castle Hill Press, Fordingbridge. 2000–2008. |
| HL | M.R. Lawrence (ed.). The Home Letters of T.E. Lawrence and his Brothers. Oxford, Blackwell. 1954. |
| JW | J.M. Wilson. Lawrence of Arabia: The Authorised Biography of T.E. Lawrence. Heinemann, London. 1989. |
| JTELS | The Journal of the T.E. Lawrence Society. |
| LTEL | A.W. Lawrence (ed.). Letters to T.E. Lawrence. London, Jonathan Cape. 1937. |
| MB | Malcolm Brown (ed.). The Letters of T.E. Lawrence. London, J.M. Dent. 1988. |
| OX | (usually followed by page number) T.E. Lawrence (Wilson, J.M. ed.). Seven Pillars of Wisdom (Oxford |

| | |
|---|---|
| | text). Castle Hill Press, Fordingbridge. 1997 (Default text for this book). |
| R | (followed by page number) or SP. T.E. Lawrence. *Seven Pillars of Wisdom: A Triumph*. Cape, London. 1940. Standard published edition based on the 1926 subscribers' edition. |
| *Secret Lives* | Philip Knightley & Colin Simpson. *The Secret Lives of Lawrence of Arabia*. Nelson. 1969. |
| *Some notes* | T.E. Lawrence. 'Some notes on the writing of the Seven Pillars of Wisdom by T.E. Shaw'. *See* Preface to *Seven Pillars of Wisdom: A Triumph*, 15–17. |

## APPENDIX 5
### KEY CHAPTER NUMERATION IN SUCCESSIVE EDITIONS OF *SEVEN PILLARS* (*overleaf*)

| Complete 1922 text 2nd ed. 2003 (OX) | 1926 Subscribers' edition | 1935 first published edition | 1940 revised edition (R) |
|---|---|---|---|
| 1  How and why I wrote | omitted | omitted | Introductory Chapter |
| 2  The Spirit of the Revolt | Chapter II | Chapter I | Chapter I |
| 5  Monotheism | Chapter IV | all chapters as for 1940 | III |
| 10  Storrs and Abdulla | Chapter IX | | VIII |
| 33  A Railway Offensive (Wadi Kitan shooting) | Chapter XXXI | | XXXI |
| 35  Strategy and Tactics | | | XXXIII |
| 51  Excursions (at Nebk) | | | XLIII |
| 81  The Serahin (sermon) | | | LXXIV |
| 87  Being taught (Dera' 1) | | | LXXX |
| 91  My Bodyguard | | | LXXXIII |
| 94-5  (Battle of Tafileh) | | | LXXXV |
| 118  A Birthday (Myself) | | | CIII |
| 134  A night of storm (Tafas) | | | CXVII |
| 135  With Barrow (Dera' 2) | | CXVII | CXVII |

# Notes

PART ONE
SEVEN YEARS OF STRUGGLE, 1919–1926
## 1  Genesis in Paris, 1919
1. George A. Lloyd to Sir Reginald Wingate, 17 August 1917, Churchill College, Cambridge.
2. T. E. Lawrence to Major R.H. Scott, 14 October 1918, DG, 258. The 'powers' meant Great Britain, France, and the United States.
3. J. Nevakivi, 137–43; M. Larès (1980), 189–90.
4. 'The aesthete in war' *in Complete Collected Essays*, 965.
5. BR, c.569. Discovered by Harold Orlans. See "The ways of transgressors", *JTELS* 6.1., 20–33.
6. Letter to Charlotte Shaw, 18 October 1927, GBS/CFS II, 178.
7. Quoted in DG, 261. Keynes' correspondent is not revealed. Probably it was David Garnett himself, the editor.
8. A special intelligence unit under the Foreign Office, where he had worked, and which officially directed his work in Arabia. The *Arab Bulletin* was published and distributed by the Arab Bureau; it had a secret status. See M. Brown (ed.), *Secret Despatches from Arabia*.
9. *Fly far away from these sickly miasmas;*
   *Purify yourself in the upper air,*
   *And drink, like a pure and divine liqueur,*
   *The pure flame of those limpid spaces.*
   Baudelaire, *Elévation* (from *Les Fleurs du Mal*).
10. The document was discovered by Knightley and Simpson. See *Secret Lives*, 162.
11. This is the earliest version; see below.
12. A.J. Clark-Kerr to R.G. Vansittart, 21 August 1919, *see JW*, 617 & note 47, 1114.
13. *JW*, 1115, notes 53 & 54 for details.
14. Not dated. Wilson dates 18 September 1919. *JW*, note 55, 1115.
15. *JW*, 622 quoting J.E. Wrench, *Struggle 1914–1920*.
16. From "Some notes on the writing of the Seven Pillars of Wisdom by T.E. Shaw" (henceforth *Some notes*).
17. June Rathbone, *Anatomy of Masochism*. The book contains a chapter on Lawrence.

18 This is substantially confirmed by D.G. Hogarth in his account of *Seven Pillars* in *The Times,* 13 December 1926, 73.
19 See M. Brown (ed.), *Secret Despatches from Arabia*, 46–54.
20 The British Library (BL), Add. MSS. 45914, 45915.
21 Now edited and published (2009) by J. & N. Wilson in *Towards an English Fourth,* 47–106.
22 O'Donnell, 1979.
23 Omitted from the Subscribers' edition on the advice of E.M. Forster.
24 *Lord Jim* and *Heart of Darkness* are both narrated by a fictional sea captain, Marlow, to an audience of friends.

## 2  Writing the Book: London, Oxford, Pole Hill, 1920

1 V.W. Richards. *Portrait of T.E. Lawrence,* 185.
2 Ibid., 184
3 27 February, 1920. DG, 299.
4 Letter to E. Garnett, 26 August 1922. DG, 360.
5 Robert Graves, *Goodbye to All That,* 308.
6 The modern Arabic name is Umm Qais; it lies just above the gorge of the Yarmouk river south of Lake Tiberias.
7 Robert Graves to John Graves, 30 October 1920. Private, quoted in R.P. Graves. *Robert Graves: The Assault Heroic 1895–1926,* 236.
8 Ibid.
9 *Goodbye to All That,* 312.
10 B:RG, 7.
11 *Goodbye to All That,* 310.
12 V.W. Richards, *A Portrait of T.E. Lawrence,* 43.
13 TEL to Vyvyan Richards. 15 July 1918. MB, 149–51. *The well at the world's end* is the title of one of Morris' romances.
14 1 September, 1919. DG, 280
15 McKenzie Smith. MS in Bancroft School archives. Published in the *T.E. Lawrence Society Newsletter* no. 90, pp. 4–6 (2009).
16 Ibid.
17 This is now in the Ashmolean Museum, Oxford.
18 V.W. Richards, 180–82.
19 TEL to Richards, 15 July 1918. DG, 243.
20 TEL to F.N. Doubleday, DG, 301.
21 TEL to F.N. Doubleday, 29 March 1920. BR.
22 Ibid., 15 May 1920. BR.
23 TEL to Richards, DG, 318.
24 These are not titles given by Lawrence but they show better the place of each piece in the story.
25 This MS is now in the Harry Ransom Humanities Research Centre, Texas. It was published by Castle Hill Press, Fordingbridge, England (March 2009) in the volume *Towards an English Fourth.*

26 F.N. Doubleday. *A Few Indiscreet Recollections*. December 1928, privately printed, p. 82.

## 3 In the Political Arena, 1920–21

1. A.J. Clark-Kerr to R.G. Vansittart, 21 August, 1919. FO 608/97.
2. The 'Rebellion' in Iraq was at its height in August 1920.
3. Patrick Seale, *The Struggle for Arab Independence*, 111.
4. George Antonius, *The Arab Awakening*.
5. Seale, 132.
6. For the story of Feisal's reign in Syria, see Seale, *The Struggle for Arab Independence*, 118–155. For Feisal's flight: Storrs, *Orientations*, 430–31.
7. Apparently. I have come across no immediate public or private reaction on Lawrence's part.
8. Record by Colonel Wigram of 31 October 1918 of Lawrence's conversation with the King the previous day, quoted by Lord Stamfordham (Private Secretary to King George V) in a letter to Lawrence 17 January 1928, *LTEL*, 186.
9. *Friends*, 250
10. Walpole, Hugh. 'T.E. Lawrence in life and death' in *Broadsheet: World Books Society Bulletin*. November, 1939.
11. T. Hoenselaars and G.M. Moore, 'Joseph Conrad and T.E. Lawrence' in *JTELS* V.1., 25–44. 1995.
12. WO 33/969, extract from 'An examination of the cause of the outbreak in Mesopotamia'. Quoted in Rush, 'Emir Zayd ibn Hussayn: Iraq's most deserving Prince' (unpublished essay).
13. Letter of 12 August 1920, *LTEL*.
14. In Charles Grosvenor, *An Iconography: The Portraits of T.E. Lawrence*, 1. I am indebted to this book for many of the details concerning the portraits and artists and Lawrence's relationships with both.
15. John Mack, *A Prince of our Disorder: The Life of T.E. Lawrence*, 505 (interview with Christine Longford, March 18, 1965).
16. *B:RG*, 131.
17. *Friends*, 229.
18. *B:RG*, 76.
19. Grosvenor, 44.
20. Celandine Kennington, on her husband; quoted in Grosvenor, 44.
21. Grosvenor, 22.
22. See Jonathan Black, '"King of the Pictures": Eric Kennington, Portraiture and the Illustration of *Seven Pillars of Wisdom*, 1920–26'.
23. 'Prefatory note' in *Catalogue of an Exhibition of Arab Portraits*. The Leicester Galleries, 1921.
24. To Edward Marsh, 17 January 1921.
25. 12 April 1921, Cairo. *HL*, 353
26. *Friends*, 267

27 André Malraux, *Le Démon de l'Absolu*, 1182.
28 Ibid.
29 Ibid., 1183.
30 See Dixon's testimony in *Friends*, cited below in Chapter 6 (Bovington Camp).
31 Letter to Kennington, 1 October 1921. Liddell Hart Centre for Military Studies, King's College, London.

## 4   From the Oxford Text to Enlistment in the Ranks, 1922

1 *Wenn Du dieses bloss nicht hast,*
  *Dieses: stirb und werde*
  *Bist du nur ein truebe Gast*
  *Auf dieser dunklen Erde.*
2 MB, 192, not dated but stated as January 1922.
3 15 February 1922, *HL*, 354–5.
4 Information about Bruce is from Knightley & Simpson, 1969, 169–171. It is a revised version of four long articles published in the *Sunday Times* in 1968 by the same authors. These were based on independent investigation and interviews with Bruce in 1968. As a result of critical comment on the articles by Lawrence scholars, notably J.M. Wilson, the book version is more cautious. There are no independent witnesses to Bruce's early (1922) accounts. The papers are housed in the Imperial War Museum.
5 Quoted in Martin Seymour-Smith, *Robert Graves: His Life and Works*, 109.
6 BR.
7 Liddell Hart Centre, published in MB, 192.
8 BR.
9 DG, 340.
10 BR.
11 *SP*, footnote in red, page 283.
12 A deposit of old ash was discovered there by members of the London group of the T.E. Lawrence Society and, we read, "one enterprising member managed to gather some of this ash, with the intention of sealing it in glass phials, for selling on to bolster Society funds." Whether any 'Ashes of the Seven Pillars' came to adorn the mantlepieces of Lawrence enthusiasts I have not discovered.
13 *Friends*, 272–3.
14 *Secret Lives*, 173.
15 *Secret Lives*, 175.
16 Mack, 429.
17 "From my slight experience of psychological warfare (of which T.E. had plenty) an elaborate fiction is more plausible the nearer it comes to fact, although the fact is unknowable to the audience." Arnold Lawrence to Mack, 23 July 1973. See Mack, note 68, page 525.

18 *Friends*, 277–8. June Rathbone has commented that Lawrence's depression or disillusionment, as narrated here, is a key feature of masochism, sometimes only alleviated by physical punishment (personal letter).
19 *Secret Lives*, 177.
20 *Sunday Times*, 8 April 1951. W.E. Johns became famous as the author of the Biggles books.
21 Letter to David Garnett, DG, 363, *circa* 1937.

## 5  Literary Mentors, 1922–24

1 TEL to Sydney Cockerell, 22 October 1923, DG, 437.
2 TEL to E. Garnett, 22 August 1922. DG, 358.
3 Ibid.
4 Ibid., 26 August 1922. DG, 360.
5 Ibid., 23 August 1922. DG, 358.
6 I am indebted to Dr Helen Smith for this and other observations on Garnett.
7 E. Garnett to TEL, 9 September 1922. *LTEL*, 87–9.
8 Ibid.
9 TEL to E. Garnett, 7 September 1922. DG, 365–7.
10 12 November 1922. DG, 379.
11 20 November 1922. DG, 383.
12 E. Garnett to TEL, 22 November 1922, *LTEL*, 91. See Chapter 103 (OX), XCIII (R).
13 E. Garnett to TEL, 23 November 1922, *LTEL*, 92.
14 In the Houghton Library, University of Harvard.
15 Ibid.
16 Bernard Shaw to Baldwin: 31 May 1923. *GBS/CFS*: Vol. 1, 41.
17 Bernard Shaw to TEL. 25 August 1922. *GBS/CFS* I, 6.
18 Shaw had over-estimated the word count by 125,000 words.
19 Bernard Shaw to TEL, 1 December, 1922. *GBS/CFS* I, 11–14.
20 Bernard Shaw to TEL, 17 December 1922. Ibid., 17–19.
21 TEL to Bernard Shaw. 27 December 1922. Ibid., 20–23.
22 Bernard Shaw to TEL. 28 December 1922. Ibid., 23–25.
23 Charlotte Shaw to TEL. 31 December 1922. Ibid., 25–28.
24 TEL to Charlotte Shaw, 8 January 1923. Ibid., 33–5.
25 Bernard Shaw to TEL. 4 January 1923. Ibid., 31.
26 A sculptress and widow of the tragic explorer of Antarctica.
27 She had a poor opinion of Garnett's critical instinct, calling him "conventional and not courageous". "I shall never forgive him for wanting to publish a maimed edition of the *Seven Pillars*". 9 April 1928, GBS/CFS, III.54.
28 Siegfried Sassoon to TEL, 26 November 1923. *LTEL*, 153–5.
29 *Friends*, 282.
30 I.e. the Arab movement.
31 Forster to TEL. Undated but February 1924. *LTEL*, 58–63.

32 TEL to Forster. 24 February 1924. BR & DG, 455–7.
33 22 February 1924. *LTEL* 63–4.
34 Letter to his mother, Alice Clara Forster, 23 March 1924. Lago & Furbank, 50.
35 TEL to Forster, 6 April 1924 from Clouds Hill. MB 263.
36 TEL to Forster, 24 July 1924. DG, 462.
37 *Friends*, 283.
38 TEL to Forster, ibid.
39 DG, 738.

## 6 Bovington Camp, 1923–25

1 TEL to Swann. 19 November 1922, DG, 381.
2 Group Captain Charles Findley, 'The amazing AC2' in *The Listener*, 5 June 1958.
3 TEL to Raymond Savage, 7 January 1923. BR.
4 TEL to Robert Graves, 18 January 1923. B:RG, 22.
5 *GBS/CFS* I, 36.
6 By Adrien le Corbeau. Published in 1924 as *The Forest Giant* by Jonathan Cape.
7 *LTEL*, 119.
8 Letter to John Mack, 25 June 1967. Mack, 346. Dixon became a writer and, like Lawrence, depicted service life (in his book *Tinned Soldier*). His contribution to *Friends* is an important account of Lawrence's life at Bovington.
9 13 June, 1923. DG, 425.
10 TEL to R.M. Guy, 21 March 1923. MB, 230.
11 Ibid., 17 September 1923, University of Harvard & MB, 244.
12 'A sea trip' essay. 18 April 1923. Bodleian Mss d230. See also *JW*, 715–16.
13 19 March 1923. MB, 227.
14 Findley, 1958.
15 TEL to Curtis, 30 May 1923. DG, 419.
16 The source is Robert Graves: *B:RG*, 27.
17 TEL to Robert Graves, 8 September 1923. *B:RG*, 26.
18 27 June 1923. DG, 420.
19 TEL to A.R.D. Fairburn, 12 May 1923. Alexander Turnbull Library, Wellington, New Zealand.
20 TEL to R. Graves, *B:RG*, 27.
21 Letter to John Mack, 25 June 1967. Mack, op. cit., 346.
22 *Friends*, 375.
23 *Friends*, 277.
24 TEL to Charlotte Shaw. 4 August 1924, *GBS/CFS*, I, 87.
25 TEL to Charlotte Shaw. 19 March 1924, *GBS/CFS*, I, 67.

## 7 The Subscribers Edition, 1924–1926

1. Lady Gregory's diary for 20 & 21 May 1923.
2. TEL to Hogarth, 13 June 1923. DG, 425.
3. TEL to V. Richards. MB, 223–6.
4. "According to legend Belisarius, one of Justinian's generals, was accused of treachery and thereafter forced to live as a beggar on the streets of Constantinople . . ." Editorial note in *GBS/CFS* I, 43. Belisarius was considered by Graves to be a precursor of Lawrence as a strategist (*B:RG*, 130).
5. D.G. Hogarth to Bernard Shaw. 4 June 1923. BR.
6. TEL to D.G. Hogarth. 23 August 1923. DG, 428.
7. Bernard Shaw to TEL. *GBS/CFS* I, 49.
8. Ibid. *GBS/CFS* I, 39. *Grangerisation*: To illustrate a book by later insertion of material, esp. prints, from other books (OED). Thus Shaw was exaggerating. The art critic Herbert Read also used the term in his review of *Seven Pillars*: "It is rather like a grangerisation album of the sixties." *The Bibliophile's Almanack*, 36. 1927.
9. Nash to Gordon Bottomly, 12 September 1922; quoted in Mack, 335. Jeremy Wilson has written that "Lawrence was gradually becoming one of the most significant private patrons of contemporary artists in Britain."
10. TEL to Charlotte Shaw, 29 November 1924. *GBS/CFS* 1.117.
11. R. Yeomans, 'T.E. Lawrence and the Visual Arts' in *TELSJ* III.1, 1993.
12. See Chapter 16.
13. Herbert Read. 'The Seven Pillars of Wisdom' in *The Bibliophile's Almanach for 1928*.
14. Grosvenor (1984): a full and erudite account.
15. Ibid.
16. Nancy Astor to TEL. 20 March 1924.
17. TEL to Bernard Shaw. 13 December 1923. *GBS/CFS* I, 48.
18. TEL to Charlotte Shaw. 31 August 1924. Ibid., 97.
19. Charlotte Shaw to TEL. 6 October 1924. Ibid., 103.
20. Bernard Shaw to TEL. 7 October 1924. *GBS/CFS* I, 103.
21. Ibid.
22. Now in the British Library: ADD 56499.
23. All three excerpts are from OX 7-8.
24. Bernard Shaw to TEL, 7 October 1924. *GBS/CFS* I, 103.
25. See my '*Seven Pillars*: Which Version?' *JTELS* XV.2, 12–42 for more examples and a more detailed analysis.
26. TEL to Charlotte Shaw. 26 December 1925, *GBS/CFS* I, 158.
27. Ibid., 31 August 1924. *GBS/CFS* I, 97.
28. Peter Wood. 'In search of the elusive Manning Pike', *JTELS* XIV.1, 69.
29. Manning Pike. 'Notes on printing *Seven Pillars of Wisdom*'. Ibid., 58.
30. TEL to Robin Buxton. 26 March 1925. DG, 472.
31. Bernard Shaw to TEL. 20 April 1925. *GBS/CFS* I, 126.

32 Andrew Boyle, *Trenchard*, 516.
33 Now Feisal I, King of Iraq.
34 TEL to Charlotte Shaw. 28 November 1925, *GBS/CFS* I, 149–50.
35 Clare Sydney Smith, *The Golden Reign*, 14.
36 Lago & Furbank, 75.
37 Letter to Dick Knowles. 3 December 1926. Private collection.

PART TWO
SEVEN PILLARS OF WISDOM

## 8 Lawrence in the Arab Revolt: A Summary

1 Patrick Seale, *The Struggle for Arab Independence*.
2 E. Brémond, *Le Hedjaz dans la Guerre Mondiale*.

## 9 Lawrence & Ronald Storrs in Jeddah

1 Ronald Storrs in *Orientations*, 157–8. He copied the extract from his report.
2 Ibid., 163.
3 Lawrence was evidently not present. His account (SP, 67) that Abdullah came to them first contradicts Storrs.
4 Ibid., 174.
5 Ibid.
6 Pages 171–180.
7 Ibid., 175. "Us all" would seem to include Lawrence but *Seven Pillars* gives a contrary impression.
8 As vividly shown in the film *Lawrence of Arabia*.
9 C.E. Wilson to G.F. Clayton, 22 November 1916.
10 *Orientations*, 179.
11 *Orientations*, 185.
12 This expression was echoed by Alec Kirkbride in his tribute to Abdullah in Chapter 4 of his memoir *A Crackle of Thorns*. He entitled it 'The King with a twinkle'. Kirkbride worked with Abdullah for thirty years.
13 Without implying anything but a coincidence, except perhaps in the langage, it is interesting to note that John Buchan's *Greenmantle* concerns a mission, a Muslim rising, a mysterious master-spirit, and a prophet. It was published in June 1916.

## 10 The Battle of Tafileh: Subhi al-Umari & Lawrence

1 This account is taken from Subhi al-Umari's book, *Lurens kama areftuhu (Lawrence as I knew him)*, 1969. Page numbers are given after each cited extract. Suleiman Moussa's long citation from al-Umari in *T. E. Lawrence: An Arab View*, 136–7, and his comments about him are *not* from the book but from an MS and letters. A number of details are different.

2 Descriptions by Lawrence (*Seven Pillars*, OX 513) and Alec Kirkbride, *The Awakening*.
3 TEL to Captain (later Admiral) Snagge, 4 March 1930. DG, 683.
4 For his original report, see *Secret Despatches from Arabia*, 176–9; for the *Seven Pillars* versions, OX 537-46, R 483-93; Lawrence also published a shortened account in *The Times* on 28 November 1918, as part of the second instalment of an article entitled *The Arab Epic*.
5 William Facey & Najdi Safwat (eds.), *A Soldier's Story*, 135.
6 Basil Liddell Hart, *T.E. Lawrence: in Arabia and After*, 272.

## 11 Kirkbride's Account

1 I.e. The 'Druze mountain' in southern Syria (now Lebanon).
2 *An Awakening*, 45.
3 Ibid., 43.
4 Omitted from *SP*, probably on Forster's advice, who found these sentences unclear.
5 Ibid., 41.
6 Ibid., 41.
7 Ibid., 43.
8 Ibid., 49.
9 Ibid., 43.
10 Ibid., 72.
11 Ibid., 74.
12 Ibid., 82.
13 Ibid., 90.
14 Changed to *our names* in the 1926 revision but how many Damascenes knew of Major Stirling? Or Lawrence?
15 However, he wrote to Stirling in October 1924, after the latter had returned the book to him with comments: "My memory of the entry into Damascus was of a quietness and emptiness of street . . . ". MB, 274–6.
16 Ibid., 95.
17 Lawrence frequently describes his movements and actions as if he was the only person there when this is not the case.
18 Ibid., 97.

## 12 The Outsider (1)

1 'T.E. Lawrence': *The Listener*, 31 July 1935; republished in *Abinger Harvest*, 169.
2 Excepting the events at Nebk (June 1917), which are presented in Chapter 17.
3 *Reminder*: in the standard editions, the introductory chapter and Chapter I.
4 When he omitted this chapter, he transferred most of this paragraph to R283, *see* below.

5 Kirkbride, *An Awakening*, 118.
6 Stephen Tabachnick, *T.E. Lawrence*, 110.
7 It is interesting that Villars, who had never seen the Curtis draft, intuits this. 'He talks of 'our men'; and one feels that he has nearly said 'us'.' Jean Béraud Villars, *T.E. Lawrence*. For Malraux it is self-evident that he is writing about himself; see the Epilogue.
8 "The masochist often regards the physical as dirty and degrading, although he is identified with the body and dependent upon a physical form of expression." June Rathbone: personal communication.
9 Boyle, *My Naval Life*, 102.
10 TEL to Mrs Lawrence. 16 January 1916. *HL*, 332.

## 13 Climax at Dera'

1 As it was in *Revolt in the Desert*. See also J.N. Lockman, *Parallel Captures*.
2 Kirkbride, *A Crackle of Thorns*, 7. He repeats the same thing in *An Awakening*, 15.
3 Antonius, 321. Antonius believed that Lawrence had more confidence in his Arabic than was justified.
4 This is the text: "Satisfactory letters have been received by Sherif Feisal from DERAA, showing that the personnel in most of the departments, including the telegraph, are Arabs". National Archives, WO 158/634, III, 138A. 15 June 1918. As far as I am aware, this was first published in J.N. Lockman, *Scattered Tracks on the Lawrence Trail*.
5 Knightley & Simpson, 215.
6 University of Texas. Published in MB, 165–7.
7 See Appendix 3, 'The demonisation of Abdelkader'.
8 See James Barr, *A Line in the Sand*, 87–89.
9 See C.W.R. Long, *British Pro-Consuls in Egypt 1914–1929*, 63.
10 J. Rathbone, *Anatomy of Masochism*, 46.
11 Ibid., 39–46.
12 Ibid., 291–302.
13 Reik, 9, in the chapter 'Freud's views'. *Cf.* "I was a standing court martial on myself" (O 683, R 583).
14 His moral masochism is discussed in Chapter 18.
15 Reik has three essential features: fantasy; the suspense factor; the demonstrative factor.
16 Reik, 44.
17 Rathbone, 41.
18 Ibid., 41.
19 Reik, 133.
20 Ibid., 72.
21 Reik, 74.
22 Rathbone, 45, but my italics.
23 The biographer Desmond Stewart devotes three pages to this incident

but his source was a reference to a "secret report" mentioned by General Edouard Bremond in his 1933 memoir of his service in the Hedjaz, *Le Hedjaz dans la guerre mondiale*, page 161. He did not know that this report was none other than St. Quentin's and that therefore the source of the story was not a French intelligence agent in northern Syria in 1912! No doubt many other stories originating with Lawrence have been misinterpreted in the same way.

24 See (T.E. Lawrence), *Oriental Assembly*, 5–62.
25 J. Lockman, *Scattered Tracks on the Lawrence Trail*, 133.
26 S.C. Rolls, *Steel Chariots in the Desert*.
27 Reik, Ch. XI, 'The secret meaning of the display in public', 145.

## 14 The Outsider (2)

1 Message from General Allenby to Emir Feisal, 20 September 1918. Hubert Young papers, King's College, London.
2 *Secret Despatches from Arabia*, 186–96.
3 I have no independent confirmation of this last allegation.
4 Quoted from Robert Bolt in 'Apologia', *JTELS* V.1, 77.
5 Unpublished notes from 1963 & 1965, *see* Mack, 237.
6 *The Observer*, 16 December 1962. Later, Arnold was less sure; see Mack, 238 (footnote).
7 *Seven Pillars of Wisdom* was the original title chosen for the film. Arnold insisted it should be changed.
8 'Apologia', 80.
9 Ibid., 77.
10 *The Independent Arab*, 252.
11 General Sir George de S. Barrow, *The Fire of Life*, 211.
12 *Le Démon de l'Absolu*, 1195.
13 See above, Chapter 5. Letter to E. Garnett, 26 August 1922. DG, 360.

## 15 The Biographical Environment and Sequel

1 Bernard Shaw, from an essay on the fly-leaf of his wife's copy of the Oxford text which he deposited in the Arents Collection of the New York Public Library. See Mack, 21.
2 Mack, 20–21, 64–66, 66.
3 OX 518, R 462, 464.
4 OX 484-6, R 440–3.
5 OX 504-7, R 458–462.
6 Hogarth travelled quite frequently between Cairo and London. Living in Oxford, he was a friend of the family. He had met Lawrence just five days before and commented in a letter to his wife that he looked "fitter and better than when I saw him last".
7 See *Seven Pillars*, Appendix 2.
8 When Sherif Hussein declared the Hejaz an independent kingdom,

stamps were minted. Lawrence played a major role in their design and production in Cairo. See Storrs, *Orientations*.
9 Reginald Wingate was now High Commissioner in Cairo.
10 Hogarth to Ormsby Gore, 26 October 1917. PRO/FO 371/3054 f.388.
11 5 September 1917. *HL*, 339.
12 28 March 1918 from Akaba. *HL*, 349.
13 MB,149. Brown added a footnote as follows: "When Richards showed Lawrence this letter seven years later (in much changed circumstances), Lawrence found it interesting enough to copy for himself. He subsequently sent his copy to Charlotte Shaw apparently believing it to be the only surviving letter of his 'Arab period'. See letter to Charlotte Shaw, 29 March 1927."
14 "Out of the turmoil of the French front I had written to him quoting part of a favourite sidenote from the *Ancient Mariner*: 'In his loneliness and fixedness he yearneth towards the journeying Moon, and the stars that still sojourn, yet still move onward; and everywhere the blue sky belongs to them, and is their appointed rest and native country and their own natural homes, which they enter unannounced as lords that are certainly expected, and yet there is a silent joy at their arrival'", Richards, 181.
15 Apsley Cherry Garrard, *Friends*, 190.
16 *Friends*, 288, 290.
17 Reik, 259.
18 This is a characteristic observed of André Malraux himself.
19 26 March 1924, *GBS/CFS*, Vol. 1, 70.
20 DG, 463. Lawrence wrote to E. Garnett that the *Myself* chapter (CIII) was "written in cipher" (DG 366). Since it is an astonishingly lucid and complex analysis of himself without any apparent effort at concealment, this is certainly a signpost pointing the wrong way. If there is a chapter written in cipher, it is elsewhere.
21 Mann's introduction to *The Short Novels of Dostoevski*. New York: Dial Press, 1945. Quoted in Harold Orlans, *T.E. Lawrence: Biography of a Broken Hero*, 65.

## 16 The Arab Mirage

1 "Toute abstraction qui désigne une collectivité humaine – nation, race, classe – lorsqu'on la charge de destin, devient mythe. Son Arabie était un mythe. *Le Démon de l'Absolu*, 871-2.
2 A Sherif is a man of noble family whose ancestry can be traced from the Prophet Mohammed through his daughter Fatima. The term is also used more loosely for a high dignitary but not, I think, by Lawrence. The term Grand Sherif refers exclusively to the ruler of Mecca.
3 Forster to TEL, February, 1924. *LTEL*, 59.
4 Hubert Young, *The Independent Arab*, 192.
5 *The Independent Arab*, 150.
6 Wilfred Thesiger, *Arabian Sands*, 81-2, 85.

7 As Lawrence implies (OX 230), only certains clans of the Howeitat (including the Abu Tayi) were 'true Bedu'.
8 Edward Said, *Orientalism*, 230.
9 Ibid., *Orientalism*, 241.
10 Ibid., 240, 241.
11 *Le Démon de l'Absolu*, 871.
12 Ibid., 870.
13 'Nationalism among the tribesmen', *Arab Bulletin*, 26 November 1916. *Secret Despatches*, 72.
14 These countries, in the formal political sense, did not exist when his report was written, still less formal frontiers, but one should not imagine that they had no reality for their inhabitants. *See* Seale.
15 Later, some years after the Churchill–Lawrence settlement of 1921, he took the view that Arab self-government would work after many years of painful trial and error, provided there was no interference from the West. The message was: 'leave them alone to learn from their own mistakes'. We have not followed his advice.

## 17 The Presentation of History

1 TEL to V.W. Richards, March 1923.
2 From 'Bias in history', see *An Autobiography and Other Essays*, 1949.
3 Tabachnick, *T.E. Lawrence*, 54.
4 Barr (2006), 117–18. *See* Appendix 2 for more background.
5 It was widely believed in the Arab world after the war that Lawrence's principal rôle was as an agent for the promotion of British imperialist ends.
6 This was well understood by Robert Bolt, the screenwriter of *Lawrence of Arabia*. We see Lawrence, on his departure from Wejh, ask Feisal if he could claim to be riding in his name. "Yes, Lieutenant Lawrence, you may claim it, but in whose name *do* you ride?"
7 *JW*, 210, 211, 213.
8 *See* Leclerc in *TELSJ* XX.1, 53, quoting Doynel de St. Quentin: 'Le Raid du Major Lawrence et l'action anglaise à Akaba': Cairo, 20 August, 1917.
9 10 July 1917. Reproduced in DG, 225–31.
10 Lawrence's own wartime notebooks show what an enormous amount of news travels round the desert far and wide. *Add Ms 45914,* BL. See also Thesiger, *passim*.
11 Suleiman Moussa. Vain attempts were made from Britain to counter Moussa's denial. BR, MS ENG c.6751.
12 Lowell Thomas, *With Lawrence in Arabia*, 84. This version is only just recognisable as the same trip. It is also reported at some length in Antonius, 222–3. Where Antonius got this from is not stated. He first met Lawrence in September 1921.
13 Lawrence had thus long ago thrown doubt on the claim later put

forward by J. Wilson (as proof of his journey) that incidents in Baalbek province, in fact a revolt by the Metawila tribe reported by a Turkish officer, were provoked by him: *JW*: Notes 41 & 48, 1070. There are also diary entries cited by Wilson as follows: "although the diary entries for 5th to 19th June were intentionally cryptic and have in places been erased, they support the account given in Lawrence's report to Clayton. The entries of 7th, 9th, and 11th June, for instance, confirm that he visited Burga, the Metawila tribe, and Ras Baalbek". I have studied the diary entries for 5th to 19th June and they read to me almost like a caricature of secret service methods. I would conclude that, given his statement to Graves that he has deliberately hidden the truth, intentionally cryptic and erased diary entries must be treated as suspicious and unreliable. Compare his diary entries for the alleged Dera' visit: *see* Barr 2006, 197–200.
14 *B:RG*, 84–90. Lawrence changes his mind again in the versions he gave to Liddell Hart (by interview and draft correction).
15 Barr (2006), 151.
16 Le Père Jaussen. See Henry Laurens, *Lawrence en Arabie*, 146.
17 Auguste Lamotte, 'Observations on *Revolt in the Desert* by the English Colonel T.E. Lauwrence' [*sic*].
Unpublished Ms. See Leclerc, C. 'French eye-witness accounts of the Arab Revolt', Part 2. *JTELS* XX.2, 2010/11, 60–72.
18 30 July 1917, FO 686/8. *see JW* 431-2 & notes 33–4, 1076–9.
19 *JW*, 404–5.
20 *Orientalism*, 242.
21 This book, *The Arab Awakening* (1938), is the most famous Arab account of the Arab national movement in English. For a historical assessment of Lawrence, see 319–24.
22 *Times Literary Supplement*, 21 January 1977.
23 'Doyen' of modern British historians on the Middle East, author of *A History of the Arab Peoples*. From 'T.E. Lawrence and Louis Massignon'. *Times Literary Supplement*, 8 July 1983.
24 *Orientalism*, 240.

## 18  The Problem of Autobiography

1 These aspects are more fully treated in the Oxford text than in the 1926 revision.
2 A. Hourani, 'T.E. Lawrence and Louis Massignon' in the *Times Literary Supplement,* 8 July 1983, 733–4.
3 Ibid.
4 Rathbone, 292.
5 For Schopenhauer, the Will is a primary force, a first principle. Interestingly, Lawrence capitalises the word in the *Myself* chapter "as if it were a separate being" (Hourani). Is this an echo of Schopenhauer?
6 To Robert Graves, 4 February 1935.

7  January 4th 1923. *GBS/CFS* I, 30.
8  V.S. Pritchett, 'The aesthete at war' in *Complete Collected Essays*, 385.
9  "A sense of grandiosity and of self-pitying deprivation paradoxically are sides of the same coin, and neither can exist without the other." Arnold Cooper, 'The Narcissistic-Masochistic character' in *Masochism: Current Psychoanalytic Perspectives*, 134.
10 Freud, 161, 166.
11 Reik, 249.
12 *Cf*. Nietzsche: "He who despises himself nevertheless esteems himself thereby as despiser." Cooper, 128. Reik, 261, has almost the same wording.
13 Reik, 139.
14 28 August 1928. MB, 383.
15 Lawrence to Sydney Cockerell, 22 October 1923. DG, 437.

**Epilogue**

1  The MS was edited by Maurice J-M Larès and published in the Pléiade edition of the complete works of Malraux, with the title *Le Démon de l'Absolu*. See *Bibliothèque de la Pléiade, Oeuvres complètes II, 817–1301* (Text) & *1666–1818* (Notes by Larès). The chapter under study here was published as Chapter XXXV (originally by Malraux) but it had long led an independent life by then, having been worked on and published by Malraux three times between 1946 and 1949, and also published three times in English between 1948 and 1956, each time in a different translation. The first translator was Dorothy Bussy, the other two are anonymous. Larès published these translations together with the French text of *La Pléiade* and an introduction for English readers in a special edition of *T.E. Notes*, December XIII.3, 2003, 1–55. The translations given here do not follow one single version throughout. A few are my own. For full details of the history, see *Le Démon de l'Absolu* (*DA*) 1672–4 and *T.E. Notes*.
2  Larès : Introduction to *Le Démon de L'Absolu*, 1677. See also Denis Boak. 'Malraux and T.E. Lawrence' in *Modern Language Review*, April 1966, 61:2, 218–24.
3  *DA*, 1189. Chapter 35 runs from 1189–1202.
4  Boak, see note 2.
5  His flight from Damascus, whence he was expelled by the French High Commissioner, General Gouraud, 28 July 1920.
6  *La Condition Humaine*, 1933; *L'Espoir*, 1937.
7  The passage within single quotation marks is in fact made up of extracts taken, according to Larès, from nine different places in the text (all from the same chapter). This illustrates well the liberties Malraux took in using quotations. However, it does nonetheless provide a perfectly valid summary. Notice also that Malraux frees the statements from the solidarity of the *we* pronoun. Here, it is always *I*.

8 E. Garnett to TEL: Letter of 18 July 1927 (*inter alia*); *LTEL*, 93–6.
9 *Ecce Homo* (1888) was the title of one of Nietzsche's last works. It was also the year of Lawrence's birth!
10 *Friends*, 272.
11 TEL to E.M. Forster, 20 February 1924. DG, 457.
12 TEL to J.B. Acres. DG, 492.
13 TEL to Kennington. 6 August 1934. DG, 814.
14 *See* Larès, *DA*, 1668–9. Larès highlights the similarity between the story of Lawrence's 'lost' manuscript and Malraux's.

## Appendices

1 *B:LH*, 129, 145.
2 Barr (2004), 241–2. FO 371/3881, National Archives.
3 TEL to Colonel Joyce, 13 November 1917. DG, 239.
4 The last statement contradicts the letter to Stirling, which runs: "The Turks ordered out cavalry to intercept us." In Lawrence's narrative of the attempt on the bridge in *Seven Pillars*, there is no sign of any special precautions.

# BIBLIOGRAPHY

## Archives

<u>British Library MSS</u>

T.E. Lawrence *pocket diaries:*
  A. *1 January 1917–5 January 1918.*
  B. *1 January 1918–8 October 1918.* Add MS 45983.
T.E. Lawrence *wartime notebooks:*
  *Army field service correspondence book with notes & memoranda relating to 30 October 1916–16 April 1917.* Add MS 45914.
  *Parts of a diary in pencil written on backs of Army messages and signals pads 17 January–28 June 1917.* Add MS 45915 (includes sketch maps).
T.E. Lawrence:
  *Typescript of The Mint with extensive Ms corrections & rewritings + accompanying MS.* Add MS 45916.
T.E. Lawrence:
  *Other:* Add MSS 45930, 46355, et al.
Charlotte Shaw:
  *Her notebook*: comments on *Introduction* to *Seven Pillars* and copyings of the text of *Seven Pillars* sent to her by TEL. Add MS 56498.

<u>Bodleian Library, Oxford</u>
Special collections: The T.E. Lawrence papers.

<u>The Public Library, Oxford</u>
Journals of the *T.E. Lawrence Society (JTELS).*
<u>Quai d'Orsay, Paris.</u>
<u>Consular Archives, Nantes.</u>
MAE Guerre 1914–18.
MAE Levant 1918–40. Arabia. Hedjaz 1918 – 29 Vol 1.

## Bibliographical

*<u>Writings of T.E. Lawrence</u>*

Lawrence, T.E. (Wilson, J.W. and N., eds.). *Seven Pillars of Wisdom. The Complete 1922 Text.* Fordingbridge: Castle Hill Press, 1997 (The default text for this book).
Lawrence, T.E. *Seven Pillars of Wisdom: A Triumph.* London: Cape, 1940.
Lawrence, T.E. 'Some notes on the writing of the Seven Pillars of Wisdom

by T.E. Shaw'. *See* Preface to *Seven Pillars of Wisdom: A Triumph*, 15–17.

Lawrence, T.E. *T.E. Lawrence to his Biographers Robert Graves & Liddell Hart*. London: Cassell, 1963.

Lawrence, T.E. 'The Kaer of Ibu Wardani' (by C.J.G) in *Jesus College Magazine,* Vol. 1, No. 2, 1913. Reprinted in *JTELS* III.1, 1993, 12–14, as 'The Kasr of Ibn Wardani'.

Lawrence, T.E. 'The Changing East' in *The Round Table,* Vol. X, No. 40, September 1920

(reprinted in *Oriental Assembly* and *Towards an English Fourth*).

Lawrence, T.E. 'Prefatory note' in *Catalogue of an exhibition of Arab Portraits by Eric H. Kennington.* London: The Leicester Galleries, October 1921.

(reprinted abridged in *Oriental Assembly* 149–57, and in *Towards an English fourth*).

Lawrence, T.E. (Pvt T.E. Shaw). 'A sea trip essay'. Bodleian Mss d230, 18 April 1923.

Lawrence, T.E. 'Private Record of the Writing, Printing & Distribution of *Seven Pillars of Wisdom.*' MS. HRC, University of Texas, 1927.

Lawrence, T.E. *The Forest Giant* (Translation of *Le Gigantesque* by Adrien le Corbeau). London: Cape, 1924.

### Edited collections of writings by T.E. Lawrence

Garnett, D. (ed.). *The Letters of T.E. Lawrence.* London: Jonathan Cape, 1938.

Lawrence, A.W. (ed.). *Oriental Assembly.* London: Williams and Norgate Ltd, 1939.

Lawrence, M.R. (ed.). *The Home Letters of T.E. Lawrence and his Brothers.* Oxford: Blackwell, 1954.

Brown, M. (ed.). *The Letters of T.E. Lawrence.* London: J.M. Dent, 1988.

Brown, M. (ed.). *Secret Despatches from Arabia and other writings by T.E. Lawrence.* London: Bellew Publishing Company Ltd, 1991.

Wilson, J.W. & N. (eds.). *T.E. Lawrence. Correspondence with Bernard and Charlotte Shaw*: Vols I to III, 1922–1926, 1927–1928, 1928. Fordingbridge: Castle Hill Press, 2000–2008.

Wilson, J.W. & N. (eds.). *'Towards an English Fourth'*: Fragments and echoes of *Seven Pillars of Wisdom* 1918–1921. Fordingbridge: Castle Hill Press, 2009.

### Masochism

Cooper, A. M. 'The narcissistic-masochistic character' in Glick & Meyers, 117–138.

Freud, S. *The Economic Problem of Masochism.* 1924. *Standard Edition 19,* 159–170.

Glick, Robert A. & D.I. Meyers. *Current Psychoanalytic Perspectives.* New Jersey: Laurence Erlbaum Associates Inc. 1988.

Rathbone, June. *Anatomy of Masochism.* New York: Kluwer Academic/Plenum Publishers, 2001.

Reik, Theodor. 'The characteristics of masochism' in *American Imago,* Vol. 1, 26–59, 1939.

Reik, Theodor. *Masochism in Modern Man.* New York: Grove Press, Inc., 1941.

*Unclassified*

Al Askeri, Jafar. (Facey, W & Najdat Safwat, eds.). *A Soldier's Story: From Ottoman rule to independent Iraq: The memoirs of Jafar Pasha al-Askeri.* London: Arabian Publishing Limited, 2003 (First published in Arabic, 1988).

Al-Umari, Subhi. *Lorens kama' 'areftuhu* ("Lawrence as I knew him") Beirut: Dar al Nahar, 1969.

Andréa, Général: *La Révolte druze et l'insurrection de Damas.* Payot, 1937.

Antonius, George. *The Arab Awakening.* London: Hamish Hamilton, 1938.

Barr, James. *Setting the Desert on Fire.* London: Bloomsbury, 2005.

Barr, James. *A Line in the Sand.* London: Simon & Schuster, 2011.

Barrow, General Sir George deS. *The Fire of Life.* London: Hutchinson, 1942.

Black, Jonathan. ' "King of the Pictures" : Eric Kennington, Portraiture and the Illustration of *Seven Pillars of Wisdom,* 1920– 26' in *JTELS* XVI.2, Spring 2007, 7–28.

Bolt, Robert. 'Apologia' in *JTELS* V.1, Autumn 1995.

Boyle, Admiral William (Earl of Cork and Orrery). *My Naval Life.* London, 1943.

Boyle, Andrew. *Trenchard.* London: Collins, 1962.

Brémond, E. *Le Hedjaz dans la guerre mondiale.* Paris: Payot, 1931.

Buchan, J. *Greenmantle.* London: Hodder & Stoughton, 1916.

Churchill, Sir W.S. 'Lawrence's great book' in *The Daily Mail.* 29 July, 1935.

Dixon, A. *Tinned Soldier.* London: Cape, 1941.

Doubleday, F.N. *A few indiscreet recollections.* Houghton Library, Harvard. 1928.

Findley, C. 'The amazing AC2' in *The Listener,* 5 June 1958, 937–38.

Forster, E.M. *A Passage to India.* London: Edward Arnold, 1924.

Forster, E.M. 'T.E. Lawrence' in *The Listener,* 31 July 1935; republished in *Abinger Harvest.* London: Edward Arnold, 1936 .

Furbank, P.N. *E.M. Forster: A Life.* Vol. 2. London: Faber & Faber, 1978.

Graves, Richard Perceval. *Robert Graves: The Assault Heroic 1895–1926.* London: Weidenfeld & Nicolson, 1986.

Graves, Robert. *Goodbye to all that.* London: Jonathan Cape, 1929.

Gregory, Lady Augusta (Lennox Robinson ed.). *Lady Gregory's Journals 1916–1930.* London: Putman, 1946.

Grosvenor, Charles. 'The Subscribers' *Seven Pillars of Wisdom*: The Visual Aspect' in Tabachnick, S.E. (ed.). *The T.E. Lawrence Puzzle*. Athens, Georgia: University of Georgia Press, 1984.

Grosvenor, Charles. *Iconography: The Portraits of T.E. Lawrence*. Pasadena: The Otterden Press. 1988.

Guillaume, Renée and André. *Seven Pillars of Wisdom: An Introduction and Notes*. Translated by Hilary Mandleberg. Oxshott, Surrey: The Tabard Press, 1998.

Hoenselaars, T. & G.M. Moore. 'Joseph Conrad and T.E. Lawrence' in *JTELS* V.1, 25–44, 1995.

Hogarth, D.G. 'Lawrence of Arabia: The Story of his Book'. *The Times*, 13 December 1926.

Hourani, A. 'T.E. Lawrence and Louis Massignon' in *TLS*, 8 July 1983, 733–4 and in *Présence de Louis Massignon*. Paris: Maison neuve et Larose, 167–76, 1987.

Howe, Irving. 'T.E. Lawrence: the problem of heroism' in *The Decline of the new*. Pp. 294–326. New York: Harcourt, Brace and World, 1970 and in *Selected writings*. San Diego: HBJ, 1990, 77–102.

Hughes, Matthew. 'What did the Arab Revolt contribute to the Palestine campaign? An Assessment', *JTELS* XV.2, 83.

James, L. *The Golden Warrior*: revised edition. London: Abacus, 1995.

Jonathan Cape Ltd. *Then and Now*. 1935.
(contains W.H. Auden. "T.E. Lawrence" pp. 21–22; T.E. Shaw. "Arabian Traveller": Preface to *Arabia Felix*, 93–96; G.B. Shaw. "*Revolt in the Desert* and its author", 121–31.

Johns, Capt. W.E. in *The Sunday Times*, 8 April. 1951.

Kedourie, Elie. *England and the Middle East*, 88, 105, & chapter entitled 'Colonel Lawrence'. London: Bowes & Bowes, 1956.

Kirkbride, Sir Alec. *A crackle of thorns*. London: Murray, 1956.

Kirkbride, Sir Alec. *An awakening: the Arab Campaign 1917–1918*. University Press of Arabia, 1971.

Khoury, Philip S. *Syria under the French Mandate: The politics of Arab nationalism 1920–1945*. Princeton University Press, 1987.

Knightley, Philip & Colin Simpson. *The Secret Lives of Lawrence of Arabia*. London: Nelson, 1969.

Knightley, P. 'Found: Lawrence of Arabia's lost text'. *Independent on Sunday*, 13 April 1997, 5.

Lago, Mary & P.N. Furbank. *Selected letters of E.M. Forster*. Vol. 2, 1921–1970. Belknap: Harvard, 1985.

Larès, J.M. *T.E. Lawrence, la France, et les Français*. Paris: Sorbonne, 1980.

Larès, J.M. (ed.). "N'était-ce donc que cela?". *T.E. Notes*, December 2003, 1–55.

Laurens, Henry. *Lawrence en Arabie*. Paris: Gallimard, 1992.

Lawrence, A.W. (ed.). *T.E. Lawrence by his Friends*. London: Jonathan Cape, 1937.

Lawrence, A.W. "The aftermath of Tafas". Bodleian Reserve MSS b56.

Lawrence, A.W. (ed.). *Letters to T.E. Lawrence*. London: Jonathan Cape, 1937.

Leclerc, C. 'French eye-witness accounts of Lawrence and the Arab Revolt': Parts 1&2 in *JTELS* XX.1 & 2. 2010/11.

Leclerc, C. *Avec T.E. Lawrence en Arabie: La Mission militaire française au Hedjaz 1916–1920*. Paris: L'Harmattan, 1998.

Liddell Hart, B.H. 'Seven Pillars of Wisdom: A Worthy Edition' in *The Times*, 29 July 1935.

Lockman, J.N. *Scattered tracks on the Lawrence trail*. Michigan: Falcon Books, 1996.

Lockman, J.N. *Parallel Captures: Lord Jim and Lawrence of Arabia*. Michigan: Falcon, 1997.

Long, C.W.R. *British Pro-Consuls in Egypt, 1914–1929*. Abingdon, UK: Routledge Curzon, 2005.

Mack, J.E. *A Prince of our Disorder: The Life of T.E. Lawrence*. Toronto: Little Brown, 1976.

Mack, J.E. 'T.E. Lawrence: A study of Heroism and Conflict' in *The American Journal of Psychiatry*, 125. 8 February 1969.

Malraux, A. *La Condition Humaine*. Paris: Editions Gallimard, 1933.

Malraux, A. *L'Espoir*. Paris: Editions Gallimard, 1937.

Malraux, A. 'Le Démon de l'absolu' (M. Larès, ed.) in *André Malraux. Œuvres complètes, Vol. II*. Paris: Bibliothèque de la Pleiade, Editions Gallimard, 1996. 817–1301 & 1666–1818 (notes).

Mann, Thomas. *The Short Novels of Dostoevski*. New York: Dial Press. 1945.

Manning Pike, Roy. 'Notes on Printing of Seven Pillars of Wisdom'. Estate of Jane Manning Pike. Published in *JTELS* XIV.1, 2004.

Massignon, L. 'Mes rapports avec Lawrence en 1917' in *Collection Recherches et documents (fragments de Opera Minora)*, Dar el Maaref, Liban, Tome III, 415–16. 1963; & in *Revue du monde musulmane*, Vol LXII, 1924; & in Opera minora Tome III, Paris: PUF, 1969.

McKenzie Smith, R. 'A memory of Richards & Lawrence in Epping Forest' in *TEL Society Newsletter* no. 90, pp. 4–6, 2009.

Meinertzhagen, R. *Middle East Diary: 1917–1956*, 32, 38–9. London: Cresset Press, 1959.

Meyers, Jeremy. *The Wounded Spirit: A Study of "Seven Pillars of Wisdom"*. London: Martin Brian & O'Keeffe, 1973.

Meynell, V. (ed.) *The Best of Friends*. London: Rupert Hart Davis.

Meynell, V. (ed.) *Friends of a Lifetime*, 340, 359. London: Cape.

Montgomery-Hyde, H. *Solitary in the Ranks*. London: Constable, 1977.

Mousa, Suleiman. *T.E. Lawrence: An Arab View*. Oxford University Press, 1966.

Nevakivi, J. *Britain, France and the Arab Middle East 1914–1920*. London: The University of London, The Athlone Press, 1969.

O'Donnell, T.J. *The Confessions of T.E. Lawrence: The Romantic Hero's Presentation of Self.* Ohio University Press. 1979.
O'Prey, P (ed.). *Robert Graves: In Broken Images.* Moyer Bell, 1988.
Orlans, H. "The Ways of Transgressors" in *JTELS*, 6.1, 20–33.
Orlans, H. *T.E. Lawrence: Biography of a Broken Hero.* Jefferson, North Carolina: McFarland, 2002.
Pritchett, V.S. 'The aesthete in war' (a review of Mack) in *Complete Collected Essays.* NY: Random House. 1991.
Pritchett, V.S. "A portrait of T. E. Lawrence" in *Books in General.* London: Chatto & Windus, 1953.
Read, Herbert. 'The Seven Pillars of Wisdom' in *The Bibliophile's Almanach for 1928.* London: Fleuron, 1927.
Richards, V. *A Portrait of T.E. Lawrence.* London: Jonathan Cape, 1936.
Rolls, S.C. *Steel Chariots in the Desert.* London: Jonathan Cape, 1937.
Rush, Alan de Lacy. 'Emir Zaid ibn Husayn: Iraq's most deserving prince'. Unpublished essay.
Said, Edward. *Orientalism.* London: Routledge and Kegan Paul, 1978.
Seale, P. *The Struggle for Arab Independence.* Cambridge: Cambridge University Press, 2010.
Seymour-Smith, Martin. *Robert Graves: His Life and Works.* London: Hutchinson, 1982.
Stewart, Desmond. *T.E. Lawrence.* London: Harper & Row, 1977.
Sydney Smith, Clare. *The Golden Reign.* London: Cassell, 1940.
Storrs, Sir Ronald. *Orientations.* London: Nicholson & Watson, 1937.
Tabachnick, S.E. *T.E. Lawrence.* Twayne: 1978.
Tabachnick, S.E. (ed.). *The T.E. Lawrence Puzzle.* Georgia: The University of Georgia Press, 1984.
Thesiger, W. *Arabian Sands.* London: Longman, 1959.
Thomas, Lowell. *With Lawrence in Arabia.* New York: Century, 1924.
Trevelyan, G.M. (The Garibaldi Trilogy) *Garibaldi's Defence of the Roman Republic.* Phoenix, 1907; *Garibaldi and the Thousand.* London: Longmans Green, 1909. *Garibaldi and the Making of Italy.* Phoenix, 1911.
Trevelyan, G.M. *An Autobiography and Other Essays,* 1949.
Villars, Jean Béraud. *T.E. Lawrence.* (Translated from French by Peter Dawnay). London: Sidgwick & Jackson, 1958.
Walpole, Hugh. 'T.E. Lawrence in life and death' in *Broadsheet: World Books Society Bulletin.* November 1939.
Wilson, Colin. *The Outsider.* London: Gollancz, 1956.
Wilson, J.M. *Lawrence of Arabia: the Authorised Biography of T.E. Lawrence.* London: Heinemann, 1989.
Wilson, J.M. *T.E. Lawrence.* London: National Portrait Gallery, 1988.
Wood, Peter. 'In search of the elusive Manning Pike', *JTELS* XIV.1, 69.
Woolley, L. *Dead Towns and Living Men.* London: Humphrey Milford, 1920.

Wrench, J.E. *Struggle 1914–1920*. London: Nicholson & Watson, 1935.
Yeomans, R. 'T.E. Lawrence and the Visual Arts' in *JTELS* III.1, 1993.
Young, Sir Hubert. *The Independent Arab*. London: John Murray, 1933.

# INDEX

Abdelhamid, Ottoman Sultan, 136
Abdelma'in, Sherif, 142
Abdullah I bin al-Hussein, *plate 4*
   camp in Wadi Ais, 132, 179
   capture of Eshref Bey, 132
   conflict with Ibn Saud, 22, 132
   Emir of Transjordan offer from British, 58, 60, 138
   image in *Seven Pillars*, 139, 230
   Kirkbride's tribute to, 308*n*
   negotiations with British (1916), 131, 136, 137, 138, 140
   occupation of Amman (1918), 58
   as overlord of the Hejaz, 242
   Storrs' impression of, 138, 140
   TEL's first trip to meet Feisal, 130
   TEL's impression of, 139, 140, 141
   TEL's visit to his camp (1921), 57
   victory at Taif (1916), 136
Abu Bakr, 294
Abu Lissan, 134, 157
Achilles, 203, 243, 244
Ageyl clan, 199, 227, 228, 234
*Ahd* secret society, 158
Akaba assault (July 1917)
   Arab tribes' support, 179–80
   epic treatment in *Seven Pillars of Wisdom*, 245
   Feisal's role, 133, 247, 248
   recruitment of tribesmen, 247
   TEL's role, 133, 247, 249, 271
al Akle, Fareedeh, 51
Ali bin Hussein, 130, 141
Allenby, Edmund, 1st Viscount Allenby
   capture of Damascus (1918), 165, 166
   ceremonial entry into Jerusalem (1917), 199, 214
   first meeting with Emir Feisal (Oct. 1918), 11, 166
   military alliance with Arab forces, 133, 134, 144, 215, 216
   offensive against Amman and Salt (1918), 155, 156, 157
   planned offensive (1918), 160–1, 163, 206, 215–16, 279
   support for Arab movement, 133
   supreme command in Syria, 14
   Turkish Army retreat (1918), 200
   Yarmuk Bridge expedition (1917), 180
Andréa, General Edouard, 295, 296
Antonius, George, 49, 183–4, 258–9, 313*n*
*Arab Bulletin*
   sources for *Seven Pillars*, 20, 26, 33, 44, 45
   Tafas incident (Sept. 1918), 201, 202
   TEL's contributions, 20, 44
   Yarmuk Bridge expedition (1917), 297
Arab Bureau (Cairo), 14, 19, 20, 133–4
Arab independence
   Abdullah's object, 139
   *Ahd* secret society, 158
   Arab regular officers motivation, 158, 175
   British promises of support, 250, 251, 258
   plea before the Council of Ten, 16
   TEL's involvement, 13, 16, 23
   Versailles Peace Conference (1919), 15, 17, 22, 23
Arab Legion, 60
Arab nationalism, 50, 52, 242, 248, 313*n*

Arab regular army
  Abu Lissan base, 134, 157
  Arab officers, 142, 157–60, 167, 175
  captured by the British, 142, 157
  development of, 133
  importance of, 167
  Jerdun railway station attack (1918), 202
  Kirkbride's role, 153, 154, 155, 157–60, 167
  Al-Umari's defection from Turkish army, 142
  TEL's liaison role, 199
  Waheidah base, 157–60
Arab Revolt (1916–1918)
  Arab-British negotiations (1915–1916), 135–41, 250–1, 256–7
  beginning of uprising (1916), 59, 129, 136
  Dera' offensive (Sept. 1918), 161–2, 164, 203, 205–8, 285, 286–7
  epic character of, 243–7
  Kirkbride's account, 152–68
  *Seven Pillars* as major source on, 3, 4
  Storrs' account, 135–9, 140, 141
  Tafileh Battle (1918), 143–51, 271
  TEL's participation, 11, 129–34, 139–41
  TEL's presentation of in *Seven Pillars*, 31, 34, 129–30, 139–41, 158, 171, 243–7, 267, 278–80
  two distinct parts of, 245–6
Arab World *see* Lebanon; Mesopotamia (Iraq); Palestine; Syria; Transjordan
Arabia, TEL's expert knowledge on, 12
*Arabia Deserta* (Doughty), 12, 80–1
Arabs
  Arab politics, 241–2
  British attitude to Arab interests, 14, 15, 19, 30
  defeat of Ottoman Empire, 13, 15
  freedom concept, 158, 174–5, 233, 234–5, 241–2
  image in *Seven Pillars*, 158, 227–34
  limited autonomy in Syria, 22, 23, 49–50
  nomadism, 167, 227, 228
  notion of allegiance, 227
  Versailles Peace Conference (1919), 13–14, 15, 16, 17, 18, 19, 22, 50–1, 218, 283
  *see also* Bedu
Ashendene Press, 115
al-Askari, Jaafar, 142, 145, 146, 148, 160
Assad, Bashar, 17
Assad, Hafez, 17
Astor, Lady Nancy, 55, 113
Ataturk, Kemal, 52
al-Atrash, Hussein, 253, 294, 295, 297, 298
Auda abu Tayi, 133, 180, 230, 231–2, 247
al-Auran, Sheikh Diab, 146, 148
Awad the Sherari, 228

Baker, Herbert, 24, 35, 52, 69
al-Bakri, Fawzi, 294
al-Bakri, Nesib, *plate 6*
  concerns about British intentions, 252
  dispute with TEL, 51, 248, 249–50, 258
  Great Syrian Revolt, 293–5
  Nebk expedition (1917), 248, 249–50, 258, 296
  relations with Feisal, 51, 248, 250, 295
  respect of Druze leaders, 294
Baldwin, Stanley, 109, 123
Barr, James, 4, 254
Barrow, General George
  Dera' offensive (Sept. 1918), 164, 203, 206–7, 208, 285, 286–7
  TEL's hostility towards, 178, 202, 203, 206, 207
Bartholomew, General William, 107
Bedu
  Akaba expedition, 133
  blood revenge, 203
  Blunt's passion for, 53
  capture of Damascus (1918), 165
  declining wartime role, 134
  Dera' offensive (Sept. 1918), 206, 207–8, 287
  enemies of the Druze, 165

Bedu *(continued)*
  freedom concept, 158, 174–5, 233, 234–5, 241–2
  image in *Seven Pillars*, 200, 207–8, 227–8, 232–7, 238, 246
  Jerdun railway station attack (1918), 159
  Kirkbride's war memories, 158, 167
  non-politicisation, 175
  Tafas incident (Sept. 1918), 162, 163–4, 201, 203
  Tafileh Battle (1918), 143, 144, 145, 147, 148
  TEL as an expert on, 132
  TEL's fellowship with, 11, 132, 174–5, 215, 234–5, 240
  Theisger's description of, 233–4, 238
  as warlike and courageous, 154, 228
Beeston, C.F.C., 211
Belisarius, 109, 307*n*
Bell, Gertrude, 16, 17, 109, 237, 239, plate 4
Beni Atiyeh tribe, 227
Beni Sakhr tribe, 155–6, 227
Binyon, Laurence, 68
Blunden, Edmund, 37, 80
Blunt, Anne, 53
Blunt, Wilfrid Scawen, 38, 53
Boak, Denis, 276, 283
Bolt, Robert, 4, 128, 183, 203–5, 268, 313*n*
Bonsal, Major, 16
Bowhay, Mr. (teacher), 287
Boyle, Admiral William, 178
Brémond, Colonel Edouard, 129, 131, 297, 311*n*
Bridges, Robert, 37
Britain
  Arab aspirations, 14, 15, 19, 30
  Arab independence, 250, 251, 258
  Mesopotamia (Iraq) ambitions, 15, 16
  Mesopotamia (Iraq) mandate, 47–9
  Middle East settlement proposals (1921), 56–9
  negotiations with Arab leaders (1915–1916), 135–41, 250–1, 256–7
  occupation of Mesopotamia (Iraq), 14, 172
  occupation of Palestine, 14
  official military alliance with Arabs, 134
  Palestine ambitions, 15, 16
  Palestine mandate, 47, 58
  Palestine policy, 58, 59, 60, 70
  Sykes–Picot treaty, 14–15, 257, 295
  Transjordan mandate, 47, 58
  Versailles Peace Conference (1919), 15, 16–17, 18–19
  withdrawal from Syria, 22–3
  Zionist policy, 60
  *see also* Arab Bureau (Cairo); Colonial Office; Eastern Committee; Foreign Office; India Office
Brooke, Rupert, 174
Brown, Malcolm, 3
Bruce, John, 64–5, 71, 72–7, 100, 188, 197, 220, 304*n*
Buchan, John, 308*n*
Bussy, Dorothy, 276, 315*n*
Buxton, Robin, 107, 109, 110, 122

Camus, Albert, 276
Cape, Jonathan, 80, 81, 89, 91, 99, 100, 122
Cecil, Lord Robert, 49
Chambers, Jock, 101, 222
Chapman, Sir Thomas Robert Tighe, 17–18
Chauvel, General Harry, 165, 178
Chaytor, General Edward, 161, 163
Cherry-Garrard, Apsley, 109
Chetwode, General Sir Philip, 100
Chirol, Sir Valentine, 17
Churchill, Winston S.
  appointed Colonial Secretary, 51, 52–3, 56
  appointment of TEL at Colonial Office (1921), 51
  image of Arabs in *Seven Pillars*, 227, 238
  meeting with TEL, 51
  Middle East conference (1921), 57, 242
  Middle East settlement proposals, 56, 57, 58, 60

release of TEL at Colonial Office (1922), 62, 64
Transjordan independence, 60
Versailles Peace Conference (1919), 16
Clark, J.C., 111
Clayton, Sir Gilbert
  image in *Seven Pillars*, 241
  'Intrusives', 239
  Tafileh Battle (1918), 148
  TEL's meeting with Nuri Sha'alan, 251, 252, 253
  TEL's telegrams, 140–1
  Yarmuk Bridge expedition (1917), 297
Clemenceau, Georges, 16, 17, 50
Cockerell, Sydney, 79, 87–8, 95, 107, 109, 115
Colonial Office
  Churchill as Secretary, 51, 52–3, 56
  TEL as Colonial Office civil servant (1921-22), 51, 55, 56–61, 62, 64
Conrad, Joseph
  friendship with Garnett, 52
  Garnett's guidance, 84
  *Heart of Darkness*, 29
  influence on TEL, 12, 29
  *Lord Jim*, 29
  meeting with TEL, 51–2, 80
  *The Mirror of the Sea*, 52
  *Nostromo*, 29, 285
  published by Doubleday, 41
  truth of fiction, 264
Constable Publishers, 88, 89
Cornwallis, Kinahan, 135
Cox, Percy, 59
Cunninghame Graham, R.B., 49, 51, 52, 53
Curtis draft, 25, 27–9, 44, 45, 175, 293
Curtis, Lionel
  correspondence with TEL, 100–1, 102, 103–4, 107
  friendship with TEL, 27
  Iraq deputation, 49
  *Round Table* political monthly, 57
  *Seven Pillars* subscribers' edition (1926), 109
Curzon, George, 1st Marquess Curzon of Kedleston, 14, 52, 160

Dahoum, 101, 195, 211, 232, 234, 273
*Daily Express*, 47, 91, 99
*Daily Mail*, 99
*Daily News*, 47
Damascus
  capture of (1918), 11, 164–6, 245–6
  Feisal's arrival (Oct. 1918), 11, 166
  Feisal's rule, 49–50, 134, 295
  French occupation, 49
  Great Syrian Revolt, 294
  Sykes–Picot treaty, 14
  Turkish barracks 'hospital', 208
Daud, 177, 232
Davenport, Major W.A., 132
Dawnay, Colonel Alan
  'Hedgehog' special unit, 134
  planned offensive (1918), 160
  *Seven Pillars* 'Oxford' text (1922), 107
  *Seven Pillars* subscribers' edition (1926), 109
  *Seven Pillars* 'Text I' (1919), 24
  TEL's acceptance in the Tank Corps (1923), 100
  TEL's thoughts on, 21
de Caix, Robert, 17
Dera' incident (Nov. 1917), 181–98, 221–5
  Barr's views, 4
  erotogenic experience, 270
  Hourani's essay, 261
  Lawrence's post-war behaviour, 210, 212
  Mack's views, 210, 221, 223
  post-Dera' letters, 213–14, 215
  *Seven Pillars* 'Oxford' text (1922), 70, 181, 182–5, 188–9, 195, 221
  *Seven Pillars* revised text (1940) (R), 181, 182–5, 188–9, 194, 195, 284
  *Seven Pillars* 'Text I' (1919), 26
  *Seven Pillars* 'Text II' (1920), 31
  'truth' of, 213, 221, 273, 281
  J. M. Wilson's views, 210, 211
Dera' offensive (Sept. 1918), 161–2, 203, 205–8, 285, 286–7
al Dheilan, Mohammed, 228
Dixon, Alec, 101, 103, 104, 124, 306n
Al-Djezairi, Abdelkader
  Arab government declared, 165–6, 186

Al-Djezairi, Abdelkader *(continued)*
  death of, 166
  relations with King Hussein, 296
  suspicion of Feisal, 166
  TEL's hatred of, 186, 282, 296-8
  TEL's treachery accusations, 186, 187, 188, 279, 297
  Yarmuk Bridge expedition (1917), 186, 296-7
Al-Djezairi, Mohammed Said, 165-6, 186, 187, 294, 296
el Dleimi, Abdullah, 144, 147, 148, 150
Doran, George, 44
Dostoevski, Fyodor
  'Creative writer', 221
  influence on TEL, 12, 33, 193, 278, 284, 287-9
  *The Karamazov Brothers*, 82, 269, 285, 288
  Thomas Mann's comment on, 225
Doubleday, Florence, 41, 42
Doubleday, F.N., 41, 42-3, 44, 45
Doughty, Charles Montagu, 12, 80-1, 83, 107-8, 234, 236
Druze, 165, 248
Dulac, Edmond, 112

Eastern Committee, 13, 14
Eisenstein, Sergei, 275
erotogenic masochism, 270
Eshref Bey, 132

Fakhri, Hamid, 137, 148, 149
Farraj, 177, 232
Feisal, Emir
  Akaba assault (July 1917), 133, 247, 248
  Arab Army, 142, 167
  Arab Army base at Abu Lissan, 134, 157
  as Arab leader of revolt against Turks, 228, 242
  as the 'armed prophet', 139-40
  arrival in Damascus (Oct. 1918), 11, 166
  arrives in France (Nov. 1918), 13-14
  arrives in London (1920), 52-3
  Augustus John's portrait of, 36
  bodyguards, 227
  Al-Djezairi brothers suspicion of, 166
  exile in Italy, 50, 52
  expulsion from Syria (1920), 50, 160, 258
  first meeting with Allenby (Oct. 1918), 11, 166
  first meeting with TEL (1916), 27, 44, 130-1, 141, 230-1
  image in *Seven Pillars*, 229, 230-1, 232, 241, 246
  Jerdun railway station attack (1918), 159
  King of Iraq proposal, 56, 57, 59
  Knight Grand Cross decoration, 14
  as later King of Iraq, 160
  limited autonomy in Syria, 22, 23, 49-50
  meeting with Nuri Sha'alan, 252
  meeting with Subhi al-Umari, 142
  meeting with Weizmann, 51
  meets TEL in London (1925), 124
  Nebk crisis (1917), 247-8
  negotiations with the Turks, 279
  post-war situation, 218
  relations with King Hussein, 295
  relations with Nesib al-Bakri, 51, 248, 250, 295
  relations with TEL, 132, 134, 179, 256
  rule in Damascus, 49-50, 134, 295
  Sykes-Picot treaty, 257
  Syria strategy, 247-8, 294-5, 296, 297
  Syrian claim, 16, 30
  Tafileh Battle (1918), 144
  TEL as liaison officer/adviser, 11, 13-14, 15-16, 17, 19, 132, 134, 139-40, 141
  TEL's personal grief, 17-18
  Thomas's Covent Garden show, 31
  Turkish Army retreat (1918), 200
  Versailles Peace Conference (1919), 13-14, 15, 16, 17, 19, 22, 50-1, 218, 283
  Wadi Yenbo defeat, 131
  Wejh expedition (1917), 132, 178
  Young's description of, 229, 231
Fifield, A.C., 89

Findlay, Charles, 98–9, 102
Foreign Office
  Arab vs. French interests, 15
  Versailles Peace Conference (1919), 15, 16
Forster, E.M., xi, 102
  correspondence with TEL, 93–7, 108, 118, 228, 272
  Dera' incident (Nov. 1917), 222
  image of Arabs in *Seven Pillars*, 228, 232
  'Oxfordisms', 241
  *Seven Pillars* 'Oxford' text (1922), 92–7, 118, 171
  *Seven Pillars* subscribers' edition (1926), 125
  as TEL's literary mentor, 92–7, 118, 125, 171, 274
  truth of fiction, 264
  visits to Clouds Hill, 103
  visit from TEL (1925), 124
France
  interests in Syria, 14, 15, 16–17
  occupation of Damascus and eastern Syria, 49
  Sykes–Picot treaty, 14–15, 295
  Syrian mandate, 47, 49–51
  Versailles Peace Conference (1919), 15, 16–17
Franco, Francisco, 278
Freud, Sigmund, 6, 191, 270

Gallipoli landings (1915), 250
Garland, Major Herbert, 136
Garnett, David, 276
Garnett, Edward
  correspondence with TEL, 81–4, 85–6, 104, 108, 114, 268–9
  Dera' incident (Nov. 1917), 190, 193, 222, 223
  friendship with Conrad, 52
  Garnett–Lawrence abridgement of *Seven Pillars*, 81, 83–4, 85–7, 89, 99, 109
  literary criticism background, 80, 278
  "Myself" chapter, 264, 268
  as publisher's reader for Cape, 80
  *Seven Pillars* 'Oxford' text (1922), 80–4, 88, 92, 93, 97, 107, 268–9
  *Seven Pillars* subscribers' edition (1926), 109, 114, 268–9
  *Seven Pillars* 'Text II' (1920), 33
  "strange free disclosures", 3, 264, 269
  as TEL's literary mentor, 33, 80–4, 88, 92, 93, 97, 107, 109, 114, 263, 268–9, 274, 284
  TEL's meeting with Conrad, 52
  TEL's self-esteem, 218–19
  *Wanderings in Arabia* (abridgement of *Arabia Deserta*), 81, 83
Garvin, J.L., 99
George V, King, 14, 31, 50, 75, 125
Georges-Picot, François, 14
Ghalib Bey, 136
Gibbon, Edward, 244
Gide, André, 84
Gill, Colin, 110
Goethe, Johann Wolfgang, 62
Gorky, Maxim, 275
Gouraud, Henri, 49, 50
Graves, John, 36
Graves, Richard Perceval, 35
Graves, Robert
  Alpine Club visit (1920), 54
  correspondence with TEL, 35, 60, 66–8, 99, 224, 253–4
  Dera' incident (Nov. 1917), 222, 224–5
  first meeting with TEL (1919), 35–6
  friendship with TEL, 35–7, 65–6
  introduces TEL to Hardy, 102
  *Seven Pillars* abridgement version (1920), 62, 66
  *Seven Pillars* 'Oxford' text (1922), 80, 118, 224
  *Seven Pillars* subscribers' edition (1926), 99, 125
  TEL as the Arab Revolt, 238
  TEL's interest in painters and sculptors, 54
  TEL's 'journey to the north' (1917), 253–4
  TEL's letter writing, 105
  as TEL's literary mentor, 62, 66, 80, 99, 118, 125, 224, 274
  TEL's *To S.A.* (dedicatory poem), 62, 66–7
  TEL's views on poetry, 82–3
Greene, Graham, 174

Gregory, Lady, 107
Grey, Sir Edward, 251
Grosvenor, Charles, 54, 55, 112
Guy, R.M., 101

Hajim Muhittim Bey, 184, 185–6, 187, 298
Halim, Subhi, 159
Hall, E.F., 6
Hall, Midge, 212
Hamma bridge, 297
Hardy, Florence, 95, 102–3, 105, 123, 124–5
Hardy, Thomas, 95, 102–3, 105, 108, 124–5
al-Hareidhin, Talal, 163, 182–3, 185, 200, 201, 202
el-Harithi, Ali ibn Hussein
  as Homeric hero, 232
  image in *Seven Pillars*, 232, 241
  Kennington's portrait of, 230
  *Lawrence of Arabia* (film) character, 230
  sermon to the Serahin, 265, 266
  Yarmuk Bridge expedition (1917), 180, 296–7
Hauran region, 161, 182, 200
Hector, 203, 243
Hemingway, Ernest, 179, 276, 283
Herbert, Aubrey, 49
Hirtzel, Sir Arthur, 48
Hitler, Adolf, 275
Hoare, Samuel, 100, 123
Hodgson, Herbert John, 121
Hogarth, D.G.
  correspondence with TEL, 101, 108, 114, 214
  difficulty in helping TEL, 38
  Feisal's relations with the Bakris, 295
  Iraq deputation, 49
  Middle East conference (1921), 57
  orientalism, 237, 239
  planned offensive (1918), 216
  *Seven Pillars* 'Oxford' text (1922), 107, 108, 109
  *Seven Pillars* subscribers' edition (1926), 109, 114
  *Seven Pillars* 'Text I' (1919), 24
  *Seven Pillars* 'Text II' (1920), 30–1
  Sykes–Picot treaty, 14

TEL in the Tank Corps, 103
TEL's health, 215, 311*n*
TEL's Research Fellowship at All Soul's, 24
TEL's role in negotiations with the Arabs (1916), 256–7
Holbein, Hans, 55
Homer, 203, 244, 245
Hornby, Charles Harold St John, 115, 136
Hourani, Albert, 259, 261, 262, 265, 266
Howe, Irving, 243
Howeitat tribe, 133, 144, 227, 228, 234, 249
Hudson, W.H., 84
Hughes-Stanton, Blair, 110, 111
Hussein bin Ali, Sherif of Mecca
  Arab Revolt against the Ottoman Empire, 129, 250
  negotiations with British (1916), 131, 135, 138, 250–1, 256–7
  negotiations with TEL (1921), 58–9
  official military alliance with Britain, 133, 134
  as overlord of the Hejaz, 228, 242
  relations with Al-Djezairi brothers, 296
  relations with Feisal, 295
  Storrs' impression of, 138
  Sykes–Picot treaty, 251, 257
  TEL's first trip to meet Feisal, 130
  Versailles Peace Conference (1919) representation, 13–14

ibn Dgeithir, 228
ibn Dughmi, Benaiah, 252
ibn Hamza, Sherif Abdullah, 156
ibn Jazi, Hamad, 145
Ibn Saud, 22, 59, 132
*Iliad*, 203, 243, 244
*Independent on Sunday*, 27
India Office, 15, 48, 56
Iraq *see* Mesopotamia (Iraq)

Jarmana village, 294
Jaussen, Father, 256
Jawdat, Ali, 160, 203
Jebel Druze, 155, 247, 248, 294, 295, 296

Jeddah
    Arab Revolt (1916–1918), 136
    Seven Pillars 'Text II' revision
        (1921), 56
    TEL's teak door, 40, 59
Jemal Pasha, Mehmet, 161, 214, 232
Jerdun railway station attack (1918),
    159, 202, 229
Jerusalem, Allenby's ceremonial entry
    (1917), 199, 214
John, Augustus
    letter to TEL, 100
    portrait of the Emir Feisal, 36
    portrait of GBS, 87, 107
    portraits of TEL, 40, 53–4, 55
    Seven Pillars subscribers' edition
        (1926), 110
Johns, Captain W.E., 77
Joyce, James, 84
Joyce, Colonel Pierce Charles
    Dera' incident (Nov. 1917), 184
    image in Seven Pillars, 241
    Middle East conference (1921), 57
    Sykes–Picot treaty, 254–5, 257–8
    TEL's relationship with Feisal, 132
    Yarmuk Bridge expedition (1917),
        296, 297
Juheineh tribe, 227
Jurf al Darawish, 143

Kanaan Bey Bejani, 146, 149
Kedourie, Elie, 259
Kelmscott Press, 36, 39, 42
Kennington, Eric
    background and character, 54–5
    correspondence with TEL, 59, 69,
        289
    first meeting with TEL, 53, 54–5
    friendship with TEL, 53, 54–5
    Leicester Galleries exhibition, 112,
        230, plate 7
    portraits of TEL, 55
    Seven Pillars 'Oxford' text (1922),
        107, 110
    Seven Pillars subscribers' edition
        (1926), 110, 111, 112, 113, 114,
        122, 125, 229–30
    TEL's views on Seven Pillars
        'Oxford' text (1922), 71–2, 79
    TEL's visit with Bruce, 76
    TEL's wish to enlist in the RAF, 63

    in Transjordan (1921), 55, 58, plate
        7
    visits to Clouds Hill, 103, 104
Keynes, John Maynard, 18–19
al Khadra, Subhi, 160
Khalil Pasha, 48
Khoury, Philip, 294
Kidston, George, 22
Kipling, Rudyard, 41–2, 80, 107–8
Kirkbride, Alec
    An Awakening war memories, 129,
        130, 152–68, 213, 308n
    as an Intelligence officer, 153,
        154–60
    Arab Army base at Abu Lissan, 157
    Arab Army base at Waheidah,
        157–60
    Arab Army role, 153, 154, 155,
        157–60, 167
    Armenian girl, 156–7
    arrival in Tafileh (1918), 152–3
    background, 153–4
    Bedu, 158, 167
    capture of Damascus (1918), 164–6
    A Crackle of Thorns, 183, 184
    Dera' incident (Nov. 1917), 183,
        184
    Dera' offensive (Sept. 1918), 161–2,
        205, 206
    description of Arabs, 238
    Feisal's sword gift, 164
    first meeting with TEL (1918), 152,
        153
    Ghor es Safi mission, 156–7
    Jerdun railway station attack
        (1918), 159
    Lawrence of Arabia (film), 203
    Tafas incident (Sept. 1918), 163,
        164, 201
    Tafileh mission, 155, 156
    TEL's description of, 153
    TEL's love of suffering, 191
    TEL's military theory and practice,
        133, 167
    TEL's sense of honour and responsi-
        bility, 173, 175, 255
    TEL's wartime role, 168, 219, 271
    tribute to Abdullah, 308n
Kirkbride, Mary, 157
Kitchener, Horatio Herbert Kitchener,
    1st Earl, 48, 250

Knightley, Philip, 27, 74, 185, 186
Kut, Battle of (1916), 48
Kut, Halil, 48

Lamotte, Auguste, 256
Larès, Maurice, 275, 276, 296, 315*n*
Laurie, Janet, 212
*Lawrence of Arabia* (film)
  characterisation, 230
  Dera' incident (Nov. 1917), 183
  epic structure of, 243, 246
  *Seven Pillars* as screenplay source, 4, 213, 240, 268
  Tafas incident (Sept. 1918), 7, 202–5, 273
  Turkish barracks 'hospital' scene, 208
  Wadi Rumm gathering, 162
Lawrence, Arnold (TEL's brother), 74, 203, 213
Lawrence, Bob (TEL's brother), 46, 213
Lawrence, D.H., 84
Lawrence, Sarah (TEL's mother)
  correspondence with TEL, 57–8, 63–4, 179
  departure from Polstead Road, 46, 63
  not married, 18
  relationship with TEL, 17, 63
Lawrence, T.E.
  ARAB WORLD
  Arab independence, 13, 16, 23
  Arab nationalism, 242, 313*n*
  Arab nationalists mixed feelings about, 17, 18, 50, 158
  Arab self-determination, 16, 18, 22, 48, 53
  articles on Middle East mandates (1920), 47, 48–9
  British mandate of Iraq, 47–9
  British withdrawal from Syria, 22–3
  as a champion of the Arabs, 116, 255
  concern over Syria, 47, 50–1
  Feisal's expulsion from Syria (1920), 50
  knowledge of Arabia, 12
  McMahon's 'pledge', 250, 251, 256
  Middle East conference (1921), 57–8

  opinion of Syrian politicians and nationalists, 50
  power-sharing in Iraq, 56–7
  pro-Arab lobbying (1918–1919), 13
  Sykes–Picot treaty, 22, 30, 47, 133–4, 251–2, 255, 256–8
  Transjordan mission (1921), 58, 59–60, *plate 4*
  ART and LITERATURE
  admiration for Doughty, 12, 80–1
  Augustus John's portraits of, 40, 53–4, 55
  classical epics, 244
  interest in book production, 39, 42, 43, 63, 111, 120–3
  interest in poetry, 37, 54
  Kennington's drawings, 55–6
  Kennington's portraits of, 55
  Kirkbride's war memories, 168
  literary background, 12
  love of being painted, sculpted or photographed, 53–4, 55–6
  McBey's portrait of, *plate 1*
  obsession with the 'great writer' idea, 79, 89, 218–19, 287–90
  Orpen's painting of, 53
  Rothenstein's painting of, 53
  teak door from Jeddah, 40, 59
  writing style, 70, 79, 91, 93, 118
  CORRESPONDENCE
  with Bernard Shaw, 80, 88–9, 90–1, 100, 114, 115, 117, 267
  with Cape, 99
  with Charlotte Shaw, 105, 115, 116–17, 120, 122, 123–4, 125, 194, 222–3
  congratulatory letter to Lloyd George, 22–3, 30, 51
  with Curtis, 100–1, 102, 103–4, 107
  with Doubleday, 41, 42, 43
  with Doughty, 80–1
  with Florence Hardy, 123
  with Forster, 93–7, 108, 118, 228, 272
  with Garnett, 81–4, 85–6, 104, 108, 114, 268–9
  with Graves, 35, 60, 66–8, 99, 224, 253–4
  with Guy, 101
  with his mother, 57–8, 63–4, 179

with his parents, 213–15, 216–17
with Hogarth, 101, 108, 114, 214
with Kennington, 59, 69, 289
with Richards, 32–3, 39, 41, 43, 45, 69, 108, 120, 217–18, 243, 244, 283
INTERESTS and VIEWS
  anti-establishment position, 172
  attitude to history, 244
  Boanerges (Brough motor-bike), 78, 103, 105, 123, 124
  Hejaz stamps, 215, 311–12*n*
  orientalism, 237–41
  Thomas's Covent Garden show, 31–2, 267
PERSONAL LIFE
  adolescence, 211
  at Polstead Road, Oxford, 13, 23, 46
  at school, 211
  in Barton Street, Westminster, 24, 31, 32, 63, 69, 277–8
  father's death (1919), 17–18
  'The Old Man' story, 72–7, 219–21
  Pole Hill visits, 40
  uncertainty period (Aug 1919–Aug 1922), 38
PERSONALITY
  as a control-freak, 25, 75, 245, 254, 267, 272, 289
  corporal punishment, 74–5, 77, 197, 210, 219–21
  desire to achieve, 210–11, 219
  emotional isolation, 210–12
  freedom concept, 126, 174–5, 233, 234–5, 241
  guilt feelings, 19, 125–6, 173–4, 175, 196, 225, 255, 257, 262, 270–1
  heroic legend image, 1, 13, 131, 243–5, 263, 266–8, 286–90
  historical responsibility, 256–8
  inability to express grief, 18
  loneliness, 198–9, 216
  masochism, 6, 25, 175, 176, 188–94, 195, 196–7, 269–72
  mental state just before the end of the war, 212–18
  notion of truth, 3, 6, 7, 75, 84, 182, 204, 253–4, 273
  positive character traits, 210–11
  pragmatism, 17, 23, 30
  self-esteem, 182, 216, 218–19, 269, 271
  sexual rituals, 191–2
  sexuality, 211–12
POST-WAR CAREER
  arrival in Cairo (June 1919), 21–2
  at All Souls College, Oxford, 24, 35, 37–8, 42, 43
  as Colonial Office civil servant (1921-22), 51, 55, 56–61, 62, 64
  departure for India (1926), 125
  dismissed from RAF (1923), 99–100
  flight to Rome (May 1919), 20–1
  Handley Page incident (1919), 20, 21–2, 101–2
  interview and medical for RAF, 77
  nostalgia for the RAF (1923), 101
  RAF alias 'John Hume Ross', 77, 91, 98–9, 100
  re-admitted to RAF (1925), 123–5
  resignation from Colonial Office (July 1922), 71
  service in the RAF (1922-23), 78, 80, 83, 85, 90, 98–9, 102
  in the Tank Corps (1923-25), 75, 76, 77, 100–4, 107, *plate 3*
  Tank Corps alias 'T.E. Shaw', 100
  Versailles Peace Conference (1919), 15–17, 18–19, 22, 50–1, 218, *plate 2*
  wish to enlist in the ranks of the RAF (1922), 62–3, 64, 82
PRE-WAR CAREER
  in Carchemish, Syria (1911–1914), 195–6, 211, 240
  first Syrian journey (1909), 240
  Khalfati imprisonment story, 195, 196
RELATIONSHIPS
  dislike of Abdullah, 139, 140, 141
  as Feisal's translator, 15
  fellowship with the Bedu, 11, 132, 174–5, 215, 234–5, 240
  first meeting with Bruce (1922), 64–5
  first meeting with Doubleday (1918), 41
  first meeting with Graves (1919), 35–6

Lawrence, T.E.
RELATIONSHIPS *(continued)*
  first meeting with Kennington, 53, 54–5
  first meeting with Kipling, 41
  first meeting with Shaw (1922), 87–8, 107
  friendship with Bernard Shaw, 55, 124
  friendship with Blunt, 53
  friendship with Charlotte Shaw, 55, 104, 124, 172
  friendship with Graves, 35–7, 65–6
  friendship with Kennington, 53, 54–5
  friendship with Richards, 31, 38–9
  friendships, 211
  hatred of Abdelkader Al-Djezairi,, 186, 282, 296–8
  meeting with Churchill, 51
  meeting with Conrad (1920), 51–2, 80
  meeting with Nuri and Nawaf at Azrak, 252, 253
  meeting with Nuri Sha'alan, 251–2
  meetings with Bruce, 65
  meets Feisal in London (1925), 124
  relations with Feisal, 132, 134, 179, 256
  relationship with his mother, 17, 63
  visit to Forster (1925), 124
WARTIME ROLE
  Akaba assault (July 1917), 133, 247, 249, 271
  Al-Umari's first sight of, 143
  Allenby's demands, 215–16
  Arab Revolt (1916–1918) role, 11, 129–34, 139–41
  Azrak imprisonment story, 196
  bodyguards, 162, 199, 215, 227, 234, 236, 281
  capture of Damascus (1918), 164, 165, 166
  criticism of Allenby, 156
  Dera' offensive (Sept. 1918), 161–2, 205–8, 285, 286–7
  diaries, 26
  difference of opinion with Vickery, 177–8
  dispute with Nesib al-Bakri, 51, 248, 249–50, 258
  as Feisal's liaison officer/adviser, 11, 13–14, 15–16, 17, 19, 132, 134, 139–40, 141
  first meeting with Feisal, 27, 44, 130–1, 141, 230–1
  historical reality of his role, 242
  hostility to Barrow, 178, 202, 203, 206, 207
  in Iraq (1916), 48
  'journey to the north' (1917), 248–9, 252–4
  journey to Wadi Ais, 194
  leaves Damascus (Oct. 1918), 11
  Nebk crisis (1917), 247–9, 263
  negotiations with the Arabs (1916), 135, 137, 138, 139–41, 256–7
  obsessed with the notion of fraud, 173, 199, 200, 254–6
  offensive against Amman and Salt, 155–6
  planned offensive (1918), 160, 215–16
  railway raids, 134, 136, 159, 161–2, 199
  relations with Arab officers, 157–8
  relations with military staff, 177–9
  resignation, 199, 216
  ride to Wejh (1917), 177–8
  sermon to the Serahin, 265, 266
  snowbound with his bodyguard in Tafileh, 199, 281
  summoned to Jerusalem, 199, 214
  Tafas incident (Sept. 1918), 44, 162–4, 201–5, 264, 273, 281
  Tafileh Battle (1918), 146–8, 149–51, 271
  Turkish Army retreat (1918), 200–1
  Turkish barracks 'hospital', Damascus, 208
  unique wartime experience, 11–12
  Wadi Kitan shooting, 202, 264
  wartime notebooks, 12, 25, 26–7, 33
  Yarmuk Bridge expedition (1917), 31, 134, 179–80, 186, 216, 265, 296–7
WORKS
  'The changing East' article (1920), 57
  *Minorities*, 125
  *The Mint*, 64, 77, 100, 102, 123

*Revolt in the Desert*, 43, 87, 92, 122–3, 125, 171
  *Some notes*, 118
  see also Dera' incident (Nov. 1917)
Le Carré, John, 174
League of Nations, 47
Lean, David, 183, 204, 268, 281
Lebanon, 14, 17, 47
Liddell Hart, Basil
  *Lawrence of Arabia* (film), 203, 204
  *Seven Pillars* 'Text I' (1919), 20, 25, 292–3
  Tafas incident (Sept. 1918), 203, 204
  TEL's archaeology work in Syria (1911–1914), 196
  TEL's heroic legend image, 6, 286
  TEL's method of composition, 27
  TEL's role in Tafileh Battle (1918), 151
Liman von Sanders, Otto, 135
Lindsay, Vachel, 37
Lloyd, George, 11, 12, 241
Lloyd George, David
  British withdrawal from Syria, 22
  TEL's concern for Syria, 47
  TEL's letter, 22–3, 30, 51
  Thomas's Covent Garden show, 31, 32
  Versailles Peace Conference (1919), 16
Lockman, J., 311*n*
Longford, Christine, 54

McBey, James, *plate 1*
Mack, John, 74, 203, 210, 211, 212, 221, 223
McKenzie Smith, Roy, 40
McMahon, Henry, 250, 251, 256
el Madpai, Jamil, 160
Mahmas (tribesman of Lawrence's bodyguard), 118–19
Malraux, André
  affinity with Lawrence, 276–7
  biography, 275–6
  *La condition humaine*, 222, 275
  *Le Démon de l'Absolu*, 275, 278, 315*n*
  *L'Espoir*, 275–6, 279
  "N'était-ce donc que cela?", 246, 274–5, 276, 277–90, 315*n*

TEL's Arabian adventure, 240
TEL's Arabian myth, 227
TEL's betrayal theme, 19, 59
TEL's silence over Dahoum, 273
Mann, Thomas, 225
Marlowe, Christopher, 29
Marriott, Charles, 55
masochism
  compulsive nature of, 191, 194
  demonstrative concealment, 194, 195
  demonstrative feature, 193–5, 197
  erotogenic masochism, 270
  moral masochism, 6, 191, 270
  sado-masochism, 175, 176, 264
  sexual masochism, 191, 192, 270
  TEL's struggle with, 6, 25, 175, 176, 188–94, 195, 196–7, 269–72
  unconscious character of, 191, 270
masochistic fantasy, 188, 189, 190, 192–3, 196, 198, 264
al-Masri, Ali Abdelaziz, 131, 137–8, 140, 158
Massignon, Louis, 213, 261
Mastur, Sherif, 148
Matheson, Christopher, 241
Matte, Marcel, 213
Mauron, Charles, 276
Maxwell, General John Grenfell, 250
Maysalun, Battle of (1920), 49
Mecca, Arab Revolt (1916–1918), 130, 132, 136, 137
Medici Society, 81
Medina, Arab Revolt (1916–1918), 136
Meleager of Gadara, 35
Melville, Herman, 12, 278
Mesopotamia (Iraq)
  British ambitions, 15, 16
  British mandate, 47–9
  British occupation, 14, 172
  Feisal as king of Iraq proposal, 56, 57, 59
  Intifada (June 1920), 48
  power-sharing proposal, 56–7
  Sykes–Picot treaty, 14
  Versailles Peace Conference (1919), 15, 16, 22
Metawila tribe, 314*n*
Monotype Corporation, 121
moral masochism, 6, 191, 270

*Morning Post*, 71
Morris, William, 38, 39
Motlog, Sheikh, 228
Moussa, Suleiman, 3, 147
Mukhlis, Mauloud, 142, 160, 175
Murray, General Sir Archibald, 178
Murray, Mr., 64

Na'amek, Colonel Ismail, 153
Nash, Paul, 110, 111
Nasir (sharif of Medina)
  Akaba expedition, 133
  capture of Damascus (1918), 165
  Dera' offensive (Sept. 1918), 205–6
  image in *Seven Pillars*, 229
  Jerdun railway station attack (1918), 159
  meeting with Nuri Sha'alan, 252
  Nebk crisis (1917), 247
  Turkish Army retreat (1918), 200
  Yarmuk Bridge expedition (1917), 180
Nebk crisis (1917), 247–9, 263
Newcombe, Major S.F.
  correspondence with TEL, 69
  image in *Seven Pillars*, 241
  railway raids, 136
  support for TEL, 19
  Sykes–Picot treaty, 254–5, 257–8
  TEL's relationship with Feisal, 132
  as TEL's successor, 179
Nichols, Robert, 37
Nicholson, William, 110
Nietzsche, Friedrich
  despising oneself, 315*n*
  *Ecce Homo*, 316*n*
  influence on TEL, 12, 33, 278, 285, 287–8
  as a prophet, 289
  *Thus spake Zarathustra*, 33, 82, 285, 288

*The Observer*, 47, 48, 99
Ogston, Dr., 64
orientalism, 237–41
Orpen, William, 53
O'Toole, Peter, 183
*Oxford Times*, 71, 277

Palestine
  British ambitions, 15, 16

British mandate, 47, 58
British occupation, 14
British policy, 58, 59, 60, 70
Sykes–Picot treaty, 14
Versailles Peace Conference (1919), 15, 16, 22
Palmer, E.S. (Posh), 96, 105
Pasternak, Boris, 275
Patroclus, 203
Peake, F.G., 60, 203, 204
Philby, Harry St. John, 22, 49, 61, 239
Pike, Manning, 113, 120–1
Pisani, Captain Rosario, 159, 161
Pole Hill printing establishment, 39–41, 59
Pritchett, V.S., 17, 270
Proust, Marcel, 84
Pugh, Sgt., 54

Qadri, Tahseen, 166

Rabegh, 130–1, 132, 137, 141
Rahail, 228
Raho, Captain, 132, 136
Raleigh, Sir Walter, 24
Raleigh, Sir Walter (professor), 37
Ras Baalbek, 253, 254
Rathbone, June, 25, 190, 192, 265, 305*n*
Rattigan, Terence, 100
Read, Herbert, 112, 274, 307*n*
Reik, Theodor
  demonstrative concealment, 194
  demonstrative feature, 193, 197
  displaying suffering, shame and punishment, 181, 182, 190, 193, 197
  *Masochism in Modern Man*, 190
  masochistic character, 271
  masochistic fantasy, 192
  masochist's high and exorbitant demands, 219
  unconscious character of masochism, 191
Richards, Vyvyan
  correspondence with TEL, 32–3, 39, 41, 43, 45, 69, 108, 120, 217–18, 243, 244, 283
  dream of medieval living, 38–9, 40–1, 45, 120
  friendship with TEL, 211, 212

# Index

*Seven Pillars* 'Oxford' text (1922), 69, 107
*Seven Pillars* 'Text II' (1920), 31, 32–3
*Seven Pillars of Wisdom* abridgement version (1920), 43, 45
TEL's notion of truth, 7
Roberts, William, 110, 112
Rolls, S.C., 196
Ross, John Hume (TEL's alias in RAF), 77, 91, 98–9, 100
Rothenstein, William, 53, 110, 219
*Round Table* political monthly, 57
Rualla tribe, 205, 247, 249, 265
Russell, Arthur, 103, 105
Russia, Sykes–Picot treaty, 14

sado-masochism, 175, 176, 264
Said Ali Pasha, 137, 140
Said, Edward, 237–8, 239, 258, 259
Said, Nuri
   capture of Damascus (1918), 164, 165
   Dera' offensive (Sept. 1918), 161, 206
   Jerdun railway station attack (1918), 159
   as later Prime Minister of Iraq, 160
   Storrs' diary, 140
   Tafas incident (Sept. 1918), 163
   Turkish Army retreat (1918), 200
St. Quentin, René Doynel de, 195–6, 252, 253, 311*n*
Saint-Exupéry, Antoine de, 276, 283
Salim Achmed *see* Dahoum
Samuel, Sir Herbert, 57, 58, 60, *plate 4*
San Remo conference (1920), 47, 58
Sardast, Rasim, 144, 145, 148
Sargent, John Singer, 110
Sassoon, Siegfried, 37, 80, 92
Savage, Raymond, 44
Schopenhauer, Arthur, 314*n*
Scott, Lady Kathleen, 91, 116
Scott, Major (base commander Aqaba), 13
Scott, Robert Falcon, 109
Seale, Patrick, 294
Serahin tribe, 180, 264–5, 266
*Seven Pillars of Wisdom*
   abstract discourse technique, 176, 264–6, 284, 285
   accuracy and reliability of, 3–5, 107, 195–6, 213, 222–4, 252–4, 257–8, 263–4
   autobiographical aspect, 5, 90, 93, 198, 246, 260–6, 282–6
   Curtis draft (Introduction and first five chapters of Book 1), 25, 27–9, 44, 45, 175, 293
   Drama of the Self, 2–3, 33, 171, 173, 177, 180, 190, 261, 262
   epic character of, 243–7
   fraud & betrayal theme, 5, 19, 30, 47, 59, 173–4, 199, 200, 247, 254–6, 257
   guilt theme, 125–6, 174, 254, 257, 270–1
   heterogeneity of, 1, 5
   historian's reviews of, 258–9
   introspective comment technique, 263
   Malraux's "N'était-ce donc que cela?", 246, 274–5, 276, 277–90, 315*n*
   "Myself" chapter, 6, 119–20, 174, 261, 264, 268, 285
   parallel texts, 2–3, 151, 171, 263
   Preface, 25, 27
   punishment theme, 181, 188, 191, 196–8, 270
   self-analysis technique, 6, 264
   as a source text, 1, 3–5, 203–4, 268
   story writing technique, 263–4, 280–2
   *To S.A.* (dedicatory poem), 21, 56, 62, 66–8
   Versailles Peace Conference (1919), 18, 19
   'Text I' (1919)
   begins writing (Feb. 1919), 19–21
   Book I 'The Discovery of Feisal', 26
   chronology of, 25–6, 291–3
   Dera' incident (Nov. 1917), 26
   Introduction and drafts of Books 9 and 10, 24
   Liddell Hart's interview notes, 20, 25, 292–3
   lost in Reading Station, 24–5, 291, 292
   method of composition, 27
   notebooks, 26–7
   sent to Dawnay, 24

*Seven Pillars of Wisdom* (continued)
  shown to Hogarth, 24
  The Spirit of the Revolt (Chapter 2), 25–6
  writings in Barton Street, Westminster (Autumn 1919), 24
  writings in France (Feb. 1919 to July 1919), 22
  'Text II' (1920), 32–5
  Book VI, 31
  ceremoniously burned (1922), 34, 71
  Curtis draft, 27
  Dera' incident (Nov. 1917), 31
  and Garnett, 33
  and Hogarth, 30–1
  piracy problem, 42
  publishing proposal, 41–2
  revisions (1921), 56
  and Richards, 31, 32–3
  *The World's Work* excerpts, 41
  writings in Barton Street, Westminster (1920), 31
  Yarmuk Bridge expedition (1917), 31
  abridgement version (1920), 42–6, 62, 66, 243
  'Oxford' text (OX) (1922), 69–72
  Abdullah's camp in Wadi Ais, 132, 179
  Allenby and Feisal's meeting in Damascus (1918), 166
  Arab regular officers, 157–60
  and Bernard Shaw, 80, 87–92, 93, 107, 108, 109
  Book VIII revision, 117
  "borrowed phrases and ideas", 29
  capture of Damascus (1918), 164, 165
  Chapter 1, 129, 130, 172–3, 213
  Chapter 92 omitted, 117
  Chapters 1 and 2, 70
  and Charlotte Shaw, 89–90, 91, 92, 107
  completed (May 1922), 70–1
  confessional aspect, 79, 82, 83
  criticism of Allenby, 156
  and Dawnay, 107
  Dera' incident (Nov. 1917), 70, 181, 182–5, 188–9, 195, 221
  Dera' offensive (Sept. 1918), 206, 207–8
  description of Auda abu Tayi, 231–2
  eight printed and bound copies (1922), 68, 71, 80
  feedback from secret readers, 107–8
  first publication ix
  and Forster, 92–7, 118, 171
  fraud & betrayal theme, 173, 199, 200, 254, 255–6
  and Garnett, 80–4, 88, 92, 93, 97, 107, 268–9
  Garnett–Lawrence abridgement, 81, 83–4, 85–7, 89, 99, 109
  and Graves, 80, 118, 224
  historical accuracy, 70
  and Hogarth, 107, 108, 109
  *How and Why I wrote* chapter, 28, 255–6
  image of Bedu, 200, 232–3, 235–6, 238
  Introduction and ten Books, 291
  'Intrusives' orientalism, 239
  and Kennington, 107, 110
  and Kipling, 41–2, 107–8
  Monotheism chapter, 233, 235–6, 237, 238
  Nisib bridge demolition, 161
  revision of, 117–20
  as revision of Text II, 34
  and Richards, 69, 107
  sado-masochistic sex, 175, 176
  sent to the printers, 46
  sermon to the Serahin, 265
  sexual confession, 175–7
  *The Spirit of the Revolt* chapter, 28, 158–9, 174–7, 234–5
  Tafas incident (Sept. 1918), 201, 273
  Tafileh Battle (1918), 149–51
  TEL's antipathy to Abdullah's character, 139
  TEL's arrival in Jeddah (Oct. 1916), 135
  TEL's execution of a Moroccan, 179
  TEL's first meeting with Feisal, 230
  TEL's homesickness, 200
  TEL's journey to Wadi Ais, 194
  TEL's loneliness, 200

TEL's meeting with Nuri Sha'alan, 251
TEL's ride to Wejh (1917), 178–9
TEL's story on Abdullah's unscrupulousness, 140
TEL's views on, 71–2, 79, 81–2, 88, 90, 108
as text of retrospective reflection, 171
textual changes, 45
*To S.A.* (dedicatory poem), 68
Turkish Army retreat (1918), 200–1
Turkish flotilla destroyed on the Dead Sea, 156
Wadi Rumm passage, 119
Yarmuk Bridge expedition (1917), 179–80, 265, 297
subscribers' edition (1926)
and Bernard Shaw, 100, 110, 114–16, 117, 121, 178
Chapter 1 *How and why I wrote* omitted, 116, 117, 255
and Charlotte Shaw, 114–15, 116–17, 121
criticism of Allenby, 156
and Curtis, 109
and Dawnay, 109
decision to publish, 109–10
first thoughts about, 99–100
and Forster, 125
fraud & betrayal theme, 173
and Garnett, 109, 114, 268–9
and Graves, 99, 125
and Hogarth, 109, 114
illustrations, 54, 55–6, 110–14, 122
Introduction and ten Books, 291
and Kennington, 110, 111, 112, 113, 114, 122, 125, 229–30
"Myself" chapter, 268
production of, 120–3
revision of the 'Oxford' text, 117–20
sado-masochistic sex, 175, 176
sexual confession, 175–7
subscription requests, 125
*To S.A.* (dedicatory poem), 68
Yarmuk Bridge expedition (1917), 298
revised edition (R) (1940)
Abdullah's camp in Wadi Ais, 132, 179

Dera' incident (Nov. 1917), 181, 182–5, 188–9, 194, 195, 284
Dera' offensive (Sept. 1918), 285, 286–7
description of Auda abu Tayi, 231–2
fraud & betrayal theme, 174, 200, 254–5
image of Bedu, 200, 232–3, 236
introductory chapter, 172–3
"Myself" chapter, 119–20, 174, 285
Nisib bridge demolition, 161
*The Spirit of the Revolt* chapter, 117, 174–7
Tafas incident (Sept. 1918), 201, 273
Tafileh Battle (1918), 149–51
TEL snowbound with his body-guard in Tafileh, 281
TEL's antipathy to Abdullah's character, 139
TEL's execution of a Moroccan, 179
TEL's first meeting with Feisal, 230
TEL's story on Abdullah's unscrupulousness, 140
Turkish Army retreat (1918), 200
Wadi Rumm passage, 119
Yarmuk Bridge expedition (1917), 297
sexual masochism, 191, 192, 270
Sha'alan, Nawaf, 252, 253, *plate 7*
Sha'alan, Nuri, 229, 230, 247, 251–2, 253
Shakir, Sherif, 135, 228
Shanghai, Communist revolution, 275, 278, 279
Sharif, Omar, 162
Shaw, Bernard
correspondence with TEL, 80, 88–9, 90–1, 100, 114, 115, 117, 267
Dera' incident (Nov. 1917), 224
first meeting with TEL (1922), 87–8, 107
friendship with TEL, 55, 124
*How and Why I wrote* chapter dropped, 117, 255
*Revolt in the Desert*, 122
*Seven Pillars* 'Oxford' text (1922), 80, 87–92, 93, 107, 108, 109

Shaw, Bernard *(continued)*
  *Seven Pillars* subscribers' edition (1926), 100, 110, 114–16, 117, 121, 178
  TEL's abilities and interests, 211
  TEL's alias in Tank Corps, 100
  TEL's departure for India (1926), 125
  TEL's display and concealment conflict, 107, 194
  TEL's financial situation, 109
  TEL's image, 91, 267
  as TEL's literary mentor, 80, 87–92, 93, 100, 107, 108, 109, 110, 114–16, 117, 121, 178, 274
  TEL's re-admission to RAF, 123
  visits to Clouds Hill, 103, 105
Shaw, Charlotte
  Augustus John's portrait of GBS, 87
  correspondence with TEL, 105, 115, 116–17, 120, 122, 123–4, 125, 194, 222–3
  Dera' incident (Nov. 1917), 194, 222–4
  friendship with TEL, 55, 105, 124, 172
  *How and Why I wrote* chapter dropped, 117, 255
  image of Arabs, 238
  literary criticism of *Seven Pillars*, 274–5
  *Revolt in the Desert*, 122
  *Seven Pillars* 'Oxford' text (1922), 89–90, 91, 92, 107
  *Seven Pillars* subscribers' edition (1926), 114–15, 116–17, 121
  TEL's departure for India (1926), 125
  visits to Clouds Hill, 103, 105
Shaw, T.E. (TEL's alias in Tank Corps), 100
Shobek, 142, 156
Simpson, Colin, 74, 185, 186
Smith, Clare, 124
Smith, Wing Commander Sydney, 124
Spanish civil war, 275–6, 278, 279
*The Spectator*, 92
Stalin, Joseph, 275
Steed, Wickham, 17, 30
Stewart, Desmond, 310–11*n*

Stirling, Major W.F.
  capture of Damascus (1918), 164, 309*n*
  Dera' incident (Nov. 1917), 186, 187, 188, 221
  support for TEL, 19
  TEL's accusation of Abdelkader's treachery, 187, 188
  TEL's letter (June 1919), 186, 187, 188, 221, 294
Storrs, Ronald
  negotiations with the Arabs (1916), 130, 135–9, 140, 141
  orientalism, 239
  *Orientations* diary extracts, 137, 138, 140
*Strand Magazine*, 32
*Sunday Times*, 47, 49, 76, 192, 304*n*
superego, 272
Swann, Air Vice-Marshal Sir Oliver, 77, 78, 98, 99
Sykes, Mark, 14, 249, 257
Sykes–Picot treaty
  Arab Bureau opposition, 19
  Arab knowledge of, 251, 257
  Britain, 14–15, 257, 295
  Feisal's knowledge of, 257
  France, 14–15, 295
  Grand Sherif's knowledge of, 251, 257
  secrecy of, 251
  Syria, 14, 295
  TEL's acceptance of, 22, 30
  TEL's anger over mandates, 47
  TEL's knowledge of, 133–4, 256–8
  TEL's meeting with Arab leaders, 251–2, 255
Syria
  Battle of Maysalun (1920), 49
  British and French occupation, 14
  British withdrawal from, 22–3
  Feisal's claim to, 16, 30
  Feisal's expulsion (1920), 50, 160, 258
  Feisal's limited autonomy, 22, 23, 49–50
  Feisal's strategy, 247–8, 294–5, 296, 297
  French interests, 14, 15, 16–17
  French mandate, 47, 49–51

French occupation of Damascus and eastern Syria, 49
Great Syrian Revolt, 293–5
pan-Arab nationalism, 52
Sykes–Picot treaty, 14, 295
TEL's concern over, 47, 50–1
Versailles Peace Conference (1919), 16–17, 19, 22
*see also* Damascus
Sysiphus, 191

Tabachnick, S., 173, 244
Tafas incident (Sept. 1918), 162–4, 193, 201–5
improbability of, 263, 264
*Lawrence of Arabia* (film), 7, 202–5, 273
Malraux's "N'était-ce donc que cela?", 281
*Seven Pillars* abridgement version (1920), 44
*Seven Pillars* 'Oxford' text (1922), 201, 273
*Seven Pillars* revised edition (1940) (R), 201, 273
Tafileh Battle (1918), 143–51, 271
Taif, 136, 137
*T.E. Notes*, 275
Tell el Shehab, 296, 297
Thesiger, Wilfred, 111, 233–4, 238
Thomas, Lowell, 4, 24, 31–2, 240, 253, 266, 267
*The Times*, 13, 22, 30, 47, 187
Tolstoy, Leo, 12, 287
Townshend, Charles, 48
Toynbee, Arnold, 49
Transjordan
Abdullah becomes Emir (later King), 58, 60, 138
British mandate, 47, 58
TEL's political mission (1921), 58, 59–60
Trenchard, Sir Hugh
Iraq deputation, 49
*Seven Pillars* 'Oxford' text (1922), 70
TEL's dismissal from the RAF, 100
TEL's proposed history of the RAF, 63, 64
TEL's re-admission to RAF, 123
TEL's wish to join the RAF, 62–3, 71, 77
Trevelyan, G.M., 244–5, 246
Trotsky, Leon, 275

al-Umari, Subhi, *plate 4, plate 5*
Arab independence, 175
capture of Damascus (1918), 165
defection from Turkish army, 142
first sight of TEL, 143
*Lurens kama' areftuhu*, 129, 158, *plate 5*
Tafileh Battle (1918), 143–6, 147–8, 149, 150
TEL in Tafileh, 199
United States, Versailles Peace Conference (1919), 16

Vansittart, Sir Robert, 20
Versailles Peace Conference (1919)
Britain, 15, 16–17, 18–19
Council of Ten, 16, 283
Feisal's presence, 13–14, 15, 16, 17, 19, 22, 50–1, 218, 283
France, 15, 16–17
Mesopotamia (Iraq), 15, 16, 22
Palestine, 15, 16, 22
Syria, 16–17, 19, 22
TEL's presence, 15–17, 18–19, 22, 50–1, 218, *plate 2*
Vickery, Major Charles, 177–8, 179, 263
Villars, Jean Béraud, 296, 310*n*
Vye, Eustacia, 102

Wadi Ais, 132, 179, 228
Wadi Arabah, 143, 154
Wadi Hesa, 144, 148, 149
Wadi Khalid, 297
Wadi Kitan, 4, 202, 264
Wadi Rumm, 119, 162, 200
Wadi Sirhan, 133, 228, 247
Wadsworth, Edward, 121
Waheidah Arab Army base, 157–60
Walpole, Hugh, 52
Wavell, Archibald Percival Wavell, Earl of, 70, 107
Weizmann, Ezer, 51
Wejh, 132, 177–8, 228
Welsh, Major, *plate 4*
Wemyss, Admiral Rosslyn, 131

Westminster, Hugh Richard Arthur Grosvenor, Duke of, 54
Whittingham & Griggs of Chiswick, 56, 113
Wilde, Oscar, 240, 267
Wilson, A.T., 48
Wilson, Colonel C.E., 107, 136, 137, 138, 254–5, 257–8
Wilson, J.M., ix, 3, 210, 211, 304*n*, 307*n*, 313–14*n*
Wilson, Woodrow, 16, 22, 47
Wingate, Sir Reginald, 131, 140, 187–8
Winterton, Edward Turnour, 6th Earl, 38, 49, 57, 124
*The World's Work*, 41, 66
Wrench, Sir Evelyn, 41

Yarmuk Bridge expedition (1917), 31, 134, 179–80, 186, 216, 265, 296–7
Yeomans, R., 111, 112
Young, Hubert
  Arab regular officers, 167
  Dera' offensive (Sept. 1918), 206, 207
  description of Arabs, 229, 238
  description of Feisal, 229, 231
  description of Zeid, 229
  Jerdun railway station attack (1918), 229
  memoir, 129–30, 213
  Nisib bridge demolition, 162
  planned offensive (1918), 161
  *Seven Pillars* 'Oxford' text (1922), 178
  Tafas incident (Sept. 1918), 163, 203
  takes up post in Arabia, 155

Zaagi, the, 228
Zaal, Sheikh, 180, 228
Zeid bin Hussein, *plate 6*
  as Grand Sherif representative, 135, 136
  image in *Seven Pillars*, 229
  Jerdun railway station attack (1918), 229
  quarrel with TEL, 199, 216
  Tafileh Battle (1918), 143, 144–5, 146, 147, 148, 150
  TEL's proposed forged telegram, 59
  Young's description of, 229
Zionists, 16, 51, 59, 60, 75